The Service City

The Service City

State and Townsmen in Russia, 1600-1800

J. MICHAEL HITTLE

Harvard University Press
Cambridge, Massachusetts
London, England • 1979

*Publication of this volume has been aided by a grant
from the Andrew W. Mellon Foundation*

Library of Congress Cataloging in Publication Data

Hittle, J.   Michael, 1938-
    The service city.

    Bibliography: p.
    Includes index.
    1.   Russia—Social conditions.   2.   Cities and towns—
Russia—History.   I.   Title.
HN523.H5   309.1'47   79-10909
ISBN 0-674-80170-9

To my mother and to the memory of my father

Acknowledgments

A FIRST BOOK affords an excellent opportunity to thank the many people who have shaped in one manner or another not only the work at hand but one's scholarly career as well. Thus my thanks go to David Joravsky, whose teaching skills and humane concerns led me to the study of Russian history, and to Edward J. Brown and Henry Kucera, who together introduced me to the riches of the Russian language and its literature. To Richard Pipes I am indebted for steering me into a little-known but rewarding corner of Russian history and for instilling in me respect for the historian's craft. John T. Alexander and Arcadius Kahan contributed helpful comments on two portions of this work, which were first presented at professional conferences. I am especially grateful for the thoughtful observations of Samuel H. Baron on my work and on the study of Russian social history in general. His encouragement and kindness have exercised a decisive influence on my scholarly undertakings.

I have drawn much sustenance in the creation of this work from many of my colleagues at Lawrence University. From them have come wit, perspective, and a willingness to listen—each at the proper season. Two, however, I must single out. Bertrand Goldgar, who took leave of Walpole—though not of his wits—so that he might give me the judicious counsel of an established scholar, has been my guide in every perplexity from the *MLA Style Sheet* to the angst of creation. And I could not imagine a finer person with whom to share the difficult apprentice years in a profession than my companion in Clio, Anne Jacobson Schutte. Her talents as a scholar are matched only by her steadfastness as a friend.

In the preparation of this work I have been the beneficiary of considerable support from institutional sources. Early research on the project was supported by a Stoufer Fellowship from the MIT-Harvard Joint Center for Urban Studies. The major portion of the writing was made possible by a Young Humanist grant from the National Endowment for the Humanities. That support enabled me to spend a year at the Harvard University Russian Research Center, where I had an opportunity to test out my ideas both in a formal seminar presentation and in daily give-and-take with other scholars. Final research on the project was completed at the University of Illinois, Urbana, under the auspices of their Summer Research Laboratory and at the British Library, London. Lawrence University summer research grants eased the burden of my many trips to major research libraries.

Able assistance in the preparation of the manuscript in its various stages came from Sharon Adams, Christine Krueger, Mary Probst, Carol Techlin, and Catherine Ulrich. The bulk of the manuscript's preparation, however, was accomplished with great patience, efficiency, and good humor by Ruth Lesselyong. To my editor, Harry Foster, I am indebted for a thoughtful reading of the manuscript and many helpful suggestions for its improvement.

Final credit properly belongs to my wife, Marcia Adams Hittle, and my sons, Alexander and Samuel. Without their gracious accommodation to the time-consuming demands of this project and their loving support, I should never have seen this work to completion. Although their sacrifice can thus be recognized, it cannot, I fear, ever be adequately recompensed.

Contents

The Service City

Introduction

STUDIES OF THE SOCIAL HISTORY of Russia from the accession of Michael Romanov through the October Revolution have focused, and rightly so, on the countryside, on the activities of an entrenched landed nobility and a massive and often volatile peasantry. The cities and their inhabitants—especially those engaged in commercial and manufacturing pursuits—have always occupied a secondary place, in part because their contributions to the national past were sporadic and often inconspicuous, in part because their impact on Russian society was not equivalent to that of their counterparts in Western Europe during these same centuries. But neither the predominant role of rural Russia nor the comparatively modest achievements of the towns and their inhabitants ought to be allowed to obscure the urban contribution to the national history. Russia was a nation of extensive city development. New cities sprang up one after another as the country's political frontiers spread across a vast continent, and its urban-situated merchants, artisans, and manufacturers provided the body social with necessary economic goods and services. Without the efforts of the townsmen, the growth of Muscovy into a vast empire would have been inconceivable.

Three protagonists dominated the history of urban Russia: the state apparatus, the towns, and the townsmen themselves. Although the townsmen must be considered the principal subject of this study, their story cannot be told in isolation. Their interaction with the state constitutes the study's central dynamic, while the towns themselves play a supporting role, setting the context for that confrontation. The complicated nature of the topic inevitably requires shifts in emphasis from one protagonist to another, but the basic relationship between state and townsmen, the reconciling of their respective interests and aspirations, is never far from center stage. In that relationship lies the key to an understanding of the urban history of early modern Russia.

The term "townsmen" needs immediate clarification. For the period under study, 1600-1800, is still too early for one to speak of a Russian middle class, certainly not if one has in mind the broad, somewhat amorphous body of urban residents that the term customarily connotes. In fact, the term "townsmen" in this study is reserved for but one of the many constituent groups of the Russian city population, the *posadskie liudi*. (I have decided on this translation partially for convenience and partly to affirm the urban character of the posadskie liudi). The townsmen may be identified, first of all, by their economic pursuits. Among their ranks could be found entrepreneurs, factors, and clerks; petty merchants; artisans; and unskilled laborers. Their preoccupation with the production and exchange of goods helps to distinguish the posadskie liudi from other city dwellers and serves to establish a degree of kinship between them and the burghers of Western European cities. But occupational characteristics are not sufficient to an exacting definition of the townsmen. In many cases occupation provided little basis for differentiating the townsmen from other city residents, from the peasants, church dependents, postal officials and petty military personnel who all engaged, whether legally or illegally, in trade and manufacturing in the cities. What really set the townsmen apart was their claim to possess exclusive rights to the urban marketplace. In a society of sharply delineated social groups, that claim amounted to an assertion by the townsmen of their status as *the* urban estate of the realm. It was an assertion that was given considerable force by the state, both when it bestowed economic privileges upon the townsmen and when it saddled them with obligations for urban administration. By occupation and by legal status, then, the posadskie liudi were the most characteristically urban estate in Russia.

The townsmen can be more precisely characterized by several of the main institutional features of posad life. First, they shared among themselves a common tax obligation, known as *tiaglo*, to the central government. It obligated them to pay taxes and to render numerous services on behalf of the local and national administration. Second, in order to administer tiaglo and to work out mutual economic problems, the townsmen of any given locality drew together into a fairly cohesive social organization, the *posadskii mir* or posad commune. This institution, uniquely the product of local initiative, stood at the center of posad political life. Finally, from the early eighteenth century, the posadskie liudi and their local commune were linked to the central government by the magistracy, an institution composed of elected members of posad society but charged basically with securing the state's interests within the cities. For the remainder of the century the fate of the townsmen was tied, now firmly, now loosely, to this offspring of the Petrine reforms.

These distinguishing features of posad society, from economic privileges to commune to magistracy, suggest the close relationship that existed between the townsmen and the central government. Such a relationship was wholly in keeping with the basic social order of the state, one marked by the continual involvement of the central government in the social relations of its citizens. What was true for the service gentry, clergy, and state peasantry was equally true for the tsar's urban estate. It is also clear that in imposing complex tax burdens and unwanted administrative institutions on the townsmen, the state exercised a profound influence on urban society. But it would be a mistake to conclude that the relationship was entirely one-sided. Posad-state relations were a two-way street: the state was dependent on the townsmen not only for their economic contributions to the country, but also for the performance of crucial administrative functions that the government could not accomplish with its own resources. At times the state even had to accede to various demands of the townsmen in order to secure the continued orderly performance of these services. The ties that bound state and posad were woven deep into the fabric of the Russian nation.

The period 1600-1800 is particularly suitable for an examination of the relationship of state and posad. First, it was during the seventeenth century that the townsmen emerged as an estate of the realm, their rights and obligations codified in law, their place in the national life precisely set out. This establishment of the estate character of the posad cannot be attributed to the efforts of the townsmen alone, though representations to the government on behalf of their interests had a long history. Instead, it was the convergence of both posad and central-government interests in urban stability that brought about the formal definition of the estate. In fact, this action was part of a still broader clarification of social relations that occurred in the seventeenth century, the central feature of which was, in every case, the relationship between a social group and the central government. Yet, dominant though the state may have been in defining estate relations generally, and those of the townsmen in particular, it cannot be argued that its actions were arbitrary or wholly at odds with the views of the people involved. In the case at hand, the townsmen seem to have accepted for the most part the characteristics of their estate life as ennunciated in the mid-seventeenth century; indeed, their behavior for the next century and a half can only be understood in terms of an estate mentality that had its roots in this very period.

If the emergence of the posadskie liudi as an estate during the seventeenth and eighteenth centuries constitutes one reason for focusing on that period, the development of the central government during that time —that is, its mounting aspirations and its increasing capacity to govern —constitutes a second. Progress toward that end was relatively slow in the seventeenth century. The main objective of the early Romanovs seems to have been the restoration of the Muscovite order, though some modifications and improvements were, of course, necessary to accomplish that goal. But the eighteenth century was another matter. It witnessed the emergence of a new, imperial Russia, its horizons European in the fullest sense of the word, its absolutist pretensions ever more forcefully advanced, and its bureaucratic machinery growing in numbers and efficacy. The implications for the cities and for the townsmen were immediate and profound. Beginning with the Petrine era the state set a number of challenging goals for the cities and their inhabitants—especially for the posadskie liudi. These goals, frequently at odds with the traditional principles of the posad estate and almost always beyond the capabilities of the townsmen, dominated the relationship between state and posad throughout the century, though the intensity with which they were pursued varied with the capacities of the government. This tension between a maturing and reform-minded state, on the one hand, and a tradition-oriented urban estate, on the other, lay at the heart of urban history in eighteenth-century Russia.

There is, however, still a third consideration that makes the chosen time span especially appropriate for a study of the townsmen. It was during the eighteenth century, as best one can judge, that the long-run secular transformation of the Russian state began. Its characteristic features— a modification in the nature of the serf economy and a related expansion of capitalistic enterprise—both had a powerful impact on the economic and social life of the posad, as well as on the entire city and all of its inhabitants. Once again the state had a number of roles to play, now as promoter of economic expansion, now as adjustor of the social and administrative consequences of that expansion. In the final analysis, the latter role entailed presiding over the decline and destruction of the old posad order, and with it of two centuries of intimate bonds between the state and its urban servitors.

The story of the posadskie liudi has many dimensions. Though not yet a middle class or bourgeoisie in the fullest sense of those terms, the posadskie liudi did represent the middle-class phenomenon in its nascent form. As such, the townsmen of the seventeenth and eighteenth centuries set the stage for their middle-class successors in the crucial modern era. But the study of the posadskie liudi goes well beyond a single stage in the development of a social class: it has ramifications for other major lines of investigation: namely, social relations among classes or estates, the character of the national government, and problems of modernization. The history of urban classes—even the weak ones in preindustrial states— opens a broad and illuminating window onto the broader societies of which they are a part.

THE HISTORIOGRAPHIC PERSPECTIVE

The historiographic tradition dealing with the Russian towns and their inhabitants remains, on the whole, rather weak.[1] As to why, one can only speculate. The urban commercial and manufacturing population never played a role of sustained eminence in the history of Russia; and in its few big moments upon the stage it proved singularly inept. One suspects, therefore, that the well-recognized penchant of historians for following winners has led them elsewhere, to the state or to the countryside, where bureaucrats or peasants and gentry set the tenor of national life. Moreover, the type of life customarily associated with the mercantile and manufacturing worlds could scarcely be said to harmonize with the ideals of most modern Russian historians, either before 1917 or after. Neither the liberals nor the Marxists have been inclined to make heroes of those who buy cheap and sell dear.[2]

The investigation of urban life in Russia begins where so many studies of that country, contemporary and historical, have begun—namely, with a sense that Russia is somehow different, that its distinguishing features are of a qualitatively different sort from those of most other societies. Each nation may be unique, but to natives and visitors alike, Russia has frequently seemed more unique than others. To be sure, several of Russia's cities could hold their own in population and commerce with their counterparts in Western Europe, and they duly impressed foreigners on these counts, but many other Russian cities appeared pitiful replicas of true urban environments. And in almost all Russian cities manifestations of what one might call civic consciousness were few and far between. If the cities thus stood out for their deficiencies, for their failure to live up to expectations, the same could be said for the townsmen themselves. Indeed, were they not odd townsmen, who bowed to a dominant landed gentry not only in society at large but in the towns as well? What kind of urbanites were they who so poorly directed the affairs of the city? Or, perhaps most telling, what kind of burghers were they who found themselves on the receiving end of the epithet "muzhik," that is, peasant?

In one manner or another the historiographic tradition was built on this image of the Russian city as unique, as a social form lacking in much that one associates with the cities of Western Europe. Prerevolutionary Russian historians accepted this line of thought, essentially an argument based on the notion of backwardness, and set to work cataloging the ways in which Russian cities diverged from the Western European models. The terms of comparison varied from the real and mundane to the political to the spirtual, that is, from the cleanliness of the streets, to institutions of urban autonomy, to independently created and enriching manifestations of high culture. On most counts Russia was found lacking.

Explanations for the apparent disparities centered on two main themes: impedimenta to the free operation of the economic process; and hindrances to the development of a proper mercantile spirit, or bourgeois mentality, if the latter phrase can be stripped of its contemporary, odious connotations. Each line of argument has a certain merit and consequently each finds its place, though duly modified, in this study. But these explanations have still broader implications in terms of the historiography of urban Russia, for each also identifies the state as the principal agent in the shaping of the urban environment. Indeed, it is not unusual to find the state cast as a veritable culprit, the single agent most responsible for the sad condition of the cities.

This theme emerges in all its clarity in the assertions, frequently encountered in works written in the late nineteenth and early twentieth centuries, that Russia's townsmen existed in a frustrating dependence on the state, one that precluded the emergence of the middle class as a powerful force in its own right. To P. N. Miliukov, "The city estate in Russia obviously was not able to present itself as an independent element of estate life. Not only did it not develop independently or even in contradiction to central power, but, on the contrary, even in its very isolation as a special social group and in its corporate organization it was wholly obligated to the state."[3] In somewhat more evocative language, P. A. Berlin contended that "the Russian upper bourgeoisie grew up . . . in fear of the government, firmly remembering that all their well-being and even their simple existence depended wholly on the favor of the government."[4] Finally, A. A. Kizevetter went so far as to suggest that the absence of true self-government in Russian cities could be explained, at least in part, by "the enserfed character of the trade and industrial order of the city population."[5] Obviously, the state was the master of those serfs. Whether as an insatiable tax collector or as a jealous and aggressive wielder of political power, the central government was cast in the role of a villain that destroyed the budding bourgeoisie on the vine and deprived the cities of that most precious of commodities, urban autonomy.[6] Stripped of their accusatory undertones, these arguments contain more than a kernel of truth. The state was a powerful influence on the development of the cities, but the point to be made here is that these arguments represent a basically negative approach, designed to demonstrate why something that should have happened did not. The specter of national inferiority, then, lurked behind a great deal of prerevolutionary work on the history of Russian cities, and it produced some strange results. These range from the implications that Russia's cities were not really cities at all, just overgrown villages, to Miliukov's assertion that "the Russian city . . . on account of the slow development of Russian trade and industrial life was not a natural product of the internal economic development of the country." Indeed, he argued, the needs of the state for services performed in and from the cities "outstripped the natural development of city life."[7] Such a position is scarcely tenable. To begin with, whatever the cities may have been like, if they appeared in Russia during its history, they cannot be considered "unnatural products" of the national history. But it seems more likely that Miliukov's real objective was, first, to suggest that *the* model of city development was that of Western Europe, where the commercial and manufacturing population dominated the urban scene, and then to show how Russia fell short of that model. But even here Miliukov's argument stands on shaky ground, for many a European city known for its trade and manufacturing achievements had its origins as an administrative center for its medieval rulers, secular and ecclesiastical, or even as a center of Roman power; and many Russian cities had more in the way of economic enterprise than Miliukov was prepared to acknowledge.

The attitudes of prerevolutionary historians toward the towns and the townsmen, especially their emphasis on the deleterious influence of the state on urban life, should sound a familiar note to those acquainted with the intellectual and political climates in Russia during the last century of Romanov rule. Beginning with the renowned mots of P. Ia. Chaadaev, Russian intellectual circles have been home to detractors and debunkers who have fed their criticism of the nation's past and present with a steady diet of adverse comparisons with Western Europe.[8] And, of course, the liberal political movement with which both Kizevetter and Miliukov— two of the foremost students of urban Russia—were so intimately connected arose in opposition to a powerful and despised autocratic government. The liberal historians thus had no difficulty blaming past national shortcomings and misfortunes on the autocracy in its earlier incarnations.

If, ultimately, the prerevolutionary historiographic tradition may be linked to broader cultural and political concerns, the same can be said of historical writing in the years since the Bolshevik revolution. Moved by a combination of Marxism and, from the early thirties, national patriotism, Soviet scholars have shied away from the negative view of the towns and the townsmen. They have argued, instead, that prerevolutionary historians overlooked or played down economic considerations that, from a Marxist perspective, constitute the truly defining characteristics of urban forms. To redress the balance, Soviet scholars have stressed the economic activities of the towns and their residents and in doing so have built a strong counterargument against those who would assert that most

Russian cities were overgrown villages. Soviet scholars have done much to modify earlier views of the towns, but their preoccupation with matters economic betrays an unduly narrow conception of what cities are all about.[9]

The affirmation that Russia did indeed have cities constitutes only a partial response to the prerevolutionary tradition. Soviet historians must also confront the problem of comparison with the West. At this point one encounters a major preoccupation of Soviet scholarship: the effort to prove that the overall historical development of Russia conforms to an inevitable process—a process, it should be remembered, that was derived from the Western European experience. That process, of course, is the shift from a feudal to a capitalistic social order, as defined in Marxist terminology. Accordingly, the principal objective of Soviet urban history has been the uncovering of economic and social antecedents of capitalism in the womb of feudal society. In such work, the stress falls on the formation of the internal market, the development of urban industry, the increasing use of hired labor, the social divisions within the city, and the growing differentiation between urban and rural life. Administrative matters tend, on the whole, to be relegated to secondary status at best, and thus the state, so important in earlier scholarly accounts based on a comparison with Western Europe, recedes into the background.[10] Much of this work has centered precisely on the seventeenth and eighteenth centuries, though there have been occasional forays into still earlier times. Ultimately, this search for the origins of capitalism amidst the disparate pieces of data on economic and social relations in the cities has taken precedence over the study of the cities as they actually functioned.

There is, of course, much more to the historiography of urban Russia than has just been outlined, yet among all its facets, the dialogue between the detractors and advocates of Russia's cities, a dialogue set against the backdrop of implied inferiority to Western Europe, stands out as its central feature. Much that is useful has emerged from this debate, but it has its negative aspects as well. The emphasis on the state, for example, although warranted by the circumstances, readily lends itself to a moralizing, reproving tone that attributes a certain malicious intent to the central government. Such an attitude precludes a thoughtful analysis of the government's relationship with the towns in general and with the members of the urban tax-paying community in particular. More broadly, this dialogue has deflected historians from the major task of assessing the functional role of cities in preindustrial Russia. The effort to analyze the urban component of early modern Russia is as little served by the identification of towns with overgrown villages or by the notion that the townsmen were abused wards of the state as it is served by the exclusive concentration on the economic characteristics of the cities. The former notions fail to do justice to the achievements of the towns and distort the role of the state; the latter unduly restricts the essential diversity of urban life.

THE SERVICE-CITY CONCEPT

One of the principal objectives of this study is to develop a conceptual or analytical model that will faithfully represent the towns and townsmen in relation to the broader state order of early modern Russia. As the historiographic review suggests, many previous treatments of the subject have been based on the notions of what might have been or what ought to have been. Such approaches are inherently unproductive. What is needed is a conceptual approach that recognizes the necessary character of many crucial features of the state-posad relationship and builds from there. One may wish, ultimately, either to lament or to exult over the fate of the Russian towns and their inhabitants, but such judgments can be properly drawn only when one has an accurate understanding of where and how the towns and the townsmen fit in Russian society.

The construction of an analytical model does not require that the existing body of scholarship be set aside completely; a careful reappraisal is called for, however. Arguments of continuing merit must be sorted out from those based on wishful thinking or disappointed expectations. In particular, a reappraisal is called for when dealing with the two areas least well handled in the past: the role of the state and the uniqueness of the Russian urban world.

Toward that end, the shift in perspective afforded by the comparative approach to the topic can be of considerable benefit. Of course, many of the adverse judgments rendered against Russian towns and the townsmen have been based on comparisons with the West. Yet the comparative approach need not be limited to the measuring of one society in terms of the achievements of another. It can—and indeed should—be used to uncover underlying similarities and differences between diverse societies in institutions, behavior, and attitude—without holding up any one society's experience as the norm. In the case at hand, the comparative method can be of particular value in gaining new vantage points from which to view the activities of the state as well as the role of the townsmen in society. Comparisons with state-building in Western Europe hold promise for a reevaluation of the state's involvement in urban matters, while world-wide comparisons seem especially appropriate to an examination of the affairs and attitudes of the townsmen. Through such shifts in perspective, then, the Russian urban context may be more precisely fixed and the

way opened toward an interpretive schema that modifies the older arguments even as it avoids the pitfalls of reflexive revisionism. One caveat is
in order, however. Though this study relies on the comparative approach
to clear up some of the troublesome legacies of earlier scholarship and to
point the way toward a new interpretative position, it would be misleading to suggest that it is consistently comparative throughout. The emphasis of the study falls squarely on the Russian state and the Russian townsmen, and the service-city concept that draws together the phenomena
discussed in this book comes directly from Russian experience.

The first step toward the creation of a conceptual schema embracing
the Russian state and its townsmen entails a reappraisal of the actions of
the central government. The manifold areas of the state's involvement in
the cities cannot be denied. The state exercised ultimate control over the
land on which the townsmen lived and worked; it established the dimensions and character of the townsmen's tax and labor-service obligations;
it regulated dozens of aspects of the social and economic activities of the
townsmen just as it regulated social relations among all the constituent
groups of the society—that is, according to its own needs and interests;
and it was in its capacity as final arbiter of social relations in the country
that the state listened to the complaints of the townsmen and acted on
them or ignored them as the situation warranted. In the absence of well-
established local law or local political autonomy, the central government
of Muscovy, and later of imperial Russia, was the final source of law and
of the political force that gave structure, continuity and stability to the
state order it officially sanctioned. It is not hard to see how easily the
state's influence on the townsmen might, especially in the eyes of those
innately given to distrust political authority, transform the state into a
kind of evil demon. Yet to succumb to such temptations is to forget that
the state itself was responding to pressures both external and internal and
that it found itself captive to the logic of its own development. To honor
that fact and to steer clear of demonology, a still broader frame of reference is called for. If the relations between the Russian state and its townsmen are set within the framework of emerging national monarchy and
viewed from a broadly European perspective, one can gain useful insights of a comparative nature into the institutional features that went so
far toward determining the relative strengths of Russian and Western
European townsmen.

In Western Europe, many of the institutions that contributed to the
strength and independence of urban life developed during the commercial revival of the late Middle Ages. Craft guilds, merchant organizations, institutions of economic self-regulation, sophisticated instruments
of commerce, a free citizenry, and a measure of political autonomy—all

these features of city life existed prior to the emergence of the nation-state. When the national monarchies began to form and to extend their dominion, the cities were a force to be reckoned with. The record of their interaction contains instances of both cooperation and conflict. In some cases the national monarchs skillfully employed the wealth, knowledge, and political power of the towns in their struggle with entrenched feudal interests. There can be no gainsaying the contributions of the cities to state-building. At the same time, the nation-state steadily encroached de jure and de facto on the powers and prerogatives of the towns, but in a manner so gradual that most of the institutions that had given shape to the late medieval cities survived in modified form to provide the foundations of bourgeois Europe.

In Russia, on the contrary, quite another sequence of events transpired. The institutional features that had characterized the cities of Kievan Russia, in particular the self-government of the *veche*, had all but been eradicated during the years of Tatar domination. When life in the cities of the northeast took a turn for the better with the lessening of Tatar control, it did so simultaneously with the growth of centralized political authority. The state and the cities developed their own institutional features in close consort with one another. There can be no finer case in point than Moscow. This once-obscure appanage town loyally supported its ruling princes in their successful quest for national leadership and became in time the capital of a vast state and the claimant to the mantle of Rome and Constantinople. Political and ecclesiastical power—not the volume of its trade nor the products of its artisans—made Moscow the city it was. The importance of administrative power could be seen clearly in the social relations of the city, where the secular and ecclesiastical lords stood well above the merchants, separated not only by the barrier of prestige, but also by legally prescribed privileges and prerogatives. To be sure, the state valued highly the mercantile community and relied heavily on its contributions to state-building; but there was no question of the merchants or of any other group of the city population ever striking out on an independent course. Ivan III made that point clear in his treatment of Novgorod.

As with Moscow, so it was with other cities of the realm. The trying process of putting together a nation-state in a hostile geopolitical setting left its mark on the institutional arrangements that took shape in the cities—on administrative organs, social relations, landholding patterns, economic activities, and the like. Purely urban interests had always to stand aside in deference to the pressing needs of national survival.

One can, of course, make a similar argument for Western Europe, but there is a crucial difference. Whereas the Western European cities had developed—thanks largely to the commercial revolution—great capacities of their own, and hence had enjoyed a strong bargaining position from which to confront the nation-state, the Russian cities never benefited from that great revival of trade and thus had substantially less leverage than their European counterparts. The difference can be epitomized by the contrast between the hard-driving, innovative leadership of the Western European merchant class and the relatively more passive, traditional Russian merchantry—the former were masters of their trade and their towns, the latter servants of their tsar. The comparison is overdrawn on both sides and countercases could easily be marshaled; but it does reflect an important truth: in their confrontation with the growing central government, the Russian townsmen operated at a decided disadvantage, one that arose primarily from the basic economic weakness of the urban commercial population.[11]

In sum, the Russian cities came out from under Tatar rule simultaneously with the creation of a nation-state. Since the townsmen did not have great wealth or power, and since the cities had not therefore developed strong institutional bases of their own, the emergent city order was molded by the nation-state to a much greater degree than in Western Europe.

Such a comparison goes a long way toward explaining differences in the basic institutional structures of Russian and Western European cities and, by extension, the differing modes of urban life that arose within them. And this comparison changes for the better the terms of analysis to be applied to the activities of the Russian state. The requirements of nation building provide a more satisfactory explanatory framework than does stress upon the insatiability of autocracy and its minions.

The pursuit of a conceptual model for early-modern urban Russia requires more, however, than a demon-free interpretation of the central government; it also demands a reassessment of the position of the towns and their inhabitants in the overall institutional structure of the state. Here, economic and sociological considerations take precedence over political ones, though the complexity of urban relationships makes it hard to separate the one from the other. And, as in the preceding step, comparison is a crucial factor, though social and economic comparisons require a far broader perspective.

In evaluating urban forms and the behavior of urban dwellers, there is good precedent for sociological comparisons based on norms that have been derived from the European experience. The works of Max Weber on the city constitute a case in point. His classification of city forms has left its stamp on Western sociology and has attracted the attention of a handful of Western scholars of Russia.[12] In his study of the city Weber argues that the "full urban community" appeared only in the occident, where there occurred a unique conjunction of market, local law, civic association, and political autonomy. Further, the true city required that control over these features of city life be exercised not by the traditional estates, but by a new estate open to all comers—essentially, the bourgeoisie. Thus, only in the nineteenth-century west did the true city make its debut.[13] Weber may well have identified the distinguishing traits of the Western European city, especially in its industrial phase, but the typology he developed can hardly be applied universally. Indeed, to judge urban forms that sprang up in other locations and at other times against the true city of the occident is an exercise of limited usefulness. In the case of early modern Russia, a much more rewarding comparative approach is that which examines the country's cities in relation to the experience of cities around the globe during the preindustrial era.

The obvious starting point for any such comparison is Gideon Sjoberg's *The Preindustrial City*. In it he makes three arguments that are especially germane to the condition of Russia's cities.[14] First, he contends that even though the dominant wealth in a preindustrial society may have lain in the hands of a rural landholding class, that class exercised its power over the society through cities. Even in vast, rural, peasant Russia, political organization proceeded through the cities. Not only were major decisions of state made in the great cities, Moscow and St. Petersburg, but their execution depended to a significant degree on crown representatives who had final authority over cities great and small. And within the cities, the elite constituted a potent force—as representatives of the crown, as consumers, as holders of large blocks of urban real estate, and not infrequently as sponsors of the urban economic activities of their rural dependents.

Second, Sjoberg claims that administrative considerations, more than economic matters, shaped the preindustrial urban order. Again, Russia's cities constitute a case in point. Much of the fragmentation of urban social and political relations can be attributed directly to service-based divisions of the population. There were no urban citizens, strictly speaking, on which to build common city institutions: there were only subgroups of the population, characterized in no small measure by their service duties. Sjoberg's argument works equally well when applied specifically to the townsmen. The administrative responsibilities the posadskie liudi bore as a part of tiaglo went a long way toward determining the structure and operations of posad society as well as the attitudes of the townsmen toward other members of society. Merchants and artisans though many of them were, the townsmen were also administrators of state and local government.

Finally, Sjoberg argues that merchants and artisans in preindustrial societies occupied a decidedly inferior social rank, not just in society at large, but even in their own bailiwick, the cities. That was surely the case for the posadskie liudi. The measures of their inferiority were many and varied. They had no recourse against the condescension and derogatory remarks of the gentry save to attempt to gain gentry status, and that avenue was open only to a few. As a group the townsmen labored without firmly articulated and effectively defended personal rights, a condition that left them prey for the agents of the crown. Even their chief avenue for the redress of grievances—the humbly presented petition to those on high—added yet another dimension to their humiliation. And, as has been argued, though the government expected much from them in the way of local administration, the townsmen proved incapable of seizing the existing institutions of urban government and turning them into instruments for their own ends. In all situations and at all times, the townsmen remained subservient to representatives of the crown, to men drawn from the landed gentry.[15]

If a comparison of Russian cities with those of Western Europe suggests important differences, a comparison of them with preindustrial cities the world over turns up a number of fundamental similarities. From a structural perspective it would appear that Russian cities were not at all unique. They were controlled by the ruling order for the purpose of maintaining its hegemony over society; they were largely shaped by the needs of state administration; and they provided a difficult environment for those whose lives were taken up with the production and exchange of goods.

These brief reappraisals of the Russian state and its townsmen, based on a comparative approach, are not intended as definitive statements. Rather they have been introduced to demonstrate that neither the behavior of the state nor the activities and social role of the townsmen are quite so unique or, as in some accounts, quite so reprehensible and dismal as parts of the historiographic tradition would suggest. With the insights they afford, the path has been cleared for a more positive treatment of urban Russia and its relationship with the state.

For all the help the comparative perspective provides in clearing the air, this study turns, nonetheless, to the Russian tradition for its guiding conceptual notion, or model, if the term does not sound too rigidly mechanical or social-scientific for some ears. I have chosen to call the urban order in which posad society was enmeshed the "service city." The notion of service is familiar to students of Russian history. In its prototypical sense, it describes the relationship between the government of Muscovy and those members of Russian society who performed military service for the crown. The serving people (*sluzhiliye liudi*) were a varied lot, ranging from exalted boyars to the great mass of service gentry to the specialized contract servitors. Most, but not all (the contract servitors were often exceptions), drew their livelihood from landed properties of various sizes and tenures. What they had in common—and what gave the system its characteristic features—was a set of obligations owed to the state. The state servitors performed a number of public functions, usually military, but sometimes civil. In return (service always entailed a quid pro quo relationship) the servitors received effective control over the land that was the source of their wealth and, increasingly as the years passed, over the peasant population who made that land productive.

The service principle arose initially because the rulers of the new principalities of the northeast lacked the resources to maintain large bureaucracies or standing military forces and because they had to honor the existing rights and privileges of the landed magnates. The principle continued to flourish even after Moscow had emerged as the dominant political entity, and it was clearly in force in the early seventeenth century, at the time this study begins. Indeed, service became not only the defining relationship between the state and its military servitors, but the distinguishing principle for all social groups. Almost every group in Russian society gained its identity and its position vis-à-vis other social groups from its service relationship with the state. The more significant the service rendered, the higher the status and rewards to those who rendered it. With national survival the principal task of statecraft, it was only natural that the military servitors should occupy the foremost position in the social hierarchy.

The service principle was no less operative in the cities than it was in the countryside, where it first appeared and where it remained so visible.[16] To begin with, the various full- and part-time inhabitants of the towns, the boyars, gentry, contract servitors, clergy, and itinerant peasants, could all be identified by their respective relationships with the state. More to the point for this study, however, is the status of the posad population: they too were defined by their service obligations to the state. In their capacities as tax and customs collectors, as in their labor for the maintenance of city property, the townsmen can best be understood as the tsar's urban servitors, men whose role was analogous in many respects to that of the rural service gentry. In return for their services, to balance the service equation as it were, the townsmen expected to be supported by the state in their claims to be the rightful and exclusive masters of urban trade and manufacturing. Again, as in the case of the military servitors, necessity gave birth to this relationship: in this instance the state's inability to maintain and control a bureaucratic establishment in the cities compelled it to enlist the services of the townsmen.

The notion of service has much to recommend it as a means of exploring the history of the Russian townsmen and their urban environment. First, the service principle leads the investigator toward those features of posad life that truly distinguish the tax-paying townsmen from other members of society, urban and rural. At the same time, by regarding the townsmen as yet another group of servitors, it becomes possible to place them in a social context in a state where the hierarchy of social values was itself largely determined by the service principle. Second, the service-city notion lends itself ideally to an investigation of the crucial links that joined the fortunes of the posad and the central government. It provides a workable set of criteria for assessing the relative strengths and weaknesses of the two parties, and it opens the way toward an appreciation of the necessities, mutually experienced by state and townsmen, that shaped the developing institutional order of the state. Third, once the issue of posad-state relations has been raised, it is but a short step to an exploration of the still broader issues of nation building that figured so strongly in the fate of Russia's cities. Finally, the concept of service stands as a measure of change, for service was indeed gradually modified and in part phased out over the course of time as the Russian state apparatus matured and as long-run social and economic conditions altered the cities. Service thus proves as useful in chronicling the end of an era as it does in characterizing that era in its full flower.

THE SPECIFIC APPROACH

To explore the history of the Russian townsmen during these crucial, formative years, I have assembled a synthetic study of some breadth. The identification of the significant features of posad life and an appraisal of the role of the posadskie liudi in the evolution of the Russian state demand an approach that embraces the widest possible set of relations bearing on posad society and examines them during an important transitional era in the history of the state. To meet the needs of such a broad-gauged study, I have drawn on materials from cities throughout European Russia for a period of more than two centuries. It would be difficult, given such a wide data base, to make the kinds of generalizations appropriate to this work were it not for the fact that custom and central government regulation made for considerable uniformity in institutional structures throughout Russia. That is not to say that no regional differences existed. In their social composition, in the nature of their economic life, and in cultural matters, the cities of Russia varied considerably. But the forms of posad organization and the common bonds of a centrally determined tax obligation gave a surprising degree of uniformity to posad society. It is regularities of that order that make possible the study's generalizing approach.

As the preceding argument implies, this study seeks to gain an understanding of the townsmen primarily through an investigation of the institutionalized aspects of posad life: the economic process, social organization, and political structures. A knowledge of the patterns and structures that direct social behavior along fairly regular lines over considerable spans of time is an indispensible element of the historical study of any society.[17] There is always the danger, however, that the study of institutions will become dry and formalized, that an emphasis on legal norms will not be matched by a commensurate attention to life as it really was. For precisely those reasons it is now somewhat fashionable to downgrade the works of nineteenth- and early twentieth-century Russian historians who were attracted to legislative memorials as a way of uncovering the past.[18] To be sure, law and life are not identical, and a study of the former without the latter can lead to sterile results. Further, there is always the temptation in dealing with legal history to adopt a lawyer's mentality and pick away at the technical flaws and conceptual inconsistencies in dead laws. In spite of these potential pitfalls, the study of legislative memorials remains a valid and essential part of any institutional analysis, as Ditiatin and Kizevetter have so well demonstrated. This study devotes particular attention to three legislative memorials: the *Ulozhenie* of 1649; the Main Magistracy Regulation of 1721; and the Charter Granted to the Cities of 1785. Each of these documents influenced directly the political, social, and economic institutions of posad life. As legal documents they speak to the problems that agitated governments and reflect the kinds of solutions that statesmen of the time thought feasible, or at least desirable. And, when executed—however imperfectly—each created a new institutional framework that shaped the fate of posad society for years to come. Even the most imperfect legislation has a way of leaving its mark upon the historical record.

But there is much more to the study of institutions than the recounting of their legislative origins. Their own operations must be carefully examined and they must be related to the broader society. To accomplish that end, I have relied upon the following simple model, or, less pretentiously put, set of assumptions. In any given society, certain functions must be performed if that society is to perpetuate itself. The types of institutions that arise to perform those functions are shaped by two factors: the nature of the function to be performed and the character of the society itself. The resulting institutional structures, therefore, are not the products of chance or of abstract institution-making; they are necessary structures, integrally related to the needs and capacities of the society. However strange an institution may appear to an outside observer, it may be well suited to the function it performs in its particular social context. The determining conditions can change, of course, and with them the nature of institutions, up to and including their disappearance.

Apart from its intrinsic merits, such a notion has a particular applicability to the study of Russian urban history, for it provides, through its stress on the necessary character of institutions, a natural and effective antidote to the proponents of what-might-have-been history, to those who lament the absence of institutions, that, however beneficial they may appear in the abstract, had no chance of taking root in Russia.[19] The stress throughout this work falls on the way in which the institutional structures that guided the lives of the townsmen were an integral part of the society, waxing and waning in relation to the long-run transformations of the national life.

More specifically, the relevant materials on posad life have been treated from two different, but closely related perspectives. The first focuses on the central institutions of the townsmen, in particular the commune and the magistracy, with an eye toward providing a typology of the institutional matrix in which the posad dwellers operated. This line of analysis is perhaps as much sociological as historical in its pursuit of the nature of these institutions and their role in society. The second, more purely historical perspective, observes the townsmen and their principal institutions over time, relating their evolution to a number of long-term developments of Russian life—that is, to the social setting, to economic conditions, and, most importantly, to the evolving structure of national monarchy. Together, these two perspectives yield an analysis of the commune as an institution and a chronicle of the changes it underwent.

It is easy enough to define the posadskie liudi in terms of their estate privileges and obligations, and it is similarly easy to identify their principal institutions. It is also possible to see the presence of the central government in the affairs of posad life through the agencies of state administration and their functionaries. It is not nearly so easy, however, to identify the townsmen's chief venue, the city—that is, to be able to say precisely what was or was not a city. The difficulties are many. First, the historical tradition has not always treated Russia's cities kindly, even going to the point, as mentioned earlier, of doubting whether the country had more than a handful of real cities. Second, the literature of contemporary sociology contains no simple definition of a city that enjoys universal assent. The urban-rural continuum is maddeningly flexible. Third, the Russian scene presents some problems all its own. One must take into account not only the *goroda* of government lists, but also a vast array of settlements of diverse nomenclature, many with developed economies, almost all of which could lay claim to city status—depending, of course, on the criteria employed. Through the better part of the eighteenth century, to take a pertinent example, some settlements of a commercial or industrial nature bore the designation *posad*, a usage that can be attributed simply to the fact that the economic activities of the settlements' inhabitants were more or less identical to those engaged in by the posadskie liudi, the urban posad inhabitants. Why the venue of the latter individuals was considered a city and that of the former not, is not always clear. The distant observer can take modest comfort from the efforts of the minister of internal affairs who in 1807 found it necessary to come up with a set of definitions that would distinguish a city from a posad in order to resolve a land-use dispute.[20]

Some useful guidance on the definitional question can be found in Leonard Reissman's notion of a "macro-social" approach to urban phenomena.[21] Rather than trying to define in a restrictive sense what is the precise nature of a city, what it is in and of itself, he shifts the emphasis to the functional, to what is done generally by the cities, either uniquely or conjointly with other institutions, for the society. Such an approach casts a wide net, gathering in not only economic activities but administrative, social, and cultural matters as well. And it assesses the city as a center of communications, a dispenser of information and misinformation of every conceivable sort to its hinterland. Function, more than form, thus defines the city.

A number of the goroda of Russia made contributions in each of these areas and thus easily qualified as cities, while others, handicapped by small populations and few resources, contributed much less. But the goroda all shared in common the performance of one or more of the functions that are traditionally associated with cities. Moreover, the very lexicon used by the Russians indicates that they understood the goroda to be entities distinct from other social organizations. With these considerations in mind, it would seem that the goroda of government lists may, for all intents and purposes, be regarded as cities. To be sure, not all goroda fit our general understanding of what cities are about and some discrimination of city types is clearly in order. Chapter 1, for example, introduces a rudimentary typology of cities to set the scene for the activities of the posadskie liudi, but an effort has been made not to let the problem of defining a city gain the upper hand. Anyone interested in this matter would be well advised to look at Ia. E. Vodarskii's discussion of the typologies employed by earlier scholars of Russia's cities, as well as his own effort—not very persuasive in my judgment—to provide a Marxian schema for classifying Russian city-type settlements.[22]

Definitional problems affect not only the abstract discussion of institutions, but also the very practical task of translating foreign words. It might ideally be desirable to restrict the term "city" to the larger and more heterogeneous population concentrations and to employ the term "town" for the bulk of Russia's medium- and small-sized goroda. Yet such a verbal division of labor might be seen to imply that only a handful of goroda were real cities. Therefore, the two terms are used interchangeably to underscore the conviction that the vast majority of the goroda do represent—in greater or lesser degrees of realization—urban forms, distinguishable functionally from villages, hamlets, and other rural settlements.

CHAPTER ONE

Towns and Townsmen
in the Seventeenth Century

WIDELY DIVERGENT IN CHARACTER, the cities of Muscovy served as centers of defense, administration, and commerce for the developing nation-state. It is not surprising, therefore, that as the state grew, the number of cities in it increased. Early in the sixteenth century, there were 96 cities; by the end of the century, there were about 170 cities of a permanent character; and by the year 1650, there were 226.[1] This steady growth over a century and a half can be attributed primarily to the territorial expansion of the state. The acquisition of settled territories in the west brought established cities and towns within the nation's borders. On the ever-changing southern frontier, new cities sprang up one after another as the border was pushed toward the Black Sea. As the frontier moved on, cities behind it took their place as administrative centers, consolidating the hold of the central government over the newly pacified lands.

The geographical disposition of Russia's cities was highly uneven. A map of late seventeenth-century Russia shows the cities concentrated in a crescent beginning in the lower Dnieper River basin and the adjacent upper Donets basin, running up through the Oka region and on along the upper Volga area. The importance of the rivers for communications, so integral to the earlier history of Kievan Rus, remained undiminished in the Muscovite period. Indeed, along the banks of the Volga and its affluents stood a substantial number of Russia's cities, including many of the first rank. In the north, the *Pomore*, cities were few and far between— understandably so, given the inhospitable climate. In the south, along the Don and east of the Volga, cities were equally sparse, but in this case, inhospitable neighbors, not weather, accounted for their paucity.

Not only were the cities unevenly distributed, they were far apart. Moscow and Novgorod, reduced to neighbors by the scale of text-book maps, are nearly 500 kilometers apart. Herberstein, speaking in praise of the Muscovite state post service (*Iamskaia gon'ba*), and in particular of its horses, noted that one of his servants journeyed from Novgorod to

Moscow in just 72 hours.[2] It is unlikely that communications to other parts of the state were as good, for the Moscow-Novgorod route was old and established. But if 150 kilometers a day were the standard, it would have taken five days to get a message from Moscow to Kazan', seven days to Arkhangel, and more than eight days to communicate with Sol' Kamskaia, seat of the Stroganov lands on the Kama River. In fact, news seems to have traveled more slowly than that. The fortress city of Kozlov, located on the Belgorodskaia defense line less than 400 kilometers from Moscow, did not receive news of the Moscow uprisings of June 2, 1648 until nine days later.[3]

The uneven dispersal of Russia's cities over so great an area had a profound impact not only on the history of the cities but on the fate of the nation as well. In the first place, the sheer size of the country—in particular the presence of a vast, moving, and relatively unpopulated frontier—dictated that city development be extensive rather than intensive, at least until about 1800. The story is not one of urbanization, of the transformation of a rural society into an urban one; rather, it is the story of the adaptation of old cities and the creation of new ones, sometimes gradually, sometimes in bunches, to meet urgent political needs of the state. For the most part, analytic categories appropriate to the study of urbanization are not relevant to seventeenth- and eighteenth-century Russia.

Second, as a consequence of the close tie between state growth and city development, Russia's cities came to perform a number of functions on behalf of the state. Indeed, the cities of the realm can be roughly typed according to their predominant function or functions; and within the cities, the inhabitants fell into distinct groupings, each of which was characterized by its state-determined tasks. Thus the social structure of the cities to a large extent derived from the exigencies of state building.

Third, the great distances involved and the limited means of communication hampered the economic development of cities. To be sure, there was trade between neighboring cities and there was long-distance trade, particularly in items of high value relative to weight; but it remained difficult for the small number of cities to establish economic hegemony over the huge hinterlands. The effect was to reinforce the self-sufficiency of the rural dwellers, and, to a remarkable degree, to encourage it on the part of city residents as well. The kind of division of labor between towns and countryside that makes for neat sociological analysis simply was not present in Russia.

Finally, the geography of the land posed special problems for those who would exercise political control. Given the distances involved, it was a continual struggle for the central government to enforce its will on the outlying areas of the state. To get information to or from the cities took considerable time. To actually do something about a local problem took even longer; and even then there was little assurance that matters would be straightened out properly. The rulers of Muscovy faced an administrative Hobson's choice: to leave local affairs in local hands was to court political disintegration; to maintain centralized control necessarily involved the sacrifice of efficiency, and in many cases the suppression of potentially constructive local initiative. This administrative dilemma has dogged the footsteps of Russian rulers to the present time, though it is now somewhat muted by the achievements of technology.

MILITARY-ADMINISTRATIVE CITIES AND THEIR INHABITANTS

As might be expected in a country so large and still growing, there was no single city type. Russian towns varied in size—from tiny, shrinking seats of ancient princely power to the metropolis that was Moscow. In social composition the cities displayed equally great variety: some contained a population made up almost exclusively of military servitors, others had a distinctly commercial population, while a few combined all social elements into the heterogeneous social atmosphere that is customarily associated with urban forms. In terms of their larger functions in Russian society, the cities performed, in various combinations, three main tasks: military, commercial, and state-administrative. The latter function was almost always present: in fact, the presence of administrative offices in a town was itself sufficient cause for it to be considered a city by government and subject alike.

Seventeenth-century Russian cities can be divided, on the basis of state function and related social structure, into two groups: military-administrative and commercial-administrative. The evidence demonstrates quite clearly that the majority of Russia's cities in the seventeenth century were military centers, inhabited by those whose principal duties concerned the defense of the state and the administration of crucial border areas.

In the west the presence of Sweden and Poland made necessary the fortification of the frontier from Novgorod and Pskov down to the Seversk lands and on through the trans-Oka region. With the acquisition of the Ukraine, of course, the greater part of this border shifted westward. To meet its defense needs in the west, the government had only to refurbish the fortifications of existing cities and to garrison them adequately.[4] In the south, however, quite different conditions prevailed. To meet the threat posed by the Crimean Tatars, the Moscow state erected a line of fortress-cities, linked by land and timber defense-works designed to deny the Tatars access to the heart of Muscovy. The core of this defense system was the *Belgorodskaia cherta*, a string of twenty-nine fortress-cities and defense-works, which ran from Akhtyrka on the river Vorskla to Tambov. Most of these towns were established between 1636 and 1648. A second wave of activity, occurring between 1648 and 1654, extended the fortified line northward and eastward. Although the chief function of these cities was to act as a first line of defense, they also served as administrative centers for areas newly come under Muscovy's control. By the 1660s their inhabitants were beginning to petition against rapidly increasing tax burdens, suggesting that the incorporation of these regions into the main stream of Muscovite life had been swift and sure.[5]

Further to the east, along the lower Volga River, defense needs of a different character predominated. There, the government's chief task lay in protecting commerce down the Volga from the depredations of the Kalmyks and their occasional allies, the Nogais. Thus the towns of the lower Volga basin maintained substantial garrisons. And the middle Volga and Kama basins were defended by an extension of the fortified line eastward as far as Menzelinsk on the Kama River. Of course, the cities of the Volga basin figured prominently in the transit trade that passed through the area.[6]

The military role of the cities can be seen clearly in their physical layout. At the center of nearly every Russian city—not just those on the borders—stood a fortress, called in earlier times a *detenets*, later a *kreml'*. Located advantageously on high ground, the kreml' contained within its walls, usually built of stone but occasionally of wood or earth, the centers of administrative, military, and ecclesiastical power. The house and chancellery of the military governor, the customs house, and the state liquor outlet represented the authority of the central government, while the offices of the police and of assorted petty administrators marked the presence of local authority. An arsenal and powder magazine, houses for leading servitors, and a stable signified the military presence. And, of course, the ever-present cathedral and a handful of dwelling places for leading clerics symbolized the power of the church. The walls of the kreml', however, were not the sole fortification of the city: the main residential area, which lay outside the walls of the kreml', was itself surrounded by a huge land wall that served as the city's first line of defense.[7]

Walls alone, however, are not sufficient proof of the military orientation of so many of Russia's cities, for the preservation of medieval fortifications long after the need for them had ceased was as characteristic of Russia as of other countries. It is in the social composition of the cities, in the dominant role in them of the servitor population, that the military presence is most evident. The tale is told graphically by the distribution among various social groups of city *dvory*, or courts (in this context the word *dvor* describes a discrete piece of property, usually delineated by a wall, a fence, or a building constructed about an open courtyard, though in other contexts *dvor* may refer to the inhabitants of such a property, in which case it is rendered "household"). P. P. Smirnov argues that in the mid-seventeenth century more than 60 percent of all city property lay in the hands of servitors of various ranks. Broken down by geographic region, the evidence is even more striking. In the west, 71.2 percent of the city courts belonged to servitors; in the south the figure was 85.3 percent, and in the east, it climbed to 87.3 percent.[8]

The bulk of these servitors fell into the category of *sluzhilye liudi po priboru*—contract servitors. In the sixteenth century, these petty servitors began to appear in princely suburbs, usually adjacent to cities, where they practiced any one of a number of different occupations on behalf of the state. Basically, however, they can be divided into two groups, craftsmen and soldiers. Contract servitors might, for example, be stonemasons or carpenters employed in the erection of fortresses or breastworks along the southern frontier or called upon to work at the court of the tsar. But by far the greater number of them were military personnel: musketeers, artillery men, city guards, and serving cossacks (*gorodovye* or *sluzhilye kazaki*) who resided in suburbs (*slobody*) associated with the towns of the southern defense line.[9]

The remuneration of contract servitors was not great, nor was it very regular. After luring men to the southern defense line, for example, with salary and promises of tax privileges, the government soon reneged on both pledges; only when enemy campaigns threatened did it come around with money, and with paltry sums at that. As a consequence of their financial insecurity, the contract servitors busied themselves when not on state duties with handicraft work or trade in the cities, or with agriculture in the neighboring countryside.[10] The occupation of contract servitors with craft and trade, traditionally urban activities, as well as with rural agricultural pursuits, helps to explain the basic provisioning of so many of Russia's towns where almost the entire population, formally at least, was connected with administration, military matters, or church administration, with few if any bona fide merchants present.

Other state servitors were present in the cities, though in substantially smaller numbers. In all regions of the state, one could find city courts belonging to the members of the state post service, and, of course, courts of *dvoriane* and *deti boiarskie* could be found scattered through the towns. All told, however, these groups constituted only a fractional part of the city population.[11]

COMMERCIAL-ADMINISTRATIVE CITIES AND THEIR
INHABITANTS

On three points of the compass, then, Russia's cities reflected the overall
military orientation of the state as it sought to stabilize some borders, to
expand others, and to provide basic defense in all cases. In the north and
center, however, a sharply different city type predominated. There, the
urban population was far more heterogeneous. Merchants, petty traders,
and craftsmen in considerable numbers joined military servitors, church
hierarchs, contract servitors, lower-level bureaucrats, and, on occasion,
small colonies of foreigners in cities of some diversity and vibrancy. Thus
it was in the ancient and populous center and in the old but sparsely inhabited north that cities of a nonmilitary cast appeared, cities that could
best be described, judging from their social composition and services performed, as commercial-administrative.

The military servitors who figured so prominently in the social make-
up of the border cities occupied a decidedly secondary position in the
commercial-administrative cities. They controlled but 23.6 percent of the
city courts in the north and a mere 13.9 percent in central Russia.[12]

In those two areas, the *posadskie chernye liudi*, literally, "taxable people of the posad," constituted the most numerous group of permanent
urban residents. Just who these people were can perhaps best be understood through a brief etymological review.

The word *posad*, as found in the sources of the thirteenth, fourteenth,
and fifteenth centuries, signified that area of a city that lay between the
walls of the kreml' and the outer land walls. Most inhabitants of the
posad engaged in crafts and trade, though agriculturalists, state servitors, and other segments of the population could be found within its confines. The land on which the posady sprang up belonged ultimately to the
Moscow prince; it was taxable (*chernyi*) state land, like the rural land
settled by thousands of peasants. Since the state demanded recompense
from those who resided on its property, it taxed these people directly.
They, in turn, came to be known as *chernye liudi*, that is, "taxpayers."

By the end of the fifteenth century, the geographical term *posad* and
the administrative term *chernyi* begin to appear side by side in the phrase
posadskie chernye liudi, or in its more commonly encountered, abbrevi-
ated form, *posadskie liudi* (here rendered variously as posad "taxpayers," "dwellers," "inhabitants," or "residents," or, simply, as "townsmen"). Both phrases denoted that part of the tax-paying population that
resided in the cities and bore a certain set of government responsibilities
known as *tiaglo*. *Tiaglo*, for its part, denoted the full scope of state impositions that fell on the posad population. It included the payment of

direct taxes in money or in kind to the central government. In fact, the townsmen were the largest single contributors of cash revenues to the Russian state; from their tax moneys the logistic support of the armed forces was largely financed.[13] Tiaglo also entailed the performance of specified services on behalf of the state or for the benefit of the town (but also at the state's direction). These services included the construction and maintenance of roads, bridges, and fortifications; tours of duty as police officials, watchmen, or firefighters; and assignments related to state administration, especially the apportionment and collection of taxes. The manifold service obligations of tiaglo that fell upon the posadskie liudi thus gave the word *posad* a second meaning, quite distinct from its original, territorial one; *posad* now came to mean the sum total of those subject to the tiaglo.[14] Thus, the posad had become a fiscal-administrative unit that was not limited either in theory or practice to a prescribed geographical area. Since, however, the bearers of this tax tended to live and work together, the old territorial sense of the word did not entirely disappear from use.

It is important to note that the language used to categorize this element of the city population is intimately connected with state service obligations. The common bond of tiaglo helped to bring together the posadskie liudi as a coherent, identifiable social group. But they were not the sole bearers of tiaglo in the state: this obligation fell on rural agriculturalists as well. Any characterization of the posad must therefore include two other dimensions—the occupational orientation of the posadskie liudi and their place of operation. The production and exchange of goods, largely in an urban setting, marked off the posadskie liudi from the rural bearers of tiaglo. The posad population may thus be succinctly described as the tsar's urban taxpayers who made their livelihood and paid their taxes for the most part from trade and manufacturing activities.

The posad population was by no means homogeneous; it, too, like the rest of society, had its social subdivisions. In cities where the *posad* contingent was sufficiently large to be divided, it was broken into three categories or ranks (*stati*) based on the total assets (*zhivoty i promysl'*) of individual members. There appears to have been no single formula for the country as a whole; each posad decided on its own the category to which a man belonged.[15] It is clear, however, that the gap between top and bottom was substantial. The third rank was composed of extremely poor individuals, mostly hawkers of wares or foodstuffs and manual laborers. The men of the first rank, on the other hand, were relatively well-off; they controlled the internal life of the posad.

The posad social order had its extremes. At the lower extreme were the *bobyli*. These men of few means worked at menial tasks or served as yard-keepers for more well-to-do posad residents. They could be distinguished from the third rank of regular posad dwellers by the nature of their tax obligation. Whereas the regular posad dweller bore tiaglo, the bobyli paid the state an *obrok*.[16] This arrangement indicates that the bobyli were not considered economically sturdy enough to bear the higher burdens of tiaglo.

At the upper extreme of posad society, one encounters a significant manifestation of the service principle: the most successful members of posad society were separated from their former compatriots by membership in one of three privileged corporations—the *gosti*, the *gostinaia sotnia*, and the *sukhonnaia sotnia*. The members of these corporations formed a state service elite, responsible for high-level fiscal and commercial administration. The most prestigious corporation, the gosti, consisted of a handful of wealthy merchants appointed by the government. Thirteen strong late in the seventeenth century, their number probably never exceeded twenty to thirty men.[17] The elevation of successful merchants to the rank of gosti had the effect of drawing them directly into service of the state, where they acted both as advisors to the tsar and as administrators of important financial and commercial undertakings. Gosti administered state monopolies, the customs collection, and the farming of liquor revenue collection; they managed the fishing and salt-making establishments of the state, purchased goods for the tsar, and operated his sable-hunting enterprise.[18] They also assisted the tsar in matters of foreign trade and in domestic economic activities. When, for example, the English sent John Merrick to the court of Michael to reestablish and even broaden their commercial privileges, which had lapsed during the Time of Troubles, the leading government negotiator, F. I. Sheremetev, consulted the gosti on each and every one of the English requests.[19]

In return for these many services of the tsar, the gosti received a number of privileges: emancipation from state tax responsibilities (tiaglo); free passage abroad for the purpose of trading; the right, up to 1666, to obtain hereditary landed property (*votchina*); subordination for administrative purposes directly to the Bureau of the Great Treasury; the right to store wine at home; and exemption from the payment of numerous customs and tariff duties.[20]

Next in rank after the gosti came the members of the Moscow *gostinaia sotnia* and *sukhonnaia sotnia*, or "hundreds." They too formed privileged corporations, though much larger than that of the gosti. In 1649, the combined membership of both hundreds totaled 274 persons.[21] In addition to maintaining their own business establishments, they served as agents of the tsar, assisting primarily in the collection of taxes and customs duties. Their privileges, less than those of the gosti but still substantial, included emancipation from state tax responsibilities and exclusion from the jurisdiction of local governmental authorities.[22]

In the gosti and hundreds one finds a logical and consistent application of the service principle on which the social order of old Russia was based. In fact, the individuals involved appear to have perceived themselves as a part of such an order. Bogoslovskii notes that in addressing state authorities the gosti and hundreders referred to themselves as slaves (*kholopy*), the term used by military servitors in such a situation, as opposed to the term orphans (*siroty*), as used by the rank-and-file posadskie liudi.[23]

Not all city residents who bore tiaglo lived in that area of the city known as the posad. Especially in Moscow, a great many taxpayers resided in the suburbs. Suburbs arose in the early centuries of settlement of the northeast as a part of the competition for a limited labor supply. Lay and secular magnates, along with princes, offered privileges and protection to those agriculturalists who would gather in settlements on their land and engage in agricultural pursuits. Later, with the rise of Moscow and the corresponding increase in the importance of cities to the administration of the state, new suburbs arose in the immediate proximity of cities, again at the initiative of princes, boyars, church hierarchs, and monasteries. As distinguished from earlier suburbs, these were centers of trade and handicraft production. In the early sixteenth century, still another type of suburb appeared under the aegis of the government: the tsars settled groups of contract servitors on discrete parcels of land adjacent to, but not within, the walled limits of the towns. This phenomenon was most highly developed in the immediate environs of Moscow and has left its mark on the place-names of the capital.[24]

State suburbs did not remain separate, privileged sanctuaries for long. By the second half of the sixteenth century, most state suburbs had been transformed into taxable property (*chernye sloboda*) and their residents found themselves on the tax rolls along with the posadskie liudi.[25] Indeed, the social composition of the suburbs, especially those once inhabited solely by contract servitors, underwent considerable change. Ordinary posad taxpayers came to reside in them, along with the military men, craftsmen, and provisioners for the tsar's court, workers in the state postal service, and the like, for whom the suburbs had originally been created.[26] Ultimately, as cities expanded, they absorbed the suburbs, and in the case of the tax-paying suburbs, essentially incorporated them into the posad. Moscow, however, constitutes an exception. There the suburbs managed to maintain their identity even after they had been physically swallowed up by the growing posad. For one thing, the majority of the residents of suburbs engaged in a common occupation or hailed from a common town or area. For another, the suburbs remained territorial units, while the posad increasingly became an administrative category. The suburbs had their own internal subdivisions for the sake of police administration. But, it should be made clear, the inhabitants of these Moscow suburbs were considered posadskie liudi and bore the full burdens of tiaglo.[27]

While the state suburbs gradually merged with posady, private suburbs continued to flourish in Russia's cities. In them one could find many of the non-posad residents of the commercial-administrative cities, both the high-born and powerful and the low-born and dependent. Sprinkled among the mean dwellings of the posad people there stood the spacious city properties (referred to both as *dvory* and as *slobody*) of great boyars and of *dvoriane*, often with elegant buildings and attractive grounds. Even greater holdings of city property lay in the hands of the church, some of it belonging to the hierarchical establishment or monasteries, some to individual members of the clergy.[28] Originally these various private suburbs had served as business offices, stopover points for a visiting lord, and as seige courts, places of safety in time of enemy invasion.[29] With the passage of time, however, the owners of these properties realized that substantial economic gains could be had if these properties, exempt from taxes, were to enter the economic life of the city. It was this change of land use that made private suburbs such an important part of the city scene. In these suburbs could be found large—but usually unrecorded—populations of dependent people, serfs of boyars, and a congeries of people who relied on the church for livelihood and protection from the vicissitudes of life. The chief occupations of these dependent people were handicrafts and trade, often utilizing rural sources of raw materials or products of peasant manufacture. Deriving benefits from the privileged positions of the owners of the properties on which they resided, these dependent people proved to be serious competitors of the rank-and-file posad population, with whom they shared common trades.[30]

Foreign citizens, though relatively few in number, constituted a distinct and often conspicuous part of the urban scene in medieval Russia, and their presence was a source of concern to many parties, among them the state, the church, and the native Russian townsmen. In Moscow proper, they could be found in the famed foreign suburbs—the Nemetskaia, Panskaia, and others. Off and on, from the reign of Vasilii III (1505-1533) the military men, artists, artisans, and adventurers who had been drawn to Muscovy had lived in suburbs, isolated from the center of Moscow. During the Time of Troubles, however, the foreign suburbs of Moscow were destroyed and their inhabitants dispersed. Michael Romanov was content to allow foreigners to settle in whatever part of the city they wished, but pressure mounted to reestablish the foreign suburb. The church, fearing the insidious doctrines of Protestantism and Catholicism, pleaded that the infidels be isolated, lest contact with them taint the purity of the Muscovite's faith. The posad people of the city also objected to the presence of foreigners in their midst, claiming that the business practices of the wily Europeans worked great hardship upon them. In 1652 Aleksei yielded to the heartfelt pleas of his countrymen and created a new foreign suburb—the Novoinozemskaia Sloboda, or Novaia Nemetskaia Sloboda as it was known in popular parlance. The suburb residents, although citizens of other states and now somewhat isolated from the life of Moscow, nonetheless fell under the jurisdiction of Russian law and administration. Those activities they performed for the Russian government were supervised by the appropriate *prikazy*. For example, foreign military personnel were handled first by the Inozemcheskii and then by the Razriadnyi prikazy. The suburb, however, exercised complete and independent control over its internal affairs. As a consequence, its inhabitants enjoyed a certain autonomy, as well as numerous privileges and exemptions from state responsibilities.[31] Yet the land on which the suburb rested belonged to the state: there was never any suggestion that the right of extraterritoriality might be applied to it. In other cities of the state, where foreigners were present, their numbers were not sufficiently large to warrant their isolation in a suburb, and they mixed freely with the local population.

In the preceding breakdown of city population by social grouping, the basic principle on which the categorization was accomplished was the relationship which each group had to the state, or to private persons who themselves stood in a clearly defined relationship to the state. A city inhabitant was either a state taxpayer, a state servitor, a dependent of a state servitor, a member of the church hierarchy, a church dependent, or a foreigner whose position in Muscovy was carefully regulated by the state.[32] But he was not an urban citizen, in the sense of belonging to a category of people who derived certain rights, obligations, and identity from their presence or participation in urban society. Instead, city inhabitants gained their identity by membership in social groups whose traits derived from principles extraneous to the city environment per se. In fact, it was not uncommon to find representatives of these social groups residing in the countryside, including even posadskie liudi.[33]

The practice of categorizing individuals by social groups, while it helps the historian to clarify the social composition of the towns, has had quite a negative impact on efforts to draw up a demographic profile of Russia's urban population. Useful data do exist on the posad population, since the townsmen were an overwhelmingly urban tax category. But other segments of the urban population, such as clergy or servitors, were recorded along with the rural members of their estate (*soslovie*) group, making it impossible to know from that data how many lived in towns and how many in the countryside. Then there were large numbers of feudal dependents who operated from private courts and suburbs, as well as a substantial population of transients; neither of these groups left any significant trace on urban administrative records. There are, however, ways to get around some of these obstacles sufficiently to make a few general observations about those urban inhabitants who were settled enough to be recorded as part of one estate of the realm or another.

In the middle of the seventeenth century, Russia had about 160 cities with posady, that is, cities where the tax rolls indicated a population of individuals obligated to tiaglo. By 1678 that figure had grown to 173. In terms of the actual number of posad registrants, the record shows 108,000 males for 1652 and 134,000 for 1678. The distribution of the posadskie liudi was such that about one-third of them lived in cities with fewer than 1,000 posad registrants, one third lived in cities with between 1,000 and 2,000 registrants, and the remainder in cities of 2,000 registrants or more. The total urban population was, of course, considerably larger. Based on an inventory of military-eligible males in the cities as of 1678, Ia. E. Vodarskii estimates the total number of male city inhabitants of all estates at 185,000. This represents about 2 percent of the total population of the country. It should be borne in mind that these estimates do not include various dependent people and transients, about whom no information exists. Any estimates of the overall city population and its relation to the population of the state must therefore remain pure guesswork.[34]

In this book I concentrate on the 160- to 170-odd cities of seventeenth-century Russia that possessed a tax-paying urban commercial and manufacturing population. Not only were these cities the center of activities for the posad population, they were far and away the most interesting and important cities of the realm, thanks to the diversity of their population and the multiplicity of functions performed in them. Although not generally large, these cities tended to be larger than the border cities and they included in their ranks the greatest city of the realm, Moscow. The presence of large numbers of posadskie liudi, men who made their living at trade or small-scale manufacturing, gave these cities a decidedly commercial cast, especially when compared to the cities of the border areas. At the same time, the presence of a host of servitors great and small, bureaucrats, and churchmen lent weight to the administrative operations performed in these cities—operations, it should be stressed, in which the tax-paying townsmen also participated. The commercial-administrative

city of the Muscovite center and north must be considered the prototype
of the emerging Russian city order.

PROPERTY RELATIONS IN THE CITY

The motley social composition of the Russian city is reflected in the property relations that existed within the city. Not only are the precise nature
of those relations unclear, but the forms of property in medieval Russia
were different from those common in Western European nations. Indeed,
until the eighteenth century the Russian language lacked a word for private property (*sobstvennost'*). Nevertheless, property relations were
regulated and did have a juridical basis.

During the Muscovite period, the only real property to which full
rights of ownership accrued was *votchina* property; it could be sold,
testated, mortgaged, or bequeathed at the pleasure of its possessor.[35] In
the appanage period, each piece of princely property was held in votchina right; upon the death of a prince, his estate was distributed among
all of his male heirs, each of whom exercised votchina rights over his own
share. The foremost votchina of the realm belonged, of course, to the
grand prince of Moscow. As he expanded his domain, he applied the
principle of votchina property to each territorial acquisition, no matter
how it came into his hands—by purchase, escheat, gentle persuasion, or
brute force. Chicherin and other legal historians have argued that the
Moscow princes never really regarded their possessions as state lands,
separate from their own personal property. In effect, the state was but a
large votchina.[36] While this phenomenon was most pronounced in the
fourteenth and fifteenth centuries, traces of it persisted well into the eighteenth century, when the sovereigns disposed of the lives and property of
their subjects as it suited their moods or needs.

The Moscow rulers, however, were not the sole possessors of votchina
property: various petty princes, the church, monastic institutions, boyars, and even a few great merchants (gosti) had them. But the votchina
holdings of these men paled before those of the grand prince, who never
missed an opportunity to increase his possessions at the expense of rival
princes or great boyars. The vicissitudes of Muscovite politics made for
considerable turnover in property, and the tsar was certainly a net win-
ner in these transactions.

Other forms of real property existed alongside votchina property, but
none of them entailed full rights of disposition. In each case, these lands
were held in right of use, or possession, but not of ownership. The most
well-known form of land possession was *pomest'e*, granted to the tsar's
servitors in return for their service. In theory, the pomest'e remained in

the hands of the servitor only so long as he continued to fulfill his obligations to the state, and insofar as he did not incur the displeasure of the
sovereign. In fact, over the course of time, the servitors increasingly be-
haved as if they had full rights to dispose of pomest'e lands. The be-
queathing of a pomest'e to a servitor's heirs, for example, became a common practice; and, so long as the new holders rendered service, the state
remained indifferent to the de facto treatment of such properties as if
they were hereditary possessions. The de jure status of pomest'e lands
was never really in doubt. The ultimate nature of the property rights of
the peasants who resided on state (chernye) lands was also conditional,
though the absence of any formal charter or grant made it seem less obviously so. The peasants, who in many cases had settled in the northeast
before princely authority had been imposed, quite understandably felt
the land they tilled was theirs by gift of God, and they completed all
manner of transactions with it. But in the last analysis, as they came to
find out, it was not God, but God's representative on Earth, the tsar,
who controlled that land by his votchina right. Thus all non-votchina
property-holding amounted to nothing more than diverse forms of tenure
—the votchinik was the true owner of the land, and others who resided
on it were of necessity dependent on him for their continued residence.
With these powers of ownership came powers of a political, economic,
and even social character—a fact of cardinal importance to the towns.[37]

In turning to property relationships within the cities, it is perhaps best
to begin on the negative side by asserting what was not. Just as there
existed no such social entity as the urban citizen, neither did there exist
any special forms of urban property. The cities themselves did not possess on behalf of their inhabitants what we would today refer to as public
or municipal property. And there was no form of urban property that
private citizens might hold in right of full ownership. Instead, the territorial space of the city was broken into numerous parcels of land of varying sizes that fell under the established rubrics of votchina property or
one of the many forms of possessional holdings.

The great votchinik of Russia, the grand prince of Moscow, was also
the dominant presence in urban property relations, for the greater part of
Russia's urban land belonged ultimately to him. As area after area came
under Moscow's sway, the prince confiscated or obtained by other means
fair or foul substantial pieces of city land and added it to his votchina.
And it goes almost without saying that new cities established by Muscovy were erected entirely on the grand prince's votchina lands, or were,
in other words, state cities. These city properties of the tsar were in turn
inhabited by various categories of the tsar's subjects, who held the land
in a variety of conditional tenures. Smirnov cites four distinct types of

conditional landholding in the cities, all of which emanated from grants, formal or merely implied, of the tsar. The first, and least prevalent, was personal grant possession. Similar in many respects to the pomest'e, it granted land to subjects for specific use—for siege courts, for stopovers, or on occasion for commercial use. A second, more common type was communal grant possession in a suburb. Contract servitors, for example, held their settlements collectively through such grants, some of which were conferred in actual charters liable to periodic renewal. Since the holders of these two types of property performed state services not dependent on the land granted them, these properties were exempt from state taxes.[38]

Other forms of conditional landholding in the cities did involve the obligation to pay state taxes. Third on Smirnov's list of forms of conditional landholding was collective possession by the posad commune (posadskii mir)[39] of the taxable (chernye) land on which its members lived. The origin of posad land varied. Some of it consisted of former suburbs attached to the princely court or of special state administrative departments (puti) that had been transformed by princely charter into posady. Other posad land, perhaps the majority, had once belonged, in formal title, to appanage princes or had been held in full right of ownership by individual citizen landholders (svoezemtsi).[40] By the sixteenth and seventeenth centuries, however, the Moscow prince had displaced these former owners and had taken title to their lands. A grant from the tsar had become the chief claim to possession of posad land, and an implicit condition of such a grant was the fulfilment by the taxpayers of their obligation to the state. The tsar's ultimate claim to the full rights of ownership of posad land went uncontested.[41]

The fourth form of conditional urban landholding was personal grant possession for the purpose of establishing some kind of business activity —manufacturing, trading, or even the holding of a fair. Properties given out for such use went to people of all ranks, with the exception of servitors of high rank, who easily subverted the prohibition by using straws. With possession of these lands came the obligation to bear state taxes, which, as Smirnov points out, made such a transaction merely the renting of state property.[42]

If, in legal terms, the tsar retained formal title under the four categories of conditional urban landholding, in actual practice the degree of control over the use of such properties by their possessors varied substantially. In the suburbs of contract servitors, for example, the tsar—or, more accurately, his bureaucratic establishment—closely regulated the land and its uses. The government surveyed suburb lands and set norms for the size of courts. The actual apportionment of courts to specific individ-

uals was a task apparently shared by the government and the local inhabitants. These courts could not be sold or bequeathed; when they became
empty, it was the government's agents who decided who was to be the
next occupant. The individual servitor could lay full claim to the use of
his property only so long as he fulfilled his specified service obligations.
This was truly a form of conditional landholding, depending strictly on
service.[43]

It was quite another matter, however, for most of the posad lands.
These properties were both numerous and widely scattered around the
state. The Muscovite bureaucratic apparatus was still growing in the
seventeenth century, and it was beyond the powers and perhaps the
wishes of the state administration—or of the city administration to the
extent that it existed—to regulate exactly who lived where, who manufactured in this court or that, what happened to a parcel of posad land
when its possessor died, and so forth. Thus it was that posad dwellers,
inhabitants of state suburbs, and even individual possessors of commercial courts performed all those property transactions that are associated
with full rights of ownership: they bought, sold, mortgaged, leased, and
bequeathed their city properties. Insofar as taxable property remained on
the tax rolls, the government was essentially indifferent to its precise disposition.[44] For all practical purposes, then, posad land belonged to the
townsmen who lived and worked on it, irrespective of the fact that it ultimately made up part of the tsar's votchina holdings.

The tsar, as noted earlier, was not the sole possessor of votchina property; boyars, gosti, and church people also held land in this way. Thus
the city holdings of these people and institutions fell into the category of
true property, entirely at the disposal of its owner. The importance of
non-state votchina lands lay in their freedom from state tax obligations—
such properties were referred to as *belye mesta*, literally, "white places,"
to distinguish them from "black," or taxable, courts—and in their relative invulnerability to regulation by state or local officials. The posad
people, as we shall see in greater detail, found it nearly impossible to
curb economic competition coming from dependent people, known as
belomestsy, working in city votchina courts or in suburbs, for the *belomestsy* labored on properties over which the posad officials, and, to a
certain extent, even crown officials in the towns, had no jurisdiction.

There were a few instances in the sixteenth and seventeenth centuries
of cities (goroda) or commercial and manufacturing posady that were the
private property of powerful votchiniki, secular and clerical. The Stroga-
novs had title briefly in the sixteenth century to two Volga River cities. In
the seventeenth century it was not uncommon for monasteries to possess
commercial posady, and a handful of secular magnates possessed forti-

fied cities. Gradually, the private cities dwindled in number as the Muscovite state expanded and incorporated them into the tsar's domains. Even so, the phenomenon of privately held cities persisted into the eighteenth century.[45]

CITY ECONOMY

The most vigorous—one hesitates to say developed—sector of the urban economy in seventeenth-century Russia was undoubtedly commerce— the wholesale trade in valuable raw materials native to Russia, a thriving transit trade in eastern luxury goods like silks and spices, and petty trade in inexpensive items for domestic use. There were abundant commercial opportunities in Russia, and, as so many commentators on the Russian scene from Giles Fletcher on have noted, everyone in the country, "from the humblest to the mightiest, traded."[46] It should be made clear from the outset that the posadskie liudi shared with many others in the society the responsibility for moving goods about the country.

As might be expected, the number one landlord of the realm, the tsar, was also its foremost trader. He possessed monopolies that managed some of Russia's most valuable commodities, among them grain, liquor, and, most notably, furs. Furthermore, he had the right of first purchase on all imported items, which of course enabled his agents to corner the market in particularly profitable commodities. Monopolization of export commodities and speculation in imported goods, both of them practiced irregularly and unpredictably, impeded the even flow of commerce in the country; and they had the additional ill effect—at least from the point of view of the townsmen—of depriving the mercantile community of important sources of capital accumulation. It was neither simple whim nor sheer cupidity that led the sovereigns to so involve themselves with the mundane world of commerce: the profits were essential to the finances of a government that ruled a vast but economically backward agrarian society.[47]

The leading secular merchants were, of course, the gosti and the members of the gostinaia and sukhonnaia hundreds. Both as assistants of the sovereign and as entrepreneurs in their own right they shared in the most lucrative ventures, particularly the wholesale movement of goods over considerable distance, often from deep in the interior to the port cities. And, like the sovereign, they enjoyed privileges that enhanced their competitive position.

Never to be outdone when it came to wealth and power, the monasteries also got into the act of commerce—using their dependent people as factors in distant cities and holding bustling little markets (*torzhki*) at which the rich and varied products of monastic lands and manufactories were traded. They too, owing to the tax-exempt status of their lands, enjoyed a competitive edge over the tax-paying traders of the realm.[48]

The Russians were not alone, however, in seeking to exploit the commercial potential of their vast land; many visitors came with the intent of amassing a commercial fortune in that limitless and untapped market. Immediately after Richard Chancellor's discovery of the White Sea passage in 1553, the British set themselves up as sole masters of Russia's overseas trade. The government of Ivan IV granted the Russian Company extremely generous commercial privileges: trade without customs and tariffs; free entry and exit from Russia; and a monopoly right to the use of Russia's northern ports.[49] Yet the days of British domination were numbered; by the early seventeenth century, ships of other nations were putting in at White Sea harbors. Next, it was to be the turn of the Netherlands. Lacking monopoly rights such as those the British had hung on to until the early seventeenth century, the Dutch established their hegemony over Russia's international trade on the basis of maritime supremacy and commercial expertise.[50]

It must have been exasperating, both for Russian merchants and the government, to stand by and watch this crucial aspect of the country's economy fall into the hands of foreign merchants. But the fact remains that the foreign presence was absolutely necessary were Russia to derive any benefits at all from its natural riches and strategic location. The Russians had no merchant marine, capital was in short supply, and the country's traders were little experienced in the ways of international commerce. This foreign presence—mounting as it did to a position of dominance in large-scale trade operations—was to become a major issue in the crucial relations between government and townsmen in the seventeenth century and even, though to a lesser degree, in the following century.

With the tsar, the guild merchants, monasteries, and foreigners controlling major commercial operations, the rank-and-file posad dwellers were confined to the roles of artisan and small shopkeeper. There were, naturally, exceptions to this rule; the successful trader with capital and influence could hope to earn appointment to one of the guilds. But by and large, the scale of operations of the posad people was quite small, their methods of business primitive, and their profits meager.

The posad people carried on their business from shops in the trade rows (*riady*) of the commercial sectors of the cities. These shops were considered the property of the tsar and rent (*obrok*) was charged for their use, at least from the sixteenth century.[51] Each trade row was supposedly devoted to trade in a specific item, such as bread, boots, or silver products, but the nature of the urban economy was such that merchants very often dealt in quite unrelated items, such as fish and bast shoes. It all depended on what advantageous purchases of wholesale goods the individual merchant could make.[52] Nor, for that matter, were the artisans beyond mixing services. According to Kulisher, "foreigners continually mention the market place where 'barbers cut the hair of the common people with the same knives with which they cut bread and other foodstuffs' and which is 'so strewn with hair that you walk about as if on soft upholstery.' "[53]

Each shop space (*dvor*) occupied about 200 square feet and was frequently divided into halves, quarters, and even eighths, with different merchants working from each section.[54] Shops selling foodstuffs, hide products, and textiles dominated the marketplace.[55] The profits on manufactured items and on food, raw and prepared, were quite small, and the capitalization of most tradesmen was correspondingly minute.

Russian craftsmen were not organized in heavily regulated, closed guilds, as was the case in medieval Western Europe. They were, however, separated into the traditional categories of master, journeyman, and apprentice. The exclusive right to take on independent work distinguished the master from the journeyman. A youth who wished to be apprenticed to a trade signed a contract in which he pledged to work for a master craftsman, usually for five years. Upon the termination of that agreement, the youth, now a journeyman, customarily remained in the employ of his master for some time longer. When he had satisfied his mentor that he knew the trade well, he too became a master, with the right to set up on his own. The scanty evidence on craft regulations and the low quality of much of the merchandise suggests that the work of Russia's artisans was not carefully controlled, either by the artisans themselves or by city officials. Nor is there any indication that the crafts had an exclusive character; it was, after all, in the interest of the urban tax-paying commune to have as many productive members as possible so as to lighten the tax burden that fell on each man.[56]

Even in the not very profitable world of artisan work and petty commerce, however, the posad people did not have the field entirely clear for themselves. On the borders of the state, where posad people were few and far between, contract servitors almost completely controlled trade and manufacturing activities in their fortress cities. In fact, the law allowed them a tax-exempt trade turnover of one to three rubles yearly.[57] In areas where the posad people were more numerous, they encountered stiff competition from peasants residing on the nontaxable secular and ecclesiastical votchina properties in the city. It was not uncommon even for churches or monastic institutions to rent shops in the trade rows of cities, where their dependents traded along with the tax-paying towns-

men. In Iaroslavl' the church and monastic institutions possessed 8.8 percent of the shop courts.[58] I have seen no evidence to suggest that these
competitors actually undersold posad people, for price determination in
the market tended to be a combination of custom and of haggling over
each individual sale. But the fact that the posadskie liudi had to share the
city market with these interlopers—who, and this was no doubt the gall-
ing point, did not bear tiaglo—was enough to draw long and agonized
cries of foul play from them.

Though commerce and petty craft manufacture predominated in the
country's economy, there were some manufacturing establishments on a
larger scale. Salt boiling, iron and steel making, and weapons production
required operations substantially larger than those needed to turn out
items of domestic use. As a rule, these heavy industrial plants were located not in the major cities, but in or near small towns or on votchina or
pomest'e estates, where they were close to the source of the appropriate
raw materials.[59] The salt works of the Stroganov family at Ustiug-Perm,
the many metallurgical factories in the vicinity of Tula, and the copper-
smelting plants on the shores of remote Lake Onega are all examples.[60]

As Liashchenko noted, the rural industries overshadowed by far the
urban ones. "The economic organization of *votchina* industrial economy
with its numerous household craftsmen and large *votchina* enterprises,
based on peasant labor, was so powerful and important that the influence of free city industry at the end of the seventeenth century remained
very limited. 'Heavy industry' of the seventeenth century arose and
developed in the nucleus of *votchina* economy and to a much lesser
degree—in city industry."[61]

The limited role of the cities—and by implication, their mercantile
population—in the development of industry is also reflected in the data
on the capitalization of Russian industry. According to Liubomirov, foreign capital sources predominated in the seventeenth century, followed
in importance by state and merchant capital.[62] State and foreign capital
investments both contributed to the development of Russia's war industries. In the 1630s, for example, the government set up two powder mills
and several arms plants, while the Dutchmen Vinius, Marselis, and
Akema established their famous metallurgical complex in the Tula area.
Relatively little capital, however, flowed into industry from the hands of
urban merchants.[63] Most posad people lacked sufficient capital to run
their own businesses effectively, to say nothing of having a surplus left
over for investment. Successful gosti and hundreders did have the resources to invest, but they seem to have preferred the familiar to the un-
known. It was, after all, easier and less risky to buy up manufactured
goods and to trade them about the country than to enter into the uncer-
tainty of manufacturing.

The industrial and commercial activities of the posadskie liudi were an integral and indispensable part of the national economy of seventeenth-century Russia. In the northern and central areas especially they appear to have held a predominant position in the manufacture and exchange of goods, and the most successful among them proved able assistants to the tsars in the management of large-scale state and crown enterprises. Moreover, they contributed substantially to the cash revenues of the state, though such benefits to the national well-being derived more from their susceptibility to taxes than to their wealth per se.

As important as these achievements may have been, the fact remains that the posadskie liudi could not, on the whole, be characterized as a wealthy and economically powerful social group. They fell far short of obtaining that degree of control over the nonagricultural sectors of the economy that one normally associates with an urban business community. They lacked the aggressiveness and independence of spirit that could have enabled them to control their own environment, the city, and to extend their influence, economic and otherwise, into adjacent hinterlands. The root cause of these limitations, of course, lay in the relative poverty of posad society. With the exception of a handful of wealthy guild merchants, most of the townsmen led modest lives indeed, turning over miniscule amounts of capital yearly, reeling from the vicissitudes of the market, and suffering from the heavy burdens of taxation. In such circumstances, hand-to-mouth living was frequently the rule, the accumulation of capital a near-impossibility. There was, perhaps, no better measure of the limited resources of the townsmen than the physical conditions of the cities in which they lived. Crowded homes, crudely constructed and modestly furnished, sat on narrow muddy streets. Amenities and refinements were few. And everything was subject to the periodic ravages of fire. Public buildings, where they existed, were equally humble, reflecting an indifference toward broader civic ends. Only the churches, marvelous in design and sumptuous in decoration, suggested the presence of accumulated wealth, and in fact many of those structures were founded by the small upper stratum of the merchantry in testimony to their piety.

The economic weakness of the Russian townsmen stemmed from two interrelated conditions: the relative poverty of the state as a whole and the restricted role of the townsmen in the national economy. As regards the first point, one must bear in mind that the formative years of the posadskie liudi as an estate of the Muscovite realm occurred simultaneously with the great commercial expansion of Western Europe. For the West, the fifteenth, sixteenth, and seventeenth centuries marked the full flowering of preindustrial commercial society, a time when the primary source of great wealth was the exchange of goods, not the efficient, mechanized production of them. But Russia was not able to participate significantly in that great era of commerce. Located on the edge of Europe, lacking convenient ports and so vast as to make overland transit a difficult and costly venture, the Russian state remained right into the eighteenth century very much a peripheral part of the European commercial world. The country was thus deprived of the bulk of the economic benefits enjoyed by the Western European states in the post-medieval period of commercial expansion.

In regard to the second point, the restricted role of the townsmen in the national economy, one encounters a curious, almost paradoxical situation. Though merchants in a mercantile age, the Russian townsmen failed to emerge as a healthy, wealthy, and powerful middle class. The most obvious obstacle was, of course, the location of Russia on the periphery of a commercially active Europe. But that obstacle might have been surmounted had the townsmen not found themselves in a society that made the practice of mercantile affairs so difficult. The many impedimenta to economic activities that were deeply rooted—one could as easily say institutionalized—in Russian society thus stand at the very center of any analysis of the economic weaknesses of the townsmen.

Perhaps the most fundamental impediment to the townsmen's enterprise lay in the nature of the economic process in Russia, in particular, in the role of the city in that process. The central point here is simple, yet powerful in its implications: namely, that the provisioning of the population with food, clothing, shelter, and items of domestic or productive use was by no means the sole responsibility of the towns. Indeed, the system of distribution that existed in the towns was supplemented not only by the numerous rural markets and periodic fairs, but by the rather substantial production which took place on both votchina and pomest'e properties. The vastness of Russia and the difficulties of transportation reinforced this tendency toward rural self-sufficiency, as did the social structure, which increasingly gave the landed elements of the state fuller powers over the disposition of the labor of their dependent populations. And, interestingly, the reverse situation also obtained. Townsmen raised crops, maintained fish ponds, and engaged in other agricultural pursuits, thus reducing their dependence on rural sources of foodstuffs and raw materials. One could argue, following the lead of Karl Polanyi, that those activities which in modern societies are neatly isolated as economic and analyzed in terms of the marketplace were in premodern societies performed by many institutions not always a part of a market economy.[64] In Russia, many modern "economic" functions were embedded in a number of institutions—self-sufficient votchina and pomest'e economies, monastic establishments, the privileged trading of the tsar and the gosti, and the garden plots so dear to the posad taxpayers. All these means of meeting economic needs helped to distort or subvert a strictly market-oriented distribution of goods. All this is not to deny the presence of urban markets, of the flow of goods over long distances—indeed, from one end of the country to the other. But it is to suggest that institutionally the posad people had to make their living in a market that was constrained both geographically and institutionally by the presence in the country of alternative means of production and exchange.

State-initiated hindrances to the free exercise of economic initiative further impeded the development of the townsmen's economic capacity. One might list in this regard such diverse considerations as the tsar's monopolies; the plethora of government regulations on matters as varied as personal mobility, behavior in the marketplace, and credit operations; the enormous burden of service, particularly for the successful merchants; and the susceptibility of merchant property to interference or confiscation by the state. In Samuel Baron's judgment these prescriptions, prohibitions, and threats left the townsmen precious little breathing space; indeed, he argues that the overall atmosphere in which the townsmen operated posed a serious challenge to the very essence of a mercantile community based on free, private enterprise.[65]

The problems of state interference were real enough, but the open and conspicuous nature of that interference, so easily accessible to the historian, makes it tempting to exaggerate its impact. To give the proper balance, one must also take into account the fact that the posadskie liudi were victims of their own relatively primitive means of production and marketing. The techniques employed by urban artisans differed in no significant ways from those of rural craftsmen; hence, the posad people produced neither better goods, nor the same quality at lower costs. And the evidence suggests that in most all cases the rudest of techniques predominated. According to Iurii Krizanich, for example, Russian carpenters rarely used saws; instead, they fashioned boards with axes. The axes, in turn, were made according to custom of a uniform size and weight and often proved ill-fitted for the task at hand.[66] Only a few items, like gold and silver jewelry, displayed quality workmanship, and they were frequently the creations of skilled foreign hands. The customary organization of production in the towns also reflected the low level of technology. Most shops consisted of an artisan, perhaps aided by a journeyman or an apprentice, and occasionally assisted by a few nonskilled hired workers. They produced either on special order or in very small quantities for general sale.[67]

In their commercial activities, most posad people fared little better. They had little if any capital at their disposal, credit was hard to come by and expensive, and, beyond that, the Russian tradesmen seemed content, according to most observations on their activities, with covering their costs.[68] The accumulation of profit for the sake of reinvestment appears to have been neither a widespread practice nor an aspiration. There were, naturally, a select number of successful merchants, but their wealth seems to have come more through exacting the maximum profits from deals, on occasion through some form of deception, than through the steady, calculated accumulation of small profits. In dealings with foreign merchants the Russians developed a reputation for being unreliable and shifty. Johann Korb, an Austrian diplomat present in Russia in 1698-99, noted that, "Whereas the Muscovites lack any good rules [of trade], then, in my opinion, deceit serves as evidence of a good mind."[69] Such an appraisal cannot be dismissed merely as the product of prejudiced and snobbish European minds, for Ivan Pososhkov, whose patriotism could not be denied, argued in the early part of the eighteenth century that the Russian marketplace badly needed improved business morals.[70] To use the Weberian dichotomy: the urban commercial world of seventeenth-century Russia was animated more by the age-old pursuit of quick riches —often to be gained through risky but potentially highly profitable ventures—than by the more moderate, rational, and calculating pursuit of gain that lay at the heart of economic development in Western Europe.[71]

Finally, it has been argued with some justification that posad society suffered both exacerbated internal relations and a loss of valuable leadership through the government's policy of drawing the most prominent merchants into service in the guilds.[72] That was certainly the case, and no doubt it worked to the detriment of the posad as a whole. Yet the numbers involved were not all that great, and surely some moderately successful established merchants and young men on the rise must have been left behind in the localities. In reality, the problem of leadership was, like the problem of economic activity, embedded in the institutional arrangements of the state—in this case, in the related areas of urban administration and national policies of taxation. The question, really, is, What power was available to whomever it was that rose to leadership within the posad population? The answer, as the next chapter shows, is that there was not a great deal.

The picture that emerges of the posad population of the seventeenth century is that of a small number of souls, two hundred thousand at the most in a country of several million, concentrated in the cities of central and northern Russia. Residents on state land, they had special obligations to the tsar's government, namely, the bearing of tiaglo—taxes and service tasks—the majority of which were associated with revenue collection. On the whole, their economic undertakings would have to be considered quite modest. Most townsmen were poor traders and craftsmen in a generally poor country, though there were a few genuinely prosperous individuals among them. In most instances the posadskie liudi dominated the economies of the towns in which they lived, but it was a precarious dominance, vulnerable to competition from without the *posad* and forever threatened by a plethora of constraints, regulations, and prohibitions imposed by the state. Moreover, they were far from being the undisputed masters of the production and distribution of goods on a state-wide basis; that was a domain they had to share with many others. Who the townsmen were and what they could and did do ultimately depended on the larger institutions that defined the character of the Russian state.

CHAPTER TWO

Townsmen and the State in the Early Seventeenth Century

IT IS IN THE AREA of administrative relations that one can see most clearly the contours of the Russian city and of its urban tax-paying commune. The picture is complex, reflecting the contributions of the towns both to the national enterprise and to the governance of the localities. Behind each of these relationships lay the tangled web of social relations that typified Russia. The powers exercised by the posad taxpayers, as well as the constraints upon them, can only be understood in this nexus. Just where the city fit, administratively, in the institutional order of the Russian state and what issues brought the state and townsmen into contact are the subjects of this chapter.

In one sense, the cities operated as agents of the central government, integrated vertically into the hierarchy of rule emanating from Moscow and reaching out toward every citizen. Like cities everywhere, Russia's cities helped to organize political space. Yet the very imperfections of the Muscovite state, its institutional immaturity as it were, showed up in this relationship. Almost never did the cities, functioning as autonomous entities, contribute to the administration of Muscovy. Instead, that job was done in part by urban-based representatives of the crown who carried directives from, and taxes and rumors back to, the capital, and in part by citizens drawn into state service from one of the social groups within the cities—most frequently from the posad. Thus, the administrative contribution of the cities to the state effort derived from geographical considerations and from the activities of select urban inhabitants. It did not emanate from the cities operating as autonomous civic entities.

In another sense, the cities were integrated horizontally into the locale of which they were a part through their inclusion in administrative jurisdictions that embraced both urban and rural areas. Other than to serve as the physical centers of such jurisdictions, that is, as the site where offices were located and administration dispensed, the city itself played no special role in the government of the localities. A similarly subordinate position was the lot of the townsmen. Local administration reflected the reality of social and political power in Russia, a reality dominated by an agrarian-based servitor population. It was they, and not the townsmen, who had the final say over both the cities and their hinterlands.

Caught in the crosscurrents of national and local interests, the Russian cities are hard to delineate administratively. With the possible exception of the frontier cities of homogeneous military population, the cities did not constitute clearly defined and delimited administrative entities, nor did they possess, administratively, any autonomous institutions. In affairs of state taxes and administration, they fit within the administrative hierarchy of the central government; in matters of a purely local character, the cities belonged to the broader localities surrounding them. But even in the latter instance, the state retained for itself final responsibility.

Three factors contributed to the shaping of this particular administrative configuration. First, the differentiation of town and countryside was not very far advanced in the early part of the seventeenth century. There was not just a lack of any historical legacy of urban identity and the appropriate institutions for its expression, but also a certain fusion of characteristics that made it difficult to sort out people and jurisdictions. In economic matters, for example, there existed considerable overlap of activities and technique in the urban and rural areas. Physically, many towns had little in the way of structures, layout, or in some cases even size to distinguish them from rural villages and hamlets. Socially, peasants and posad taxpayers moved from rural to urban communes and back again with the greatest of ease, sharing as they did common occupations and more or less identical tax burdens. Such mobility was particularly in evidence in those areas of the state where the cities were located among great tracts of state lands. But even in areas where votchina and pomest'e estates prevailed, the activities of state servitors—both their roles in local, urban-based administration and their maintenance of urban properties for residence or business—tended to blur lines of interest between city and countryside. Finally, one might mention the nearly ubiquitous presence of parcels of state land, in towns and countryside alike, that stood in need of some measure of uniform management. In the presence of so many common features and shared interests, it is not hard to understand the advantages of some form of administrative arrangement that did not draw a sharp distinction between urban and rural affairs.

Second, administrative arrangements in the cities reflected the social order of the Muscovite state. The requirements of service meant that each social group had a unique set of responsibilities, ultimately defined by state needs. In such a setting, good administration was tantamount to the proper regulation of these service responsibilities. In the case at hand, the tax-paying townsmen had various services to perform; and one of the functions of the crown's chief representative in the localities, the *voevoda*, or military governor, was to make sure that these services were performed and the state's interests protected. A system of this sort, once it was fully in place, could tolerate no independent loci of power, social or political: to have done so would have risked the integrity of the state. Urban autonomy, like civil or political rights, had no place in such a scheme of things and was never really an issue.

The state, however, was far from all-powerful, and this very fact leads to the third consideration affecting administration in the cities: the need to go outside the formal administrative structures to secure assistance in the governance of the country. The seventeenth century witnessed great strides by the nascent Russian bureaucratic apparatus. The signs of growth were everywhere—in the number of offices (*prikazy*) and in the number of officials working in them. In some cases bureaucratic staffs doubled or even tripled. But, for all these gains in staffing, the absolute numbers remained small. N. F. Demidova contends that in the second half of the seventeenth century the bureaucratic establishment in Moscow employed, in addition to a few hundred judges and clerks, about two thousand scribes. The number of scribes working as assistants to military governors in provincial cities she places at about one thousand.[1] It is obvious that with such limited numbers only the most important matters could receive the attention of the bureaucracy. And, in fact, it was precisely in the area of setting major state policy and rendering crucial judgments that the budding Muscovite bureaucracy operated best. At that level the precious commodities of continuity and expertise that a bureaucracy can provide were of maximum value to the nation-state. But there was no way in which such a small establishment could accomplish, through its own machinery, the total administration of so vast a state.

The administrative needs of the state could have been met, of course, through reliance on autonomous centers of political-administrative power, of which the cities were the likeliest candidates. But the Russian autocracy was unwilling to share authority and responsibility with any other center of power, real or potential. It was jealous of its political power and distrustful—rightly so—of the capacities of the society or any of its parts to engage constructively in self-government. By the process of elimination, therefore, it became necessary for the government to rely on relatively weak local institutions, such as the rural and posad communes, to perform certain tasks that were properly the province of formal government agencies, in particular, revenue collection and the administration of justice. In the communes the government found institutions of long-standing that had internal strengths adequate to the jobs entrusted to them, but which lacked the financial and social power that might have enabled them to threaten the dominance of the bureaucracy. It was this union of central direction and supervision with local, communal execution that made possible the administration of Russia; in the absence of effective and trustworthy independent sources of social or political power, such as strong, autonomous cities, it was not an entirely unsatisfactory manner of governing so vast a land.

The very nature of this administrative system, however suited it was to conditions in Russia, at the same time precluded the appearance of administrative institutions that dealt uniquely with urban issues. While there were administrative institutions responsible for different social categories of city residents and other institutions in charge of geographical areas both larger and smaller than the cities, there was no such entity as "city government." A cursory examination of book titles and tables of content reveals that Russian historians have for the most part eschewed the category of city administration; rather, they employ the term local administration (*mestnoe upravlenie*), which more accurately reflects the most immediate level of the institutional structure in which the city found itself enmeshed. But even this term is misleading, for it suggests a geographical basis for local government, and in doing so it ignores many instances in which administrative arrangements ran from individuals or social groups directly to the central government, bypassing as it were the local government apparatus, just as it overlooks miniscule, socially restricted administrative units. It is, nevertheless, probably most fruitful to approach the administration of the city and its residents in terms of the rubric of local administration, if only because the principal figure of authority in the seventeenth-century city, the military governor, exercised powers over the entire citizenry of the district entrusted to his care.

LOCAL GOVERNMENT: THE MILITARY GOVERNOR AND THE ELDERS

The military governor appeared on the scene as a part of the efforts of the Romanov dynasty to restore some measure of stability to the state in the wake of the Time of Troubles. Local government had collapsed in many areas of the state, and it was crucial that it be shored up. In the military governor the state had an official ideally suited to the task. Combining in his hands both military and civil power, the military governor exercised his authority over an entire district, or *uezd*. Though he shared his authority with other government officials in the countryside, he was in undisputed command of the city and its affairs. His responsibilities included caring for city fortifications and superintending mobilizations, supervising revenue collection, repairing roads and bridges, and watching out for the morals and welfare of those entrusted to his care.[2]

The military governor was, of course, an appointed official, selected from among the ranks of the tsar's military servitors.[3] He, in turn, was subordinate to the many prikazy, which had ultimate responsibility for the administration of the country. In most cases, a military governor in carrying out his duties dealt with a number of prikazy, depending on the nature of the business. For one affair it might be a prikaz that handled money matters, for another one that dealt with military affairs. In some cases, the military governor was subordinate to a single prikaz. This arrangement prevailed on the southern border, where the Razriadnyi Prikaz, which managed the affairs of the military servitors, controlled many of those frontier cities that were inhabited almost exclusively by contract servitors.[4]

Both the powers of the military governor and the extent to which the central government, through its representative, was involved in the details of city affairs were dramatically illustrated by the procedures followed when one military governor superseded another. After receiving the town keys from his predecessor, the new man took an extensive inventory of the human and physical resources of the town, checking his tallies against past records to make sure that the tsar's wealth had not suffered diminution. As head military man in the district, he had to know the location and condition of the arsenal and powder magazine; as chief supervisor of taxation, it was crucial that he know how many taxpayers fell under his jurisdiction. As a part of his installation ritual, the military governor inspected the town guards to make certain that they were on the job and alert, ready to sound the tocsin should fire, that great bane of Russia's cities, break out.[5] From the point of view of the central government, the military governor was the town's protector in every respect. It should be remembered, however, that his powers extended beyond the city limits, and thus the office could not be considered, strictly speaking, a city institution. Moreover, the functions of the military governor amounted essentially to the defense of the state's property and other interests, not the management of the town for the benefit of its residents.

While the office of military governor watched out for Caesar's interests, other institutions managed the day-by-day affairs of the locality. In particular, strong roles were played by police elders (*gubnye starosty*) and land elders (*zemskie starosty*), official positions born of a reform of local government undertaken between 1551 and 1556 by the government of Ivan IV. The police elders were truly local officials; they were elected by the entire population of the county or township, and assumed police powers over the whole territory. The broad jurisdiction of this office, both territorially and socially, did not prevent the government from restricting eligibility for office to gentry or to petty servitors (*deti boiarskie*). Yet the institution could not be said to have a strictly class basis, for representatives from the neighboring peasantry and from the local posad assisted the police elders in their work.[6]

The land elders, in contrast, were elected by smaller constituencies—in the case of a city, by the posad or by suburbs. They dispensed justice and collected state revenues from the posad and suburb residents or from the township peasants (in the rural areas) who elected them. Military servitors could neither run for the office of land elder nor participate in elections for posad elders. Since his constituency was limited and his competences were confined to that constituency, the land elder has to be regarded as something less than a "local" official.[7]

The arrival of the military governor resulted in a curtailing of the judicial powers exercised by the land elders, so that the energies of the latter came to be concentrated on tax matters. The government had traditionally levied a lump sum of taxes against the whole commune and left it to the taxpayers themselves to decide who would bear what burden. In the last analysis, the difficult task of tax apportionment fell on the land elders. In cities where the posad was large, the elders were aided in this undertaking by subdivisions within the commune. Sometimes these smaller units were known as quarters (*storony*), but more commonly as parishes, streets, suburbs, and in the case of Moscow, hundreds. Each of these units formed its own small tax union, with its own elder (or in the case of Moscow, a *sotskii*). With the assistance of sworn men (*tseloval'-niki*), the land elders were also responsible for collecting the tax revenue and delivering it to the military governor.[8]

The presence of elective officials on the urban scene implies a measure of self-rule or autonomy for city dwellers, but a closer look at the operations of these institutions suggests otherwise. To begin with, the institution of police elder had little, if anything, to contribute to genuine self-rule. When the reform was initiated, one of its goals was to free able-bodied servitors for important military or central administrative posts, and hence the government restricted candidacy for police elder to those men who were no longer in active service. Thus local law enforcement fell to the lot of old, wounded, or otherwise infirm servitors. And in fact, even these dubiously qualified men were not always elected to the office of elder; they were frequently appointed by the central government, and their subsequent "election" merely served to confirm them in office.[9] In an extreme example of how badly the police elder institution could serve its community, Solov'ev cited a petition directed to the tsar from the residents of Kashin. In it they complained that law and order were not present in the city, that there was no voevoda to manage affairs, and that the police elder had "neither hands nor feet."[10] It is unlikely that such an expression had metaphorical connotations; the elder may well have lost the appendages in military service. Even in less dire circumstances, however, the reliance on aged servitors to perform police duties and the frequent interference by the central government in their selection argue against any notion that the police elder was an institution of self-rule. Moreover, the district-wide jurisdiction of the elder made him something more than a city official.

It is equally impossible to see in the land elder the makings of urban autonomy. For one thing, the narrow basis of candidacy excluded servitors, who, though not numerous, were often wealthy and powerful in the localities. Local government with independence and backbone would surely have to be based on the strongest groups in society, not the weaker ones. Moreover, the land elder's restricted jurisdiction limited the resources at his disposal, so that even had he been inclined and empowered to act on behalf of the community which elected him, little could have been done.

In the last analysis, these elected officials were completely overshadowed by the tsar's representative, the military governor. The relationship between the military governor and the land elder transcended the mere supervisory powers that were entrusted to the military governor, and which in theory left the land elders and the local communes with substantial freedom. In fact, as the government continually pressed the communes for more and more revenues, the military governor found himself intervening increasingly in posad affairs, an area that had traditionally been the exclusive prerogative of the communes. In the cities, for example, he ruled on the qualifications of those seeking to enter the communes, and he apportioned out residential courts and sites for shops and warehouses. In such cases his decisions were made with an eye to maintaining or increasing the tax-paying capacity of a city, not with an eye to ensuring the welfare of the posad dwellers.[11] There can be no doubt that the military governor completely overshadowed the local institutions, making them but small links in the conveyor belt that poured revenues into Moscow. In local administration, it was ultimately the interests of the central government that were served first.

Given the priorities, it is not surprising that local interests suffered. The military governors, once on the job, found themselves far from Moscow and the watchful eyes of their superiors. Many became, in the space of a few months, local satraps, greedily gouging their hapless subjects. The central authorities were fully aware of the situation, informed as they were by a steady flow of petitions from the plundered cities, but their efforts to curb the abuses were not eminently successful.[12] Great distances and the prevailing low standards of official morality rendered supervision by the central bureaucracy over its local agents notoriously weak. The government had to be content if the military governors turned in the required revenues, kept minimal order in the cities, and looked after the defense needs of the country.

Since the preoccupation of the military governor was with matters of a state nature, it is not surprising that he gave short shrift to many crucial areas of administration, in particular those dealing with public welfare. Inevitably, the burdens of fire prevention and fire fighting, on-the-street police protection, road repair, regulation of the marketplace, and a number of other activities that should, in the ideal scheme of things, have fallen under the jurisdiction of city government, fell instead into the lap of the posad commune. As was so often the case, tasks that affected the lives of all inhabitants of the city, and to a certain extent the lives of the neighboring rural dwellers as well, became the responsibility not of the entire community, but of one segment of it. Since the military governor's office had only the most limited funds available for civic use, and since the posad commune was financially depleted after the payment of taxes, these crucial public services became added service obligations for which the posad dweller received no recompense and which imposed still further upon his time and energies.[13] One does not have to search far for an explanation of the poor quality of public services in the cities.

The perspective of local history reveals that the cities were not independent entities, but were enmeshed institutionally in local and state administrative structures. It also suggests that that relationship had certain costs, in terms of poorly developed services for the cities and towns. Beyond that point, however, the value of the local approach is limited to the identification of particular social or economic configurations of this or that town. To get at the broader functional role of the cities and their inhabitants in Russian society, one must turn back to the dominant force within the towns, the state. The Muscovite government used the towns— more precisely, their tax-paying inhabitants—as agents for the performance of crucial state administrative functions.

THE REGULATION OF SERVICE

In its administration of the cities, the state was primarily interested in regulating service responsibilities, which boiled down to making sure that all persons and institutions involved in revenue collection pulled their full load. Toward that end, the government pursued a number of courses of action, from updating cadastral records, to tax reform, to minor alterations in administrative relationships. A few brief examples will serve to illustrate this facet of government activity.

The performance of a number of key financial tasks fell, as noted, to the members of the select corporations of merchants, the gosti and the sukhonnaia and gostinaia hundreds. It was the government's responsibility, and not an easy one at that, to keep up the membership in these corporations. In spite of the privileges that accompanied their status, the corporation members found their tasks extremely burdensome. Indeed, the obligations often matched, or even outweighed, the privileges. A hundreder's tour of duty lasted for one and one-half years and frequently took him far from home. On occasion, such prolonged absences meant the ruin of his business. Moreover, the corporation members were held personally responsible for the fulfillment of their state-appointed jobs; if revenue collections did not meet the established quota, the difference had to be made up out of the pockets of these officials. Since the government selected only one or two dozen men from each hundred for service in any given year, it was naturally to the advantage of the hundreds to keep their membership rolls as large as possible, thus reducing the frequency with which men were called to duty.[14]

Yet the matter of filling up the hundreds was not so simple as it might seem. For one thing, there is evidence to suggest that many wealthy merchants preferred not to participate in these privileges. In the 1670s F. I. Surovtsov and his brothers, who were salt processors from Sol' Kamskaia, were listed in various documents as, alternatively, members of the gostinaia sotnia, posad people, hundreders once more, and finally as plain posad people. It seems highly unlikely that a prosperous merchant family would have sought exit from the hundred had they not considered it detrimental to their own affairs.[15]

A more frequently encountered difficulty arose when local posad communes and hundreds complained bitterly about the loss of their most wealthy taxpayers to the corporations. Since taxes were apportioned within posad society on the basis of ability to pay, the removal of rich men burdened still further those who remained behind. In 1647-48 there occurred a classic example of the conflict between the corporations and the posad for well-to-do merchants, a conflict that the government had to mediate. The depredations and economic chaos of the Time of Troubles had so thinned the ranks of the gostinaia and sukhonnaia hundreds that by the year 1630 these corporations had about half the manpower they had had in the late sixteenth century.[16] To restore their depleted ranks, the government during the period 1646-1648 enrolled some 245 families into the two corporations. This action in turn brought forth a petition during the troubled summer of 1648 from the elders of the Moscow suburbs, demanding that the local merchants impressed into the hundreds be returned to the tax rolls of the suburbs and that the impressing of people into service in faraway cities be terminated.[17] The gosti and gostinaia sotnia replied with a petition of their own, noting that the current crisis had been ruinous to them and that they desperately needed new blood in the corporation. The sukhonnaia sotnia chimed in with a petition of its own, pointing out that only 112 men were registered in the hundred, whereas the total had once been 357. And of the 112, only 42 were wealthy enough to serve and 18 of them served yearly. The remaining 70 could not serve because of complete poverty.[18] Again, the Moscow posad rank-and-file petitioned the government, calling to its attention the impoverishment suffered by suburbs and posady throughout the country because of the loss of their best men.[19]

The government responded with a compromise. It would continue to have Moscow gosti and hundreders perform services wherever the tsar commanded, especially in Moscow, Arkhangel, and Kholmogory. Iaroslavl' traders taken into the corporations were to perform the same services in Iaroslavl', Astrakhan', and Kazan'. For residents of other cities, taken into the corporations in the last year, however, the government eased up on their obligations and canceled some privileges. It ordered them to remain in their towns and to perform state services there, namely customs and liquor collections, and to bear tiaglo along with the rank-and-file posad people.[20]

This sequence of events not only illustrates government regulation of its urban service personnel, but also underscores the extent to which entry into corporations split tradesmen off from their former posad colleagues. Another, still more thorny problem of administration concerned the handling of the tsar's chief representatives in the localities, the military governors. As noted earlier, the military governors tended to get out of hand, using and abusing their broad powers to line their own pockets. There could be no question that willful actions of these officials were detrimental to the posady, reducing their ability both to pay and to administer effectively their service obligations.

Government efforts to place restraints on the military governors were a patchwork of ad hoc measures, each designed to counter one or another of the well-known abuses, but in the end these reforms were of limited success. The source of the difficulties lay not in isolated features of the rule by military governors, but in the almost total control over the localities with which the government found it necessary to invest them. The government, for example, limited the terms of the military governors to three years on the assumption that they would not have time to become sufficiently entrenched in their domains to get the processes of

graft fully in motion.[21] But, of course, they responded simply by speed-
ing up the timetable of their extortionate activities. In 1661 the government undertook a massive reshuffling of personnel, but that again was
only temporarily effective.[22] In 1672 the state forbade the appointment of
a military governor to preside over a locality in which he owned landed
property.[23] This measure was more substantial than those preceding it,
but still it was only a partial solution.

The townsmen had their own particular grievances with the military
governors, who interfered both in business and financial matters. In
1645-46, in response to numerous petitions, the government deprived
military governors of their jurisdiction over townsmen who were departing on business trips, thus freeing the traders from infringements on this
crucial aspect of their work. The merchants were placed under the jurisdiction of customs chiefs, chosen from among the sworn men of the communes and suburbs. Bakhrushin goes so far as to state that this reform
gave to the posad people "a certain degree of estate self-rule in the sense
of exclusive subordination in trade affairs to a court of persons of their
own rank, and elected at that." It is hard to agree with such an interpretation, however, which sees self-rule in the management of certain aspects
of commercial relations. At any rate, the law was rescinded in 1651-52.[24]
The problem of interference by the military governors in the business affairs of the townsmen remained, however, and it was only in 1667 that
the New Trade Regulation (*Novotorgovyi ustav*) forbad the military
governors to meddle in mercantile affairs.[25]

The increased meddling of the military governors in posad affairs, as a
result of their watchfulness over the fulfillment of tax levies, also aroused
the ire of the townsmen. Ultimately the government was forced to take
action. In the years 1679-1681, there occurred a major reform of the tax
structure, which reduced the four main direct taxes to three and apportioned the burden more equitably among various groups of the population.[26] The important aspects of the legislation for our purposes, however, were the procedural changes it introduced. Responsibility for delivery of tax revenues (as opposed to their collection on the spot) was taken
from the military governors and given to the local elders and sworn men.
Moreover, control over customs and liquor collections was also entrusted to elected local officials.[27] The motive for such an administrative
rearrangement is not hard to ascertain. Substantial amounts of tax revenue were finding their way into the pockets of the military governors, a
condition that worked to the detriment both of the state and of the local
residents, who were taxed enough without having to pay an illegal luxury
surcharge to subsidize the greed of the local satrap.

The preceding examples have two points in common. They demonstrate clearly that the predominant, if not the sole reason for government intervention in city affairs was concern for the most effective possible management of state revenue collections. Whether it was a matter of filling up the hundreds or curbing the military governor, fiscal considerations dictated the need for and the course of action. Second, the problems derived from the very nature of the service system, that is, from the incompletely developed administrative structure of the state. On the one hand, the reliance on merchants as unpaid administrators was bound to have repercussions within the commercial community, which would demand government regulation. And, on the other hand, the broad civil and military powers of the voevoda, which made him such a threat to the local populace and hence a man in need of continual restriction, stemmed from ineffective local government and from an urgent need on the part of the central government to secure some kind of control over the localities.

THE STRUGGLE TO PRESERVE POSAD SOCIETY

The involvement of the state in the affairs of the cities went well beyond efforts at regulating their service functions to include the preservation of the posad from threats to its very existence. Such state intervention could come in the form of special policies designed to meet critical moments in the life of the towns, such as Godunov's posad reconstruction activities. Or it could take the form of state aid to the townsmen in their prolonged struggle with hostile social and economic forces. Both cases bear directly on the nature of the relationship between state and townsmen.

From the reign of Ivan III on, government involvement in the affairs of the posady had steadily mounted, though for the most part its actions had been prompted by petitions of grievance from the townsmen. It was only in the aftermath of the oprichnina, when the countryside lay wasted and the towns were depopulated and in ruins, that the government seized the initiative and began to give legislative support to the integrity of the urban commune. The first steps were timid and limited to specific cities or regions, but as precedents for future actions, they were of some import.

In 1586, for example, a charter given by Fedor Ivanovich to the city of Sviiazhsk prohibited posad people from giving themselves into the protection (*zakladnichestvo*) of secular and ecclesiastical magnates. There is no indication, however, that this stricture applied elsewhere in the state.[28] In 1591 an enabling charter to the town of Toropets forbade exit from the posad, arguing that the prohibition on peasant departure introduced during the "forbidden years" (*zapovednye gody*) applied to the Toropets posad as well. This was the first known total abridgment of the mobility of the posad dwellers, though it pertained to but one posad.[29] These first, isolated measures fell far short of stemming the flow of taxpayers from the posady of the realm.

A more vigorous policy was pursued by Boris Godunov, first as regent, then as tsar.[30] Not content merely to defend the helpless remnants of the shattered posady, Godunov worked hard to rebuild them, which meant, first and foremost, filling up the thousands of empty households with able-bodied men capable of bearing the all-important tiaglo. Godunov's agents, most of them dvoriane, were not particularly choosy about where they found the bodies; they even took individuals from the courts of secular and ecclesiastical votchiniki. Such a measure did little to enhance Boris's stature in the eyes of the disapproving old-line aristocracy, and he was surely aware of the dangers inherent in this course of action. That he pursued it so vigorously attests to Godunov's understanding of the urgency of posad restoration.

The significance of Godunov's labors lies not in their success, for with his death in 1605 posad construction came to an abrupt end long before its completion, but in the emergence of a working definition of who was to be considered a taxable city dweller. These were people who (1) previously lived in the posad; (2) engaged in trade and industry; (3) had been born to posad parents; (4) lived in contiguity with the posad.[31] Persons falling into any of these categories immediately became candidates to fill vacant posad courts. The governments of the first two Romanovs were to fall back on these precedents as they embarked on their own policies of posad reconstruction.

The cities profited from the policies of Godunov, and they proved strong enough to contribute to the military operation that drove the Poles from the country and defeated the Cossack rebels. It remained to be seen how the posady would be rewarded for their services to the state during the *Smuta*, or Time of Troubles. As it turned out, their reward was a policy that picked up where Godunov's labors had been broken off, that is, with efforts to fill up the posady with taxpayers and to make sure that these people stayed put. There was precious little in the way of innovation during the reign of Michael: the reconstruction of the state was undertaken along the same lines as those that had guided state policy prior to the Troubles.

The government did not act alone in these matters. It was joined by the townsmen in efforts to keep the posad registers full, and hence to combat the declining urban population. The posad elders devoted a goodly portion of their energies to locating and trying to retrieve individuals who had for one reason or another departed from the communes. A few taxpayers had simply moved to different cities and were bearing tax responsibilities there. While Caesar was justly rendered his due in such cases, the posady these men had abandoned were short of valuable taxpayers. Some townsmen sought to escape tax obligations altogether by enlisting in one of the various groups of military specialists—musketeers, cannoneers, and the like. Still others found gainful and less-taxed employment as artisans in state suburbs of stonemasons, bricklayers, or carpenters. There were also posad people who simply lived in their city of registration and refused to pay taxes.[32] Finally, some of the posad population, usually the poorer elements, resorted to the ultimate in medieval Russian tax-dodging; they fled to the country's great, ever-expanding frontier. It was clearly and unambiguously to the advantage of the government to see that such fugitives from posad law, order, and taxes were returned to the fold, and both local and central government officials willingly assisted the posad elders in bringing back errant taxpayers. Petitions to the government on these counts usually met with favorable responses.[33]

There is, of course, another side to this coin: the perceived right of the townsmen, a right sanctioned by tradition, to come and go freely from a posad, that is, to change residences at will. So entrenched was this tradition that posad elders and central government officials alike could move against it only gingerly. Thus, even though the government assisted in identifying and returning errant individuals to the posady, it pulled up short of instituting blanket prohibitions against movement by the townsmen. According to Smirnov, there is no evidence that entry into or exit from the posad was in any way restricted between 1497 and 1550.[34] The decisions of the Stoglav council, however, restricted departure from the posad to the same period around St. George's day in which peasants were allowed to move.[35] Though a major restriction of the townsmen's mobility, it did not constitute an absolute abridgment of their right to come and go from the posad. Indeed, as late as 1617 the inhabitants of Sol' Vychegodsk could remark, "We have an old custom, a man can go live where he wishes, and previously there was no prohibition about this."[36] One should keep in mind, however, that conditions in that remote area were not necessarily identical with those in the center of the country.

Maintaining the tax-paying capabilities of the posad also tended to draw the state slowly but inevitably into the running battles that raged between the tax-paying townsmen and their competitors. Some of their competition was economic and came from foreign shores. The large-scale operations of British and Dutch factors made the going rough for Russia's wholesale merchants, and the increasing tendency of foreigners to enter retail operations worked to the detriment of the average posad trader. It was to the central government that the townsmen turned in search of protection from foreign merchants, but it was to be some time before the government responded to their pleas.[37]

The greatest thorn in the side of the townsmen, however, was of domestic origin—it came from the *belye mesta*, the nontaxable urban households of votchiniki. As noted earlier, the peasants and dependent people who traded from their masters' tax-exempt property in the towns constituted a major threat to the economic enterprise of the townsmen.[38] Moreover, the possessors of such property engaged in yet another encroachment on the interests of the posad: namely, the seizure of communal meadows and plowlands on the outskirts of the cities and the transfer of these lands to the exclusive use of the votchiniki.[39] The posad people claimed, with justification, that their very survival depended on the prompt return of these properties. Though petitions in which this grievance found expression contained the usual share of hyperbole, there can be no doubt that the posad people were deadly serious about this matter. The economic crisis of the sixteenth century and the depredations of the Time of Troubles had rendered agricultural land all the more important to them.

As if the economic competition of the nontaxable votchina properties were not annoyance enough to the townsmen, these properties were also implicated in the manpower problems of the posad. Many inhabitants of the votchina courts were former members of the posad who had entrusted themselves to the protection of secular or clerical lords or occasionally to gosti or hundreders. Such persons were known as *zakladchiki*, a word derived from *zakladyvat'sia*, to mortgage oneself. A townsman, crushed by excessive taxation, would go to a monastery or a rich servitor, seeking asylum. The latter would grant said request, thereby removing the petitioner from the posad commune and freeing him from the responsibilities of tiaglo. In return, the zakladchik promised to work for this benefactor for a finite period of years—five, ten, sometimes twenty. The Soviet scholar A. M. Pankratova notes that most historians describe this relationship as one of "protective dependence."[40] While the dependence may initially have sprung from the need for protection, it was not necessarily a degrading relationship. There were, for example, zakladchiki who worked as factors for the Iaroslavl' Spasskii monastery, whose trade turnover was in the vicinity of 10,000 rubles annually.[41]

The practice of zakladnichestvo was widespread; in 1637, about one-third of the Moscow posad people had left the commune via this route.[42] Obviously the posad leaders did not stand by idly and watch their fellow taxpayers siphoned off, only to return to haunt them as competitors with what seemed like outrageous privileges. They complained to local officials and petitioned Moscow. Although the government had, in the crisis period of the late sixteenth century,[43] issued at least one outright prohibition against zakladnichestvo, in the seventeenth century the response of the state to this posad tale of woe was not nearly so sympathetic as it was in the matter of returning simple fugitives to the tax roles. It was one thing to drag a single, unwilling taxpayer back from the forest or steppe to the posad, and quite another to take fifty or a hundred productive zakladchiki from a servitor, a bishop, or an old and wealthy monastery.

The weakness of the townsmen and the lack of authoritative urban administrative institutions to defend their interests drew the central government into contact with the townsmen on nearly every matter of substance and made the state's presence in the towns a commanding one. Where the central government's interests were most directly involved, as in the instances of service regulation and local administration, the initiative for involvement arose from the center. Likewise, when major civil disorder threatened to destroy the cities, the state moved aggressively to check the sources of tension and unrest. In matters concerning the immediate economic or social welfare of the townsmen, however, the stimulus for state action—and that action was limited—came from the townsmen themselves. Their never-ending stream of petitions to the central government is itself a reflection of the institutional arrangements that governed the lives of the townsmen. Lacking urban administrative institutions to embrace all the social interests in the cities and to take effective action on behalf of the socially powerful in the towns, the townsmen had no recourse but to band together as a separate urban subgroup and turn, petition in hand, to the Muscovite bureaucracy. Only when their pleas coincided with the interests of those social groups that enjoyed greater prestige and exercised more political influence—often the very groups with whom the townsmen were in conflict—could they expect a sympathetic hearing, and that was not a frequent occurrence. No relationship between two social organizations can go only one way, but neither can there be any doubt that in the interaction of state and posad the scales tipped heavily, through action and inaction, to the side of the state.

CHAPTER THREE

State Policy in the Seventeenth Century and the Emergence of the Service City

THE PROBLEMS OF MAINTAINING the posad's tax-paying population and defending posad interests against domestic and foreign competition persisted well into the seventeenth century, increasingly attracting the attention of posad and state alike. For their part, the townsmen grew more forceful in their search for redress of grievances. The ever-flowing stream of petitions directed to the center, petitions that were similar in style and substance regardless of their point of origin, suggests that townsmen all over the state were developing a sense of what constituted their self-interest as well as a consistent notion of what state policy measures ought to be taken to protect those interests from encroachment by hostile social groups. Out of this struggle by supplication there seems to have emerged a sense of identity and common purpose among posad leaders, which helped to lay the groundwork for the estate mentality that was to characterize this group through the later seventeenth century and on through the eighteenth.

The state, for its part, responded to the mounting pressure from the towns with major administrative actions and with legislation, the effect of which was to give the state's imprimatur to de jure, if not always de facto, answers to the plaints of the townsmen. The ultimate consequence of state action, however, was to institutionalize the kind of city order that had been emerging for over a century. The relationship of state and townsmen was now fixed in the tsar's law.

THE FIRST ROMANOVS AND THE POSAD

The dire fiscal straits in which the government of Michael Romanov found itself demanded that measures be taken swiftly to augment the tax-paying capabilities of the posady of the realm. The empty courts had to be settled with craftsmen and merchants sufficiently prosperous to bear tiaglo. To achieve this goal, a special government bureau, the Prikaz of Search Affairs, was set up and it swung into action in 1619. The prikaz remained in business two years, long enough to right some of the worst imbalances between taxable posad land and the nontaxable votchina properties located in the cities. Then it closed down.[1]

From 1620 until Filaret's death in 1633, the government followed a cautious, conservative policy toward the social conflicts in the towns. Filaret's government went so far as to forbid in 1621 the alienating by posad people of their courts (the land, not the buildings on it) to nontaxable people. But there was no legislation that forbade the latter from buying or accepting mortgages on such property, which they continued to do.[2] The effectiveness of legislation depends to a large extent on the disposition of those charged with enforcing it, and in this instance, the government did not demonstrate any noticeable zeal. Tal'man points out in his study of the Iaroslavl' posad that during the 1620s petitions directed by the townsmen against the Iaroslavl' Spasskii Monastery received little sympathy from the central authorities. In fact, government investigators, sent to check on posad petitions demanding the return of zakladchiki, discredited the testimony of a few residents of votchina courts who were so honest—or naive—as to state openly that they had previously been enrolled in the Iaroslavl' posad.[3] The disinclination to enforce the law, based, no doubt, on the influence that many holders of nontaxable city properties had over the government, also explains why a proposal of 1627 to exclude all belomestsy from the territory of posady was stillborn.[4]

The motives of Filaret's conservative policies are not hard to discern. Once his chief objective, the restoration of the Russian body politic, had been achieved, all policies were directed at the maintenance of the status quo. In the cities, that meant leaving untouched the existing balance between posad and non-posad social forces. Moreover, Filaret could scarcely be expected to pursue an urban reconstruction policy that would be unpalatable either to the church or the boyars—however desirable such a course of action might have been for fiscal reasons. As patriarch of Moscow and All the Russias, Filaret had a vested interest in preserving church properties, including thousands of courts located in the cities. As a member of a great boyar family, one with huge holdings of city property, he was not likely to dispossess his fellow aristocrats of their urban real estate.[5]

Although the posad population came off second best during the period Filaret controlled the government, subsequent events suggest that it had not only revived from its moribund state by the end of the Troubles, but also gained a new sense of identity. The leaders of the posad put even greater pressure on the governments of princes Cherkasskii and Sheremetev, who succeeded Filaret as the powers behind Michael Romanov, and this time the government made substantial concessions to the plain-

tiffs. Indeed, within a year of the death of Filaret, the government instituted criminal penalties for the alienation of urban courts to belomestsy,
a law which, even if it was still directed only at the seller, suggests a
much tougher attitude on the part of the government.[6] But the big gains
of the posady were linked not so much with the righteousness of their
cause as with broader reasons of state.

The disastrous Smolensk war had been entirely Filaret's doing and had
received virtually no support in Russian society.[7] His successors quickly
dropped this enterprise and redirected Russian policy to the south, where
it appeared that the Cossacks, by their seizure of Azov from the Tatars,
were about to draw Russia into a conflict with Turkey. Urgently needed
improvements in the defense lines of southern Russia were sure to be
costly, and a Russo-Turkish war, should it have broken out, would have
been an even greater drain on the country's resources.[8] Money as well as
manpower were in demand, and the bulk of it came from posad taxes. It
stands to reason that the government should have lent a sympathetic ear
to the pleas of its urban taxpayers.

The posad population was not alone, however, in its efforts to persuade the government to return its lost taxpayers and to limit the encroachments of the belomestsy. The dvoriane, growing in size and political importance, also bore a heavy burden of state responsibilities. Each
new military campaign required more and more of their resources, derived ultimately from the labor of the serfs on their pomest'ia. Just as the
posad was losing members in zakladnichestvo, so, too, were the gentry
losing peasants who sought protection on the estates of the great secular
and clerical landowners. The townsmen and the dvoriane thus shared a
common interest in stopping the flights of fellow taxpayers and laboring
hands, respectively, into privileged sanctuaries.

In February 1637, the gentry and the petty nobility presented the government with a petition outlining the grievances of the servitor population: the flight of their peasants, excessive military burdens, and unfair
treatment by the courts. In suggesting remedies, the petitioners made two
recommendations which, if accepted, would have served the interests of
the posad population as well as their own. First, the petitioners sought
the elimination of the statute of limitations on the recovery of fugitive
peasants and posad people. Second, they called for the establishment in
the cities of civil courts composed of elected members from the gentry
and from the *zemskie*, the local people, which must have meant—at least
in part—the posad population. In pressing their own case, the gentry had
argued at the same time on behalf of the posad—hoping, no doubt, for
support in their battle with the powerful.[9] In May of the same year, a
petition from the Moscow posad elders and hundreders sought the return

of all zakladchiki to their proper communes and, to aid the government, listed all the fugitives by name and by present place of residence.[10]

In the face of growing pressure from townsmen and servitors alike, the government moved immediately to mollify each group. It prohibited the powerful landowners from acquiring land in southern areas of the state where small pomest'ia predominated, and it increased the statute of limitations on the recovery of runaway serfs from five to nine years.[11] At the same time, it ordered the Vladimir Court Prikaz to undertake a general search for all posad zakladchiki, with a statute of limitation on recovery of twenty-five years; accordingly, any townsman who had departed his commune from 1613 on was liable to recovery and return. The instructions also broadened the circle of those who could be taken into the posad to include persons who had engaged in trade or crafts in the employ of a posad dweller. Thus, any free laborer who had hired himself out became eligible for enrollment in the posad tax ranks.[12]

In 1638 the search was shifted to a newly resurrected Prikaz of Search Affairs, under the control of Prince B. A. Repnin. This prikaz functioned vigorously until 1642, when the tsar curtailed its activities by decree and sent Repnin off to perform important state business—in Astrakhan'.[13] On the basis of the extant materials, Smirnov concludes that the search was extremely successful; in the cities for which there is evidence, between 33 and 72 percent of the zakladchiki named on the posad petitions were brought back to the fold.[14] On the practical level, Smirnov attributes these favorable results to the fact that the searchers often worked in the lesser cities of the realm, where the magnates were fewer and could not intimidate them. In the larger cities, the investigators turned their attentions to the vast clerical holdings, which they happily plundered. But the overriding reason for the successful outcome of the search of 1637-1642 was the government's disposition to do the job right, an attitude ultimately determined by the needs of the fisc.

When the young Aleksei assumed the throne in 1645, management of government affairs was entrusted to the boyar B. I. Morozov, the new tsar's tutor. Faced with a severe financial crisis, Morozov's first moves were typical exercises in fiscal conservatism. He purged the prikazy of unnecessary bureaucrats, reduced the salaries of many who remained in service, and even held some in service without compensation. As noted earlier, to improve revenue collections he took new blood into the ranks of the gosti and hundreds, and sought to loosen the control of the military governors over the trade activities of the posadskie liudi. Perhaps the most famous—or infamous—act of the Morozov government was the introduction of the salt tax, a highly regressive indirect levy.[15]

With the same fiscal goals in mind, Morozov worked hard to strengthen the posad communes. In the city of Vladimir, for example, his agent, P. T. Trakhaniotov, recovered zakladchiki, registered hired hands into the posad, and annexed to the posad lands belonging to neighboring votchiniki. Morozov then broadened Trakhaniotov's authority to include looking after Vladimir's "justice," that is, protecting the town from all suits seeking the recovery of land or dependent persons.[16] Such activities, supplemented by numerous searches elsewhere in the state between 1646 and 1648, constituted major victories for the tsar's urban taxpayers.

In 1643 the citizens of Suzdal', impressed by Trakhaniotov's work in Vladimir, asked the tsar for their own protector (*oberegatel'*). This request for a single official responsible for the affairs of the city—even though appointed or confirmed by the tsar—was clearly aimed at obtaining an urban administration favorably disposed toward the trade and craft element of the community. The citizens also asked that the privileged votchiniki be driven from the city and demanded that the government recognize the exclusive right of the posad people to engage in trade and industry. Finally, the petitioners sought to insure whatever concessions they might obtain from the tsar by recommending that they be spelled out precisely in a charter.[17] In short, estate rights and privileges granted and guaranteed by a benevolent sovereign were the goal of the citizens of Suzdal'.[18] Although the petition failed, nonetheless it represents the heightened sense of self-interest—social maturity one might call it—that characterized the posadskie liudi at mid-century.

THE ULOZHENIE OF 1649: THE TOWNSMEN'S ROLE DEFINED

The long conflict between the posad and its nontaxable neighbors at last came to an end—legally, at least—with the publication of the *Ulozhenie* of 1649. The new law code was the outgrowth of a *Zemskii Sobor* that Aleksei felt compelled to convene in the wake of serious popular uprisings in Moscow and in other cities throughout the state. Several elements of the Moscow populace participated in the rioting and bloodshed. The posad people vented their anger on the gosti and members of the hundreds, as well as on government officials generally. The musketeers and other contract servitors, who had much in common with the posad people, joined them in protest. But it was the participation of the Moscow gentry in these disorders that ultimately persuaded the government to summon a Sobor and to undertake major reforms of the state order.[19]

In many of its articles, the *Ulozhenie* granted long-standing requests of the townsmen. It eliminated forthwith all nontaxable votchina courts in the cities; they were annexed to the posady and the state suburbs, along with most of their inhabitants. Many votchina suburbs on the outskirts of the cities were also seized by the tsar. Henceforth there were to be no suburbs aside from state ones.[20] The *Ulozhenie* granted each posad the right to recover all former members who had escaped taxes by seeking refuge with great magnates or by joining the ranks of the contract servitors. The practice of zakladnichestvo was sternly forbidden; anyone in the future who gave himself to the protection of another was to be beaten with a knout and exiled to Siberia; magnates accepting dependent people were to fall into the tsar's disgrace and, incidentally, to have their lands confiscated by the tsar.[21] The code ordered peasants who held courts in the cities and traded or did craft work on them and who did not wish to pay posad taxes to sell their courts to state-taxable people.[22] Peasants were permitted to trade in towns only on bazaar days, with items of their own production, and from carts, not from shops or stalls.[23] The *Ulozhenie*, then, created for the posad population a monopoly right to trade and craft activities in the towns. On paper, at least, the posady had gained victory over their most persistent and irksome competitors.

Just as the government moved to protect its tax-paying townsmen from outside forces, so too, did it move to safeguard its own fiscal interests in the towns. The *Ulozhenie* contained a number of articles aimed at maintaining the cities in their present size and condition and averting any future depopulation such as they had experienced in the late sixteenth century. All posad people were to register in that posad in which they resided at the time of the publication of the new code.[24] Under no circumstances were they to leave it, even if they planned to bear their fair share of taxes in some other city.[25] If the members of the posad commune could not exit from it,[26] and if peasants could no longer abandon the land for the cities, then the posad was destined to become a closed institution, hereditary in nature. Sons would follow fathers as bearers of tiaglo. As of 1649, the people of the posad had become an estate of the realm. That is, they constituted a precisely defined social group, entry into and exit from which was tightly controlled; they possessed monopoly rights to urban trade and manufacturing; and, like Russia's other estates, they bore their share, and a large one it was, of state obligations.

Historical interpretations of the *Ulozhenie* of 1649 and its effects on the posad population tend toward one of two extreme positions. On the one hand, there is the traditional view, based on the prohibition on exit from the posad, that it was the intent of the government to draw the townsmen into the web of state service, just as it had done to the gentry servitors.[27] Behind this argument lies the assumption that the initiative for the *Ulozhenie* came solely from an omnipotent and calculating government, eager to obtain authoritarian control over the country for the purpose of milking the last drop of tax money from an exhausted population. At the other extreme stand the arguments of Smirnov and Syromiatnikov, who contend that the new law code was not only a victory won from the government by an increasingly powerful urban population, but that it contained the seeds of freedom for the urban dweller.[28]

Unquestionably, ever-broadening foreign-policy commitments compelled the Muscovite government to search high and low for newer and better sources of revenue. It was only natural that the maintenance and enhancement of the tax-paying potential of the cities should have figured in its deliberations. Yet the whole history of social relations in the Russian city, beginning as far back as the reign of Ivan III and culminating in 1649, cannot be dismissed as so many manifestations of excessive zeal on the part of the state for tax revenues. While it is true that the tax structure —in the broad sense of each group's obligation to the state—determined the limits within which social conflicts had to be worked out, parties other than the state had their share of influence on the course of events.

In the first place, the composition of the government and the social bases of its support underwent considerable change between 1500 and 1650. The old princely families and established boyars declined in influence, while the service gentry rose in importance. This is not to say that boyars and princes disappeared from major government positions: Romanov, Morozov, and Repnin are cases in point. But it was the dvoriane, not the boyars and princes with their retinues, that formed the military basis of the Muscovite state. For that reason the demands of the gentry could not be ignored by the chief policy makers of the realm.

In the second place, the posad people, through their long struggle with unfair competition, had gained some sense of their identity as urban tradesmen and manufacturers. Their petitions to the tsar and his officials in the second quarter of the seventeenth century reflected this growing awareness. In fact, as the principal source of money taxes, the city taxpayers were not without leverage on the government, although their exercise of it may have been somewhat crude. It was, after all, an urban disturbance in Moscow in which the posad people played a leading role that galvanized Aleksei's government into calling the Zemskii Sobor of 1648.

The demands of the gentry and those of the posad population coincided on a number of important points: the recovery of workers from the privileged landowners; the elimination of arbitrary governmental interference in their affairs; and the establishment of institutions of self-rule. This coincidence of interests greatly enhanced the bargaining position of each group, for the government needed both servitors and cash. One, without the other, would have been useless.[29]

Thus it would seem that all parties involved—the government, the dvoriane, and the posad people—had something to gain from the reforms introduced by the *Ulozhenie*. The events of 1648-49, as they affected the city, cannot be viewed as the willful enserfment of the urban population, nor can they be interpreted as a major concession forced on an unwilling, semireactionary government by the street mobs of Moscow.

There remains the question of whether the townsmen moved in the direction of freedom. Certainly, the terms of the *Ulozhenie* freed the tradespeople from infringements on their rights by the privileged orders of society. But the very same document bound each and every posad dweller to one town—forever. That can hardly be called freedom. Nor did the townsmen, in spite of their protestations, receive any form of self-rule. If anything, their fortunes suffered a reverse along those lines, for in 1648 the government had restored the military governor's control over the trade activities of the posad population. Government officials, operating from the capital or in the localities, continued to exercise close control over the posad.

One might argue, as B. I. Syromiatnikov does, that the posad people obtained the right of free trade in the cities, if by free one means the absence of unfair, privileged competition.[30] But here a distinction must be drawn between the letter of the law and the actual execution of it. Although 10,095 acres of nontaxable lands, with 21,036 inhabitants, were incorporated into the state tax registers in compliance with chapter XIX of the *Ulozhenie*, tax-exempt lands remained a part of the urban scene.[31] In 1686, a government decree approved the possession of city courts and shops by non-posad people, provided that the taxes due from the property were paid.[32] Furthermore, the townsmen found no relief from the crushing burdens of state taxes, burdens so great as to limit severely their economic freedom. Finally, there existed a glaring contradiction between the exclusive privilege to carry on urban trade and manufacturing in towns, which was granted the posad people by the *Ulozhenie*, and the obvious fact that everyone in Russia, at one time or another, had a hand in the production and distribution of goods. The *Ulozhenie* bestowed upon the townsmen rights that had no basis in reality and which could not have been brought into being, no matter how much energy was expended. Even by Syromiatnikov's definition, the posad people did not experience free trade. Neither in the social, economic, nor political spheres could it be said that "posad air made free men."

THE NEW TRADE REGULATION OF 1667:
PROTECTION FROM FOREIGN COMPETITION

If the government did not have the capacity to eliminate once and for all the many forms of domestic competition that plagued the townsmen, it did have the powers to curtail the activities of foreign merchants, who, through the possession of privileges and superior business techniques, dominated those commercial transactions in which they took part. The hegemony of the foreign merchants was recognized by all. When, early in Michael's reign, the boyar F. I. Sheremetev assembled the gosti to discuss John Merrick's proposal that Britain's trade privileges be renewed and even extended, these wise elders of Russian commerce argued strenuously that English merchants were so rich and powerful that the Russians could neither compete with them nor even cooperate with them. In the long run, the gosti claimed, both Russian merchants and the treasury would suffer from any preferential treatment of the British.[33]

There followed, over the years, a series of petitions calling to the attention of the government the hardships inflicted upon Russian merchants by this or that group of foreign traders. The government, however, was reluctant to take action, for it depended on foreign commerce both as a means of obtaining much-needed arms and as a source of silver and gold currency.

The first indication of a change in policy came in 1646, when, in response to a petition, the government abolished the tariff-free trade of foreign merchants, thus forcing them to pay the same duties on the sale of goods that Russians paid.[34] Just three years later all English commercial privileges were canceled. The government expelled British merchants from the interior of the country and limited their trade to Arkhangel and other border cities. The excuse for this action was that the British had shown inadequate respect for their own monarch, but this explanation was simply a cover for the abolition of a policy that had outlived its usefulness.[35]

The complaints of Russia's merchants did not cease, and the troubled years around mid-century witnessed their share of petitions directed against foreigners. In 1653 the government went beyond establishing equal conditions of trade to the introduction of mildly protective tariffs. The customs regulation of that year, designed primarily to regulate internal collections, also contained provisions that discriminated slightly against foreign merchants. On trade transactions in interior cities they were required to pay a 6 percent tax, as opposed to the 5 percent Russian merchants paid, and if the goods they traded emanated from port cities, there was an additional 2 percent charge for bringing them into the country. At port cities, however, Russians and foreigners paid identical duties.[36]

It was only in 1667, with the promulgation of the New Trade Regulation, that the basic demands of the Russian merchants vis-à-vis foreign competition were met. The New Trade Regulation did not really break new ground; what it did was to restate firmly many rules that had not previously been enforced. In the first place, it sought to prescribe what types of commercial activities were permissible to foreigners and where they could operate. It restricted foreign merchants to trade in port or border cities, except when they had specific charters from the tsar permitting them to enter the interior of the country. Once in the country on permission, they were not to attend local fairs and they were supposed to trade only with Russians native to the city in which they found themselves. Under no conditions were foreigners to engage in retail trade, nor were they to trade among themselves. In effect, then, foreign merchants were restricted to wholesale trade in border cities, an arrangement that the Russian merchants found much to their liking. The second aspect of the regulations concerned customs duties, and here the New Trade Regulation refined and strengthened the protective aspects of the statute of 1653. It clearly separated import and export operations. For the former, foreigners paid the same duty as Russians at port cities, but if they took goods into the country the combined port and internal duties amounted to 16 percent. Also, goods purchased by foreigners for export were subject to a 13 percent duty.[37]

The New Trade Regulation appears to have been effectively executed, for it was defended in 1676 by the Moscow gosti, while foreign commercial interests sought to revise it, as did Peter Marselis, who may well have written the basic draft of the regulation.[38]

Although merchant voices had long been raised in chorus against foreign competition and a petition to that effect was delivered in 1667, it appears that the initiative for the drafting of the New Trade Regulation came from the government.[39] For one thing, the time appeared right for a major overhaul of foreign trade relations. Russia's trade with the states of Western Europe was now well established, and the privileges granted to make the Russian market more attractive were no longer needed. Moreover, the Andrussovo treaty seemed to promise a period of peace on the Polish border. Thus, should any European state retaliate against a tariff reform by withholding arms from Russia, the danger to Russian national security would not be all that great. For another thing, the need for tariff reform and for measures to strengthen the Russian merchantry was widely recognized. Foreign trade was Russia's main source of valuable metals; both an increased trade turnover and higher duties would serve the goal of increasing Russia's store of precious metals. And, in fact, one of the key features of the New Trade Regulation was the provision that foreign merchants had to make payments for goods or for customs duties in silver currency of Western European origin. Such monies were routed directly into the Russian treasury, where they were restamped or reminted as coin of the realm.[40]

It should also be pointed out that the ideas on which the new regulation was based were already in the air in Russia. Bazilevich has argued
that there were several proponents of mercantilism in seventeenth-century Russia, men like Jan deGron and Iurii Krizhanich, who were fully
conversant with the literature and practice of mercantilistic policies in
Western Europe. Both personal connections and a certain correspon-
dence between their ideas and steps taken by the government suggest that
they were not without influence.[41] The foreigner with the greatest impact
on Russian trade policy was, without doubt, Peter Marselis. The talented
son of a Hamburg merchant, Marselis had been in Russian service since
1629, holding down important posts in the government, assisting the tsar
in commercial operations, and even performing key diplomatic missions.
Bazilevich argues persuasively that Marselis authored the major part of
the New Trade Regulation, though it would appear that other parties,
most likely some prominent Moscow merchants, sponsored the tougher
restrictions on the activities of foreign merchants.[42]

THE PSKOV REFORM OF A. N. ORDYN-NASHCHOKIN

For all the contributions of outsiders, it is quite possible that the driving
force behind the New Trade Regulation was a native Russian, A. N.
Ordyn-Nashchokin. Again according to Bazilevich, both the style and
the ideas of the statute argue strongly that Ordyn-Nashchokin had a
hand in its drafting, and he may well have been, as a creative and able
administrator with a keen interest in trade matters, one of the chief proponents of tariff reform at this time.[43]

The activities of Ordyn-Nashchokin were not, however, limited to this
single contribution. For the student of city history it is the reform work
he undertook as military governor of Pskov that commands attention. In
it one can see an effort—albeit annulled quickly by higher powers—to
come to grips with some of the key economic, social, and political problems that confronted the townsmen.

The goals of Ordyn-Nashchokin's reform were twofold: to improve
the conditions of the local merchants and, in time-honored Russian administrative fashion, to increase the flow of silver currency into the state
treasury. Toward the former goal, Ordyn-Nashchokin moved to transfer
to the local posad population much greater power over their own affairs.
A local duma was elected to manage the affairs of the city. Of its fifteen
members, elected for a three-year period, only five actually served on the
duma in any one year. They were to handle all civil suits among posad
people and church peasants, and they were to join the police elders in
dealing with criminal offenses. In suits involving posad people and

church peasants on the one hand, and dvoriane on the other, a mixed court was to sit in judgment. The objective here was to free the towns-men from the oppressive judicial system, which was controlled almost exclusively by the gentry.[44]

Strengthening the local merchantry also entailed the suppression of the internecine conflicts that weakened the ranks of Pskov posad society. The poor and middle elements of the commune felt that they were preyed upon by the rich merchants, and the latter were often vexed at the poor for selling goods so cheaply to foreign merchants. Nashchokin's solution was an ingenious one. He sought to limit trade with foreigners to the wealthy members of the posad, hoping in this way that the smaller num-ber of Russian merchants could control the market better, driving up the selling price of their goods. And, to aid the poor, he recommended that they become clients of the rich; provided with loans from the town hall, the poor were to buy up exportable goods and turn them over to the rich merchants. When the latter made their big sales at fairs or in the local market, they then gave to their clients a suitable return based on the prof-its of the transaction. Were everyone to have fulfilled his role, bigger returns should have accrued to all.

To secure money for the treasury, Ordyn-Nashchokin felt that at least one-third of the payments made by foreigners for Russian goods should be in *efimki*—foreign silver coinage. This money was then to be sub-mitted to the treasury, which, after the deduction of customs tariffs, would return the remainder to the merchants in rubles. He also seems to have felt that duty-free trade during a strictly defined period of the year would be beneficial for Russian commerce, both domestic and inter-national.

Making use of the broad powers at the disposal of the military gover-nor, Ordyn-Nashchokin put his plan into effect in advance of approval from the central government. Shortly thereafter, however, he was re-called to Moscow to assist in working out the 1665 treaty with Poland, and the position of military governor in Pskov fell to I. A. Khovanskii. After a quick look around, he canceled the entire reform, reporting to the tsar that the interests of the gentry had suffered greatly and that pass-ports abroad were given freely without the military governor's approval. The tsar's response was predictable. He encouraged the reestablishment of the previous order, noting that one "cannot have such an order in Pskov alone, or there will be a big disturbance [*smuta*]."[45] To have al-lowed one city's merchants a special set of administrative arrangements would have opened the floodgates to demands from other posady for just the same privileges. To have yielded to such demands was unthinkable, for they necessarily entailed a loss of control on the part of the state over its urban population—a loss that neither the government of Aleksei nor the governments of his successors for a century to come were prepared to suffer.

The Pskov reform of Ordyn-Nashchokin reflects leading ideas of the day, ideas that influenced attitudes and policies toward Russia's urban tax-paying population not only during the reign of Aleksei, but on into the reign of Peter I. The need to strengthen the Russian merchantry, both through improved commercial techniques and through protection from hostile interests, became a standard component of government thinking, if not always the object of successful policy making. On the other hand, Ordyn-Nashchokin accepted the basic realities of the Muscovite state: he was not a revolutionary. The fundamental divisions of society—and the services each performed for the state—were not subject to challenge by his plan. Even the most radical of his measures, the introduction of a local duma, did not create what one could call a genuinely urban government: it simply transferred jurisdiction over certain matters to elected representatives of two groups of the city population. And all his work is characterized by a clear devotion to the interests of the state. To the extent that this stance derived from existing practice in Russia it could be called traditional; to the extent that it derived from an acquaintance with notions of political economy emanating from Western Europe it could be called mercantilistic. In any event the two reinforced one another, for the power of the state was the ultimate objective of his policy.

The outcome of Ordyn-Nashchokin's labors, though unsuccessful from his perspective as a government functionary-cum-reformer, makes it abundantly clear that in the state-posad relationship, the state was the senior partner. Whether one considers property relations, social structure, tax-gathering operations, local governmental arrangements, or military organization, the state made its presence felt in the cities at every turn. As for the townsmen, they encountered the state most directly through the many service obligations imposed on them. Since local administration and tax-gathering—two of the chief forms of service—are essential functions of any government, and since they embrace so many aspects of men's lives, the door lay wide open for extensive state involvement in the affairs of the registrants of the posad communes. One need not read a malicious or sinister intent into this situation, though of course abuses of power by government officials were endemic. Rather, the role played by the state should be understood as integral to the service system. It was, after all, a system that made use of each subgroup within the society for the purposes of state administration, without, at the same time, surrendering to these groups the political prerogatives of the autocratic state. But if that system were to function properly, the state had no option but to oversee as vigorously as possible the townsmen's performance of their crucial service operations. Any failure of the state to exercise such vigilance would have been to court administrative confusion, if not downright anarchy and the disintegration of the state order.

If reasons of state thus served to reinforce the townsmen's status as junior partners in their dealings with the state, so too did the shocks administered to the posad economy, already suffering from a number of inherent weaknesses, by the Time of Troubles and its prolonged aftermath. Moreover, there can be no gainsaying the fact that the posadskie liudi, in spite of their temporary alliance with the dvoriane in the years prior to 1648 and in spite of their demonstrable influence on affairs of state during the Troubles and again at mid-century, occupied an inferior place in the social hierarchy, well below the born aristocracy and the broad mass of servitors, most of whose wealth lay chiefly in landed property.

With these economic and social weaknesses came, of course, a corresponding political weakness, the prime example of which can be found in the townsmen's failure to mold to their own ends the institutional features of their natural environment, the city. There was, in short, no city government shaped and dominated by the urban mercantile population. Its absence left the townsmen in a precarious position, unable to control adequately the very base of their operations. The way was thus further opened to the state, whose institutional foot was already in the door, to treat the cities as it chose.

On that score, matters were clear. If the state was everywhere in the city, acting now to protect the townsmen from some threat to their wellbeing, now to exact some service from them, the city itself was nowhere in the eyes of the state. True enough, the language of the prikazy or of the sovereign's legislation included the word "city," but there was never, either in bureaucratic practice or in legislative memorials, any understanding of the city as a totality, as the sum total of the inhabitants within a given territorial area (with the noted exception of border military cities, and, of course, cities that disappeared behind enemy borders as a consequence of the misfortunes of war). Naturally, since the city was not conceived as an entity, there was no notion of the city's possessing autonomy or even limited rights of its own. To the Russian state, the city had geographical, demographic, fiscal, and military meanings; but the word "city" carried with it no uniquely urban institutional connotations, no notions of mayors or town councils. Going back to the time when the center of the Russian state shifted from Kiev to the northeast, there had been no effective urban autonomy, Novgorod and Pskov excepted; and there was no need to create some intermediate and undoubtedly troublesome institution—city government—that would interpose itself between the state and those who served it. Even had the government been so in-

clined, it is difficult to imagine precisely what would be the contours of
an institution that could deal with dvoriane, clergy, craftsmen, merchants, contract servitors, and peasants and which would not, at the
same time, be destructive of the very service principle on which the state
was based.

There is always the temptation when dealing with societies famed for
their bureaucratic ways to attribute variations from known institutional
patterns to confusion and incompetence within the system. The cities of
Muscovite Russia provide just such a temptation, for their conflicting
and confusing administrative jurisdictions and the absence of genuinely
local authorities with competence over an entire town seem to suggest a
breakdown in or aberration from the familiar pattern of Western European city administration where the concept of the city as an entity in and
of itself was strongly rooted and where someone—be it town council or
secular or clerical lord—acted on behalf, if not always to the advantage
of, the collective citizenry. But to succumb to such an explanation is to
ignore a basic reality: namely, that the institutional features of Russia's
cities as they developed in the sixteenth and seventeenth centuries derived from the exigencies of state building in a most demanding setting.
The service system enabled a growing national monarchy, short on
executive capacity at the center and unable to fall back on the localities
for effective assistance, to make do with the limited resources available
to it. The institutional contours of the state that thus emerged, and in
particular the ties that bound state and townsmen, did not represent a
departure from the norm, but constituted the norm itself and were so
understood by tsars and townsmen alike. To the extent that these institutional arrangements assisted the townsmen in the performance of their
state-service tasks and thus contributed significantly to the survival and
expansion of the state, they must be considered successful responses to
the given conditions. Of course these arrangements also had their costs,
for the constraints and burdens that fell upon the townsmen must surely
have encumbered the growth of their economic, social, and political
capabilities—though it is impossible to know how much. However one
strikes the balance between the positive and negative aspects of service—
my own inclination is to argue that the service relationship was on the
whole a reasonable and effective principle of state organization for Muscovite Russia—one point seems incontrovertible: institutional developments in Russian cities were not artificial or inorganic or inappropriate to
the particular state structure that evolved in Russia. Though the shape of
urban life was to change significantly during the eighteenth century, the
point of departure for the study of Russia's cities during the early imperial years must be the service city.

CHAPTER FOUR

The Urban Reforms of Peter I

By ONE SET OF INDICES, the reign of Peter I did not substantively alter life in the posad. The tax-paying townsmen continued to represent only one segment of the urban population, and a decided minority at that in the big cities of the realm. They pursued their livelihood in much the same manner as they had done in the past. They performed state services and paid taxes in the traditional manner. Even their problems had a certain constancy. They complained of foreign competition, though to little avail, for the government preferred to encourage the merchants to compete rather than to afford them protection through discriminatory trade rules. They also objected to the presence of belomestsy in the towns. On this issue, the townsmen did gain some ground, as government policy tended over time to incorporate nontaxable courts into the posad registers.[1] There were, in short, no radical changes in the posad or in the townsmen's role in society.

By another set of measurements, however, the Petrine era stands out as a time of considerable innovation. Its distinguishing feature was a steady flow of decrees and regulations whose intent was to reshape both towns and townsmen, to bring them to the point where they, like other elements of society, could meet the increasing demands of a country that was rapidly emerging as a major European power. The story of the posad in the early eighteenth century, then, is told more forcefully than ever in terms of government policy.

Although a common theme, the enrichment of the treasury, ran through all Petrine urban legislation, the means whereby this objective was pursued varied considerably. Initially, the government operated within the rather narrow confines of the Muscovite understanding of the townsmen, seeking merely to increase the cash flow from this valuable segment of the population. By the last years of the Petrine epoch, however, the tsar had formulated—and expressed in legislation—a much broader vision of the character and contribution of the townsmen. They were to become, in effect, burghers, Russian style. Finally, with the creation of St. Petersburg, Peter set before his countrymen a model, however imperfect, of city life as he felt it ought to exist. It was a model that departed in conspicuous and challenging ways from Russian tradition.

EARLY ADMINISTRATIVE REFORMS

Three major administrative reforms formed the core of Petrine urban policy: the *burmistr* reform of 1699, the provincial reform of 1708, and the magistracy reform of 1721-22. Each came in response to the fiscal problems endemic to Peter's reign, and each sought to make the cities more responsive to the needs of the treasury. But the very existence of three separate reforms in a span of twenty years attests to the failure of the institutions created by them to keep up with the rising costs of financing a militarily aggressive imperial state.

These reforms are important in several ways. First, they demonstrate the heavy hand of tradition, the extent to which the key features of existing relationships between state and townsmen remained intact, in spite of external appearances of more substantial change. Second, they reflect Peter's belief in the efficacy of administrative rationalization as a means to achieve important state goals. Third, they represent the clearest expression of the tsar's maturing understanding of how the cities and their inhabitants could make their maximum contribution to the good of the state.

The institution of the burmistr was introduced for fiscal reasons. The cities had traditionally been the principal source of cash revenues, but it was believed that they could contribute still more if obstacles to the healthy operation of the urban economy and the smooth functioning of local tax-gathering were eliminated. In particular, the government was responding to the long-standing problem of abuses of power by the military governors, actions that had on many occasions impaired the ability of the townsmen to meet their tax obligations. The problem, of course, was not new. The government had previously undertaken, on a limited basis, to restrict the powers of the military governors over certain specific economic activities of the townsmen. But those efforts had failed, and it remained for the government of Peter I to put forward a more decisive remedy for this enduring problem.

No doubt Peter was aware of the need for substantial reform of local administration. When he visited Amsterdam in 1697 he learned about the administration of that great city from his friend Nicholas Vitzen, *Bürgermeister*.[2] The tsar also instructed his representative to the Karlowitz Congress to find out about the operations of Magdeburg Law cities. Magdeburg Law, German in origin, provided for institutions of municipal self-government, capable not only of administering state law, but of legislating for the community as well. Magdeburg Law had spread eastward through Poland, beginning in the thirteenth century, and on into Lithuania in the fifteenth century. Peter could as easily have consulted the Malorossiiskii Prikaz for the desired information, for that agency had its hands full with Magdeburg Law cities.[3] If it was characteristic of Peter to set out in hasty pursuit of information about a pet project, it was scarcely less typical of him to act impulsively without waiting for all the evidence to be in. And so it was in the case of his first city-related reform. In the year 1699, the burmistr reform appeared, a badly worded, sloppily constructed series of decrees whose function was to increase revenue by eliminating the interference of military governors in cities and by giving to the townsmen slightly more control over their own affairs.[4]

The burmistr institution cannot be easily characterized, for it addresses itself to the unique position of the city in the Russian state. It had some of the trappings of an urban reform: it called for the election of local administrators, burmistry, for each city and entrusted them with management of financial and judicial matters. But the reform also had some features of social legislation, focused as it was on the problems of a single estate of the realm, the posad taxpayers. The burmistry exercised jurisdiction over the posad dwellers only, but not over servitors, clergy, and other residents of cities. If the reform were no more complex than what has just been related, one could accept it as an institution providing for locally elected leadership of the tax-paying townsmen. But in fact the jurisdiction of the burmistry extended beyond the city to include state and crown peasants in the countryside. Certainly the urban tax-paying population was the largest social group directly affected by the new institution, and it was their tax-paying potential that the government had foremost in mind in drafting the legislation. But the inclusion of non-posad people within the embrace of the burmistry is an anomaly that stands in need of explanation.

The coherence and unity of conception of the burmistr legislation derives from a very simple notion indeed: the removal of the posad people and of the state and crown peasants from the jurisdiction of rapacious military governors.[5] By this action the government hoped to improve the economic environment of these taxpayers and thereby to raise their tax-paying potential. The means to this end—replacing hard-to-control representatives of the central government with elected or appointed officials from the local population—was not new. Ivan Groznyi's government had done as much and with the same end in view: increasing the take of the treasury.[6] That the burmistr institution cost the government little could scarcely be considered an innovation either. Unpaid state service by the posad population was an established practice. In sum, the burmistr reform can be most aptly described as a reform of the tiaglo system.

The functions assigned to the Moscow Burmistr Chamber further attest to the fiscal orientation of this reform. This body, the heart of the new institution, had two main tasks: it served as the chief administrative organ of the commercial population of the capital; and it functioned as a central administrative organ supervising burmistr activities throughout the state. In this latter capacity, the chamber performed duties that were primarily fiscal. All revenues collected by the local burmistry went directly to the Moscow chamber, which allocated them to those governmental agencies responsible for the maintenance of the army. So it was that Peter reorganized the tax-gathering apparatus of the state, combining local control over the first stages of collection with centralized accumulation and disbursement.

The burmistr reform was no overnight success. Among other things it met with resistance or indifference on the part of those it was intended to aid. The government had made acceptance of the reform voluntary; any city that wished to be done with its voevoda and elect burmistry could do so—providing it paid taxes at twice the previous rate. Presumably the government reasoned that locally controlled administration, even at the cost of double taxation, would still be considered a bargain by the beleaguered citizens. As it turned out, the reform encountered a decidedly unenthusiastic response: only eleven cities adopted the new institution and agreed to the double tax.[7] The government swiftly countered by making the reform mandatory.[8]

As one might have predicted from the reform legislation, the burmistr elections proved to be neither exclusively urban nor exclusively the affair of the posad population. In the north, numerous rural merchants and artisans, some of them peasants, were elected to office, whereas in the south, where posad people were scarce, contract servitors often found themselves serving as local burmistry.[9] The intent of the reform, however, was not to reshape the definition of a city or to realign social groups. Its purpose was fiscal, and in that respect it was a success, at least in the short run. In 1701 the burmistr institution (or *ratusha*, as it came to be known in a Petrine corruption of the German *Rathaus*) collected some 1.3 million rubles, nearly one-half of the state's income for the year and much above the government's expectations.[10] After revenues dropped sharply in the next two years, Peter appointed A. A. Kurbatov to head the Moscow Burmistr Chamber and to supervise its entire operation. With Kurbatov at the helm, the chamber steadily increased its take. In time, though, even Kurbatov's effective management of the ratusha proved inadequate in the face of spiraling military expenditures.[11] In 1708 the institution was nearly buried under the provincial reform.

If the needs of the treasury had earlier pointed toward centralization, they now led the government in the opposite direction. The provincial reform divided the country into eight provinces and made each one responsible for the total maintenance of a fixed number of troops. The goal of the legislation was to reduce waste by eliminating an entire level of administration. The new arrangement afforded no special place for the cities, just as it introduced no separate institutions for them. Instead, they were assimilated into the overall administrative structure of the provinces, and, as such, they fell under the jurisdiction of governors, military governors, and a variety of lesser officials with slightly Russified German titles.[12] In spite of this proliferation of bureaucracy, the provincial reform did not entail the abandonment of the ratusha, only its modification.[13] The Moscow Burmistr Chamber formally lost its role as the central collector and disburser of revenues, but continued as a local organ of the townsmen. It even appears to have maintained some supervisory authority over burmistry in the localities for several years.[14] Right up to the introduction of the magistracy in 1722-23 local posady continued to elect their own burmistry, though these officials were, in the new scheme of things, subordinate to the local representatives of the crown.[15]

As far as the townsmen were concerned, the provincial reform did little more than alter some of the procedures for revenue collection. But its impact on the broader environment of the townsmen—the city—was more substantial. The institutional identity of the cities, never crystal clear, became still more difficult to discern. When the Moscow Ratusha had been in full operation, direct lines of communication had existed between the state and a substantial portion of the urban population, the posad taxpayers. That element of centralization had made possible the relatively successful execution of the 1699 tax reform. But with the provincial reform, it seemed that everyone had a hand in city administration, though clearly there were no city administrators per se. The closest thing to a specific assignment of responsibility for city administration came in an instruction of 1719 that called on all major officials—governors, military governors, *ober-komendanty*, and *komendanty*—"to maintain everything in the city in suitable order."[16] Such admonitions, especially when accompanied by diffusion of responsibility, were essentially meaningless. In effect, the towns and their tax-paying inhabitants were fully integrated by the provincial reform into the local revenue-processing machinery, along with a large number of rural taxpayers. For more than a decade, Russia's cities languished in a kind of administrative limbo.

THE MAGISTRACY REFORM AND CITY ADMINISTRATION

The principle of administrative centralization, in the background since the early part of Peter's reign, was soon to reassert itself. The establishment of the Senate and the increase of its power, the collegial reform of 1717, and yet another provincial reform of 1718—all pointed in that direction. The harbinger of things to come for the posad was the publication in 1719 of the Commerce College Regulation.[17] This statute gave to that state agency broad powers over the cities. It was made responsible for the economic and social affairs of the townsmen, and it was given responsibility for policing each city and its entire population.[18] While it is not hard to see why the college, whose primary function was the encouragement of commerce, was made responsible for supervising that estate of the realm involved in commercial activities, it is not clear why it was put in charge of urban police affairs. What is most interesting, the regulation gave to the Commerce College full power over the magistracies in the cities, though no magistracies existed at that time and no definition of them could be found in this document or elsewhere.[19] Through all the inconsistencies and confusion, two points clearly emerged: after a decade of decentralized administration of the towns and their inhabitants, Peter had resolved to reinstitute central control over the trade and manufacturing population and had chosen to make magistracies, or town councils, the basis of this change.

In spite of the urgent need for a new urban administrative institution, the birth of the magistracy proved to be prolonged and difficult. The problems were many: Peter had a new, more mature view of the needs of the city, which made for a most ambitious piece of legislation; the old hasty and slapdash methods of drafting and executing the law complicated its implementation; the absence of qualified and willing personnel weakened the institution at its very inception; and, more generally, it was imposed upon a population too exhausted by war, taxation, and assaults on tradition to reverse direction for yet another of Peter's grand schemes. The story of the magistracy is not just another page in the lengthy and often depressing administrative history of the Russian city; it is also a classic study in Petrine reform.

As early as 1718 Peter had declared his intention "to establish magistracies in all cities and to provide them with good rules drawn up on the basis of the Riga and Revel regulations."[20] In the same year he established the St. Petersburg Magistracy with a noted merchant, Ilia Isaev, at its head. Isaev did nothing, however, and two years later the tsar found it necessary to rename the institution—it became the St. Petersburg Main Magistracy—and to place a new man, Prince Iu. Iu. Trubetskoi, in the president's chair.[21] Isaev remained as the new leader's assistant. Still, the institution remained lifeless, so the impatient tsar, to prod his appointees into action, issued in January 1721 the Main Magistracy Regulation.[22] This document embodied his ideas on the nature and purpose of the institution and repeated an earlier charge to Trubetskoi and Isaev to draft rules for other magistracies and to see to their creation. But progress came slowly, and the tsar ultimately had to threaten these men with exile before they finally published, in 1724, an instruction that outlined the specific tasks of local magistracies.[23]

The two documents, especially the regulation, provide a final statement of Peter's understanding of the nature of the city, its role in the state, and the institutional features that should shape its life. To be sure, the regulation pertained first of all to the establishment of the St. Petersburg Main Magistracy, but it also discussed explicitly the extension of the magistracy institution to other cities of the realm. Moreover, in discussing desirable features of city life, the document by no means restricted them to the capital. For these reasons, it seems fair to argue that the principles laid down in the document represent Peter's objectives for all cities, not just for his new capital.

The heart of the reform was the magistracy, or town council. It varied in size from one president and four *burgomistry* (not *burmistry*) in the larger cities—2,000 households or more—down to a single burgomistr in towns of less than 200 households.[24] The regulation betrayed no awareness of the contradiction inherent in a one-man council. These officials were to be assisted by councillors (*ratmany*) whose number also varied with the size of the city and the need of the magistracy for additional assistance. The presidents, burgomistry, and councillors were selected by the "first rank, good, wealthy and clever people."[25] For most towns, that meant in practice that the majority of urban citizens were not allowed to vote.

Anchoring the reform was the St. Petersburg Main Magistracy, which not only governed the affairs of the townsmen in the capital but also supervised magistracies in cities throughout the country. It confirmed the election of officials in local magistracies, watched over their activities, and served as a court of last resort for the townsmen.[26] Obviously these arrangements limited the magistracies' ability to evolve into independent agencies of local self-government.

The Main Magistracy Regulation outlined succinctly the areas for which all magistracy institutions were responsible: "to judge the citizens, to supervise the police, to gather from them [citizens] prescribed revenues and to deliver them wherever the state revenue college directed, to manage the economy of the city, the merchantry, all crafts, arts, and other such things, and to make useful suggestions to the Main Magistracy about all those necessities that would serve the citizens' welfare."[27] Each of these areas received further elaboration both in the regulation itself and again in the instruction. For example, it was the stated objective of the law to free posad people from dependence in legal matters on gentry-dominated courts and bureaucratic institutions. Accordingly, the local magistracies took jurisdiction over all criminal and civil cases involving regular citizens, with the exception of important crimes against the state.[28] Moreover, governors and military governors were specifically enjoined from interfering with the magistracy's handling of legal matters and of the city economy.[29] Another area of traditional importance, revenue collecting, received scarcely any mention in the regulation, an oversight that was more than compensated for in the instruction, which devoted one-third of its articles to tax-collecting procedures.

In terms of its underlying institutional assumptions, the magistracy reform constituted no break with the past. In the first place, although it modified slightly the social organization of urban society, basically it left the towns as they had always been, that is, comprised of a number of social groups, each of which ultimately gained its identity from its relationship to the state. The reform did not establish a category of urban citizenship that would embrace all inhabitants of the city.

Second, the authority of the magistracy was limited, again with exceptions that will be discussed in the following section, to the trade and manufacturing population of the towns—the posad dwellers. It became, in effect, an instrument of estate administration for the townsmen; and in that capacity it came closer to fulfilling—on paper—their aspirations than any legislation that was to appear after 1649. The sovereign himself had written of the need to gather the "scattered building of the Russian merchantry," and the magistracy reform was an effort to do just that.[30]

Finally, the exercise of supervisory power over the system by the St. Petersburg Main Magistracy is reminiscent of the centralizing principle that characterized the burmistr reform. Indeed, the entire magistracy system can best be defined as an effort to extend the state's administrative apparatus more directly to the cities through a series of hierarchically ordered agencies. The inclusion of certain magistracy officials in the Table of Ranks corroborates this view.[31]

THE MAGISTRACY REFORM AND SOCIAL ORGANIZATION IN THE POSAD

If the magistracy reform, for all its borrowed forms and labels, departed little in principle from past administrative structures linking the central government and its townsmen, it did contain some innovative features with respect to the social organization of the posad. In delineating the various categories of urban citizen, the legislation set aside the traditional tripartite division of the posad, based on the total assets or tax-paying ability of each townsman, in favor of a new scheme, in part based on wealth, in part on profession. It separated those subject to the magistracy institution—basically the posad population, with a few additions—into two groups, regular and irregular citizens.[32] The regular citizenry, in turn, was to be comprised of two guilds (*gil'dii*). The first guild, separated from other posad people by "privileges and advantages," embraced bankers, wealthy merchants, doctors, apothecaries, skippers of merchant ships, gold and silver craftsmen, icon painters, and artists. To the second guild belonged those engaged in petty trade or in the sale of produce, and craftsmen—tailors, bootmakers, and the like.[33]

Organization and structure within the guilds was to be provided by elected elders. They were responsible for taking the concerns of their constituencies to the proper authorities and, in the case of the first guild elders, for assisting the magistracy officials when needed.[34]

Those posad dwellers who did not qualify for membership in either of the guilds fell into the category of irregular citizens. Though subject to the authority of the magistracy, they were given considerably less standing in the urban community. Known as the base people (*podlye liudi*), these were hired laborers who performed unskilled or semiskilled work.[35]

The less important groups, the second guild citizenry and the irregular citizens, appear to have been little more than the traditional second and third ranks (*stati*) of posad society, renamed. But the first guild citizenry was another matter. No established sociological concept comes to mind that would embrace such a diverse lot of people. It is likely that this particular feature of the reform can best be understood in terms of Peter's own understanding of cities and their potential within society, an understanding that was strongly shaped by Western European influences.

Whether it be Peter's frequent visits to the *Nemetskaia sloboda* in Moscow or the inquisitiveness that marked his visits to foreign states, there existed from the beginning of his reign an attraction to the world of the European burgher. This attraction led him not simply to commerce and to those who expedited the exchange of goods, though Peter displayed strong interest in mercantile issues, but also to those occupations that either did not exist in Russia or were present only on a limited, imperfectly developed basis. That Peter respected and valued skippers, engineers, boatwrights, doctors and the like is borne out by his efforts to recruit men with such talents to the service of the Russian state.

The first-guild citizenry under the magistracy regulation, therefore, might best be described as "valued urban dwellers," people capable of contributing through specialized skills to the commercial, productive, hygenic, and aesthetic life of the state. By segregating these people and granting them privileges the tsar held them up to public honor and perhaps emulation; by securing for them a dominant role in the operations of the magistracy he made certain that such powers as inhered in that institution were exercised by the cream of the urban lot.

That Peter sought to divert the posad population from its narrow, tradition-bound ways and to encourage it to develop along the lines of a Western European bourgeoisie can be seen in other, related actions he took. It was during Peter's reign that the two privileged merchant corporations, the gosti and the gostinaia sotnia, began a rapid decline into oblivion. Although both groups were explicitly excluded from the ranks of the urban citizenry by the magistracy instruction of 1724, in the very same year the Moscow magistracy ordered the gosti and hundreders under its jurisdiction to register in the appropriate guild.[36] In 1728 the Senate decreed that gosti and hundreders in all cities should register in the local posad tax rolls, thus terminating the privileges of these groups.[37] Apparently Peter had become disenchanted with these corporations for two reasons: first, the expanded state bureaucracy made unnecessary their service functions of advising the sovereign and managing select aspects of the economy; second, as merchants, members of the corporations had proved too conservative, relying on their privileges for personal gain and avoiding adventurous, potentially risky ventures.[38] Peter's policy of allowing the privileged corporations to slowly die out neatly complements the social policy of the magistracy reform, which moved to the forefront of urban society the best of the tax-paying merchantry and other men of talent, without so burdening them with privileges as to render them self-satisfied and cautious.

Reliance on guild-type social organization constituted a second emphasis of the magistracy reform that can also be traced to Western European origins. Not only did Peter provide guilds for the more successful members of the posad (these were, despite the theoretical breadth of first-guild membership, basically merchant guilds), he also ordered that each art and craft establish its own guild (*tsekh* or *tsunft'*). In keeping with their prototypes, the guilds were instructed to elect aldermen or elders, keep books outlining their rules and privileges, and supervise the activities of their members through their elected officials.[39]

Craft guilds, as called for by the Main Magistracy Regulation and subsequent Petrine legislation, were far from being exact replicas of Western European guilds. They differed most significantly in not being compulsory for all artisans, in that membership was not an exclusive right, passed on by inheritance, and in not enjoying special privileges in the marketplace.[40] Indeed, the absence of features attractive to artisans, coupled with the fact that the guilds were a creature of the government, not of the craftsmen themselves, signaled rough sailing ahead for this Petrine innovation.

Historians have been of one mind in interpreting the Petrine guild legislation as a means of enhancing governmental regulation over an important segment of the population. Polianskii, in his study of city crafts, argues that the introduction of the guilds followed from "fiscal-police needs" and from a desire to establish "state control over production."[41] Yet he goes on to argue, with justification, that Peter was seeking through the guilds to raise the level of output and the quality of Russian artisan production. The call for regulation of the master-apprentice relationship, heretofore left to custom, is a case in point.[42] With the craftsmen, as with the guild merchantry, Petrine reforms seem to bear the same basic message: these are important, productive members of society whose contritutions might well be enhanced by organizational structures successful elsewhere and adaptable to Russian conditions. That Peter did not introduce western guilds in all their purity should come as no surprise. Even had he been willing to copy Western European guilds in toto, which he was not, the guilds that had survived into the eighteenth century bore only a pale resemblance to their medieval progenitors.

To return to the initial point: the magistracy reform and related legislation was socially innovative, in the sense that it called for a reordering of posad society and afforded to each group some corporate life of its own. More significant, however, was the intent of the reformer to transform the townsmen—be they merchants or craftsmen—into something much closer to their Western European counterparts.

The same objective lay behind a host of public welfare tasks entrusted to the magistracies by the regulation. In this instance the legislation engaged in some primitive social engineering, attempting to upgrade the life of the townsmen by improving the environment in which they lived. A productive society needs educated people, so the magistracies were instructed, in a curious turn of phrase, "to avoid hindering" the establishment of schools. In fact they were to give aid wherever possible, especially to the lower schools (*malye shkoly*) that taught reading, writing, and arithmetic.[43] To improve the lot of the less fortunate in society and perhaps even to restore them to productive labor, the magistracies were directed to set up hospitals for the sick, injured, and aged; homes for women living in a disreputable fashion; and houses of correction where idle, troublesome men and petty criminals could be reformed through hard labor.[44] These measures pale, however, before the charge to the police:

> And exactly, it [the police] assists in the laws and in justice. It dispenses good order and moral admonitions, gives to all safety from robbers, thieves, ravishers, tricksters, and similar persons, drives away disorderly and indecent living, and compels each to work and to honorable industry, makes good householders, careful and good servants, looks after the correctness and the construction of homes and the conditions of the streets, prevents high prices, and brings satisfaction in all that human living requires, stands on guard against all occurring illnesses, brings about cleanliness in the streets and in the houses, forbids a superfluity of domestic luxuries and all manifest sins, looks after the poor, the sick, the crippled and other unfortunates, defends widows, orphans, strangers, according to God's commandments, educates the young in chaste purity and honorable sciences; in short, over all these things the police is the soul of citizenship and all good order, and the fundamental support of human safety and convenience.[45]

This conception of police power has come under criticism as a manifestation of tsarist police-state tactics, but such a view is not tenable.[46] Peter's travels to Western Europe had brought him face to face with cities of quite another character from those of his native land, and it became one of his goals to abolish the many forms of blight that marked Russia's cities—the mud, the smoky and cramped houses, lawlessness, disease, and so forth. In their stead he envisioned well-ordered cities with straight, paved streets, neatly kept houses of sound construction, and thriving commerce and manufacture. In keeping with the general European practice of the day, Peter employed the term "police" to signify that institution entrusted with drawing up and administering the rules and regulations that would make this dream a reality. The proper context of the Petrine police is the eighteenth, not the twentieth, century.

Restructuring posad society and establishing institutional means for upgrading the city were but two of the tactics used by Peter to transform the posad population. Perhaps his greatest efforts along this line were directed at modernizing the institutions of manufacture and commerce. The Main Magistracy Regulation had a great deal to say on this point. It called on magistracies to promote trade, crafts, and water transport and made them responsible for the execution of orders sent down by the Manufacture and Commerce colleges; and it encouraged them to report to the appropriate college or colleges ideas for new rules or other forms of assistance for local commerce.[47] Such general assignments were to be expected, for the regulation was, after all, only a guideline for those who would actually set up the new institution and provide it with more detailed rules of operation. But the document went on to make specific recommendations for the stimulation of the urban economy. The law called for the establishment of exchanges in the major port and inland trading cities and suggested that leading merchants be present at the local exchange for at least one announced hour each day. The exchange was to serve both as a site for the completion of commercial deals and as a convenient location for the spread of information useful to merchants and manufacturers, such as the time and place of arrival of merchant ships.[48] The law also called upon magistracies in leading cities to appoint brokers to officiate at commercial transactions and even specified the manner in which their rates were to be set.[49] Considerable space was devoted to touting fairs as a means of encouraging trade and, not incidentally, of raising more revenue.[50] This concern for the fundamentals of economic development clearly distinguishes the magistracy reform from earlier Petrine legislation dealing with the townsmen.

The magistracy regulation remains, nevertheless, a piece of prescriptive legislation, the embodiment of the tsar's hopes for Russia's cities. It is not a description of real achievements. More concrete evidence of Peter's strategy of making the townsmen into effective burghers can be seen in a variety of governmental policies designed to stimulate commerce and manufacture.

As early as 1699 an imperial decree urged Russian merchants "to trade as they do elsewhere, that is, in companies."[51] Later in his reign, following the examples of the famed Western European trading companies of the seventeenth century, the tsar organized one company with exclusive rights to the China trade, another for trade with Spain.[52] Even more attention was devoted to creating manufacturing companies, sometimes in a genuine effort to develop a needed area of production, sometimes to dump an unprofitable government industry into private hands. Whatever the motivation, the principle of joint ownership was a persistent feature of Petrine industrial development, if not always a popular one with those impressed into entrepreneurship. It should be noted, of course, that company ownership was not limited to townsmen. Select members of the gentry could and did find themselves placed in managerial roles.[53] But the basic targets of these attempts to introduce joint ownership to Russian business were naturally the townsmen, especially the guild merchants.

Other governmental encouragement to commerce and manufacture, though it unquestionably influenced the conduct of business, belongs more properly to economic history than to social. Loans, reduced taxation, tariff exemptions, monopolistic concessions, assistance in securing laborers, and the creation of a merchant marine fall into this category.

The preceding evidence must, of course, be kept in perspective. Peter's main aim was to increase the economic capacity of his state and with it, its military power. Developing the urban economy per se could hardly be considered an ultimate objective. Indeed, many of those drawn into the economic arena came from outside the ranks of the tax-paying townsmen, so it cannot be argued that these actions impinged exclusively on the townsmen. Nonetheless, Peter's economic and social programs had a great impact on the towns. The tsar clearly counted on the townsmen, in particular the upper strata of the merchantry, to take the lead in developing a backward Russian economy. To that end he attempted to alter the social organization of the townsmen, to make the towns themselves more conducive to economic activity, and to improve business technology through a variety of government programs. In all these areas the influence of the tsar's Western European contacts can be seen, especially his respect for the good burgher and the skilled craftsman. His understanding—however accurate or inaccurate—of their contribution to the strength of Western European states informed his major efforts to tear the Russian townsmen from the traditional patterns of posad life, patterns that obstructed the ambitious plans of Russia's most vigorous sovereign.

THE CREATION OF ST. PETERSBURG

Still more evidence, and this of a particular kind, on Petrine urban policy can be drawn from the early history of St. Petersburg. The story of the city's foundation has attracted the attention of historians, novelists, and salon intellectuals, and it has captured the popular imagination of Russia as well. Indeed, St. Petersburg stands as a symbol of the first order of magnitude in modern Russian cultural history. It can also serve as an exemplar of Peter's urban policy, for the construction of this showcase city conformed in most respects to the objectives set out for all cities of the realm in the magistracy legislation.

Initially, the import of St. Petersburg lay in its strategic location in the estuary of the Neva River. The city's most noted landmark, the fortress of Peter and Paul, was constructed to take advantage of the site. But, as it turned out, the Swedes, whom the fortress was intended to repel, were soon to be driven beyond Vyborg, and other defenses were erected further out in the Baltic. The Peter and Paul fortress was never called upon to defend either the newly acquired territory or the city that arose behind its ramparts. Still, Petersburg retained military significance throughout the eighteenth century in another capacity: it became the center of Russia's efforts, sporadic to be sure, at becoming a maritime power.

Under Peter, the seaward orientation of Russian policy led directly to the development of a vast shipbuilding establishment in the new capital. In addition to the yards of the admiralty, numerous supportive enterprises appeared, such as the arsenal and powder works. By 1715, some ten thousand workers are believed to have been engaged in shipbuilding or related activities.[54]

It was also a part of Peter's vision that the city become a great center of commerce. The task was not an easy one to accomplish, however. For one thing, overseas trade was firmly rooted in Arkhangel. For another, Petersburg was poorly equipped to compete. The harbor was shallow and dotted with hazards to shipping; only a primitive road connected the city with the remainder of the country; and, of course, there was no indigenous merchant community. Although the government lacked the technical capacity to overcome the natural disadvantages of the site, it was able to resolve the human and economic problems by the means it knew best: compulsion. It ordered merchants to move to the new capital, and it set a number of trade and tariff regulations that strongly discriminated in favor of St. Petersburg. In a matter of years, the ancient White Sea port had been eclipsed by this Baltic upstart.[55]

One could argue that Peter's interest in the economic development of the city had been dictated largely by geographic considerations. But such an explanation would not hold for the tsar's efforts to give his new capital a pleasing physical appearance, to provide it with necessary public facilities, and to ensure that its inhabitants led orderly, civically responsible lives. On this count there seems to have been a conscious emulation of other European cities. Trezini and Leblond were asked to submit master plans for the physical development of the city, though only one of their recommendations, the making of Vasilevskii Island into the residential center of the city, was acted upon by the tsar.[56] Paved and lighted streets, safely and solidly constructed homes, stone embankments on the rivers and canals, and a host of other improvements—these, too, were integral parts of Peter's vision. And, of course, there was a steady flow of legislation regulating the daily activities of the citizens for the greater glory of the city: streets were to be swept in front of homes, missing paving blocks replaced, refuse delivered to appointed places, no horses ridden along certain quays lest their emissions pollute the waterways, and so forth.[57]

Obviously, regulations were one thing, reality another. In fact, Petersburg grew in a haphazard manner; its streets were crooked, muddy, and littered; most housing consisted of the traditional wooden structures; and fire protection was limited, to put it generously. The city budget, dependent for the most part on allocations from the state, could not begin to cover the expenditures that fulfillment of all the laws would have entailed.[58] But the issue here is policy, and on that count Peter must be credited with far greater foresight and imagination than any of his predecessors had shown in their management of Moscow.

Human resources are just as important as material ones, and Peter paid due attention to this aspect of city-building. He made a conscious effort to populate the city with men of varied skills and backgrounds, each selected for the particular contribution he could make. Though foreign specialists are the most conspicuous examples of this policy, the bulk of the population, naturally, was drawn from Russia. The call went out for skilled and unskilled laborers, for merchants, for gentry, and for men of any rank whose flair or talent qualified them for one of the tsar's pet ventures. Because the city had little inherent appeal, situated as it was in an area more suited to be a game preserve than to be the capital of a continent-spanning empire, it took more than a casual invitation to get most people there. From 1708 to 1718 conscript labor poured into the city at the rate of 24,000 men or more each year, few of whom chose to remain after their time was up. The gentry proved equally reluctant to abandon hearth and home for the chill Baltic coast; they came only because their sovereign commanded them.[59] Force had conquered the site; force populated the city.

Securing a diverse population and putting them to work at their appointed tasks might be considered a job well done by the city builder, but for Peter there was yet another related task to be performed—to broaden the intellectual horizons of the Petersburg citizen. Generally speaking, cities have distinguished themselves from rural or village societies by their encouragement of a more intense exchange of ideas and information among a heterogeneous population. It would, of course, be ridiculous to suggest that Moscow or a number of other pre-Petrine cities failed totally in this respect, but the job seems to have been done better in Petersburg than at any other place or time in Russia's past. The appearance of the *Vedomosti* and schools of engineering and naval science helped to institutionalize the transfer of knowledge. The *kunstkamera* accomplished the museum's time-honored function of arousing interest in the world of man and nature. And there were the assemblies. Not only did they give diverse elements of Petersburg society an opportunity to meet and mix; they helped to break down the barriers of the terem. The groundwork had been laid for the brilliant social life that was to characterize the Russian court and high society during the reigns of Peter's successors.

So it was that Peter, presumably operating without theories of urban sociology, assembled the basic building blocks of urban society. St. Petersburg had large-scale industry, international commerce, the seat of government, the central institution of the church, educational institutions, a development plan, and a heterogeneous population. And to make it all work, to smooth out and shape social relations, Peter provided the city with a vast corpus of regulatory legislation. Many of the dominant motifs of St. Petersburg—in particular the emphases on commerce and manufacture, on merchants and skilled craftsmen, and on regulations affecting public welfare—echoed policies advanced by the Petrine government on a state-wide basis and were in accord with the tsar's general conceptions of cities and their contributions to the state.

It is doubtful that Peter had the interests of his subjects foremost in mind while erecting this city: the physical suffering attendant upon its early years argues for his indifference to human costs. More likely, he was moved by egoistic considerations to create the grandest possible capital for the empire whose borders he had extended. Whatever the motives, though, the creation of this city set before the Russian people new standards of urban life, and it presented them in a manner more graphic and challenging than all the urgings and admonitions contained in documents such as the Main Magistracy Regulation.

THE PETRINE LEGACY

As often happens, this summary implies a carefully conceived and consistently applied governmental policy. That is far from being the case. As with so many Petrine activities, elements of haste and carelessness, even a certain haphazardness, permeated Peter's urban reforms. Moreover, to the extent that matters can be systematized, the evidence suggests that Peter's attitude, and hence his policy objectives toward the cities and their inhabitants, evolved noticeably over time. If at first he regarded them as rich veins of revenue to be protected from hostile forces so that the state might exploit them all the more, by the end of his reign Peter recognized that prosperous, tax-rich cities required much more than the protection of an outmoded city order from the excesses of venal crown officials. They needed an educated, socially alert, and economically sophisticated population; and they needed institutions that would enable that population to perform its designated tasks with facility. Nowhere can this position be found more forcefully expressed than in the Main Magistracy Regulation, the principal document of Peter's reform of the state-townsmen relationship. Not only did the regulation undertake to rearrange the tax affairs of the townsmen for the greater interest of the treasury, it was normative and prescriptive in relation to nearly every imaginable aspect of urban life. The document is a curious collection of the sovereign's pet notions, and one is hardly overwhelmed by its conceptual underpinnings. Yet, for all its inadequacies as a legislative guideline, the regulation evinces a more comprehensive view of the problems of Russia's towns and townsmen than did the tsar's earlier efforts in this area.

If Petrine legislation had its impressive features, the actual achievements of his reign were clearly less dramatic. The efforts to transform the posad dwellers into full-fledged burghers failed. Traditional social arrangements within the posad commune prevailed, largely negating the tsar's efforts at restructuring that segment of Russian society. The fundamental elements of the service relationship of the townsmen also remained unchanged, with the relatively insignificant exception of the phasing-out of the privileged corporations. And, in spite of observable increases in manufacturing output and commerce in the post-Petrine era, the posad people retained, for decades, their accustomed forms of doing business. It was not until the third quarter of the century that signs of the impending demise of the age-old posad order stood out sharply. The traditional patterns of behavior proved too deeply rooted to be altered in a few decades, even by a ruler as dynamic as Peter.

The principal instrument of Peter's reform objectives, the magistracy, was a dismal failure in the short run, and in the long run it did little more than serve as an adjunct of the central government's administrative and revenue-gathering operations. Weaknesses in the enabling legislation certainly contributed to its difficulties, as did the death of its creator and the subsequent period of governmental drift, both of which occurred soon after the magistracy's inception. But the basic weakness of it lay in the absence of two conditions, each dependent on the other: for the magistracy to be successful it had to enjoy a substantial measure of autonomy; and for there to be autonomy, there had to be the proper social and political conditions to guarantee that the exercise of urban autonomy would not be detrimental to the state. Neither condition was present during the Petrine reform era.

The Soviet scholar Ia. E. Vodarskii argues that in the process of working out the magistracy regulation, the gentry-controlled government conceded to the townsmen "autonomy on questions of city administration."[60] To be sure, the regulation thrust upon the magistracy a whole host of urban administrative tasks, but that is hardly tantamount to entrusting it with responsibility for making policy. To execute policies determined by others is not to exercise autonomy. It is also true that the regulation called for the creation of local police, subject to the magistracy's supervision, and gave to those police broad competences in local administration. Even as the government was in the process of spelling out the duties of the new police, it was hard at work creating its own centrally controlled, hierarchically ordered police system.[61] There can be no question as to which agency had the greater power. Thus, in light of the imposition of this institution upon the townsmen, of the detailed listing of its duties, of the supervision to be exercised over its actions and personnel by the Main Magistracy, of its narrow estate basis, and of the presence of partially competing institutions, it seems reasonable to ask whether the term "autonomy" is misleading, if not entirely hollow. It would be too strong to say that the townsmen had no latitude whatsoever under this new institution, but the framework in which they had to operate had clearly been determined for them by the state. When the going got rough, they had to repair to their traditional weapon—petitioning higher authorities. That was no formula for autonomy.

As for the posad inhabitants, one could scarcely argue that they were prepared to exercise control over the cities. Ensnared in the net of service, they regarded government as a burden to be avoided, not as an opportunity to be seized upon. Moreover, their tradition of seeking redress of grievance by petitioning the center, combined with their weak social position relative to official representatives of the crown and local gentry, made them poor raw material for leadership of an autonomous urban institution. Finally, it should be noted that the very conception of the magistracy emerged not from the midst of posad society, but from official Russia, from the tsar, his foreign advisor von Fick, and the Senate. The townsmen lacked both the qualifications and the inclination needed for real urban autonomy.

But even if the townsmen had been ready and eager to seize control over their milieu, it is hardly conceivable that Peter would have bestowed urban autonomy on them. Peter I fit the pattern of a mercantilist ruler. With the goal of enhancing the power of the state, he sought to control nearly every aspect of Russian life. Indeed, one could argue that during his reign the machinery of an absolutist state was set in place, even if its design far exceeded the capacity of the society to maintain it at the level of operating efficiency the tsar expected. In the face of this advancement of the bureaucratic powers of the state, the granting of self-rule to any segment of society was not only unthinkable, but potentially dangerous. Local self-rule could only encourage the play of centrifugal forces on the body politic, leading to an almost certain loss of revenue, if not to graver consequences still. Alterations of the system to make it function better came readily to Peter's mind, but it was not a part of his thinking to challenge deeply rooted social institutions—at least as far as posad society was concerned. The absence of local autonomy in the magistracy reform does not, therefore, bespeak Peter's ignorance of the political structures of the Baltic cities that served as models for his reform, nor does it reflect incompetent borrowing; rather, it reveals his consistent understanding of the functions of the state, as well as his astute reading of Russian conditions.

Like so many Petrine reforms, the magistracy undertook a modification of the traditional. It was an attempt at rationalizing Muscovy and not a radical break with the past. The legacy of the Petrine era remains one of goals and aspirations for a new city order, coupled with institutional changes that only slightly altered the social realities inherited from the preceding century. The service city may have taken on a new exterior and forces were certainly at work that would eventually undermine it; but for the time being, its essential character persisted. In fact, it could be argued that the apogee of the service city lay ahead—in the decades immediately following the demise of the great tsar-reformer.

CHAPTER FIVE

The Posad Economy in the Eighteenth Century

THAT THE REFORMS of Peter I were far too ambitious, given the human and physical resources available to him, is almost an axiom of Russian historical writing. Yet the same could be said for many of history's great reformers, for it is their very nature to envisage social or political transformations far in excess of what one man, or even one generation, might reasonably expect to achieve. In fact, it is possible for the historian to become so wrapped up in the comparison of attainments with goals that he overlooks the reform process itself, that all-important interplay between dream and reality that often holds the most fruitful lessons. In the case at hand, the kind of energetic urban mercantile and manufacturing class that Peter so prized did not appear on the Russian scene in the eighteenth century—or ever, for that matter. But the really telling aspects of the story lie not in the grandiose goals of the tsar, nor in the disparity of goal and achievement, but in the characteristics of Russian society that thwarted the reformer's objectives and shaped the contours of those portions of his work that did survive. Peter's efforts to rationalize urban life floundered for a host of reasons: Russian governments after him lacked the drive and forcefulness to pursue his reforms effectively; the basic structure of state administration reinforced the need for the posad commune to perform its accustomed service role; and society itself, for a number of reasons, social and economic, was not ready to abandon its traditional way of life. To understand properly the fate of the Petrine urban reform and to come to grips with the essential character of the posad commune and its role in eighteenth-century Russia, it is necessary to examine more thoroughly select aspects of posad society: the economic activities of the townsmen, the institutions that gave posad society structure and the power to act, and the social attitudes and social relations of the posad dwellers.

Economic arrangements within the posad demand first consideration, for they, more than any other force, shaped both the institutional structure of the posad and the social relations of the townsmen with the rest of

Muscovite society. Moreover, it is in the world of the posad economy that one can see most graphically the enormous diversity of occupation, wealth, and power among the townsmen. To understand the commune is to know first the diversity of the economic interests that lay within its compass, a diversity that was ultimately to place an unbearable strain on the communal character of posad society.

One must note from the outset that the economic configuration of posady varied widely. Some cities, like Moscow and Tula, had flourishing merchants, merchant-manufacturers, and a full complement of townsmen engaged in less exalted pursuits. There were other cities and even whole provinces that, in contrast, could count only a handful of posad dwellers, almost none of whom had sufficient capitalization to be considered true merchants.[1] And, of course, there were significant regional variations in the items of trade. Taking Russia as a whole, then, there can be no economically average posad, and care must be taken not to build arguments wholly upon the evidence of Moscow's flourishing merchants or, alternatively, upon the meager traces of merchants' activity in the more remote reaches of the country. Fortunately, the majority of Russia's posady, from small to large, did contain men of varying ranks, occupations, and wealth. Thus it is entirely possible to speak in general terms of the economic diversity that existed within the posad commune while at the same time recognizing the kinds of distinctions that must be drawn among the economic configurations of different posady.

THE PROSPEROUS MERCHANTRY

At the top of the pecking order in posad society stood the first-guild merchants. With their large-scale operations, their wide-ranging contacts, and their capital resources, they set the tenor of life in the commune. These advantages enabled them to dominate, directly and indirectly, the economic activities of their less successful posad brethren, and they provided the basis for the first-guild's hegemony in social relations and posad politics. Moreover, the first-guild merchantry served on many an occasion as the face of the posad to the outside world. Foreign merchants, though they dealt at one time or another with all ranks of townsmen, had their most lucrative dealings with the great guild merchants. And the Russian government, for its part, turned to these talented and successful townsmen for assistance in state economic and fiscal administration. It is not surprising, then, that in Russian economic history observations on the merchantry have been based largely on this most conspicuous element of the posad commune.

The first-guild merchants were not numerous, constituting everywhere a small minority within posad society. In 1764 they composed 11.4 percent of the merchants in Moscow, 2.1 percent in Iaroslavl', and 15.8 percent in Kazan'.[2] When the tax reform of 1775 restructured posad society according to wealth, only 11 percent of those formerly considered merchants qualified for the first guild under the new capital qualifications.[3] The distribution of first-guild merchants about the state was predictably uneven. The two strongest centers of their activity were Moscow, whose merchants were, among other things, the nation's leading importers of foreign goods, and Tula, whose merchants proved particularly aggressive in the exporting of Russia's agrarian products. Lesser cities, such as Vologda, Velikii Ustiug, Kaluga, Olonets, and others also had their share of first-guild merchants, but not in numbers to compare with Moscow or Tula.[4] Curiously, data from the 1760s show that in St. Petersburg the guild merchants were not nearly as numerous or strong as one might expect, given the city's predominant position as Russia's "window on Europe."[5] This anomaly can be accounted for in part by the traditional unattractiveness of the city to Russian merchants, dating to the forced settlement in the capital of many of their numbers during the Petrine era, and in part by the preponderant role of foreign merchants in the trade affairs of the city. Even so, one might have expected a bigger concentration of Russian commercial magnates in Petersburg than were in fact present.

It was not, of course, numbers, but economic power that made the first-guild merchants such a force in posad society, and nowhere was that power more evident than in their import-export activities. In the 1760s, a mere 1.9 percent of Russia's merchants carried on trade in port cities or abroad, but they were among the country's most capitalized individuals.[6] According to data for 1764-65, eight St. Petersburg import-export merchants had a total trade turnover of 590,000 rubles (though 500,000 rubles of that figure represent the turnover of a single individual, Savva Iakovlev); forty-five Moscow merchants had a total overseas trade turnover of 1,176,000 rubles; and thirty-four Tula merchants turned over 860,000 rubles. The data on Moscow merchants afford a good look at the variety and volume of their international trade. A. I. Turchaninov, who dealt chiefly in silks, had commercial contacts with Holland, England, Germany, and Italy totalling 25,000 rubles; D. A. Zemskii, a dealer in diverse goods, traded with Amsterdam, England, and Persia to the sum of 50,000 rubles; and V. V. Surovshchikov, trading with Constantinople via Temernik and with Amsterdam and Gdansk through St. Petersburg, turned over 90,000 rubles a year in Russian and foreign (especially Chinese) goods.[7] In the absence of dependable price tables it is impossible to make comparative judgments about wealth in another time and place;

but the sums are sufficiently large to dispell any notions that the Russian merchants—at least at the summit—were only so many trading peasants.

The dynamic of the import-export trade in Russia lay in the broad international demand for Russia's raw materials and, of course, in the growing Russian market for luxury goods. Almost half of the exports through Riga in 1768 consisted of flax, hemp, and tallow, and this was typical of Russian imports throughout the century.[8] There was one noteworthy deviation from the rule of the export of raw materials. During the second half of the century Russian merchants encountered a growing market for two categories of semifinished goods: bar iron and linen cloth, coarse for sails and fine for clothing. Both these areas of trade flourished in the last decades of the century, only to collapse in the nineteenth century in the face of competition from a fast-industrializing England.[9]

As for imports, the Russians sought mostly manufactured goods and select foodstuffs. The following list, arranged in descending order according to value, reflects the luxury character of items imported into Petersburg during the decade 1780-1790: raw sugar, silk items, wool cloth, broadcloth, spiritous liquors, tobacco, coffee, haberdashery, cotton fabric, English beer, lemons, fresh and dried fruits, oysters, and anchovies.[10]

There was, of course, a thriving domestic trade; indeed, the bulk of Russia's merchants confined their labors to the domestic market. But the absence of records comparable to those involving import-export merchants makes it impossible to speak with the same precision about their wealth and the nature of their business. What is certain is that trade in agricultural products, both for the table and for the factory, made up the overwhelming bulk of commodities traded by the large-scale merchants.[11] Things could hardly have been otherwise in a preindustrial society.

The organization of Russian commerce does not appear to have been particularly complex. With the exception of a handful of Moscow merchants who dealt in specialized lines of goods, most merchants traded in whatever items were available, however diverse.[12] As for the structure of commercial enterprises, the single-owner firm predominated. There were a few efforts, usually involving government instigation and assistance, at organizing joint-stock commercial companies, but these proved singularly unsuccessful.[13] Judging from customs records and from the list of creditors of the only merchant bank, single-owner firms and simple partnerships accounted for almost all of the enterprises of the guild merchants.[14] This is not to say that operations were handled in their entirety by the principal figure or figures: in fact, heads of firms employed numbers of other commune residents of all guilds to fill the many managerial, clerical, and manual labor positions that their large-scale operations demanded. Thus, many townsmen owed their living directly to the first-guild magnates, a condition that enhanced the power of the wealthy over their neighbors.[15]

The principal venue of large-scale commercial operations was the merchants' court (*gostinyi dvor'*) in each city. An arcade of wood or stone, it contained both shops and storage areas for the use of exporters and importers, of wholesalers and retailers. The centralization of so many commercial operations in the court served the interests of both the government and the first-guild merchants. For the former, it facilitated collection of numerous customs and tariffs, and for the latter, especially the wholesalers, it provided an opportunity to manipulate to their advantage the prices at which they sold goods to the small retail merchants who worked out of adjacent trade rows. The controlling position of the first-guild merchants in the court further enhanced their hegemony over their fellow commune members.

Another venue of large-scale merchant activity also warrants attention: the great trade fairs. These fairs met once a year for prescribed periods of time, with the overall scheduling of dates staggered so that merchants could make their rounds from one fair to another. About twenty-five such fairs occurred each year, located in or near cities and villages. Among the most famous were the Makarevskaia (later moved to Nizhnii-Novgorod), the Svinskaia (Orel), Troitskaia (Orenburg), and the Irbitskaia fair in the Urals.[16] At these fairs first-guild merchants could be found dealing with foreign merchants or their factors, with small and middle-level operators from various posady, as well as with swarms of trading peasants eager to unload their agricultural produce and the products of long winter months spent in handicraft work. Indeed, the predominance of agricultural goods—about one-third of the turnover of the great Makarevskaia fair was in foodstuffs—tended to give the fairs a seasonal character. Other goods for which demand was high included furs and hides, textiles, and metal items.[17]

Not all first-guild merchants sustained themselves wholly on transactions in the marketplace: a number chose the lucrative route of state-related business enterprise, where a substantial return on investment was almost assured. Such arrangements could take one of three basic forms: state-granted monopoly privileges; contracts for the delivery of goods to the state; and contracts to handle the collection of various government tax levies.[18]

Private monopolies had enjoyed their greatest vogue during the reign of Elizabeth, when government economic policy fell under the guiding hand of P. I. Shuvalov. For Shuvalov, the granting of exclusive commercial rights to an individual or to a group of individuals was a useful way to encourage much-needed economic development, especially in some of the less-populated but resource-rich areas of the state. That Shuvalov himself stood to profit from operations of this type was, perhaps, not entirely accidental.[19] By way of an example of a private monopoly, one might cite the patent granted in 1749 to the Moscow merchant Kuz'ma Matveev to sell tobacco in Great Russia and Siberia. For that right he paid the state some 42,891 rubles yearly.[20]

Contracts for delivery of goods usually involved supplying the armed services with foodstuffs, uniforms, or weapons. According to law, such contracts limited profits to 10 percent, but there seems little doubt that many merchants did far better as a result of various machinations.[21] Fiddling with government contracts is, after all, an enduring tradition.

Where revenue farming was concerned, perhaps the best-known and most lucrative contracts involved the farming of liquor sales. Here the prospective farmer bought from the state the right to sell liquor for a given market. In concluding his contract with the state he negotiated a fee for the privilege of being the sole seller in a given region and worked out the retail price of his sales. Such an arrangement guaranteed both to the state and to the farmer assured revenues. Some idea of the size of the income to be derived from such an operation can be gained from the example of Savva Iakovlev, who in 1750 gained the liquor monopoly for Moscow and St. Petersburg. It netted him no less than 300,000 rubles annually.[22] Through the middle years of the century these various monopolistic and farming arrangements brought vast sums to the coffers of the first-guild merchants who had the capital available for the initial securing of the requisite contracts, and they contributed substantially to capital accumulation by Russia's merchants. Indeed, Pavlenko argues that contracts and farming raised more capital than did the profits of manufacturing enterprise.[23] By the early years of the reign of Catherine II, however, government policy had undergone a major change.[24] Monopolies fell from favor, in theory at least, and many were in fact terminated. Where Catherine did choose to grant them, as in the case of the exclusive right to distill liquor, she favored the gentry. Even so, gentry possessors of monopoly patents often hired experienced merchants to manage the actual operations.[25]

The presence of state-sponsored monopolies, delivery contracts, and revenue farming raises an important question: How dependent were Russian merchants on the state for their economic well-being? From the evidence just cited, it would be easy to conclude that many of Russia's mercantile fortunes arose directly from the cozy, privileged relationships of a number of merchants with the central government. And, of course, there were still other ways in which the state assisted the merchant community, or at least its upper orders. To encourage Russia's merchants to undertake broader commercial operations and, especially, to direct their efforts into manufacturing, the state provided loans, assigned peasants to serve as factory workers, and enacted from time to time protective tariff legislation. Yet, for all these examples of government concern for and assistance to Russian merchants, the case for close economic dependence is not an easy one to make. To be sure, a handful of first-guild merchants did prosper mightily from state contracts, but the bulk of the posad community received no tangible economic benefits from the state. Moreover, even the assistance to first-guild merchants can be exaggerated, for the amount of state credit supplied the merchants in the eighteenth century was not all that great, and the other forms of state aid to the merchant community fluctuated wildly according to the whims and capacities of the sovereigns and their advisors. For the bulk of the posadskie liudi of all ranks, the principal source of capital accumulation, as indeed of their very sustenance, continued to be what it had always been—commercial transactions in the marketplace.

If there is an argument to be made for the impact of state involvement on the economic activities of the commune, it would have to be made in terms of its influence on leadership. Those men who ended up with state contracts and patents for liquor sales did invest substantial amounts of their capital in the initial securing of patents and it could be argued that monies that might otherwise have been invested or paid out in wages within the posad community were thus siphoned off. But even that argument has its limits, for more capital was generated through the exercise of economic privileges, and the operation of monopolies ultimately resulted in the employment of townsmen in the procuring, manufacturing, or delivery of commodities under contract. Perhaps a stronger argument can be made to the effect that these individuals ultimately tended to see their own economic prospects more closely connected to the state than to the posad marketplace. To the extent that such was the case, undoubtedly the posad would have suffered from, at the very least, the conflicting allegiances of some of its leading figures. Yet the effects of such a relationship can easily be exaggerated. After all, commercial and industrial magnates the world over have ever gravitated toward political power, without, in every event, causing great damage to the economic milieu of which they have been a part. What makes the Russian case unique, however, is that the leading merchants were not just independent businessmen attaching themselves to the state for personal gain—though there was obviously an element of that involved—but they were also the guiding figures of the major institution of the urban commercial and manufacturing class—the posad commune. In the latter role they profoundly affected the economic life of the commune as they interpreted and executed the fiscal-administrative demands of the state. Thus it was in the realm of fiscal-administrative concerns that the influence of the state on the posad economy—however indirectly exerted—was greatest, there that the strongest ties between state and posad were forged. And it was there that the leading guild merchants served as the principal instruments of that influence.

THE PROBLEMS OF COMMERCE

The economic enterprise of the first guild merchants had its positive aspects: wide-ranging trade, an apparently high level of capitalization, and lucrative government contracts for a small number of aggressive, well-capitalized merchants. Then, too, there was the leadership in communal affairs that came in the wake of commercial success. But all was not profit, prestige, and power. The Russian merchantry—in particular the prosperous members of the first guild—faced a number of obstacles to their effectiveness as men of commerce, obstacles that placed severe limits on the posad's capacity for economic development.

To begin with, the commercial market was limited by the very nature of the Russian state. The serf and peasant economy remained substantially self-sufficient in the eighteenth century. Peasants continued to provide themselves with many of the necessities of life, and, through their own marketing activities, disposed of large portions of their marketable produce. As Iakovtsevskii notes, the presence of periodic fairs is itself evidence that rural Russia did not need continuous contact with the market: that is, it needed the market only in the spring to unload winter handicraft products and in the fall to sell the summer's crops.[26] That picture ought to be modified somewhat to take into account the presence of local markets (*torzhki*)—the weekly and biweekly markets in small towns and villages where peasants sold their craft goods and agricultural produce—for these suggest a more regular need for market outlets. From the perspective of the large-scale merchant, rural Russia must have presented a paradoxical appearance. On the one hand, the peasant countryside provided a most inhospitable market for their wares, especially imported luxury goods. Yet the first-guild merchantry turned precisely to rural Russia for the agricultural produce and raw materials that formed such a major part of their trade.

At first glance it might appear difficult to reconcile this argument for peasant self-sufficiency with the current emphasis of Soviet historians on the formation of an all-Russian market during the eighteenth century, for surely the emergence of such a market implies the growing integration of producers and consumers throughout Russia. That a market system embracing all of Russia, with Moscow as its central entrepôt, was taking shape seems beyond question.[27] But the mechanism of the market, the means of linking any one part of the country with all other parts, constitutes only half the story; the kinds of commodities traded also speak to the character of the market. Here the evidence is clear: the bulk of the trade in Russia was in agricultural products. The countryside was dependent on the broader market for the disposal of its products, yet, as noted earlier, this dependence was often periodic in character and it remained part of a one-sided relationship. That is, while the market absorbed large quantities of agricultural products, it is unlikely that it returned to the countryside a proportional amount of manufactured goods of urban origin—at least not on a regular basis. The widely noted propensity of the Russian merchants to try to corner the market in whatever goods were available—as opposed to establishing themselves as regular dealers in fixed lines of merchandise—speaks to the irregularity of eighteenth-century commercial relations.[28] The middleman, playing his role in a steady, stable relationship between producer and consumer, had yet to find his place in the economy, no doubt largely as a result of the basic self-sufficiency of the country's vast rural population. In short, a steady reciprocal relationship between manufacturing and commercial cities, on the one hand, and their agricultural hinterlands, on the other, did not obtain in Russia, or, at least, was present only in embryonic form.

This state of affairs was fraught with implications for Russia's merchants. While the first-guild merchantry did in fact deal in agricultural raw materials, both within the country and as exporters, so too did other parties, most notably the peasants, who operated at both national and local levels. The merchants, for all the power of their leading members, were not really capable of securing monopolistic control over the movement of goods throughout the country. To the extent that the rural market offered little demand for manufactured items, that peasant traders afforded strenuous competition, and that some areas of the country were so remote as to be unprofitable for city merchants, the area of trade open to the guild merchants of the posady remained thus limited.

There was, of course, the attractive outlet of foreign trade, but there, too, the merchants ran into difficulties. Right through the century, foreign merchants dominated the export trade as they had from the days of Chancellor and Jenkinson. Their advantages lay in several areas: in their domination of shipping, in their capital, and in their generally higher level of business acumen.

The merchant marine that Peter I had so fondly encouraged proved a short-lived phenomenon. Vessels flying foreign flags continued to carry the overwhelming bulk of cargo to and from Russia. The following figures, which represent all international commercial transactions in St. Petersburg for the indicated years, bear out this point.[29]

	All ships	Russian ships	English ships
1752	425	5	180
1755	414	17	236
1787	2,015	141	767

Even the increase in Russian ships between 1755 and 1787 must be evaluated cautiously, for some foreign ships flew Russian flags in order to secure customs advantages.

The strength of their maritime fleets benefited Russia's trade partners in two ways. First, the revenues from shipping helped to offset their negative balances of trade. For the entire century, the evidence argues that the Russians enjoyed a favorable balance of trade, with the export of raw materials and semifinished goods consistently outstripping in value the import of manufactured goods. But, and here the figures—and the historians—are less persuasive, Russia appears to have experienced a negative balance of payments. Whether shipping costs in fact outweighted trade surpluses is unclear; but that they severely diminished the balance is a certainty.[30] Second, control over shipping gave foreign merchants leverage that they would not have been able to exert in more competitive conditions when it came to negotiating prices, especially for goods they bought up for export. Russians had virtually no choice but to ship with foreign agents.

That bargaining advantage was strongly reinforced by the dominant role of foreign capital on the Russian import-export scene. It was not just a matter of foreign firms, with their relatively higher level of capitalization, doing business on a large scale; in fact, foreign capital penetrated domestic commercial relations as well. Many Russian merchants with port connections, particularly the middle- and lower-volume operators, relied almost exclusively on foreign credit. They secured loans in advance—with healthy rates of interest deducted on the spot—from foreign factors and then proceeded into the interior to buy up goods which they then sold to their creditors the following shipping season. With the sale the principle was paid up, but profits were so small that another advance became immediately necessary. And so the pattern went.[31] In other cases, foreign firms simply hired Russian merchants as their factors, and the Russians traded on behalf of their employers, using foreign capital.

Indeed, it remains unclear just how many Russian merchants, even among the well-capitaled first-guild members, actually themselves engaged in international commerce, in the sense of visiting foreign markets or of maintaining factors or offices abroad. V. N. Iakovtsevskii, even in the face of certain pressures to argue for the emergence of Russia's bourgeoisie, makes the following assessment of the power of foreign merchants: "We often meet indications that Russian merchants were occupied with 'wholesale trade overseas', but this often amounted to trade with foreign merchants in Russian port cities. Factually, the trade of Russia abroad in the eighteenth century was largely found in the hands of foreign merchants and the role of Russian merchants consisted in the buying up of goods in border ports from foreign merchants and in the sale to them there of goods of Russian production."[32]

The Russians were not unaware of the disadvantages inherent in foreign domination of their external trade. The merchants for their part continued to complain to the government, much as they had done throughout the preceding century, about the damage being done to the country. In one petition the Moscow merchantry observed that Russia exported raw materials and then imported the same materials as finished products at prices "hundreds, even thousands of times" higher.[33] The central government did undertake some measures designed to curb foreign merchants, ranging from prohibitions against their retail trade to a ten percent tax on the capital of all foreign merchants departing the country.[34] Working in a different vein, the state encouraged Russian merchants to enhance their competitiveness through the formation of joint-stock commercial companies, but these efforts, confined mainly to the reign of Peter I, met with little success.

Ultimately, it would seem that reponsibility for meeting foreign competition fell on the shoulders of the merchants, and it must be said that they manifested precious little ingenuity when it came to manipulating the price of goods, either through collaborative actions, such as company formation or collective withholding of goods from the market, or through individual actions, such as attempting to free themselves from foreign capital control. To take an example: in 1768 the government granted to members of the Arkhangel posad an exclusive right to trade in the products of the Arkhangel hinterland. Instead of building ships, sending agents abroad, or even withholding goods till better prices could be secured, they simply sold their goods to the ever-present foreign merchants—just as they had always done.[35]

Just why Russia's merchants failed to combat foreign domination more effectively is a question that permits no easy answer. No doubt the power of tradition, of the accustomed way of individual merchant enterprise,

served to hold back innovation, especially in the formation of companies. But it is more than likely that the principal cause of the Russian merchants' timidity was the absence of capital. So dependent were the small
and middle merchants on foreign capital that such tactics as pooling resources or withholding goods to drive up prices were simply unavailable.
Of course, there were first-guild merchants whose level of capitalization
should have enabled them to engage in such activities. Their failure to do
so must be attributed to a combination of two factors: their tradition-
bound outlook and the associated unwillingness to risk the loss of the
adequate and reasonably certain returns they derived from their existing
relations with foreign factors for uncertain gains from potentially dangerous new forms of commercial activity. And, when confronted by the
Western European trading firms, even these men may have been sensitive
to their relatively limited resources.

The level of capitalization attained by the Russian merchantry during
the eighteenth century has not been determined with any precision. Indeed, scholarly opinion seems to be of two minds on the subject. While
Kulisher, along with other prerevolutionary historians, stressed the
shortage of capital, Soviet scholars have been at pains to demonstrate the
presence of a number of well-capitalized merchants.[36] Yet the existence of
such individuals, even if their capital were commensurate with that of
leading British or Dutch merchants, does not speak to the broader question of the capitalization of the Russian merchantry as a whole. Quite
apart from the evidence of the capital impoverishment of the lower strata
of the posad population, there is a considerable body of data suggesting
that capital was in relatively short supply even among first- and second-
guild merchants. Based on information gathered in the first years of the
century from the Volga basin, E. I. Zaozerskaia argues that even the elite
merchants of that time, the gostinaia sotnia, led precarious economic
lives. Among thirty-seven men who responded to government queries
about their economic affairs, seven claimed that they were totally desti-
tute, others asserted that they had but a few rubles at their disposal,
while only a few had sufficient wealth to have favorable economic prospects. The rapid rise and fall of business firms was a simple fact of life for
the hundreders.[37] Another study of merchant economic fortunes, this one
set in the Pereiaslavl'-Riazan region in the 1730s, points out that only a
handful of merchants avoided deep indebtedness, and they were the ones
with safe government contracts.[38] Things had hardly improved by mid-
century. Kizevetter notes that in 1759 the average capitalization of Iaroslavl' first-guild merchants was 32 rubles, 21 kopecks, and that of second-
guild merchants a mere 3 rubles, 6 kopecks.[39] Though Iaroslavl' was no
Moscow, Tula, or St. Petersburg, it was nonetheless an important trad-

ing city. Clearly the merchants mentioned earlier in this chapter who had trade turnovers in the tens of thousands of rubles yearly constituted the exception rather than the rule. The same was true at the end of the century when, in spite of the considerable sums in the control of the great merchants, merchants in general suffered a decline in fortunes and numbers.[40]

There are many explanations for the modest capital of the Russian merchantry. The limitations inherent in the domestic market must surely have been the ultimate factor in restricting the growth of capital, but there were other, more immediate problems faced by the merchants. The various demands of the fisc, a subject that will be dealt with more fully in the following chapter, undoubtedly hindered capital accumulation among posad residents of all ranks. Then, too, the vicissitudes of business life took their toll. Most Russian firms had their capital tied up in goods, a condition that rendered them susceptible in the extreme to fire, theft, or poor management.[41] Short on capital and without the benefit of insurance, the single-owner firm was a fragile entity. Yet taxes and shifting business fortunes are predictable—one might say inevitable—concomitants of the business scene. What made them particularly hard to bear in early modern Russia was the difficulty of securing credit, credit with which new ventures might be launched or the errors of past ones overcome. The old adage, "it takes money to make money," was never more true.

Until 1754, when a government decree set a six percent interest rate on borrowed money, lending at interest was legally forbidden, thanks to the law code of Aleksei the Pious. Obviously, Russian merchants did not abandon the pursuit of credit because of a mere legal prohibition, but they did have to pay dearly for it. During the seventeenth century wealthy merchants, landowners, and monasteries charged rates that ranged from 30 to 120 percent per annum.[42]

There was only modest improvement in the following century and what changes came about can be attributed to the efforts of the central government rather than to the initiatives of the merchants. Apart from the legalization of lending at interest, the government's actions took two forms. The Commerce College, charged by its founding document with responsibility for commercial credit, did give direct assistance to a few firms, for the most part to large enterprises of a quasi-industrial character, such as those in mining or fishing.[43] Then, in mid-century, the government sought to provide Russian commerce with its first formal institutions of commercial credit, the St. Petersburg Bank for the Restoration of Commerce (1754) and the Astrakhan' Bank (1764). The former bank operated only until 1770, when, with its reserves depleted and massive arrears outstanding, it was forced to close its doors. The Astrakhan' bank, a much smaller undertaking, remained a going concern until the second decade of the nineteenth century. Although these banks did make possible a number of foreign trade ventures, they never became part of a broader, regularized system of commercial credit, and they contributed practically nothing to the development of internal trade crediting. Thus Borovoi, in his study of credit and banking during the eighteenth century, concludes that Russian merchants in the period 1760-1780 basically had to get along without any established credit institutions.[44] The evidence suggests that an extensive network of private credit was in operation, but the rates remained high, ranging from 10 to 40 percent per annum, with short-term rates as high as one percent per week. Foreigners and wealthy merchants remained the chief source of credit, though many a big merchant obtained goods from small-scale suppliers on the promise of later payment with interest.[45]

Foreign merchants were quick to point out that defaults on loans, owing to bankruptcies and deceitful actions, drove up the price of credit in Russia beyond rates that obtained elsewhere in Europe. Single-owner firms were no doubt as susceptible to bankruptcy then as they are now, yet even so foreigners found the frequency of such collapses so great as to lead them to believe that Russian merchants had a most casual attitude toward such a grave action. This feeling that the Russians operated on quite a different set of standards was strengthened by what foreigners took to be the Russian propensity to shady or outright fraudulent practices.[46] Just where the truth lies in this matter is difficult to say. Most likely the Western European merchants felt they were dealing with commercial inferiors and happily generalized upon every instance of local chicanery; and the Russians, for their part, may have responded to an oppressive foreign economic domination with demonstrations of their own brand of cleverness. In any event, the perceived risk does seem to have elevated interest rates.

Closely related to matters of credit is still another obstacle that stood before the Russian merchant: the presence well into the century of a cumbersome cash economy. Copper coins were so large and weighty that, according to one estimate, it would have taken some 25,000 carts to convey to Moscow the tax revenues of just one year.[47] The merchants, to be sure, operated on a smaller scale, but even so they incurred substantial expenses in transporting and storing huge quantities of cash. The situation was somewhat alleviated by the provisions of the Exchange Act of 1729, which made legal the use of bills of exchange and set up a network of exchange offices around the country. The law's prohibition against peasant endorsement of bills, along with the absence of sufficient legal safeguards for commercial operations in general, however, limited the effectiveness of the legislation. The government also hoped that the appearance of assignats would alleviate the problem of a copper coinage economy, but their rapid depreciation led to another whole set of problems. And, as if these were not difficulties enough, there existed no banks in which monies might be deposited for security and in which assets might be shifted from the account of one merchant subscriber to another. Both the Petersburg and Astrakhan' banks confined their services to lending only from a pool of government-provided assets.[48]

There were, of course, other encumbrances on the mercantile art, of less import, perhaps, than those just cited, but capable of having an impact nonetheless. One might cite the restrictions placed on the townsmen's mobility by their obligations to their posad of registration and the near-impossibility of securing land within or adjacent to cities for the purposes of commercial development. Strictly speaking, the origins of these constraints lie outside the realm of economic relationships, but suffice it to say here that they most assuredly interfered with the flow of commerce and helped to curb innovative activities on the part of the merchants.

The problems confronting the Russian merchant community were serious indeed. Limitations on the market, foreign competition, problems of capitalization, the difficulty of securing credit, inadequate organization and business practice—all these conditions acted as a brake on development and help to explain the modest progress of the posad economy over the course of the eighteenth century. Perhaps nowhere can the effects of these problems be seen better than in the turnover among the top ranks of the mercantile community. N. P. Chulkov, in a study of the leading merchants of Moscow, notes that none of the prominent merchant families of the Petrine era occupied significant positions in the mercantile world of the late nineteenth or early twentieth centuries.[49] Economic factors alone cannot wholly explain this phenomenon: the urge to move up the social ladder led some men away from mercantile pursuits, family misfortunes or bad health affected others, and the burdens of tiaglo still others. But at bottom, difficulties of an economic sort—in particular the scramble for capital in a highly competitive situation—rendered sustained economic performance over time a hard goal to achieve. The paucity of Russian industrial and commercial houses of great longevity speaks to the parlous conditions of the Russian mercantile economy.

MERCHANT-MANUFACTURERS

Not all of Russia's prosperous merchants confined their operations to trade alone: the merchant-manufacturer was to become a fixture of the eighteenth-century economic scene. The stage, of course, had been set by the vigorous promotion of manufacture by the Petrine government through the establishment of state enterprises, through loans to private companies, and, toward the latter years of Peter's reign, through the transfer of state enterprises into private hands. Peter's efforts and those of his successors did not transform Russia into an industrial power overnight, but they did manage to root industrial enterprise firmly in the Russian soil. St. Petersburg had its share of government-owned manufacturing works and a handful of large private ones. Moscow became in the post-Petrine era Russia's leading center of light industry, that is, of the production of shoes, clothing, household items, and the like. Many other cities, such as Iaroslavl', Kostroma, Tula, Shui, Kaluga, and Voronezh, became known for one or more manufacturing specialties. Care must be taken, however, not to exaggerate the impact of this period of nascent domestic manufacturing, for neither in scope nor in character did it have the capacity to alter dramatically the traditional economic aspect of the cities—with the possible exception of the capitals. But it was a new presence and its promoters, the *fabrikanty*, were harbingers of the future.

Although lists of company owners during the Petrine era include such conspicuous court figures as Menshikov and Shafirov and an occasional member of the gentry, and in spite of the introduction of government capital into some enterprises, the fact remains that private capital, largely accumulated by Russia's merchants, was essential to the development of domestic manufacture.[50] Families such as the Evreinovs, Tretiakovs, Batashovs, and Demidovs, prominent in the circle of eighteenth-century industrial entrepreneurs, had gotten their start in mercantile or artisan-trader activities, and their ranks were joined by scores of other merchants with small, but still important interests in manufacturing enterprise. It should be noted, however, that only a relatively small number of merchants transferred some or all of their assets to manufacturing enterprise during the century—fewer, it seems, than development-minded historians expect should have been the case. The most common explanation seems to be that profits from successful mercantile operations were so great as to discourage diversification of capital investment.[51]

This capital found its way into manufacturing enterprises of diverse organization and scale. Single-owner firms, so dominant in trade, were overshadowed in the manufacturing sector of the economy, at least during the first half of the century, by various types of companies ranging from simple partnerships to organizations of shareholders. Capitalization varied from a few thousand rubles to well over a hundred thousand rubles, though any one merchant was likely to provide no more than ten thousand rubles.[52] A. S. Lappo-Danilevskii argues that toward mid-century the more complex forms of ownership began to fade and the single-owner firm came to predominance, the result of company failures and of decisions to break up existing partnerships.[53]

Although many industrial operations were truly impressive in scale, throughout Russian industry, from metallurgy to textiles, production continued to be based on traditional, nonmechanized handicraft techniques. Thus, a big concern might in fact consist of dozens or even hundreds of separate units of production, be they smelteries or attic workshops. Even the famed Tula metalworking industry was so arranged.[54] Craft production placed a premium on skilled labor, the short supply of which constituted the principal problem confronting the would-be manufacturer. Once the small pool of available hired laborers had been exhausted, manufacturers turned to the government in search of assistance in securing workers. The government responded in two ways. In some instances, it directed state peasants to work in industrial enterprises (the so-called assigned peasants).[55] But it also acted to enable factory owners to obtain their own peasant laborers (possessional serfs). A law of 1721 granted merchant-manufacturers the right to purchase populated villages, a concession that an outraged gentry gradually managed to whittle down until in 1762 the government reversed itself and reserved the privilege to the gentry alone.[56] Throughout the century, then, Russian manufacturers relied on a mixed labor force, in part freely hired, in part compulsorily bound. In neither instance was the level of skills particularly high, which, coupled with problems of poor labor-management relations, meant low-quality goods at high cost. Government commissions found Russian goods inferior in quality and higher in price than imports, and Russian merchants often found it hard to peddle items of domestic manufacture.[57] It should be pointed out, however, that many manufacturers were kept busy by government contracts, and the consumer who stood to lose most in such cases was the army quartermaster corps.

In many ways the activities of the merchant-manufacturer belong more to the broad history of the eighteenth-century economy than to the limited confines of the posad. Unlike trade, the traditional occupation of the leading townsmen for generations, manufacturing pursuits were relative innovations, whose initial encouragement came from an active Petrine state and whose regulation over the next fifty years was in principle, if not always in enthusiastic execution, the concern of subsequent governments. Moreover, the often conspicuous gestures of state encouragement served to identify the manufacturers more closely with the government and, at the same time, to enhance the separation of their fortunes from those of the posad. The occasional receipt of fixed capital assets from the state and the odd infusion of state capital—one-time boons— were joined by other forms of economic privilege: the right (granted in special cases) to import raw materials duty free; exemption from internal customs and duties; and, in mid-century, the acquisition by some manufacturers of monopoly rights.[58] As if this catalog of advantages were not sufficient, the manufacturers also benefited from lessened fiscal-administrative obligations (see Chapter 6).

These two sets of privileges combined to alienate the merchant-manufacturer from nearly all elements of society. Peasant small producers objected to their privileged competitors and their plaints were increasingly backed by the gentry as the century wore on. Merchants did combat with manufacturers when the latter pushed poor quality goods on them, received tariff exemptions, or used their privileged positions to expand into retail markets.[59] And, as one might expect, all posad members had cause for jealousy over the reduction of tax and service obligations for factory owners. Thus, the merchant-manufacturer, in spite of his posad origins, quickly found himself separated, economically and socially, from the milieu that had provided the capital foundation for his new endeavor. One cannot help but suspect that the isolation into which the merchant-manufacturer fell might well have prevented others from following in his path. At the very least, the manufacturers represented an altogether different set of interests from those of the first-guild merchants—to say nothing of the rest of the townsmen. Their contribution to the diversity of the commune was also a contribution to the weakening of its economic coherence.

TRADERS, CRAFTSMEN, AND HIRED LABORERS

In sharp contrast to the prosperous merchants and the merchant-manufacturing elite stood the great mass of the posad dwellers—traders, craftsmen, and the posad "black" people who eked out a bare existence through manual labor of one kind or another. For these men there were no privileges and no cozy relationships with the state, just the perennial balancing act of the marginal operator or the desperate struggle for survival of the impoverished laborer. Yet without them the economy of the posad, even of the city, would have been unthinkable.

Traders and craftsmen occupied the middle rung of the posad economic ladder. They were not an insignificant group in terms of numbers: Kizevetter claims that in the 1760s small and middle traders made up some 40 percent of the posad, while craftsmen made up another 14.5 percent.[60] Nor were they insignificant in function, for it was this group that provisioned Russia's urban residents with food for their tables, with boots and sheepskin coats, with utensils of domestic use, with the ever-present icons. But it is important to stress the limited scale of their operations. To repeat a figure cited earlier, the average yearly turnover of a second-guild Iaroslavl' merchant was but 3 rubles, 6 kopecks. For artisans generally turnover ranged from 1 to 10 rubles yearly, with 3-5 rubles being close to average.[61] Thus, an enormous chasm of wealth separated the posad trader from the first-guild merchant.

The manner and locus of operation of the posad merchants and artisans varied greatly. Some worked as itinerant peddlers, whose presence on the street corners added color and enjoyment to the lives of city dwellers—and visitors. The British observer William Tooke remarked that "in towns and great village stations, women sit in the street near public houses, with tables having roast and boiled meat, fish, piroggees, cabbage soup, cucumbers, bread and quas, consequently a superb and everywhere a cheap repast, which is taken standing, and always accompanied with a glass or two of brandy."[62]

The presence of hawkers and peddlers, it might be noted, left its impact on art as well as on travel literature. Lithographs of urban scenes frequently contain the figures of the itinerant seller of foodstuffs, his wares displayed on a tray suspended round his neck.

Small traders and artisans also appeared at the torzhki and the large periodic fairs, though they had to share these sites both with the powerful merchants and with the swarms of trading peasants. The principal venue of the small trader, however, remained the benches, stalls, and shops of the trade rows. There, amidst the hustle and confusion of a crowded market could be found the commercial center of Russia's towns. According to William Coxe, all the retail shops in Moscow—and they were most numerous—were located in a single section of the city, Kitaigorod.[63] That was an exaggeration, but only slightly, for Kitaigorod was indeed a thriving mass of shops and stalls where all manner of goods could be purchased. The importance of the trade rows to urban life can hardly be overestimated, though there is a decided tendency in the literature to overlook them in favor of the more visible large-scale export trade or manufacturing. To be sure, the latter provide better indices of economic change, but the history of the trade rows in the eighteenth century is the basic story of the retail provisioning of urban dwellers of all social categories.

It was in the trade rows that the consumer came into contact not just with those who were merchants in the strict sense of the word, but also with a wide variety of artisans. Polianskii suggests that by 1769 there may have been as many as 36,000 artisans, both guild and nonguild, plying their trades throughout Russia. They tended to be concentrated in Moscow, Petersburg, and thirty-nine provincial cities.[64] These figures appear somewhat less impressive, however, when viewed against the total population of Russia. Assuming that population to have been in the vicinity of 25 million for the year 1770, just one person in every 625 called himself an urban artisan.

The variety of trades represented was quite large. By the early eighteenth century specialization had progressed to the point where 153 guilds were represented—on paper at least—though most cities had nothing like a full complement of trades.[65] A list of tradesmen in a typical city might include tailors, coppersmiths, bootmakers, fishermen, bakers, smiths, joiners, chandlers, silversmiths, turners, potters, goldsmiths, makers of sheepskin clothes, icon painters, furriers, tanners, carpenters, millers, glovers, lacemakers, and piemakers. In Moscow in the 1770s haberdashery, metalworking, and smithing were the three leading areas of artisan activity.[66] Generally speaking, smiths and tradesmen who dealt with comestibles appeared most frequently.

Unsophisticated methods of production and the lack of effective institutional arrangements to improve them plagued craft production through the century. Foreign observers from Perry to Coxe remarked on the antiquated techniques and poor quality of workmanship of the Russian craftsmen. Perry claimed that good men hid their talents lest they be impressed into onerous state labor service, while Coxe echoed the words of Iurii Krizhanich, written a century earlier: "Though I often saw the carpenters at work, I never once perceived a saw in their hands."[67] Great proficiency with an axe is possible, but it is slow, wasteful, and inefficient work. The guilds (to be discussed institutionally in the next chapter) made poor use of such traditional means to enhance craft skills as long apprenticeships and high standards for promotion to master craftsman. In the 1720s a full 82 percent of the St. Petersburg artisans were masters, while only 3.4 percent were journeymen and 14.6 percent apprentices.[68] Such figures imply the absence of a highly skilled craft tradition. Indeed, in his study of craft guilds, Polianskii argues that "city and rural crafts in their economic nature were scarcely distinguishable one from the other."[69] That is not an unexpected conclusion, since many urban artisans had rural origins, especially early in the century.[70] The fact that urban crafts operated at the same technical level as rural ones meant, of course, that the guild craftsmen were susceptible to fierce competition from the countryside, for they could produce neither better nor cheaper goods.

The small tradesman functioned both as the producer and as the seller of his wares, and, not infrequently, as the seller of any other goods he might get his hands on. The diversity of his activities betrayed not the strength, but the weakness of his undertaking, for so uncertain were the revenues from his own specialty that he eagerly sought auxiliary means to supplement his income. Most craftsmen turned out goods in extremely small quantities, usually on special order only.[71] A magistrate's report from Kiev noted that what little craft production occurred in that city went for personal use or for a small domestic market.[72] In the latter decades of the century, however, production for the urban market or for middlemen became an increasingly common phenomenon in the more advanced cities.[73]

As is customary for those who produce on order, the Russian artisan could not afford to keep on hand a stock of raw materials. Instead he obtained them on credit as need arose. Upon completion of the product and its sale, the artisan then settled his accounts with the supplier.[74] Only a few artisans turned a profit on their labors; most just barely broke even.[75] In the face of the posad powerful and a capricious market their position was precarious.

It might be argued that in an ideal world, the operations of the first-guild merchants and those of the petty merchants and tradesmen would have complemented one another, with the former handling wholesale and large retail deals and the latter doing the day-to-day provisioning of the population. But it was not so in the real world of seventeenth-century Russia, where considerable friction existed between the two, thanks mainly to the efforts of the powerful merchants to draw the small fry into the web of their operations. At the center of the conflict stood government policy toward the trade rows.

In the seventeenth century, Moscow merchants had persuaded the government to outlaw all trade outside the rows and to prohibit all trade on Sundays. Designed chiefly to curtail the activities of peasants and foreigners, both these regulations also discriminated against the small merchants and direct producers who lacked the money to rent shop spaces or who needed Sunday to peddle the wares they made during the week. In the course of the eighteenth century, further legislation denied the right of urban retail trade to manufacturers, *raznochintsy*, and "foreigners not registered as Russian citizens and not in merchant guilds."[76] The effect was the same: in protecting posad enterprise against outside threats, the leading guild merchants enhanced their own power within the posad. The Soviet scholar Polovnikov argues, "In this way, all retail trade steadily was concentrated in the hands of the organized, predominantly guild merchantry, which had become a monopolist in retail trade and which seized conditions for the management of wholesale trade."[77] A strong seconding voice comes from Iakovtsevskii, who argues that the first-guild merchants gained a virtual monopoly over urban commerce in the first half of the century—though one that would break apart under a rural challenge in the latter decades of the century. The evidence adduced, aside from legislative memorials designed to secure the economic position initially granted the townsmen in 1649, includes capital concentration in the hands of a relatively few merchants; the guild merchantry's stranglehold over shop spaces in the trade rows (which occasionally took the form of letting shops to peasants in order to drive small operators from the posad); and control over all retail commerce within the towns.[78] Forced from the trade rows and denied by law any other form of contact with consumers, the tradesmen and small merchants had no choice but to deal with the large merchants if they were to find outlets for production and wholesale sources of merchandiseable goods. Indeed, many of the second-guild merchants who worked in managerial capacities for the great mercantile firms may have found such employment the only refuge in the face of the assault on the trade rows by the first-guild merchants.

Impressive as this evidence may be, the argument for the monopolization of urban trade by the first-guild merchants cannot be accepted without serious qualification. It is one thing to argue that the prosperous merchants dominated the urban economic scene and quite another to argue that they exercised monopolistic control. Unquestionably the powerful first-guild merchants did overshadow their brethren and rarely missed an opportunity to tighten their hold on them. But whether they monopolized the urban market is less clear. Iakovtsevskii's argument that they did rests on two main points: that the legal guarantees of the townsmen's exclusive rights to urban trade and manufacture in fact cleared the urban market of all non-posad competitors; and that therefore de facto control of the trade rows by the first-guild merchants was tantamount to monopoly control of urban trade. There are problems with each step of the argument. First, the various prohibitions on retail trade by peasants and foreigners did not succeed in eliminating their activities, a fact borne out by the frequency with which legislation was repeated and by the persistence of merchant complaints. It may be true that between the Petrine era, with its efforts to eliminate the nontaxable urban courts (*belye mesta*), and the heavy onslaught of peasant competition in the second half of the eighteenth century there was a period of relatively greater merchant control over the urban market, but monopoly seems a strong word in light of the continued presence of competitors—however illegal they may have been.[79] Second, it is difficult to sustain the claim that guild merchants monopolized retail trade. Other elements of the posad population continued their commercial activities even though squeezed by the guild merchants, and many of them felt independent enough to petition the government against the encroachments of the powerful on the trade rows. Problems there were, but again, monopoly is a strong term for what seems more like hegemony.

At any rate, many small merchants and artisans failed to knuckle under and chose instead to set up benches and stalls in other locations, often near their own homes. They were encouraged in this practice, as were many others, by the example of foreign merchants. The latter, in spite of prohibitory legislation, carried on retail trade in their homes, turning them into regular Western European shops—complete with window displays. The Russian government, embarrassed by some of the concessions it made to foreigners, began to allow Russian merchants and artisans to work out of their homes, especially in new or expanding cities where existing market facilities were inadequate. Finally, in 1782, the government abandoned all efforts to regulate the sites of retail trade: all merchants could "have shops in their homes and trade in them."[80] By 1790 the old Moscow trade rows lay in ruins, soon to be purchased by private merchants for their own use. One cannot help but wonder just how much of a monopoly the first-guild merchants had if it were so quickly and easily broken.

Occupying the bottom rung of the posad economic ladder were the third-guild merchants. As is usually the case with the lower orders of a society, this group left the fewest traces in the historical record, yet they constituted the largest single group within posad society. Kizevetter estimates that they accounted for about 42 percent of posad registrants in the 1760s; and Iakovtsevskii claims that in the second half of the century they amounted to 48 percent of the Moscow merchants and 62 percent of the merchants in all Russia.[81] Although some of these individuals lived in abject poverty, the majority supported themselves, however modestly, in occupations manual and menial, in recognition of which they earned the name "black people" (*chernye liudi*).

What is clear from the meager record is that these individuals had virtually no declared capital (the average capital of the Iaroslavl' third-guild merchant in 1759 was 42 kopecks) and no business operations of their own, except, perhaps, for those who made their living through farm gardening and marginal peddling operations.[82] Essentially they formed an urban labor pool, available to manufacturer and merchant alike. There is some evidence to suggest that in the 1720s and 1730s newly established manufactories, desperately in search of working hands, quickly absorbed the available posad poor; these individuals from the lower depths of the posad became the nucleus of a small but growing freely-hired industrial labor force.[83] Their departure from traditional posad enterprise can thus be tied to incipient changes in the national economy. But a good many other third-guild townsmen made their living in the mercantile world, serving as shop assistants, loaders, carters, bargemen, and the like. Just ninety-three large Moscow merchants employed nearly 30 percent of the third-guild merchants in that city, and, as noted earlier, those same merchants had control over an even larger percentage of the second guild.[84]

Obviously the term merchant is a misnomer for the overwhelming majority of the third-guild townsmen. These were the small change of urban society, too poor and subordinate to the wealthy to have any independent political voice. They were destined to remain pawns of the powerful.

It is not easy to draw up a balance sheet on the eighteenth-century posad economy. If one can point to the achievements of some of the well-capitalized merchants and to a handful of successful merchant-manufacturers, it is also possible to cite the inability of the Russians to meet foreign mercantile competition on even terms or the limited quality and output of Russian manufacturing—and craft—production. But if one abandons the effort to draw up a balance on the posad economy as a whole and turns instead to an assessment of its predominant features, more decisive judgments are possible. Indeed, among those features of the posad economy that most affected the behavior of the townsmen and shaped the fate of their communal institutions, two stand out sharply: the overall poverty of the posad and the diversity of its members.

The wealth at the disposal of a few merchants was truly impressive, but if one excludes the first-guild merchants in the top half-dozen cities, the remaining posady did not display great wealth. And even in those cities, the vast majority of posad registrants had only trifling amounts of capital. The frequent collapses of companies, the bankruptcies, the high rates of interest, and the tax records all speak to the limited national capital resources. The physical condition of the cities further reflected the poverty of the posad. There may have been gains in the total mercantile capital in Russia in the eighteenth century, but even that observation cannot be made with certainty.[85]

In the absence of a really convincing study to the contrary, one can only hold fast to the abundant evidence that the posadskie liudi had to share among themselves, however unequally, less than abundant wealth. To the extent that wealth and power go hand in glove, it was not an advantageous position from which to confront the remainder of society.

From a purely economic perspective, the diversity of wealth and occupation in the posad—manifest in the presence of hawkers and factory owners, of carters and opulent merchants—appears altogether natural. After all, an urban economy, including one in eighteenth-century Russia, offers a multitude of jobs of varying attractiveness and reward. From a social perspective, however, these individuals appear to have such diverse—and often conflicting—sets of interests that it seems hard to imagine how there could exist any institution that might embrace them all and still purport to speak for their collective interest. Yet that is precisely what the posad commune sought to do. It may well be that in the seventeenth century and earlier, the posad economy was simpler and more coherent, making for greater unity of interest among its members—though the disparity between gost' and humble craftsmen, as well as the intra-posad squabbles of the time, render even that notion suspect. What seems clear beyond doubt is that the strains upon the always tenuous cohesiveness of the posad mounted during the eighteenth century as a result of changing economic circumstances. The increased power of the guild merchants over posad retail trade during mid-century; the privileged role of the merchant-manufacturers; the presence of both commercial and industrial monopolists; and the advantageous position of the tax farmers and other contract operators—all these features of the eighteenth-century economy worked against the few natural ties that held the townsmen together. Common concerns with nonagricultural mercantile and manufacturing pursuits and a common locus of operation in the towns were hardly sufficient to overcome the innate divergences of wealth and occupational interests. In fact, the two principal forces working for posad unity—government imposed responsibilities and economic competition from the outside—could rightly be regarded as external in origin. In combination these forces galvanized the energies of the commune and, as the following chapters will make clear, gave coherence to its actions and shaped a reasonably consistent world view. But in the underlying economic and social diversity of the commune lay some of the seeds of its destruction.

CHAPTER SIX

The Posad Commune
in the Eighteenth Century:
Organization and Operation

UNLIKE THOSE INSTITUTIONS whose orgins lay in conscious reform activity and whose contours—or at least intended contours—can be roughly sketched from legislative memorials, the posad commune received no formal legal definition. It arose and evolved spontaneously, in response to the needs of the urban tax-paying population—needs that derived from their particular relationship to the central government. By the eighteenth century the commune had become such an integral part of the urban scene that it was not even mentioned in government decrees: its existence, and in particular its mode of operation, were simply assumed.

It is not just the commune's cloudy origins that make an assessment of its character difficult; the commune embodies that peculiar kind of complexity that so often accompanies institutions that have grown like topsy, reconciling in the process seemingly contradictory principles. From that complexity there emerges an institution with many faces: it presents one to its members, another to the remainder of society, and still another to the government. If at times the commune appears a spokesman for the private interests of its members, at other times it resembles an administrative agency of the central government. And on occasion it even appears to have donned, at least partially, the guise of an instrument of local government. It does not, in sum, fit neatly into the standard categories of institutional analysis.

In an effort to pin down the elusive nature of the commune, this chapter will concentrate on that institution during the middle years of the eighteenth century. During this period the commune reached its fullest development—though that phase was soon to be followed by a gradual process of decline. Thanks to the Main Magistracy's supervisory role over the communes of the country, there exists for this period the fullest body of information available for any era in the history of the posad. For analytic purposes, the chapter will examine first the institutional structure of the commune in order to identify those features that gave it coherence and the capacity for concerted action. It will then review the functional role of the commune, focusing primarily on its quasigovernmental activities. But it is only when these two aspects of the commune, its structure and its function, are taken together and set against the broader frame of Russian social and administrative history that any firm assessment of its character becomes possible.

THE POSAD COMMUNE

By the eighteenth century, the term *posad* had undergone considerable evolution since the time of its first appearance in the 1500s. For the most part, the word posad no longer referred to a specific physical area within or adjacent to a city, but, instead, to an abstract, arbitrarily defined administrative category. The posad, or to put it completely, the posad commune (*posadskii mir*), of a given locality (city or *uezd*) consisted of all persons registered in the census books as bearers of a certain set of state taxes (*posadskoe tiaglo*). Eligibility for enrollment in the commune depended on one of two principles: inheritance or profession.[1] Children of posad dwellers inherited their parents' status, a condition clearly fixed in law by the *Ulozhenie* of 1649. The commune also included those who wished to ply a craft or to trade in a city *and* who were willing to become subject to the tiaglo in return for permission to engage in the city economy. There can be no denying the predominance of the central government in establishing the underlying principle of posad organization. First and foremost, tax obligations, broadly construed, drew together in the commune the mixed bag of urban dwellers who passed under the name of merchant.

Although common tax liability provides the basis in principle for the posad commune, the actual organizational structure of the commune was based on territorial subdivisions and social groupings. In cities of any size, the commune was broken into territorial units, suburbs (*slobody*), and hundreds (*sotni*); and every member of the commune had to register in one of them. Each suburb and hundred had its own communal gathering (*skhod*) and elected elders. The elders' responsibilities ran the gamut from keeping records of the social composition of their unit to collecting taxes to supervising the welfare of the area under their jurisdiction.[2]

With the establishment in the 1720s of the three guilds of merchants, each with its own gathering and elder, the nature of the posad commune became still more complex. Generally speaking, the guild organizations tended to subordinate to themselves the suburb and hundred administrations, no doubt as a result of the powerful position of guild members in the community. It was within the capacity of a merchant-guild elder, for example, to order a suburb elder to take action with respect to a guild member residing in that suburb.[3] To the merchant guilds must be added another constituent element of the commune—the craft guilds, themselves products of the Petrine era. Although functionally similar to the merchant guilds, they carried substantially less weight in the overall affairs of the commune. The relatively lower status of their members left them no match in power politics for the first-guild merchants.

Just as the posad evolved from a territorial to an administrative unit, so did the balance of power within the posad swing from the territorial units to the merchant and craft guilds, particularly the former. An examination of the working of those guilds thus becomes indispensible to this study of the organizational structure of the commune.

MERCHANT SOCIETY

For most of the eighteenth century it was common practice for citizen and official alike to refer to the posadskie liudi as merchants. The widespread use of this term served the social function of discriminating, roughly on the basis of occupation, the townsmen from other major social groups—from nobles, peasants, and clergy. Yet, as the evidence presented in the previous chapter makes clear, the term "merchant" was, as often as not, a misnomer. Strictly speaking, it described the occupation of less than half of the posad registrants. The craftsmen and hired laborers of the posad fell under the rubric of merchant only formally, for the sake of social organization and the administration of taxes. As it happened, common parlance became increasingly attuned to the social realities in the posad, and by mid-century the term merchant, heretofore used loosely to cover the diverse elements of posad society, found itself a competitor. The west Slavic expression *meshchane* (singular, *meshchanin*) gained wide acceptance as a synonym for *posadskie liudi*, especially for the less wealthy third-guild townsmen. A formal legislative recognition of this distinction between the substantial guild merchants and the rank and file townsmen, or meshchane, emerged in the 1775 tax reform.[4]

The hierarchical arrangement of posad society that had existed in the seventeenth century continued on into the mid-eighteenth century, though not without a slight interruption during the Petrine era. As noted earlier, the Main Magistracy Regulation applied a new set of criteria, based on profession rather than simply on wealth, for discriminating among the ranks of the posad people. This attempt at restructuring posad society along new lines never took hold, and traditional social divisions soon reasserted themselves. By the late 1720s, the two Petrine guilds (defined by occupation) had been replaced by three, whose membership was determined as before on the basis of the total assets of each townsman. In

1742 Elizabeth's government gave formal sanction to this practice in an instruction to the Moscow merchants that called for their division "into three parts, which are to be called guilds [*gil'dii*]."[5] Not uncharacteristically, the form, if not the essence, of Peter's reform hung on; the term *gil'dii* continued to be used interchangeably with *stat'* in official business throughout the century.[6]

Little is known about the actual operations of the merchant guilds, with the exception of the upper guilds of Moscow merchants. There, it appears, each guild met separately to deal with the business of its own members. Such business might include the discussion of common economic problems and possible courses of action to meet them; the working out of the details of taxation or labor service that had fallen upon the guild; and the handling of questions of membership, passports, and the like. For the most part the business of the guilds centered on their membership alone and in so doing helped to give some cohesion to each subgroup of the posad. But there were occasions when the Moscow guilds, at the behest of the powerful first-guild elders, met jointly to act on matters that affected the whole city. In such instances the guilds became, as Kizevetter put it, "the representative of all posad society."[7] The Moscow case, however, remains an exception. In other cities the exercise of authority that went beyond the parochial interests of each separate guild was exercised not by the first-guild merchants, but by the gathering of the posad society, an institution that will be examined later in this chapter.[8]

The guilds must be viewed as an indispensible feature of posad life. Not only did they constitute a recognition of the inevitable kinds of social distinctions that exist within a society, but they also made possible the coexistence of that diverse lot of urban residents who had been brought together under the umbrella of tiaglo. By enabling the prosperous merchant, the petty trader, and the hired laborer or farm gardener each to associate with his peers, the guild system gave formal structure to natural economic and social relations and facilitated thereby the operation of the commune, both in terms of the private business of its members and of the collective interests and obligations of the whole. But this is not to say that the guilds remained isolated from one another or that the lower two were exempt from pressures and control by the first guild. Since first-guild merchants controlled the wealth, they tended to dominate all proceedings in the posad, manipulating the poor for their own ends. And, of course, it was the first-guild merchants who most often stepped forward as the spokesmen for the interests of urban society.

The hegemony of the wealthy guild merchants over the poorer members of posad society was not limited solely to the political power and social status that money bestowed upon them; it also found legal expres-

sion in a manner that could only be considered degrading to the less fortunate members of posad society. So dire were the economic straits of the
poor, the chernye liudi, that many became legal dependents of their
richer neighbors. In 1736 a government decree regulated, and hence gave
the force of law to, the practice of *otdacha v zazhiv*, the indenture of a
debtor to a creditor. According to this law, an impoverished person with
a small public or private debt could seek out a benefactor who would
assume the debt and for whom the debtor would work until he had re-
paid his benefactor with interest. The period of indenture could run any-
where from a few months up to fifty years.⁹ While such a practice cannot
be precisely equated with the mortgaging of persons (*zakladnichestvo*) so
prevalent in the seventeenth century, it developed in response to the
same underlying social conditions. In both cases, men who had been
crushed by the weight of taxes or the vicissitudes of commercial life
found it necessary to take refuge with the strong. The legalization of
otdacha v zazhiv gave governmental sanction to an arrangement that enhanced still further the power of the wealthy over the posad poor.

CRAFT GUILDS

Craft guilds were the second social group of consequence to be formed in
the posad commune. Unlike the merchant guilds, which had been a part
of posad society for more than a century and which had been only mar-
ginally affected by legislation, the craft guilds were wholly products of
government initiative. Originating in the magistracy legislation of Peter
I, they had been called into being to bring some measure of organization
and regulation into the lives and labors of the urban artisans. Undoubtedly Peter had been moved to create in Russia the kind of talented guild
artisans he had admired and from whom he had learned so much on his
Western European expeditions. But, as was often the case with Russian
institutions, especially those established at the behest of the state, the
craft guilds served primarily as an adjunct of state administration and
only secondarily—and poorly—as a vehicle for the improvement of
workmanship.

The government's administrative-oriented objectives can be seen most
clearly in the area of guild membership. Setting aside the principle of
membership based on inheritance that had been at the core of medieval
Western European guilds, the Russian government placed no restrictions on entry. In fact, the state encouraged artisans to join. Yet, at the
same time, enrollment was not mandatory for all who engaged in craft
work. According to Kizevetter, "*posad* people who were already occupied with craft work in the *posad* were obliged to register in guilds; crafts-

men of all ranks who did not belong to *posad* society were free to enter or not to enter a craft organization. In other words, the law did not establish obligatory concentration of all crafts in the *posad*, but those who wished to do craft work in the *posad* had to be enumerated in the guilds."[10] The government's resolution of the question of guild membership appears to have been a compromise between the principle, espoused by the townsmen, that they possessed the exclusive right, from the *Ulozhenie* of 1649, to be the manufacturers and traders of the realm, and the principle, espoused by the peasants and supported by the gentry, that peasants should be allowed to carry on nonagricultural activities wherever they chose. Guild membership regulations enforced the claim of the townsmen to monopoly rights within the towns, but left the crucial realm of peasant artisanship unchallenged. It follows, then, that the objective of the state in establishing craft guilds was not to concentrate artisan activity in the towns, but to provide convenient institutions for regulating the affairs of existing urban artisans.

That argument receives support from the few, but significant, activities that the guilds performed. Here, the parallels with merchant society are strong. The elected heads of the craft guilds, the aldermen, looked after the registry books and thereby assisted the government in classifying one segment of the population for what were essentially tax purposes. But the principle function of the aldermen consisted in serving as administrative agents of the central government, apportioning and collecting taxes from their fellow guildsmen.[11] As if these contributions were not sufficient, the guildsmen frequently found themselves plying their skills on behalf of urgent state needs, such as repairing the Winter Palace, though one can hardly agree with Kizevetter that "in the eyes of the government, the existence of guilds should first of all guarantee the presence of craftsmen whom it would be possible at any given minute to call on for fulfilling state tasks."[12] That reservation aside, the guildsmen clearly paid their dues to the service system.

That the government was not primarily concerned with the development of the crafts themselves can be inferred from the relative absence of regulatory legislation on matters related to the quality of production. Relations between a master and his journeymen and apprentices, so critical to the transmission of skills from one generation to another, received no treatment in legislation until 1785. In that year, the Charter Granted to the Cities laid out in exhaustive detail the manner in which guilds should be operated.[13] Up to that time, the relationship between master and subordinate had been left to custom. Similarly, legislation had little to say about the quality of merchandise sold or the manner in which it could be marketed.[14] Actual practice reflected this basic indifference:

guild aldermen apparently had a casual attitude toward the quality of the products of their associates.

Although the craft guilds were an integral part of the posad commune, filling a role in the organization of the posad roughly analogous to that of the merchant guilds, they were far from being a ubiquitous presence on the urban scene. Barely established during the reign of Peter I, the guilds fell into such disarray in the decades immediately following the tsar's death that it was necessary for Elizabeth, in trying to breathe new life into the Russian economy, to remind her subjects what guilds were about and to urge their resurrection.[15]

In the period 1743-1747, guilds could be found in only 92 of 202 posady about the country.[16] Elizabeth's encouragement met with some success as guilds reappeared in a number of cities, but the overall picture remained quite varied throughout the century. St. Petersburg, with its high level of demand for luxury goods, had sixty-nine craft guilds in 1766. Significantly, thirty-four of them were composed entirely of foreign artisans.[17] Moscow, on the contrary, had only 663 artisans registered in the guild book as of 1786. The population of the city at that date stood in the neighborhood of 175,000.[18] Many cities, even in the last quarter of the century when guilds again had the formal imprimatur of the sovereign, had no guilds whatsoever.[19] In cities lacking formal craft-guild organizations, the merchant guilds organized the entire posad society, including small craftsmen.

The failure of craft guilds to take better hold in eighteenth-century Russia stems from two related causes: they were not compulsory and they did not offer sufficient benefits to attract members. Had the guilds been the possessors and jealous guardians of trade secrets and had they served as transmitters of specialized skills, they might have lured ambitious artisans seeking advantages over their competitors. As it was, the technical level of production in the guilds stood at or near the low level of peasant handicrafts. Nor did membership in a guild bring freedom from government taxes and service obligations. The guild artisan shared posad taxes and bore the burden of special labor assignments for the government. Finally, the artisan could not find that sense of social fraternity that marked the guilds of the medieval west. The Russian city was not sufficiently differentiated, either in an economic or in a political sense, from the countryside to nurture among its craft population a strong sense of identification with urban interests. Indeed, the guilds themselves consisted predominantly of men of peasant origin.[20] Moreover, as creatures of the government, and a gentry-controlled government at that, the guilds could not provide a haven for their members against the depradations of the ruling orders of society in or out of government. The understanding of the Western European guildsman that his interests differed sharply from those of the rural population and his recognition that these interests could be protected through fraternal institutions were ideas that most likely did not cross the minds of eighteenth-century Russian artisans.

Interestingly enough, craft guilds took root best not in the older areas of the state, where the posad population was concentrated, but in the border areas. There, where agriculture was most profitable and peasant labors were directed toward the fields, not the workbench, peasant reliance on goods manufactured in the towns seems to have been somewhat greater than in the central areas of the state, where the peasants were themselves such vigorous craftsmen. Even so, that fact explains only the strength of handicrafts in the border areas, not the success of the guilds in those areas. According to F. Ia. Polianskii there are two explanations for this phenomenon. In the first place, the relatively limited development of peasant craft and trade activities afforded the guilds a better opportunity to establish a monopoly position. Second, a large percentage of the border-area craftsmen were fugitives from other parts of the empire. Enrollment in guilds gave them a stronger legal position from which they could fight off attempts at extradition.[21]

THE POSAD GATHERING

The merchant and craft guilds, along with the territorial subdivisions present in larger cities, constituted the basic units of posad organization. On their shoulders fell the responsibility for the actual execution of many of the tax and service burdens borne by the commune and for the regulation of a number of aspects of the social and economic life of the townsmen. But the locus of power within the commune lay in the institution that brought together all the townsmen for the purposes of resolving the key issues of posad life—the posad gathering, or *posadskii skhod*. The gathering made the key decisions on state service requirements and apportioned the corresponding obligations to the appropriate groups and individuals within the posad. Its broadly representative composition and the breadth of its purview made the gathering the true center of political life in the posad commune.

At sessions convened in the local posad hall (*izba*), all members of the commune had the right to take part in the proceedings, except when magistracy officials were being elected. At that time both franchise and eligibility for office were restricted. In theory, attendance at regular posad gatherings was mandatory; those who failed to appear often found themselves being dragged bodily to the meetings. On occasion the com-

munes meted out stiff punishments to chronic absentees. Only in the
north, where so many posad people resided in rural areas, was the principle of obligatory attendance relaxed. There, the rural members sent delegates to the gatherings to represent their interests.[22]

Broad rights of participation and obligatory attendance notwithstanding, posad gatherings rarely convened with a full complement of eligible
members. Since no quorum figures existed in law, business could proceed
legally with only a handful present. At times the turnout was substantial,
but in general only ten to fifty members seem to have been present.[23] At
one epic posad gathering a faction seeking to control the deliberations
drove out by force 260 of the 300 members present. The remaining forty
then transacted the business of the day, which, it should be noted, took
the force of law since all those present at the gathering had approved it.[24]

Had the democratic spirit been stronger and the power of the merchant
guilds less pronounced, the attendance record might have been a good
deal better, for the gathering laid claim to responsibility over a vast portion of posad life. According to Kizevetter, the posad gathering exercised
its authority over the following matters: "(1) Regulation of the composition of the *posad* commune; (2) management of the *posad* economy [in-
cluding taxes]; (3) elections of officials of the commune and supervision
of those taxpayers who have been sent off to perform state services; (4)
supervision over the activity of elected officials; (5) [administering] dis-
ciplinary penalties to *posad* taxpayers; (6) concern for local welfare; (7)
representation before higher institutions about various matters related to
local needs."[25] Unquestionably the most important functions were those
connected with state service obligations—the apportionment of taxes and
the selection and supervision of posad residents who served as state revenue collectors. It was in the making of these decisions that traditional
principles of posad communal life asserted themselves: wealthy merchants were selected for the most responsible posts and taxes were apportioned on the basis of the ability of each household to pay.

In addition to settling affairs related to state service, the gathering also
attended to local matters. The gathering had the power to issue orders,
obligatory for all taxpayers, concerning matters of local welfare, that is,
the various projects and obligations described earlier under the rubric of
city administration. The gathering also enjoyed, in principle at least, the
right to supervise its own elected officials. It should be noted, however,
that these local responsibilities, presumably the prerogative of the gathering, were not beyond the reach of the government. Matters of local
welfare often got tangled up in the conflicting jurisdictions of the magistracy, the police, or the military governor's chancellery. The right of the
gathering to supervise its own officials was often violated by the magis-

tracy, which, in its capacity as a representative of the central government, dispensed approbation and condemnation on the zemskii elder and his subordinates in the posad.[26] The one local right of the gathering that appears to have escaped interference was that of directing petitions about local needs to higher authorities. So frequently did the gatherings draw up lists of grievances and possible remedies that these documents came to resemble form letters, a situation that no doubt facilitated the preparation of city reports to the Great Commission and which may, in part, explain the similarity of their content.[27]

The basic organizational structures of the commune, the guilds and the gathering, belonged solely to posad society. They represented the posad itself at work on its problems and tasks; they were emphatically *not* direct extensions of the bureaucratic arm of the central government. Though scarcely autonomous, the commune, through these institutions, exercised a measure of self-administration—though over a limited and in part externally prescribed set of affairs. But posad society, if it handled many of its affairs on its own, was not isolated; nor did its institutions of self-administration exist in a vacuum. The influence of the state continued to permeate all of posad society, just as it had always done. The common denominator of tiaglo provided the raison d'être for the commune's existence and in so doing bound the commune in principle into the service system. Moreover, the central government was never really far from the scene, regulating the merchant guilds, creating the craft guilds, and forever interfering with the operations of the posad. Still, in terms of organization, the guilds and gatherings, with their latitude for self-administration, remained at some remove from the central government. What was needed if the activities of the posady were to be coordinated with the changing policies of the state and if the government were to be kept abreast of matters in the urban community was an institutional link between the posad and the formal hierarchy of state administration. During the middle years of the eighteenth century, that link was provided by the magistracy.

THE EMERGENCE OF THE MAGISTRACY

The magistracy that came to mediate between the commune and the central government during the middle years of the eighteenth century was not the same institution that Peter I had striven to introduce: it was much more an agency of government regulation than one of civic rejuvenation. The Petrine administrative system—complex, expensive to operate, and demanding of more skilled personnel than the country could begin to supply—began to unravel almost immediately upon the death of its creator. Not surprisingly, the magistracy reform, one of the last undertaken by Peter, was among the least well established and hence most susceptible to alteration. The initial step in the process came when the Supreme Privy Council, as a part of a general review of domestic policy matters, decided to revive the office of military governor "for the purpose of improving [*ispravlenie*] court and investigative affairs."[28] That action was followed by a decree issued early in 1727 that deprived the magistracy of its independence from local authorities by subordinating it in administrative affairs to the governor and to the newly reinstituted military governor. That same law also stripped from the magistracy many of its judicial competences, especially in the area of crimes of violence, and entrusted them to the governor and military governor. The latter officials were also empowered to hear appeals from citizens dissatisfied with those legal decisions that the magistracy was still in a position to render.[29] In August of the same year, the Main Magistracy was abolished on the grounds that local magistracies were already administratively subordinate to the governors. Local magistracies remained in existence, but under the appellation *ratusha*.[30]

The new administrative chain of command read, from top to bottom: Senate, governors, military governors of provincial cities, military governors of small cities, and ratushy. Thus Peter's efforts to foster a vigorous, prosperous urban population through the agency of a centrally controlled estate institution came to naught just two years after his death. The ratusha, as constituted by the legislation of 1727, took its place subserviently at the bottom of the administrative hierarchy.

The placing of the magistracy under the watchful eye of the military governor has been interpreted as a reaction by a conservative government against the rather timid local freedoms implicit in the magistracy reform.[31] But a much more likely explanation is that the magistracy institution never established itself solidly enough to perform its appointed tasks. The problems encountered by Peter in establishing the St. Petersburg Main Magistracy have already been recounted. The situation was scarcely any better in Moscow, where quarrels over eligibility for office and over procedure caused substantial delays.[32] It is not hard to imagine the difficulties that attended the establishment of magistracies in the lesser cities of the empire. In fact, councils were never set up in a number of localities. Such a shaky institution simply could not dispense satisfactory justice to the merchants and collect the full sum of state taxes levied against the townsmen. It was, then, in response to a genuine administrative crisis in the towns that the government moved to place one of its own appointed officials, the military governor, in complete control of the towns.[33]

In 1732, a commission under the leadership of Count Osterman convened to discuss the deplorable state of Russian commerce and to devise ways to remedy its ills. One recommendation of the commission called for the reestablishment of a magistracy in St. Petersburg. Shortly thereafter, the enabling legislation appeared: "For the spread of the merchantry and commerce it is necessary to institute in St. Petersburg a magistracy, on the example of Riga, and to supply it with a regulation and other appurtenances due it."[34] The similarity between these instructions and those given by Peter I to von Fick are striking. They suggest, both in the Western orientation of the model and in the specific content of the legislation, that the basic principles of the Petrine urban policy had not entirely disappeared from the thoughts of Russia's rulers.[35]

The Empress Elizabeth, who seems to have taken seriously her proud lineage, set out to reassemble the shattered pieces of Peter's legislative legacy. Immediately after coming to the throne she ordered the full reinstatement of the magistracies as they had been defined in Petrine legislation. The task was not easy, for memories of the institution, now some sixteen years extinct, had all but faded from the minds of the townsmen. Several decrees had to be issued, explaining to the existing government agencies what the magistracy was and where they stood in relation to it.[36]

The principle of centralization that had lain at the heart of Peter's reform was both improved upon and weakened in the revived magistracy. In a characteristic exercise in abstract institution-making, a statute was drawn up that called for the ranking of Russia's cities, although the criteria on which this ranking was to occur remained unclear. The "lesser" cities of the realm were subordinated (ascribed) to those deemed more important, and the latter, in turn, were subordinated to the Main Magistracy, which thus became the controlling organ of the entire system. Local magistracies had to seek permission from the center before making any decision, or had at least to secure approval after the fact.[37] A. A. Kizevetter's monumental history of the posad commune, based on archival sources, demonstrates unambiguously that most decisions of importance and many trivial ones were made in the office of the Main Magistracy.

While the ranking of cities in a kind of urban *mestnichestvo* rendered the institution more perfectly centralized and capable of control from the capital, the new magistracy was not so well buffered as its predecessor had been from infringement at the local level. The law lacked precision on this point, but both the legal historian Ditiatin and the socioeconomic historian Klokman have argued that the governors and the military governors stood over the magistracies. "In reality, in life, the relations of the military governors, governors, and police organs to the city magistracies were conditioned by the personal character, good will, and force of the former, by the helpless position of the latter."[38] Thus, the protection that had been afforded the commercial population in the legislation of Peter I —that is, an administrative system staffed primarily by merchants and shielded from external pressures, was not provided them by the recreated magistracy.

Even though the revived magistracy fell far short of being the vigorous instrument of the merchant class that Peter had intended, it soon became the single most critical institution in the lives of the townsmen. The post of burgomistr, standing as it did between the central government and the local posad society, brought to its holder considerable power and some sobering obligations. In the end the attraction of power outweighed the liabilities attendant on its exercise, and the pursuit of office became a central feature of posad life. Just how the burgomistry were elected is a matter that warrants careful attention, for it reflects the relationship between the magistracy and posad society as well as the inner workings of the commune.

From the very beginning of the magistracy's existence, it seems clear that the government understood its principal function to be tax collection. To make certain that the greatest possible revenue flowed into the treasury, a decree of 1731 made the election of burgomistry strictly an affair of the first two merchant guilds on the theory that only the most prosperous individuals should hold positions for which they were personally financially responsible.[39] From the government point of view, then, magistracy elections amounted to little more than the selection of tax agents by local posad society.

The office of burgomistr would not, at first glance, appear to have been particularly appealing. Not only was it associated with a rapacious central government, but the risks were substantial, the work hard, and the term in office long (for much of the eighteenth century, magistracy officials served terms of indefinite length).[40] One might reasonably expect a paucity of candidates for such a position. But the power to tax is the power to destroy, and the wealthy merchants considered it a wise precaution, if not an absolute necessity, to control the magistracy office. Vigorous, even violent, election struggles broke out between contesting groups of rich merchants and their followers. Frequently, neither faction accepted the results of an election and two separate sets of returns were forwarded to the Main Magistracy for adjudication. By and large the decision was awarded to that party which seemed best able, on the basis of mutual pledges, to guarantee the financial responsibility of its candidates.[41] Thus, the central government, both in setting the qualifications for election to the magistracy and in resolving disputed elections, reinforced the state-service character of the office while at the same time reserving for itself the right to interfere in the internal workings of the posad commune.

Magistracy elections tended, on the whole, toward the confirmation in state posts of a few oligarchs, but not all posady meekly acquiesced in such practices. In Arkhangel, according to the testimony of one of its leading posad figures, V. V. Krestinin, the middle orders of the population engaged in a continual struggle with the rich and powerful over the collection of taxes and the apportionment of services. The principal weapons of the rank-and-file townsmen were, of course, petitions, which were sent now to the *guberniia*-level magistracy, now to the Main Magistracy.[42] In some posady the lower social elements actually revolted— seizing control of the magistracy office, locking up the incumbent leaders, and setting up their own administrative apparatus. On occasion, these insurgents managed to retain power for a considerable period, while the government moved ponderously to restore law, order, and "proper" leadership to the rebellious posad.[43]

However colorful these short-lived revolts may have been, they failed to alter significantly the character of magistracy elections. Any real change depended on new government attitudes toward the magistracy. During the early years of the reign of Catherine II several measures pointed in the direction of broadened franchise and improved procedural practices for local elections. The guidelines laid down in 1766 for the selection of deputies to the Great Commission and for the mayors who would assist in this process called for elections in which the entire city population would participate.[44] Picking up the theme of broader franchise, the Main Magistracy shortly thereafter ordered that all elections of magistracy officials be carried out on that same basis.[45] Indeed, formal elections would have been an innovation for many a posad where cliques of merchants cynically manipulated candidates for the magistracy office. Krestinin pointed out with great pride that in 1776 his posad at last held an election in which people wrote on a piece of paper the name of the candidate whom they favored.[46] A formal government decree of 1773 extended the notion of orderly election procedures still further by announcing that judges in the local magistracy offices should be elected "by balloting according to the form established by Her Majesty for the election of deputies for the working out of a new legislative code."[47] Kizevetter points out that all these reforms encountered stubborn resistance. Many communes continued to restrict eligibility and franchise to outstanding members of the first two guilds of merchants, while others suppressed free balloting entirely.[48] Nonetheless, the government, by encouraging open elections for the magistracy, had taken a step toward relinquishing some of its considerable control over this institution at the local level. It was a breach of the state-service principle and a harbinger of changes to come.

Though the magistracy brought some order to a limited range of governmental activities in the towns over the course of four decades, it remained a far cry from what Peter had envisioned. The development of the merchant class, the extension of public services, and the creation of aesthetically pleasing urban surroundings—hopes embodied in the Petrine reform—received virtually no attention from the magistracy. Instead of proceeding to direct its efforts toward a broad range of urban problems, the magistracy became, as if obeying some inertial law of Russian administrative life, another agency devoted to feeding revenues to the center. Tax collection and the supervision of various tax-related services absorbed most of the energies of the burgomistry. The exercise of a limited number of judicial functions occupied the remainder of their time. Supervised from above by the Main Magistracy, itself responsible to the Senate, and watched carefully at the local level by governors and military governors, each local magistracy was constantly reminded that its first obligation was to the central government. Even if one sets aside problems of financing local projects, of traditional adverse attitudes toward participation in government, and the like, the very institutional structure of which the magistracy was a part precluded its becoming the dynamic organ of local government that Peter had intended it to be. The record of the magistracy during the mid-eighteenth century, then, amounts ultimately to the history of an adjunct agency of state financial administration, though one into which the townsmen themselves had been co-opted.

The concern shown by the state, as tax collector, and the leading merchants, as principal taxpayers, over the process of electing magistracy officials reflects the crucial intermediary role of the institution. Of course, there had always been some connecting link between the state and the commune: the military governor, perhaps, is the most conspicuous example. But with the appearance of the magistracy the relationship took on its most rational form ever, crowned, as it were, by the Main Magistracy with its supervisory responsibilities for townsmen throughout the realm. There now existed a chain of organization extending from the smallest units of posad self-administration to the central government. To refer to this arrangement as a hierarchy would surely be inappropriate, for that term implies gradations within a single institution, which was clearly not the case. The magistracy institution reached out from the center to touch, but not to embrace or absorb, indigenous posad administrative institutions. It was an advance of central government control, but it did not yet represent the direct extension of central government agencies into the posady. Similarly, by placing their own men on the magistracy, the posady sought to exert as much control as possible over the institution, though the limits of their power were obvious. Its capacity to resolve these conflicting interests—though almost always to the benefit of the state—made the magistracy a truly intermediary institution.

To understand this peculiar relationship, however, it is not sufficient merely to describe its constituent parts and to detail their interaction; a proper understanding of the institutional matrix in which the townsmen found themselves awaits a closer examination of its central function—service.

In the period of urban dislocation and turmoil that followed Peter's death, as well as in more stable times during mid-century, the posad commune continued to perform its traditional twofold service role. On the one hand, the commune served as an adjunct of central government administration, assisting primarily in the process of tax collection; on the other hand, the commune shouldered—weakly and reluctantly—many of the responsibilities of city management, responsibilities that fell largely on the posad taxpayers but which benefited all residents of the cities. So dominant were these matters of service in the life of the commune during the middle years of the century that one can speak of this time as the apogee of the service city.

TIAGLO: THE SERVICE COMPONENT

Of the two functions performed by posad society, by far the most important was the commune's role as an agency of state fiscal administration. This function proved to be the most demanding of human and financial resources and consequently had the greatest influence on posad society. The locus of this state-administrative function lay in the discharge of the commune's tiaglo obligation, which remained essentially unchanged from what it had been in the preceding century. For the sake of the following analysis, tiaglo has been separated into its constituent parts, service and taxation; but it is important to remember that both sets of duties were regarded as part of one and the same obligation to the state.

Following the precedents so well elaborated in the seventeenth century, the townsmen of the eighteenth labored long and hard on behalf of state administration. They worked as accountants, appraisers, inspectors of manufactured items, and as sworn-men (locally elected officials who assisted in the collection of various taxes and customs duties).[49] They managed the state liquor and salt monopolies, served at customs houses and toll points, and collected both regular and extraordinary taxes for the government. These services might be carried out in a taxpayer's city of residence or in the surrounding countryside, or even in some distant part of the country. In fact, whenever possible the government preferred to send revenue collectors to distant localities on the dubious theory that they would be more inclined to defend the interests of the fisc among strangers than among friends.[50]

Something of the flavor of service responsibilities can be gathered from the following decisions passed by the Moscow guild merchantry: "during next year, 1772, to send to the treasury chamber to receive sums from tax-farming and liquor money, [there should be] elected a good, wealthy, and ordinary man and his election [should be] reported to the Moscow magistracy"; "to select a man from the first guild for supervision over an inventory of forests and over grain prices"; "to replace a man previously elected to the oral court because he was not literate"; "for supervision over nontaxable properties and over other inspectors, [there should be] elected from the first guild one man of good literacy, able to write."[51]

Service obligations weighed heavily upon the posad. In some cities, one-quarter to one-half of the eligible men found themselves performing administrative duties of one kind or another. According to the instruction from the city of Arkhangel to Catherine II's Great Commission, out of 342 mature posad members, 80 rendered service to the central state, 27 worked in city administration, and 34 put in time as local policemen.[52] In Kazan' at one point there were forty-two more service positions to fill than men to fill them.[53]

The burden of service was made all the heavier because it was not equitably shared. According to law, the most important jobs were to be held by the wealthier members of the posad, not in recognition of their business acumen, but in deference to the fact that holders of government posts were financially responsibile for the fulfillment of the assigned tasks. A poor man who bungled a tax-collecting job could not be expected to make up a deficit; a rich man might be able to do so. While the rich were saddled with the tougher, more responsible positions, the less well-off posad people, who could ill afford to take time away from their own not-very-profitable business pursuits, filled the majority of service positions. Long tours of duty and the prospect of being sent to some faraway town rendered service still more unattractive.

Needless to say, the townsmen regarded state service as a hateful and ruinous part of their lives, and they never missed an opportunity to petition the government for the elimination of particularly unpalatable services or for an end to them all. Occasionally a positive response was forthcoming. In 1714 and again in 1722 government decrees forbad the appointing of posad taxpayers as accountants, noting that the additional work load was ruining the merchants. The legislation apparently failed, for accountants figure in lists of posad services performed at mid-century.[54] A similar fate befell legislative efforts of 1732 and 1736 to forbid service away from home. That practice continued through most of the century.[55]

Service obligations began to decline, starting in 1754 with the elimination of internal customs (see Chaper 8), but even so the townsmen still objected vigorously to them in their reports to the Great Commission. Their instructions pointed out that the filling of state posts seriously depleted the manpower resources of the posady and argued that the taking of the "best" people into service deprived the local magistracies of competent leadership. They also called attention to the dangers involved in state service, noting, for example, that the government had the right to punish severely those who failed to perform their duties as specified.[56] Several instructions asked that all service responsibilities be abolished outright and that the tasks in question be performed by hired government officials whose salaries would be financed by a special tax. The inventive citizens of Voronezh recommended that the merchants be replaced in service jobs by retired army officers, who, presumably, had nothing better to do with their waning years. Still other reports contended that certain tasks, especially local ones like policing, should not fall on the shoulders of the posad people alone but should be extended to all segments of the city population.[57] These petitions may well have been submitted with a cynicism engendered by years of unsuccessful pleading with the government for redress of service-related grievances. But times were changing in Russia: before Catherine's reign ended many of the townsmen's demands were realized, and, ultimately, the service system broke down.

TIAGLO: THE TAX COMPONENT

Along with service obligations, indirect taxes constituted the other main element of the tiaglo.[58] In the late seventeenth century and in the very early years of the eighteenth, the townsmen had been subject to a wide range of taxes: a tax on their households, a tax on their total assets, special levies for specific government needs, and a whole series of indirect taxes. The burden had been heavy, but it was only in the eighteenth century that the Russian citizens found out what it really cost to be a European power.

Indirect taxes, often insidiously disguised, took a big bite out of the income of the posad. These levies can be subsumed under three general headings: liquor (*kabatskye*), customs (*tamozhennye*), and chancellery (*kantseliarskye*). The latter category drew on a wide variety of sources: manufacturing and craft production; the rental or leasing of land or shop spaces; governmental concessions, such as the management of ferries; excise taxes; and an all-purpose collection to cover petty governmental expenses. Of the three, the duty on liquor proved to be the most productive, bringing in nearly half of the total indirect tax revenue.[59]

The manner of assessment made these taxes particularly burdensome for the population. Unlike most indirect taxes, which are based on a percentage of the value of business transactions, these were lump-sum taxes. In a given province in a given year, for example, the liquor revenue had to attain a figure determined in advance by averaging the revenues for that locality from three of the best recent years. Basing a tax on good years proved to be as foolish as it was greedy, for any economic downturn led immediately to budgetary imbalance and to massive arrears.[60]

Partial relief from the burden of indirect taxation came in 1754 with the end of internal customs duties and the elimination of seventeen articles of the chancellery taxes. That these taxes had been excessive relative to the paying power of the townsmen is evident from the fact that in canceling these tax categories the government had to write off an arrears of 1,144,975 rubles.[61] The decision of 1754 did not, however, bring an end to all indirect taxes, let alone represent an abandonment of the principle. A new series of indirect taxes went into effect in 1763, only to be abolished piecemeal in the 1770s.[62] The revenues were too substantial and the psychological advantages too great for the government to resist this means of filling the treasury.

As far as the townsmen were concerned, indirect taxation was doubly onerous. Not only were they affected as producers, consumers, and transporters of goods, they had also to administer these taxes as a part of their service obligation. Since penalties were severe if collections came up short, those charged with that responsibility often had to gouge their compatriots in order to gather sufficient cash to save their own skins. Existing social divisions within the posad could only have been exacerbated by this arrangement.

As for direct taxes, the system in effect during the seventeenth century had proved unsatisfactory to collector and payee alike. In addition to the basic direct tax on each household, the government relied increasingly on special levies to meet specific needs. Difficult to anticipate, they complicated the financial management of businesses. Moreover, if merchants lacked cash reserves at the time of a new special assessment, a likely circumstance, the government failed in its objective. It was the urgent need to reform this antiquated system that prompted Peter I to introduce the poll tax. For posad dwellers, a single tax of one ruble and twenty kopecks per person replaced the many and disparate direct taxes. By design, the poll tax should have covered all contingencies, making ad hoc levies unnecessary. In fact, the latter continued to be imposed through the century.[63]

The poll tax certainly had its advantages—it facilitated assessment, collection, and accounting. But from the point of view of the townsmen it was a mixed blessing. In order to obtain enough revenue to replace defunct taxes and to provide Peter with the vast sums needed to finance his ambitious state policy the poll tax assessment had to be large. Revenues from it exceeded by far those gathered under the previous system. The Kaluga posad, for example, saw its total payments rise at an alarming rate during the Petrine era, especially after the introduction of the poll tax:[64]

Period	Total Tax Assessment (in rubles)
1690s	908
1695 (Azov campaign)	1,705
1700-1721 (Northern War period)	2,443
1724 (poll tax)	7,243

So burdensome was the new system that arrears mounted rapidly from its very inception. In the first four years of collection, 1724-1727, poll tax arrears in the posady of Russia amounted to 64.3 percent of the assessment.[65] Apparently the amount of unpaid taxes declined after the second census, taken in 1744. Kizevetter suggests that this census may have been more accurate and hence the subsequent tax assessments more realistic. He also speculates that collection methods improved over the course of time.[66] It also seems likely that the ability of the population to pay their taxes improved somewhat over the course of the century.[67] Even so, arrears continued to be an ever-present part of the poll tax operations. As might be expected, this new imposition brought forth a flood of petitions from the tsar's subjects, demanding relief from its burdens. To the standard complaint that the tax impoverished the people and ruined the posad, there was added in the 1760s a new line of appeal. Many of the reports to the Great Commission contended that payment of a poll tax was beneath the dignity of merchants. "The Russian merchants, because they are subjected to the poll tax, find themselves in great contempt in the eyes of the bourgeoisie [*meshchanstvo*] of other European nations."[68] Relief from this humiliation was just around the corner for the more substantial elements of the posad, in the form of the 1775 tax reform.

The actual administration of the poll tax deserves careful attention. In the first place, it was the final link in the revenue-gathering hierarchy of the state, the point at which the service system touched all inhabitants of the posad, regardless of wealth or social position. Second, because apportionment and collection were strictly a local matter, these processes yield added information on the internal life of the posad, in particular on the relations between rich and poor.

The poll tax was levied not against individual taxpayers, but against the posad of a given town, and the members of the commune themselves apportioned the burden. The government, in setting the assessment, used the basic unit of a taxable person (*okladnaia dusha*), which had a value of one ruble and twenty kopecks. For every person registered in the last census, the posad was assessed one taxable person. Since many a merchant, craftsman, and hired hand did not see one ruble and twenty kopecks in a year, they could not be expected to bear a full unit of taxation. Hence the commune took upon itself the task of apportioning the tax according to ability to pay. Taking into account land, trade, and industry, the commune assessed each household as many taxable persons as it was deemed capable of paying. Thus the tax records show that some households were assessed one-half or even one-fourth of a taxable person, while the share of others came to several dozen.[69]

Prosperous merchants, because of their ability to pay the taxes of their indigent neighbors, were prized equally by the government and by their fellow taxpayers. The government sought to keep them in the communes to ensure the full payment of taxes, and the posad poor regarded the rich as insurance against excessive rates for themselves. When wealthy merchants left a commune, as many did when ordered by Peter to take up residence in St. Petersburg, the tax assessments for those who were left at home shot up disastrously.[70]

The rich were not above exploiting their position as valued taxpayers. Indeed, the ability to meet large tax payments enhanced their already substantial power, derived from mercantile success, over the poorer members of the posad. There was even some juridical basis for such domination. A law of 1742 gave the well-to-do posad taxpayers the right to look after the poor whose taxes they paid and to encourage the latter to industry and thrift.[71] It is doubtful that the wealthy needed such assistance in maintaining control over most posady, but the existence of this law is itself graphic evidence of the extent to which tax matters, themselves an integral part of the service relationship, shaped social relations among the urban taxpayers.

THE POSAD COMMUNE AND CITY ADMINISTRATION

The second major function of the commune, less clearly defined and markedly less well executed than its state service tasks, consisted of participation in the administration of the cities themselves. Standard treatments of urban administration focus, and rightly so, on the powers of crown officials, particularly governors and military governors.[72] Unquestionably these individuals exercised authority over all the inhabitants of the cities, irrespective of their social status, as well as over the magistracies.[73] But these important crown officials lacked the manpower, the financial resources, and the inclination to care adequately for local needs. With the state's many interests to protect, they could hardly be expected to develop strong programs of civic development.

The central government was not unaware of the needs of the cities for basic services and it chose to entrust responsibility for fulfilling those needs, as Peter I had, to the police. The duties that confronted the police —the maintenance of law and order, the development of crucial public services, and the supervision of morality—could by no means be placed on any single group within society. The police, an all-estate institution in its competences, was the logical candidate to shoulder this responsibility. Moreover, there was an added advantage from the government's point of view: the police could be readily controlled through the establishment of a central police agency and the hierarchical subordination of local police offices to it.

In fact, however, vigorous police departments emerged only in St. Petersburg and Moscow, where government financing and bureaucratic continuity made possible their pursuit of a wide range of activities.[74] Elsewhere in the country there were but a handful of chiefs of police, and they were men who had little in the way of staff besides a few clerical assistants.[75] For the most part, the government chose to entrust police work to the local magistracies, supervised, of course, by governors and military governors. The reasons for this policy were obviously fiscal, as this excerpt from a Senate decree of 1737 indicates: "If one appoints to these [city] police special officers and gentry, then it is necessary to give them salaries, and to appoint for them clerical assistants and messengers with their salaries as well and from this there will occur fiscal loss."[76]

In conditions such as those, it is obvious that someone other than the officials of the police hierarchy or of the magistracy office had to do the vast amount of routine police work. Not surprisingly, it fell to the lot of the urban residents to provide the needed service. Soldiers from the local garrison often found themselves charged with apprehending, detaining, and transporting particularly dangerous persons: murderers, rapists, robbers, and the like.[77] Soldiers in the capital cities manned the few pieces of fire apparatus available. But the vast majority of police work, at least in terms of hours spent, was performed by the regular inhabitants of the cities, mostly by the posadskie liudi. It was they who stood watch duty at night, enforcing curfew and sounding the tocsin should fire or mayhem break out; it was they who showed up at neighborhood fires with axe, shovel, or bucket in hand; and it was they who cleaned the streets in front of their homes.[78]

Similarly, in areas of public works and welfare, the townsmen were called upon to provide the facilities or to perform the services required by central government representatives. Bridge maintenance, for example, an essential function given the location of so many cities on important waterways, was carried out by the local populace at local expense. Some obligations, such as the construction of sidewalks and the disposal of waste and rubbish, fell directly on the individual property holder. The central government was charitable enough to assume these responsibilities for public buildings.[79]

In most cities, the authority charged with the actual supervision of these activities was the local magistracy; but a case history from Kaluga suggests that at least one magistracy was more than a little reluctant to accept that responsibility. Apparently the Kaluga police had sent several memos to the local magistracy, urging it to execute its lawfully appointed tasks of supervision for clean streets, markets, bridge repair, night guard duty, and so forth. And, according to the police, they received neither action nor even an acknowledgment of their communications. Thus frustrated, the Kaluga police informed the Main Police Chancellery in St. Petersburg about their difficulties and asked for assistance. The Main Police Chancellery in turn appealed to the Main Magistracy, asking the latter to issue directives to local magistracies about their duties as executive arms of the police. The decree in which this history is recorded duly orders the Main Magistracy and other city magistracies to carry out these functions as the law requires.[80]

What one has here is an almost classic formula for administrative inaction: a central government, eager to endorse and prescribe through legislation an upgrading of the material conditions of the cities; a disembodied local police establishment, capable of transmitting to local society the legislative objectives of the central government, but utterly incapable of accomplishing them by itself; and the magistracy, an already overburdened estate institution, whose constituency wants not more, but less in the way of services to city and state. Those who have authority have no power, and those who have the power, seek to escape the burdens of its exercise. There existed a nearly infinite capacity for buck-passing.

Precisely why the magistracy, an elected body of representatives of the townsmen, or the posad commune itself did not take the initiative and create the needed institutions of urban administration is a question that has many answers. The overall cultural level of the country tended to keep expectations low: the weight of a traditional society was felt as strongly in the cities as in the countryside. The age-old practice of the central government of identifying problems and creating institutions under its control to rectify these problems may well have dampened, if not entirely squelched, local initiative. In a related vein, the townsmen's hostile attitude, born of the bitter experience of service, toward the very action of government might also be cited. But it is not necessary to resort to such vague and difficult-to-demonstrate explanations for the townsmen's failure to secure effective control over the urban environment. It is enough simply to look at the financial problems involved.

The posad did, in fact, have a number of sources of income with which urban administration might be financed. Revenues were available, for example, from posad-owned properties, real and movable, from government loans and nonrepayable assistance, and from private loans. All these sources taken together, however, yielded little cash for the commune's treasury.[81]

Traditionally, a bigger source of posad revenue had derived from the commune's right to keep all revenues it had collected for the state in excess of the prescribed amount. In 1737, though, the government ordered that all surplus taxes be sent directly to the state treasury. The posady protested bitterly, for this regulation not only deprived them of money that could be disbursed for local expenses, it also took away a reserve that could be called upon in years when collections failed to meet assessments. In 1745 a compromise solution was arrived at: local surpluses could be applied to local arrears, but they could not otherwise be disbursed at the discretion of the posad.[82]

In the last analysis, if a posad were to raise enough money to care adequately for local needs, the task would have to be accomplished through the exercise of its right of self-assessment, granted by law in 1728.[83] But all such revenues did not go to cover useful services for the cities. Of course, repair of roads and bridges and other similar projects funded with posad revenues benefited the townsmen, and the more the money the greater such projects could be. Yet most of the cash that flowed from posad treasuries defrayed the costs of obligatory expenditures assessed against the posad by the state. Posad moneys paid for the room and board of traveling officials of the central bureaucracy—census takers, searchers of arrears, and the like; for the care of exiles or captives placed in the cities; and for the maintenance of doctors.[84] While it is true that some of the expenditures of posad funds contributed to the welfare of the townsmen and of the cities as a whole, the fact remains that other expenditures did not. Moreover, control over these many expenditures resided with agents of the central government and not with local posad society. It is not surprising, then, that the townsmen, so heavily burdened with state taxes and obligatory expenditures, should have proved reluctant to tax themselves further to create progressive institutions of urban government.[85]

THE SERVICE RELATIONSHIP

Historians of medieval Russia have pointed to the fusion of public and private functions in the actions of the country's princes and have argued that the Russians, unlike most Western European peoples, never drew sharp distinctions between the two spheres of action.[86] Certainly the operations of the posad commune suggest that the indiscriminate mixing of public and private functions in a single institution was a practice alive and well in the eighteenth century. Communal action concerning economic matters, whether it be the supervision of guilds, the allocation of shop spaces, the management of the merchants' court, or the regulation of property relations, touched directly the private interests of the posad inhabitants. Another set of activities, embracing registration into the posad tax rolls, the election of local officials, and taxing for posad needs, while they certainly affected private interests, also influenced the collective body of the posad. And some activities of the commune, though basically the business of its members, at times had an impact beyond the abstract confines of the posad, reaching other groups within the cities. Watch and fire-fighting duties, along with road and bridge repair work, fell into this category. There the posad verged on becoming an institution of local government.

On still another level, the performance of a number of administrative tasks on behalf of the state, chiefly those connected with revenue gathering, lent the posad the unmistakable air of a public institution operating on the national level. Fiscal management, after all, is a public function, and in the nation-state it is usually the job of public officials. When the townsmen set off to port cities to collect tariffs, or took up stations at bridges to gather tolls, or traveled from tavern to tavern in pursuit of liquor taxes, they acted out public roles; and the commune, in selecting them and supervising the discharge of their duties, itself performed as a public institution.

There were many situations in which the private and public interests became inextricably intertwined. The personal financial responsibility of a tax official elected from the posad is a case in point, for he was liable from his private fortune for any shortcomings in his public office. So, too, did the principle of mutual responsibility for the posad's own tax burden mix public and private interests in each and every apportionment decision. These many facets of the commune's operations (private, public, and mixed) are best understood as functions of service, for that principal accomodates the activities of the commune on behalf of its own members as easily as it accomodates the performance of public duties by individuals who never wholly lost their private identities, who remained merchants and artisans even as they collected customs tolls in the name of the tsar. Service, then, was the defining feature of the commune.

To define and to characterize an institution, however, is not to explain why it appeared and endured. The posad commune arose from the interaction of a socially weak, economically poor urban commercial and artisan class with an administratively underdeveloped state. The townsmen, while indispensable to the nation both for their economic activities and for their revenue potential, were not really powerful enough to exercise control over the cities and towns of the state, either on their own behalf or on the behalf of all the residents of the city. The establishing of genuine urban autonomy was a task beyond their capabilities—even had the central government been favorably disposed to this idea, which it was not. Indeed, the townsmen could not even defend themselves satisfactorily from their economic competitors. Thus, in the process of organizing the polity, the central government could not rely on strong, indigenous local administration, but had to fall back on its own resources.

There were problems at the center as well. Although the central government of Muscovite and early imperial Russia so dominated the political life of the country that it could successfully prevent potential rivals for political power from gaining a toehold, the fact remains that the central government was not sufficiently mature to administer the country wholly through its own institutions. Its bureaucracy had neither the financial nor the human resources to reach out directly to each individual citizen. Thus the government had to deal with groups rather than with individuals, and in so doing conceded to those groups many responsibilities that are usually considered the task of those in political authority. The landed gentry, for example, were drawn as a group into state military and civil service and were granted administrative control over their rural dependents. In return for service the government secured for the gentry the source of their livelihood. In an essential way, however, the government was in default of its political responsibility, in that it had entrusted nearly half of the population to the administrative control of a single social group, the gentry.

The fiscal and urban administrative functions of the townsmen were as necessary to the well-being of the society as were the military, civil, and rural-administrative activities of the gentry. Thus it is not surprising that there existed between the state and the townsmen an arrangement similar to that that obtained between state and gentry. The townsmen's contributions to the fiscal system and to local administration were matched, in principle at least, by a formal recognition of their socioeconomic place in society as well as by a modicum of control over their own intra-posad affairs. That the townsmen did less well than the gentry in their service relationship with the state only reflects their relatively weaker social role in a society where wealth and power were firmly rooted in the land.

When seen in terms of the mutual strengths and weaknesses of posad and state, the service system that governed the lives of the townsmen seems less simplistic. Kizevetter's notion that the townsmen constituted an "enserfed" element of the population, held in bondage by the central government, cannot be accepted as a fair description of this relationship. There were constraints and burdens on them, and serious ones at that, but the townsmen were not without compensation. That the state's support of their prerogatives proved in the end to be of limited value is as much a result of the posad's own internal weakness as it is of government indifference or bad faith.

To be sure, the system had its shortcomings. The business enterprises of individuals and the overall economic picture in many posady were adversely affected by the demands of service. Social divisions, wide enough to begin with, were exacerbated. And most importantly, the service relationship drew the attention of the townsmen away from local problems and toward the concerns of the central government. In both time and money, the drain of service was thus considerable, and the cost to local initiative correspondingly great. Yet, what alternative was there? The fate of the Petrine reforms demonstrated that the country was not yet ready for fully bureaucratized central government, and the revenue-collecting operations had to be accomplished somehow. The service system, resting on traditions that dated back to Muscovy, was at the disposal of those who would administer Russia during its emergence as a nation-state and then as an imperial power.

CHAPTER SEVEN

The Posad Estate:
Attitudes and the Social Context

THE ECONOMIC PURSUITS of the townsmen and their service relationship with the central government go a long way toward defining the character of posad life in the eighteenth century, but no characterization could be complete without an examination of the attitudes of the townsmen. Their sense of identity and social place, their perception of fundamental posad interests, the defenses put forward on behalf of those interests, their aspirations, and, finally, a sense of their limitations—all were crucial elements of the outlook that guided the actions of the townsmen in the complex and competitive world in which they found themselves. Obviously, in a society as diverse as the posad, everyone would not share a single perspective on the world. Yet the evidence suggests that in certain vital areas, especially those which touched on the posad's relationship with the rest of Russian society, including the central government, there was sufficient agreement within and among posady to make it possible to speak of a posad "estate mentality."

The posad mentality derived largely from the specific economic interests of the townsmen and from their service relationship with the central government—with an added fillip from the general atmosphere of restraint that pervaded Russian society. There was more to this mentality, however, than the identification and defense of special interests: the townsmen also betrayed an acute awareness of their position in the broader arena of national life. The townsmen's self-image was shaped by the conscious comparison of their social standing to that of other estates, particularly the dominant landed gentry. Such comparisons spawned a cautious, narrow, and often backward-looking approach to the world, which seems out of keeping with the aggressive, progressive traits that might be expected of a nascent bourgeoisie—at least judging by the experience of Western Europe. Yet, when the activities, relationships, and attitudes of the posadskie liudi are viewed from the larger perspective of comparative urban history, the apparent uniqueness of the Russian experience is diminished. As it turns out, the posad population had much in common with urban commercial classes in many other societies during the preindustrial phase of national development.

THE RECORD

Documenting the attitudes of the townsmen is not the easiest of tasks. Illiteracy in the posad ran high; consequently, there do not exist the bountiful memoir and epistolary sources that might shed light on the personal and public thoughts of the posad inhabitant. There are a handful of works of a public character, devoted largely to economic matters, from the pens of such men as Pososhkov, Krestinin, and Desnitskii—"bourgeois publicists," as Soviet historians are wont to call literate advocates of the commercial and manufacturing class.[1] Of the three, however, only Krestinin seems to have given expression to the posad perspective; the other two fall more into the category of *projecteur*, assuming an air of detachment from special interests and proposing broad reform principles. Outside sources provide only limited assistance. The gentry had little to say about the townsmen that was not tinged with disparagement, and the peasants left no written record of their views on the townsmen, though their vigorous economic competition was a forceful commentary in its own right.[2] Foreigners took some notice of the townsmen, but more with an eye to singling out the peculiarities of mind and practice that distinguish Russian merchants from their European counterparts than to presenting an analysis of the attitudes and perceptions of the townsmen in the context of Russian society.[3]

In the last analysis, the best sources for the views of the townsmen in the eighteenth century are those documents of an official nature that contain their positions on major issues affecting the posad. A number of lines of communication linked the townsmen with the central government, making it possible equally for the townsmen to inform the government of their views and for the state to gather information from and to dispense instructions to the posad. From these various contacts there has emerged a useful historical record. Proceedings of administrative institutions, such as the magistracy and the commerce and manufacturing colleges, provide a running record of a good many administrative and economic concerns of the towns. Petitions drawn up at the initiative of local merchant guilds, along with depositions presented on request to special government agencies such as the Commission on Commerce of 1758-1762, the Codification Commission of 1754-1766, and the Great Commission of Catherine II, outline specific problems that confronted the posad and offer remedies for them.

Among the extant materials, the richest source for the attitudes of the townsmen is the collection of instructions from the cities to the Great Commission convened by Catherine II in 1767 to codify the laws.[4] These documents from cities great and small yield an abundance of complaints, proposed improvements, and general observations concerning life and labor in the posad. While these reports were all drafted in the early 1760s, the appearance in them of a number of perennial themes, along with the very nature of the drafting process that relied on earlier petitionary documents, suggests that the attitudes they expressed can be considered characteristic of the posad world view for the greater part of the century, certainly from the time of Peter I. The following reconstruction of the outlook of the urban taxpayers is based primarily on the instructions to the commission, supplemented when appropriate by other materials drawn from mid-eighteenth-century petitions and depositions.

Any effort at characterizing the outlook of the townsmen that is based largely on the Great Commission data carries with it an implicit bias in favor of the leading guild merchants. The wealth they enjoyed, coupled with their power over the rank and file townsmen, which the tax system did so much to reinforce, made these more aggressive and articulate merchants the natural spokesmen for the interests of the cities. Almost all city instructions to the Great Commission were drawn up by men who were true merchants by profession and reflect their annoyances and desires. It is not clear how well the voice of the little man comes through the instructions, but this much seems certain: the instructions do not favor the extraordinarily successful (the instructions are particularly hostile to the merchant-manufacturer and his privileges) nor do they ignore some of the concerns of the posad poor (their need for land is cogently argued). The instructions, then, may well represent a broad middle ground onto which a majority of the posad, rich and poor alike, were forced to stand in defense of the interests that they did have in common.

THE ESTATE MENTALITY

The overall image of the posadskie liudi is not particularly flattering to them. More is at issue here than their failure to become more effective, competitive merchants and manufacturers or the subservient and often degrading role forced on them by the service system, though these were surely contributing factors to that image. More broadly speaking, their demeanor betrayed a striking narrowness of vision and timidity of action. When threats to their interests arose, the townsmen eschewed direct action that might have made them masters of the situation and chose instead in almost every instance to reassert their claims to a traditional position and to seek assistance from the state in enforcing those claims.

In the exceptional case when opportunity did knock, during the Time of Troubles, the townsmen seemed content to rest upon their contribution to the expulsion of the Poles, for they did not follow that achievement by any noteworthy efforts to extend their power or will over either local or national affairs. And when the Petrine reforms presented, albeit in quite different circumstances, an opportunity for the townsmen to forge a new city order, they once again failed to seize the chance. The image gains added strength from the accounts of foreigners, which often tend to make the townsmen appear not just traditional-minded and cautious, but downright slowwitted. But there is no reason to believe that the Russian townsmen constituted an innately inept lot of individuals, or that they willfully pursued policies contrary to their perceived interests. Beneath the timidity and apparent narrowness of vision there was an approach to the world that was not at all unreasonable. The estate mentality of the townsmen was a rational response to the situation in which they found themselves.

The defense of their interests, persistent and consistent across the better part of the eighteenth century, reveals the deep roots of the townsmen's estate mentality. Centuries of history had shaped their role as Russia's urban commercial and manufacturing estate, and the Law Code of 1649 had formally confirmed that role, giving the force of law both to the privileges of the posad and to the closed character of posad society. It is, perhaps, a measure of the appropriateness of the settlement of 1649 that the principles on which it was based still galvanized the energies of the townsmen more than a century later. Whether in economics, in the structure of posad society, or in the political sphere, the eighteenth-century townsmen strove to preserve and to strengthen their traditional estate rights. Moreover, the manner in which they pursued this end was no less traditional: that is, the townsmen sought assistance from the central government. The long, intimate relationship of posad and state, in which the former party had been most often supplicant and the latter party the benefactor—and a fickle one, at that—had conditioned this approach. Given the internal weaknesses of the posad and the state's position as ultimate arbiter of social relations in the country, no other means for achieving posad objectives seems possible.

Economic considerations lay at the heart of the posad estate mentality. The precarious nature of the posad economy called for the most scrupulous protection of the townsmen's mercantile and manufacturing interests. All threats to the urban economy had to be combatted forthwith, not only from feelings of class or estate pride, but also from the belief that survival itself was at stake. And the townsmen saw the best hope for their economic survival in securing the privileged position they had won in the seventeenth century, one that had given them virtual monopoly rights within the cities. It is not surprising, then, that in their complaints and recommendations to the government, the townsmen came on most vigorously in opposition to interference in the posad economy by other social groups. The peasantry, of course, were a favorite—and perennial —target of posad ire. Objections to their nonagricultural pursuits were raised throughout the century, but nowhere more eloquently nor more fully than in the city instructions to the Great Commission. Among the peasantry, the Nizhnii-Novgorod merchantry pointed out, "many are occupied with commerce, buying courts from various ranks of people in Nizhnii-Novgorod and constructing on them stone and wood buildings, many live on posad lands and also have in the various trade rows their very own shops and warehouses, and willfully call themselves merchants."[5] Vartanov notes that not all objections to peasant commercial activity sprang from such a clear-cut feeling of pure class interest, that is, from a sense that humble agriculturalists were infringing on the estate rights of the merchantry. On the one hand, he notes, some merchants from small cities spoke out most strongly against the right of peasants to trade in village markets and at rural fairs. Apparently these merchants found the local city markets inadequate to support themselves and turned of necessity to rural operations. Peasant competition thus struck at their very livelihood. On the other hand, large-city merchants found their profits lowered by the high volume (and hence lower prices) of raw materials and manufactured items unloaded onto the big-city markets by the numerous trading peasants attracted to the bustling trade centers.[6] Whatever the motive may have been, complaints directed both to the Commission on Commerce (1758-1762) and to the Great Commission displayed the merchants' broadly based hostility to the commercial activities of the peasantry.

Peasants did not constitute the sole source of competition, however, for other social groups engaged in trade and manufacturing as well. Some of the instructions to the Great Commission attempted to rule out competition from all corners in defense of the estate rights of the merchants. The Arkhangel instruction, for example, staked out a broad claim to the effect that the merchants "alone are to be occupied with trade, manufacture, and workshops, with the full exclusion from this right of all other ranks in the state and under the threat of confiscation."[7] The Simbirsk report went a step further, asking that in the future only merchants be allowed to own factories and shops, with the exception of mining enterprises.[8]

It was not just direct, open competition from other social classes that imperiled the posad's urban economic privileges; there were other, less visible but no less crucial constraints on their business undertakings. One of the chief complaints of the townsmen concerned the inadequate land resources at their disposal. No less than forty-one of the fifty-seven city instructions to the Great Commission cited the scarcity of usable urban real estate and beseeched the government to redress the situation.[9]

The townsmen needed additional land for two radically different purposes. On the one hand, instructions from many cities pointed out that the merchants had no sites on which to establish stalls, shops, and warehouses. In Rybinsk, for example, commercial activities were hemmed in on all sides by gentry land. And the gentry, for their part, were unwilling to surrender these valuable lands within or near cities, preferring to use them for farming or as locations from which their own peasants could engage in trade in competition with the townsmen.[10] In either case, gentry land prevented the expansion of a commercial or manufacturing suburb and sharply curtailed the expansion of posad economic activities.

On the other hand, many city dwellers wanted, and needed, agricultural land—meadows, forests, pasture land, and the like. And they expressly stated that such property would be put to use for the raising of crops and livestock. The Soviet historian Iu. R. Klokman suggested that cities of the Russian south suffered most from a shortage of agricultural land because truck gardening figured prominently in the economy of that region,[11] but persuasive arguments on the need for farmland came from posady in the relatively infertile north as well. The Kargopol' instruction, for example, noted that "Among those possessors [of land in the *volost'*] there are even posad people [from Kargopol'] who have no home or merchant activities, but live by farming on their own rural parcels of land, like peasants."[12] Finally, even the Moscow instruction, representing one of the country's most highly developed commercial and manufacturing centers, called to the sovereign's attention the need for more pasture land at the disposal of the urban dwellers.

A long time ago a vast space for the pasturage of cattle was set aside for use by the inhabitants of this city, according to the size of their households, but since that time, the city has expanded and most of that space has been settled and built up, and such a small part of the meadow land remains that it is almost impossible to feed cattle in the summer. Because of our extreme need we seek to bring to the hearing of Her Imperial Majesty this, our most humble request, that from the highest mercy would be granted to our city, according to need, an addition to this pasture land.[13]

The conclusion seems inescapable that in the 1760s many Russian townsmen depended wholly or in part on the produce of their own agricultural pursuits.

The many uses—commercial, industrial, and agricultural—to which the townsmen put land meant that an adequate land fund had to be at their disposal if the posad economy were to thrive. The defense of traditional rights to land and the concomitant attack on encroachments on that right thus constituted an integral part of the economic dimension of the townsmen's estate mentality. Moreover, the practice of petitioning the sovereign for assistance in retaining old land or securing new reflected the suppliant nature of the townsmen's outlook. Even in areas as vital to the health of the posad economy as land relations, the townsmen were unable, by themselves, to control their destiny.

The townsmen's economic problems were not, strictly speaking, those of the marketplace alone—they had a strong social character as well. Whether they were merchants in need of shop space or impoverished laborers in need of a few acres to eke out a living, the townsmen were constrained in their pursuit of land by a property system controlled by a powerful landed gentry unwilling to make sacrifices of wealth or principle to urban interests. It was to be some time yet before the axe rang out in the cherry orchard. And it was this same landed gentry which, through the instrument of its enserfed rural population, competed directly in the marketplace with the townsmen, or, at the very least, gave protection to the initiatives of their serfs who so competed. With the social hierarchy what it was, the townsmen could not confront the gentry head on, but had to turn once again, petition in hand, to the state. But that was hardly an adequate recourse, for even though a number of Russian statesmen were sympathetic in principle to the needs of the merchants, as members of the gentry they could hardly be expected to set aside their own class prerogatives.

Frustration with gentry-built roadblocks in the path of posad economic development were real enough and certainly contributed to the formation of the posad world view. But the social concern that most shaped the estate mentality of the townsmen had to be the perceived need to defend at all costs the basic structure of the posad commune. Not only was the commune the focus of fiscal-administrative affairs, it was the organization that gave coherence and a voice to the diverse lot of the tsar's urban taxpayers. Threats to its integrity struck at the very foundations of posad society, putting at risk its continued, stable existence. In particular, the townsmen looked with horror on any breach of the principle of mutuality that governed the commune's inner workings. The clearest expression of this concern can be found in the townsmen's opposition to privileged manufacturers. The government, eager to promote industrial expansion, had bestowed a number of privileges on those who obtained licenses to manufacture. In addition to the economic privileges mentioned in an earlier chapter, the manufacturers enjoyed reductions and exemptions from taxes and often complete exemption from service obligations. Frequently their employees shared in these boons. These benefits to the manufacturers were perceived by the townsmen to be detrimental to their interests, as the following instruction from Moscow relates:

> Not only the local merchants, but even the whole meshchanstvo in general bear not a little burden from the emancipation from all services and civil taxes of factory owners and shop owners and company owners, as well as those promoted to various ranks, for not only they themselves, but even those entrusted to them are free from this. Your most humble subjects ask that all of them, as city inhabihants, without exception exist under one law with the meshchanstvo and bear equal taxes.[14]

The departure of an able-bodied man from the tax rolls was serious enough, but there were still other problems that stemmed from the privileged position of the manufacturer. In legal matters the factory owner was subject directly to the Manufacture College or to the Mining College, depending on the nature of his business. Hence, in a dispute between a merchant and an industrialist, the issue was resolved in one of those two colleges, and, to hear the merchants tell it, the decision always favored their adversaries.

The following tale from Syzran' shows just how troublesome a factory owner could be to the posad. An enterprising local merchant entered into a partnership with a local manufacturer and on the basis of that relationship persuaded the Manufacture College to release him from the tax rolls and from legal jurisdiction of the Syzran' posad. In addition to the loss of a substantial taxpayer, the posad had to suffer further insults from the man. Although technically a manufacturer, he continued his mercantile operations at a considerable advantage over the tax-paying merchants of the town. Anyone who objected too strenuously ran the risk of a physical beating and forced employment in this man's factories for little or no recompense.[15] At times, the privileged position of a manufacturer could lead to outright political control of a locality. In Kazan', for example, a successful cloth manufacturer paid the poll tax assessments for a hundred individuals who then dutifully voted for his candidates for the local magistracy.[16] So it is understandable that the posad fought against the privileges of the factory owners and demanded ultimately that all manufacturing be located in the hands of the tax-paying townsmen.

These are, perhaps, extreme examples of the misfortune that could be visited upon posady by privileged manufacturers; for the most part, it was simple resentment on the part of the townsmen over the tax and service privileges of the manufacturers that provoked their hostility. This reaction represents but an updated version of earlier posad opposition to those who broke the bonds of the commune, either by becoming privileged corporation merchants or by simple flight. The principle remained the same—the need to hold all taxpayers, especially the more prosperous, within the fiscal administrative embrace of the posad, lest unmanageable burdens fall on all who remained. It was the seventeenth century repeated, only the privileged manufacturers replaced the gosti and hundreds as the offending parties.

The social component of the estate mentality—namely, the defense of the communal order of posad society against all manner of infringement —directly reflected the influence of the central government on the formation of the posad world view. First of all, the state granted privileges to manufacturers that exacerbated social frictions within the posad. Second, and of far greater importance, the state laid upon the posad registrants a vast array of tax and service burdens. It was the weight of these burdens that forced the commune to retain within its grasp, in self-defense as it were, men of radically different social and economic interests, often against their will. The refusal of the townsmen to countenance the departure of commune members lest the burdens on those remaining be too great had its origins in pressures from without, in the demands of tiaglo. Similarly, external pressures were at work in shaping the economic component of the townsmen's estate mentality. The need to protect the whole range of urban economic enterprise from outside competition compelled men of diverse interests to unite in defense of their estate rights, though here one cannot help but suspect that the townsmen were motivated by an inner consistency of purpose. The frequently complementary nature of their commercial activities and their officially sanctioned—if not maintained—position as *the* urban mercantile and manufacturing class must surely have given them a sense of identity independent of outside threats to it.

In addition to economic and social concerns, still another component of the posad estate mentality can be identified in the political aspirations of the townsmen. Although they had not compiled a distinguished record for initiative and originality in political matters, they did have strong views concerning the weaknesses of local government and the ways in which it could be improved. Dissatisfaction with existing institutions, especially the post of military governor, was widespread. The abuses of office perpetrated by the military governors and their gentry cohorts had become legendary. Numerous stories could be adduced, though one should suffice to illustrate the point. In Briansk the military governor, General Medem, confiscated without cause the lands and movable property of one Klimov, a member of the local posad commune. When Klimov dared to protest this brazen plundering, Medem rewarded the poor fellow with a public beating, and there the matter rested.[17]

To eliminate such mistreatment at the hands of military governors drawn from the gentry, the merchants called in their instructions to the Great Commission for an estate institution, composed wholly of posad people, which would administer the entire population of the city. In their search for precedents and principles with which to design an ideal city government, the authors of the instructions referred back to Peter's magistracy legislation. They called for the creation of a magistracy, or ratusha, its members elected from the local posad population, which would become the sole administrative organ in the cities. Subordinate only to a Main Magistracy at the center, the local institution would be freed from the noxious jurisdiction of provincial authorities. The new magistracy was to have both judicial and administrative functions. As a court it would operate strictly on an estate basis, handling cases involving posad people only. To protect court proceedings from outside influences, all magistracy decisions were to be final, with no appeals beyond the Main Magistracy. Administratively, the magistracy's competence would embrace the entire city population. In this respect, the most important power of the new institution would be its complete control over the local police.[18]

What the townsmen were advocating in these instructions was not city government to be managed by an institution composed of all inhabitants of the cities. Rather, they were espousing an estate institution, fully in the hands of the tax-paying townsmen, that would administer the entire city. As Latkin has argued persuasively, this demand parallels exactly the desire of the gentry at that time to govern the entire population of the countryside by means of estate-based gentry institutions.[19] In terms of content, the townsmen cannot be accused of radical innovation: plagiarism would perhaps be a better description, for they sought to recreate the magistracy much as Peter I had conceived it. Yet the act of claiming for the posad estate the right to govern the cities represented a step forward, a new assertiveness of the posad mentality. If the townsmen had been cool to the original Petrine reforms, it would appear that by mid-century they had come not only to accept some of the broader implications of an estate-oriented society, but to recognize the need for political action to obtain the maximum benefits for their own estate. It is, however, an ironic commentary on the political mentality of the townsmen as well as on their position in the political order that their efforts to extend posad political power were confined to a time-honored if not time-proven channel—the petition to sovereign authority.

Economic, administrative, and political considerations thus combined to give form and substance to the posad mentality. There was, however, yet another influence at work that reinforced the basic contours of that mentality: namely, the atmosphere of constraint that engulfed the townsmen. There were restraints on mobility, both the short-term annoyance of passports and the long-term difficulties of transferring place of business and residence; there were restraints on property acquisition and restraints on the securing of a hired labor force; there were constraints on the amount of time and energy a townsman might devote to his work, owing to the weight of service obligations; there was the ever-present risk to the fortunes of the wealthy arising from their personal financial responsibility for important state fiscal posts; and there were restraints arising from the precarious legal position of the townsmen, which left them subject always to capricious action by the government.[20] As if all this were not enough, one must add the difficult-to-measure, but no less real, constraints imposed upon the activities of the townsmen by their limited education and experience. It is hard to imagine that the Arkhangel posad, the majority of whose members were illiterate, was prepared to make the maximum contribution possible to urban economic development.[21] In the case of the townsmen, whose fortunes depended on a multitude of transactions best negotiated in free, open, and informed settings, these constraints proved particularly costly. To be sure, some posadskie liudi did surmount these hostile conditions to amass fortune, fame, and real influence. But as a group the townsmen suffered greatly from the infringements on their freedom of action. It seems only natural that they would proceed cautiously, looking askance at ventures that would in all likelihood founder in their constrained world.

The estate mentality the townsmen displayed in the mid-eighteenth century emerged naturally from their historical experience in the preceding century and a half. As such, it exhibited many of the hallmarks of a conservative approach to life: the protecting of existing conditions; hostility to change; and innovation within accepted, traditional boundaries and then only for the purpose of preserving the status quo.[22] This backward-looking mentality of the townsmen has come in for considerable criticism from historians. It has been held responsible for the failure of the townsmen to develop ideas and slogans suited to the dawn of the free-trade era and for their more general inability to take the lead in ushering in the capitalistic order. Soviet historians have had a particularly difficult time with the "unprogressive" aspirations of the posad. N. L. Rubinshtein, for example, in his impressively thorough study of the codification commission of Elizabeth, manages to dredge up a trait or two of progressive thinking among the merchants—for example, their hostility to monopolies—but eventually is forced to admit that by and large the estate mentality ruled. Rubinshtein's problem is of less interest, however, than his explanation for the persistence of the estate mentality within the posad: he attributes its longevity and hardiness to the defensiveness of the posad in the face of a number of potentially damaging challenges.[23]

It may seem unduly negative to focus on the defensiveness of the commune as a prime force in shaping the outlook of its members. But it must be borne in mind that the commune was composed of individuals forced, whether they liked it or not, into a collective life together. With the pressures of economic competition and of state responsibilities bearing ever more heavily upon them, they can be forgiven for circling the wagons in defense of the privileges they could rightly claim and of the social organization that kept them whole. One could hardly expect new ideas to come from the posad in such circumstances. Moreover, if innovation and change were to arise within the posad it is likely that they would appear among those groups pressing at the edges of communal existence. Yet preservation of the commune demanded that precisely those individuals be drawn back into the center, if at all possible. Those who argue, as does Pazhitnov, that the Russian bourgeoisie failed in their historically appointed mission, thanks in part to internal divisions in the posad, surely hold a mistaken notion of social change.[24] It was not the center of an often conservatively-oriented Western European bourgeoisie that pushed history on; it was its more adventurous leading edge. Similarly for Russia, it was not division within the posad, but an enforced and in many respects artificial unity that kept the townsmen operating in their accustomed fashion. Communal membership was, in effect, the lowest common denominator among posad registrants. The estate voice with which the commune spoke did not begin to represent the broad range of opinion within the posad, but it is quite likely that it did represent an almost reflexive response of the bulk of the townsmen to the challenges of the outside world.

THE SOCIAL STATUS OF THE TOWNSMEN

Repairing to their notions of estate, the townsmen found firm ground from which to advance their claims to a unique role in Russian society, one embedded in the lawful order of things and deserving of support from the central government. But for all their rights and privileges, in law at any rate, the townsmen were keenly aware that they were not the first estate of the realm. Again, the various formal expressions of posad sentiment, especially the city instructions to the Great Commission, are most revealing. In them the townsmen—especially the leading guild merchants—sounded a persistent theme: they suffered intolerably from a number of legal disabilities that surely were not appropriate to men of their worth and dignity. Of course, this reaction was brought on in part by the real economic or personal hardships that were the by-products of these disabilities, but it was also based on the denigration of the townsmen's social status that was implicit in them. Indeed, a number of complaints were of a purely social character and unquestionably reflected the humiliation the merchants felt at having to accept crumbs at the gentry table of social prerogatives. The instructions, typically, went on to argue that the state should lift these disabilities and take further steps to raise the status of the townsmen.

The poll tax, from Peter's time the basis of personal taxation in Russia, turns out to have been not only economically harmful to the merchants, but socially degrading as well. By subjecting them to an imposition borne also by the peasantry, the argument went, the poll tax reduced the merchantry to the social level of the peasants: that was reason enough for the townsmen to want emancipation from it.[25] A similar annoyance was conscription, to which the merchants were also subject along with the peasantry. Because of the dislocation that conscription brought to businesses when an owner or principal agent had to depart for the army, the merchants tried to persuade the government to free them from the obligation or at least to allow them to substitute a money payment for actual service. For a brief period, 1722-1726, a merchant could buy his way out of the army for a fixed sum, but thereafter either he or a substitute individual had to bear arms personally.[26]

The quartering of soldiers must surely rank as one of the most onerous responsibilities to fall on the shoulders of the merchants. Not only did the cost of feeding the troops strain to the breaking point many a domestic budget, but the soldiers often reduced to shambles the homes of humble citizens. Whole kennels of hounds on occasion joined officers as unwelcome, but unavoidable, house guests. The quartering obligation also entailed feeding and housing civil officials while they were performing their duties in the cities and towns.[27]

Another source of annoyance to the townsmen lay in the area of jurisprudence, both criminal and civil. Many instructions to the Great Commission argued that corporal punishment was unbefitting the dignity of a merchant and that in its place monetary fines should be instituted. Some instructions cited abuses of the townsmen's property rights and inadequate relief from such actions, while others asked that their homes be made inviolable by all persons excepting policemen in pursuit of criminals.[28] Clearly, the townsmen did not feel that they were receiving either fair or fitting treatment before the law.

In addition to the burdens and restrictions imposed upon them by law, the townsmen suffered the cruelest kind of snobbery directed by a condescending gentry. So low was the repute of the merchant's calling that Peter I found it difficult to persuade talented young men to pursue a mercantile career. To counteract the prevailing mood, the tsar ordered that "when any cadets from gentry families wish to enter the ranks of the merchants . . . neither they nor their families are to be placed in any dishonor [*bezchestie*], orally or in writing."[29] At the time of the Great Commission, the instruction from Karachev asked that "the gentry be prohibited from scorning the merchants and calling them peasants [*muzhiki*]."[30] Though the merchants took umbrage at such treatment, there must surely have been some justification, especially in the smaller cities, for their being confused with peasants.

The antagonism between noble and merchant was clearly apparent to foreigners, if one can judge by the following encounter of the British traveller William Coxe shortly after his arrival in Russia in 1772.

> The service being finished, we presented ourselves to the governor, who to our surprise, received us with an air of coldness, which made much of an impression on our interpreter, that he could not be persuaded to utter a single word. At length a gentlemen in the governor's train accosted us in French, and inquired our business. Upon informing him, that we were English gentlemen who desire a passport, and an order for horses, he told us with a smile that the plainness of our dresses had raised a suspicion of our being tradesmen: but he was not ignorant that English gentlemen seldom wore lace on their clothes, or swords on a journey.[31]

For those further down the ladder of posad society, the contempt of the gentry was even greater. The very term *meshchanin* appears to have carried strong overtones of social inferiority.[32]

Given such feelings, it is not surprising that the city instructions put forth several recommendations whose purpose was to enhance the social status of the Russian merchant. One very direct way to begin an assault on the privileged position of the gentry was to demand the right to possess domestic servants, and some instructions did just that. There was nothing innovative about this request; through most of the eighteenth-century merchants had owned domestics and many did so at the time of the Great Commission. As free citizens of the country, the merchants felt they were entitled to secure the services of the unfree. And, of course, there was the added benefit of having ready substitutes for military obligations. Quite understandably the gentry opposed this encroachment on their prerogatives and continually pressured the government to deny merchants the right to have domestics. The government yielded partially in 1746 when it ordered all posad people to dispose of serfs not registered to them at the time of the first census and forbade them to obtain new ones. It was in hopes of securing the repeal of this law that the city reports laid claim to the merchants' right to own domestic serfs.[33]

To ensure more social respect, the merchants called for stiffer penalties than those in effect for actions that brought dishonor to them or to their families. Suggested fines ranged as high as 200 rubles for insults to first-guild merchants.[34] The merchants further sought, apparently as an outward sign of their worth, the right to wear swords, although the authors of these requests could not decide whether the honor should be restricted to magistracy officials or granted to all posad people of average standing or better.[35]

However much the townsmen may have felt themselves worthy of honor and respect—and again, it should be stressed that these opinions emerged from the leadership of the guild merchantry—their humble petitions to a gentry-controlled government betray a deep-seated sense of inferiority. The surest sign of this negative self-image can be found in the desire of successful merchants and manufacturers to escape the posad milieu: that is, to become gentry. However much men may seek the power that money confers, they also seek the recognition and respect that only proper social position can bestow. In early modern Russia, as elsewhere, the landed gentry retained a firm hold on their position as the premier estate of the realm, with all the political, social, and economic benefits that followed from it. Wealthy, socially ambitious merchants had but one road open to them, and that was the rocky, but ultimately passable road to ennoblement.

During the reign of Peter I, noble status could be obtained relatively easily, for the tsar was eager to reward those among his subjects who contributed to the advancement of the country by successful participation in commerce and manufacturing. As the century progressed, however, and the political power of the gentry waxed, more and more obstacles to ennoblement sprang up. Still, a number of Russia's wealthier businessmen, through means fair and foul, gained access to the promised land of gentry Russia. The following examples, drawn largely from the reign of Catherine II, show that even while the leading guild merchants were enumerating their estate rights and proclaiming their worth, a handful of their wealthiest compatriots were scrambling up the social ladder.

Many roads led from posad society. For A. F. Turchaninov the good will of the sovereign opened the way. The owner of a few, moderate-sized metallurgical plants, he armed his workers and led them in the defense of their towns against the onslaught of Pugachev's armies. For these labors in behalf of the existing order, he was elevated to gentry status by a grateful Catherine.[36] More commonly, the establishment of a vital industry opened the door to ennoblement. In 1744 the government made A. A. Goncharov a collegiate assessor in appreciation for the sailcloth and cotton factories he had set up. Similarly, in 1758 the copper magnate I. V. Tverdyshev achieved noble rank for his role in the development of Russia's metallurgical industry.[37]

Ambitious merchants and manufacturers did not sit humbly on the sidelines, waiting for an omniscient and benevolent government to recognize their contributions to society. The honors and economic privileges that flowed from gentry rank constituted a powerful incentive to pursue social advancement by a wide variety of means. The struggles of the Batashov family for ennoblement provide a colorful and instructive case history.

Ivan and Andrei Batashov were the developers and owners of several steel-producing plants in Orenburg province. Along with two other industrialists from the area, they petitioned the Mining College in 1765 to grant them gentry status and to release their workers from the poll tax. The college responded favorably, but the Senate turned them down. A second effort involved suggesting to the admiralty that prompt fulfillment of contracts might be impaired if similar conditions were not met. Again, they received support from the government agency to which they turned, but were rejected by the final authority, this time by the State Council.

On their third attempt, the brothers abandoned a direct frontal assault on gentry status in favor of a more devious route. They had a genealogy prepared demonstrating that the roots of their gentry rank were sunk deeply in the soil of seventeenth-century Russia (1622 to be precise), even though the document indicated, without explanation, that the last five generations of Batashovy had been tax-paying residents of the Tula arms suburb. Depositions from forty-six gentry families supported their case. In the face of such empirical evidence, the Senate yielded and the empress concurred. In 1783 Andrei and Ivan Batashov received patents of nobility.[38]

According to N. I. Pavlenko, this strategy was followed often in the last quarter of the century, though not always with the same result. In the process, hundreds of thousands of rubles passed from the hands of merchants and manufacturers into the outstretched palms of government officials, indigent gentry, and clever genealogists.

Apparently, the nouveau gentry spared neither effort nor expense to imitate slavishly the gentry mode of living. In fact, the new initiates had at their disposal far greater resources than did the overwhelming majority of the gentry. As a consequence, they lived in a manner matched only by a small group of the oldest and wealthiest hereditary nobles. They built large manor houses complete with libraries, elegant furniture, and works of art. They surrounded themselves with a full complement of domestics, done up in the finest livery, and they learned to hunt to hounds.[39] And, as Prince Shcherbatov pointed out gleefully in one of his diatribes against the practice of ennobling merchants, the new gentry went through their fortunes with lightning speed.[40]

On the basis of the case histories that Pavlenko has studied, some of which have been recounted above, the movement of urban taxpayers from the posad to gentry status appears to have followed a fairly well-established route. From humble beginnings as posad craftsmen or merchants, the townsmen moved on to become privileged manufacturers and then finally achieved the rank of gentry. Such a pattern might suggest that those who so advanced might well have been motivated by a desire to gain the gentry privilege of purchasing inhabited property so that they might exploit the serf labor on it in various industrial enterprises. Petitions of those seeking ennoblement testify to this intent, as do the recorded purchases of land and serfs by newly arrived gentry. But the fact remains that only a minority of those who made the jump to gentry society enjoyed the right to buy peasants, for that privilege was jealously guarded by the aristocracy of birth. It would appear, then, that the overall attractiveness of gentry rank—not just its economic perquisites—prompted commercial and industrial magnates to abandon their own social origins.[41]

In the hierarchy of Russian society, the gentry had long been predominant, but the appeal of gentry society to outsiders surely varied over the years. In the middle of the seventeenth century, for example, there must have been few incentives for the townsmen to abandon their estate (however troubled it was) in pursuit of gentry status, for the middle service gentry were experiencing severe problems of their own at that time. But a century later and beyond, the signs of gentry ascendancy lay all about, too conspicuous to be ignored. Their state service obligations had been steadily reduced in the post-Petrine period and finally abolished completely. They exercised virtually exclusive rights to the possession of landed property and controlled a preponderant share of the country's work force. Catherine II had granted them a monopoly over liquor distillation and allowed them freely to enter the world of commerce and manufacture. Gentry held the most important positions in the government and used them in defense of their estate interests. Moreover, the gentry had from time immemorial enjoyed the lion's share of the privileges of station, those social honors and prerogatives that do so much for the ego. As a merchant, a clever man could amass a fortune—but little more. As a member of the gentry, all things seemed possible.

Obviously the sense of social inferiority that led successful members of the mercantile and manufacturing community to seek ennoblement stands witness to the supreme role of the gentry in Russian society. But the townsmen's understanding of their own relative status was not the product of simple envy: it also had deep roots in the frustration and weakness of the posadskie liudi in the very spheres of activity that pertained specially to their class. In spite of being what one might call the "official" town dwellers of Russia, they were not even masters of their own environment, the town. Subject to political control by agents (usually gentry) of the central government, continually harassed in one manner or another by the social groups resident in the towns, and burdened with a set of services for country and city that brought them little in return, the townsmen could lay no claim to full and substantial control of the towns. Even those who arrived at the summit of posad society found themselves masters of a small hillock in what was often hostile territory. It was this deeper reality, of an enfeebled posad society unable to dominate its own ambience or to satisfactorily reward its best, that gave force in social reality to the pretensions of an ascendant gentry.

Such were the influences that shaped the attitudes of the townsmen. Though these attitudes have struck many observers as peculiarly Russian, in fact they reflect a far more widespread phenomenon. The narrow, defensive, and suppliant approach to the world that so permeated the thought of the posadskie liudi goes hand in hand with the subordinate economic, social, and political status that has characterized commercial classes in preindustrial societies the world over. For the majority of the mercantile population in such surroundings, accommodation with society's powerful—usually on the latter's terms—holds first priority, though for an aggressive minority the possibility of escape from subordination by ascent into the dominant class or estate exercises a certain attraction. The feeling of inferiority and the actions that flow from it proved as difficult for the townsmen to relinquish voluntarily as they have proved difficult for reform-minded sovereigns to stamp out.

In these circumstances, one feels compelled to view with some sympathy the plight of the townsmen. Limited in their resources, pressured by competition from all sides, and hemmed in and weighed down by state regulations and demands, they lived a life of many necessities and few choices. The estate mentality that emerged must, therefore, be regarded as a reasonable and understandable reaction to a harsh reality. The posad simply did not have the capacity to do much more than it did in any area of life, and to have made exaggerated claims on its own behalf would have amounted to ludicrous posturing. Given this context, the cautious, tradition-oriented outlook of the townsmen was to serve them well for more than a century. It was to become a handicap only when the basic conditions that brought it into being changed.

CHAPTER EIGHT

The Transitional Era:
1750-1770

THE POSAD ORDER that reached full flower during the second quarter of the eighteenth century had deep roots in the experience of early
modern Russia. It had evolved gradually over more than a century,
shaped by three of the most powerful forces in national life: the basic
poverty of the country and in particular the poverty of the cities; service-
oriented social relations; and the ever-expanding apparatus of the autocratic state. The posad order occupied a firm and apparently stable place
in the institutional structure of the land. But such deeply rooted institutions, however traditional and resistant to change they may be, are not
immune to alterations in the complex of forces that bring them into being
and sustain them. Even as the posad order reached its fullest development, forces were at work in the society that would erode and eventually
destroy it. New directions in economic life, demographic movements,
and modifications of the service system that foreshadowed more profound changes in state administration—all stood witness to the forces of
change. In combination they challenged the economic basis of the posad,
altered the character of the cities, and weakened the crucial service relationship that had lain at the heart of the posad order.

It is impossible to identify a single agency that might be held responsible for these changes. Although the government, for example, did have
a hand, through legislation of one kind or another, in shaping the new
directions of city life, there seems to have been no conscious policy behind its actions; indeed, the government leaders neither desired nor
planned a phasing-out of the service-oriented posad order. It would be
equally erroneous to see the posadskie liudi, or any other element of the
city population for that matter, as the driving force of innovation. Not
only did the townsmen lack the means to initiate and sustain social
change, by attitude and interest they found themselves largely in opposition to the course of events that every day impinged more noticeably on
their traditional way of life. The real key to the breakdown of the service
city lies, therefore, neither in government policy nor in the urgings of

posad society, but in the long-term economic and social transformation
of Russia.

THE ENLIVENING OF THE RURAL ECONOMY

From the mid-eighteenth century on, a number of economic forces appeared, which, combined with those set in motion by the Petrine reforms, imparted new directions and greater vigor to the national economy. This impetus for economic change came from rural Russia. In the
world of manufacture, stiff competition for the fabrikanty came from a
growing number of gentry entrepreneurs. Their challenge was particularly strong in textiles, most notably woolens. In 1773, for example,
nearly half (nineteen of forty) of the registered woolen mills belonged to
gentry.[1] The economic rationale is plain: the gentry possessed both the
raw materials and the labor force. The nonmechanized character of production meant that little in the way of capital goods was required. Before
entering competition with the existing merchant-owned industries, the
gentry faced only the relatively simple task of organizing production.

Even more significant in terms of its scope and impact on the national
economy was the upsurge in what is called peasant manufacturing. Peasants had, of course, traditionally engaged in the handicraft production of
all kinds of goods, both for their own consumption and for sale in villages and at nearby markets and fairs. This domestic craft activity continued to supplement agricultural activity right into the mid-eighteenth
century. P. A. Khromov estimates that more than 60 percent of the peasants in the Moscow district took part in domestic industry in the 1760s.[2]
But there were also signs of still more intensive peasant manufacturing
activity. By the middle of the century, ambitious serfs and state and economic peasants had begun to establish manufacturing enterprises that
produced not only for local consumption but for broader markets as
well.[3] Indeed, they proved themselves fully capable of competing with
enterprises in the hands of gentry or merchants. In some instances the
scale of peasant manufacturing was truly impressive. Grachev and Gare-
lin, serfs of Count Sheremet'ev, employed hundreds of fellow serfs—in
conditions of near-servitude, it should be noted—in their calico-printing
and linen-weaving factories.[4] Usually, however, the scale of peasant
enterprise was considerably smaller: it was the sheer number of operations that gave peasant manufacturing its impact.

A number of manufacturing settlements (variously called posady, slobody, and *selenniia*) sprang up, especially in the central areas of the
state. Many of these settlements were devoted to the manufacture of a
single product, such as semifinished woolens, but others had much more

diversified economies. An example of the latter would be Ostashkov, one of the most famous industrial suburbs. Located on the south shore of Lake Seliger and belonging in part to the Joseph Volokolamsk Monastery and in part to the Patriarch (to the Synod after 1729), Ostashkov's economic life embraced shipbuilding, tanning, metalworking, and fishing industries, along with a thriving role in the Volga basin transit trade.[5] The presence of such settlements did not go unnoticed at the time. Radishchev, in one of his commentaries on the domestic scene, took cognizance of them and provided an explanation for their emergence. "In other lands such a multiplication of crafts takes place among the city inhabitants, but in Russia the long winter, the small crop yields of several provinces, and poor agriculture transform the majority of villages into cities."[6]

Strictly speaking, many of the undertakings of the peasantry were illegal (*bezukaznyi*), for their founders were not properly licensed and registered by the Manufacture College. But in spite of numerous laws aimed at curbing or eliminating such businesses, they proved impossible to eradicate. Among the staunchest supporters of peasant enterprise were the landlords, who were no doubt pleased to see their *obrok*-paying subjects gainfully employed in manufacturing. Not only did the landlords prosper financially, but they also appear to have reaped a certain snob value from the possession of wealthy serf-enterpreneurs.[7] In time even the government recognized the futility of opposing peasant enterprise. In 1755, for example, the government forbad further export restrictions on narrow linen cloth—the product of rural cottage industry—thereby giving encouragement to rural enterprise, gentry and peasant alike, to expand production and broaden its markets.[8] Still another form of state support for rural manufacturing was embodied in three decrees aimed at reducing manufacturing enterprise in St. Petersburg, Moscow, and their immediate environs. While the ostensible reason for such a move was the shortage of fuel (both industry and domestic users relied heavily on wood fuel), there is also reason to believe that the presence of large numbers of factory workers in the big cities gave rise to fears of social unrest.[9] Whatever the motivation, this legislation countered the natural tendency of industry to concentrate in the leading cities of the state and in so doing gave a further boost to peasant enterprise. In the final analysis, however, the strength of peasant manufacturing lay not in assistance or encouragement from outside, but in the vigor and initiative of the peasant communities themselves.

The same driving entrepreneurial spirit manifested itself equally strongly in peasant trade operations. Such activity was, of course, nothing new, though it encountered a mixed reception from officialdom and unrelieved hostility from the townsmen. For the better part of the century, the peasant trader had to swim upstream against a current of restrictive legislation designed to keep each estate functioning in its own proper sphere, or, where that was a wholly impractical objective, to prevent one estate from unduly encroaching on the sphere of interest of another. Over the course of the century, however, the peasantry were net winners in their struggle for the legalization of their diverse forms of nonagricultural enterprise.

The legal story began with the reign of Peter I. In 1711 the tsar-reformer, impressed by the phenomenon of peasant trading, raised the question of opening up commercial opportunities to the entire population, and the Senate responded by bestowing its blessings on freedom of commerce. But angry merchants protested so vigorously that the government felt constrained to abandon its new policy.[10] A little more than a decade later, a resolution clarifying the responsibilities of the magistracy forbad peasants to trade in posady without first registering in the commune; a definite measure of turnover capital was made a prerequisite for registration.[11] This policy and the accompanying complicated process of registration remained in effect until the 1740s, when pressure for its revision mounted. In July 1743 the publication of a decree that routinely confirmed previous legislation on peasant trading aroused unexpectedly strong resistance from the peasants at Ostashkov, who, working through one of their nominal masters, the Synod, secured a government review of the whole issue.[12] Two years later, the government responded by permitting the peasants to trade in villages and hamlets along the major roads of the country, but only in goods that met specifically rural needs —plows, axes, sheepskin coats, and the like, and those in limited amounts.[13] While its stated intent was to safeguard the interests of the merchants, the law definitely contained a concession to the peasants, especially when seen in light of the longstanding blanket prohibition against their trading unless they were registered in a posad commune.

Still other concessions to the reality of peasant trade were to follow shortly. The elimination of internal customs duties in 1754, a move strongly supported by articulate guild merchants, also found favor among gentry with diversified economic interests who sought greater freedom of economic activity for their serfs. The small-scale peasant trader who operated on a narrow margin of profit had suffered from the many bridge and ferry tolls. Once relieved of them, he was able to trade in a much larger area.[14] The customs regulation of 1755, also a part of this massive overhaul of the revenue system, made yet another concession to the peasants, allowing them to trade in imported grain and in other foodstuffs, though it did prohibit them from trading at wharves in port cities.[15] All this was clearly a case of the law, always a step or two behind, trying to catch up with life.

In the second half of the eighteenth century, peasants traded a wide range of goods over a wide territory. They dealt in agricultural produce; in raw materials such as flax, hemp, and wool; in semifinished textiles; and in the products of local manufacturing, including clothing, household utensils, and farm implements. The geographic scope of their activities was equally broad. The peasants who traded in towns and those who sought formally to become tax-paying townsmen were only the tip of the iceberg.[16] A far larger number of peasants could be found in the weekly and biweekly markets in small villages, as well as at the great periodic fairs. A list of trade-fair sites in the 1780s, as compiled by M. D. Chulkov, shows that noncity fair sites outnumberd city sites by three to one.[17] As indicated earlier, some posad merchants and tradesmen did visit fairs of all types, but it is also true that many small fairs and markets attracted only peasant traders.

A quantitative evaluation of peasant trade is not now available and may never be, given the problems of evidence. But the record that does survive makes it abundantly clear that the movement of raw materials and finished goods across the vastness of Russia, in the eighteenth century as before, relied on the efforts of vast numbers of peasants, and, it should be stressed, not just small peasant operators dealing from packs on their backs. Klokman argues persuasively that the scale of operation of many peasant traders rendered their enterprise "indistinguishable from that of city merchants."[18]

The importance of peasant trade and manufacturing to the national economy argues forcefully against the notion that there existed a neat division of economic responsibilities along estate lines, with merchants and craftsmen handling goods production and exchange while the peasantry confined their labors to strictly agricultural pursuits. That situation had never existed in Russia, and it came no closer to reality in the eighteenth century—no matter how much emphasis one places on the apparent monopoly right of the guild merchants.

Why did the posad dweller and the peasant so often play the same economic roles? Surely the size of the country and the uneven spread of cities made it almost impossible for urban merchants alone to meet the needs of the rural population. Of equal or greater impact, however, was the relatively low technical level both of manufacturing and commerce during the eighteenth century. The townsmen, as a consequence, had little in the way of a competitive edge, either in the quality of product or in the cost of its manufacture, over peasant entrepreneurs. Thus while the townsmen had difficulty maintaining their economic estate rights, the peasants seized upon the competitiveness of their position to expand into non-agricultural pursuits. A merchant complaint to the Commission on Commerce in 1764 illustrates the ease with which peasants could move into manufacturing. It tells of peasants learning the nail-making trade in a city and then returning to their native villages to set up nail factories there.[19] So long as production remained labor-intensive, relied on relatively unskilled, unspecialized labor, and required little capital to set up, the door remained open for peasant enterprise.[20] In commercial matters the situation ought to have favored the merchants, if only because of their traditional connection with mercantile affairs, domestic and international. But, as argued earlier, they did not prove themselves particularly innovative in the face of competition at home and abroad. By and large the peasant trader and the townsman went about their business in much the same fashion—subject to high interest rates when they could obtain scarce capital; relying on cash or exchangeable commodites when it came time to close a deal; lacking support from more advanced forms of business organization; and working without many of the instruments of commerce that were fast becoming a regular feature of the Western European mercantile world.

If those were the general, background conditions that made feasible the upswing in peasant nonagricultural activities in the second half of the eighteenth century, one must look elsewhere for its more immediate cause. If shifting government policies are also relegated to the background—and appropriately so, since they tended to follow and reflect economic change, not lead it—then it seems likely that the principal impetus to change came from a growing money economy. Increasingly the presence of a cash economy diminished the importance of a host of feudal arrangements—especially payments in kind or in labor service—and gave incentive both to lord and peasant alike to deal in cash. Indeed, where proprietary serfs were concerned, the trend toward meeting their quitrent (*obrok*) obligations with cash was pronounced enough to cause Catherine II to comment about it—unfavorably, it should be noted, because it led to the breakdown of the old estate order. Of course, the money was to be made at fairs and in market villages and towns, and it was to those sites that the peasants flocked. At first they came with products of the soil or of rural manufacture, later they tended to settle down as traders, craftsmen, or simply as unskilled workers. As one might expect, peasants from the less fertile areas were the driving force in this movement away from agricultural pursuits. In the last years of the century, according to Blum, twenty percent of the men in Iaroslavl' guberniia and ten percent of the men in the Moscow province had passports. According to one observer, in many homes on the property of Prince

Golitsyn near Kaluga two-thirds of the work-age adults had jobs away from home.[21] Although these figures are drawn from Catherine's reign, the trend they represent was well under way at mid-century. Needless to say, the growing money economy also attracted state and economic peasants into its orbit; they, too, moved into nonagricultural pursuits along with the more enterprising proprietary serfs. In fact, judging by the rate at which they provided recruits for the guild merchantry, the latter two categories of peasants proved to be most successful; but one must bear in mind the legal obstacles that faced proprietary serfs seeking to transfer into the merchantry.[22]

This enlivening of the rural economy, and especially the accelerated pace of peasant nonagricultural activities, yields a portrait of the economy that seems radically at variance with the accepted wisdom that economic development goes hand in glove with a rising bourgeoisie. It is a picture that needs clarification.

THE EIGHTEENTH-CENTURY ECONOMY
IN HISTORICAL PERSPECTIVE

What precisely was the state of the national economy during the eighteenth century? The answer to that question has varied dramatically over the years. Early studies gave the century rather poor marks, except, of course, for the Petrine efforts to develop industry and commerce. More recent studies, their scope broadened to include peasant enterprise, have rendered a more positive evaluation. An emerging synthesis, based on works undertaken from a number of different perspectives, suggests that what was taking place in the Russian economy was a development of major moment. It is only in relation to that development that the economic fate of the townsmen can be properly understood.

Both prerevolutionary and early Soviet-period economic historians tended to be preoccupied with explanations for Russia's backwardness. Accordingly, they focused on structural weaknesses in those areas of the economy that have been traditionally associated with the emergence of modern economies—mercantile pursuits and manufacturing—and on government policies that either helped or hindered economic growth.[23] They paid particular attention to descriptive accounts of economic affairs, an approach that, given the technological level of Russian trade and manufacturing, reinforced their generally negative assessment of the country's economic development. Kulisher, for example, turned to accounts of Russian sharp practice and poor company organization to help explain the inability of the nation's merchants to meet foreign competitors on equal footing, and both Tugan-Baranovskii and Liashchenko emphasized primitive technology and poor quality of output in their analyses of eighteenth-century manufacturing.[24]

Much that these scholars uncovered, in particular their descriptive work, has retained its validity over the years. Russian industry was technologically primitive; the guilds on the whole did not maintain high levels of craftsmanship; and commerce was not as advanced as in the leading mercantile states. Yet this emphasis on the failures and weaknesses of urban-based trade and manufacture led these men, if not to ignore, then to misread the broader movements of the eighteenth-century Russian economy. They were certainly aware of the changing pattern of peasant economic pursuits, and, at least in Kizevetter's case, concerned about its adverse effect on the posad.[25] But their overall attitude toward economic growth prevented them from seeing the long-run potential in such developments. From their perspective the burgeoning of peasant commerce and manufacture seemed but an aberration from the prescribed course of things—from the well-known path of Western European bourgeois-dominated economic growth.

More recent scholarship, however, has had quite a different focus. Soviet economic historians, in studying the eighteenth century, have been wise enough not to confine their investigations to the activities of posad merchants and manufacturers only, but to take into account as well the flourishing enterprise, commercial and productive, of rural Russia, a task they have accomplished in meticulous detail.[26] Two main themes have emerged from their labors. First, when the entire national economy is taken into account, productive activity in Russia was definitely on the upswing during the century. The data show rising numbers of factories and workers as well as an increased volume of output.[27] Second, an ever more complex market system was in the process of formation, ranging from the markets of a single city and its hinterland, to regional markets, and on, finally, to the all-Russian market.[28] By the latter term Soviet scholars have in mind the appearance in the middle eighteenth century of a national market centered about Moscow, one that linked, however imperfectly, the remotest regions of the country with Moscow, and through Moscow with each other. The capacity to move goods was growing apace—or even ahead of—manufacturing capacity. Some aspects of this body of scholarship are open to question, but its basic thrust—namely, that the Russian economy was on the move in the eighteenth century—seems beyond challenge.

It is in the general assessment of that movement that the most interesting contributions of Soviet scholarship are to be found. Rather than looking askance, as their predecessors had, at rural economic activity as if it were an intruder on the proper order of things, they have chosen to look upon the spread of peasant trade and manufacturing as a salutary phenomenon, as a measure of the extent to which the peasantry had been drawn out of the nexus of the feudal economy and into the growing capitalistic order. In short, the rise of peasant nonagricultural activities implies the undermining of the social basis of the serf system. Pushing on from that point, a number of Soviet scholars now regard the years from 1750 on as the decisive moment in the formation of the capitalistic *uklad*. Though the term *uklad* remains somewhat vague, particularly in light of its central position in a system of scientific exposition, it refers to the appearance of sufficiently developed productive and market relations to provide a base for the definitive arrival of capitalism in the following century.[29] The significance of this argument lies in its recognition that whatever may have been the condition of the Russian economy relative to those of Western Europe, it was an economy unquestionably in the process of evolution. Slowly but surely, the serf-based economic order was giving way to an advancing capitalist order.

Even if one does not accept unquestioningly all of the Marxist framework, many of the observations and much of the data adduced in support of it mesh well with other scholarly perspectives on developing national economies. The dispersal of budding manufacturing establishments across the countryside, to take one example, fits in well with the patterns of growth associated with what some scholars choose to call the proto-industrial stage of development in Western Europe, that is, the stage of economic development that immediately preceded full industrialization.[30] During that stage, increases in population (and Russia's population more than doubled during the century) ran parallel with an increase in rural production of semifinished products, such as textiles. In Russia, as elsewhere, this broadening of production made it possible to supply a growing population with its necessities in the period prior to machine production. Moreover, it equipped a basically rural and agricultural work force with skills that they could take with them from cottage industry into concentrated urban factory settings—though in the case of Russia these were rudimentary skills indeed. In Russia, of course, the process had the added impact of contributing to the breakdown of the serf system, as the peasants were drawn into a growing market economy.

Another example of the parallels that exist between Soviet and non-Soviet studies of preindustrial development can be found in Gilbert Rozman's work on urban networks in eighteenth-century Russia. Rozman draws upon the vast body of socioeconomic data compiled by Soviet historians and reinterprets it in light of contemporary sociological theory, specifically, central-place theory.[31] In his judgment, the economic and demographic data indicate that Russia possessed a highly developed urban network, one that compared favorably with urban networks in England, France, and Japan—what the author calls "advanced premodern societies." Indeed, Rozman argues that this network was so well established by the end of the century that one can no longer describe Russia as backward, a claim that would surely have come as a surprise to a good many nineteenth- and twentieth-century advocates, from Witte to Khrushchev, of the idea that Russia needed to catch up with the modernized states. Nevertheless, Rozman's study does confirm from yet another perspective that powerful forces for change were at work in the second half of the eighteenth century. Thus, whether one writes of the capitalistic uklad, or of a proto-industrial period, or of Russia's progress from stage to stage in the evolution of its central-place hierarchy, what is described is an economic and social system in transition. The groundwork was being laid for the still broader transformation of the following century and a half.

If Soviet scholars have taken the lead in isolating the transitional era and in identifying its properties, they have not kept pace when it comes to describing the effects of this change upon the townsmen. One might say that a kind of love-hate relationship toward the posadskie liudi infuses the work of Soviet historians: on the one hand, the townsmen are the forerunners of the bourgeoisie and hence by definition a progressive force in the eighteenth century; on the other hand, the bourgeoisie are the great enemy of the socialist future. This ambiguity has produced in its better moments a variety of studies defending the Russian merchants against charges of utter incompetence and arguing that the urban economic scene was far more vigorous than earlier scholars had given it credit for being.[32] At other times, this ambiguity has resulted in bizzare attempts to demonstrate the unfair—almost infamous—nature of mercantile profits.[33] But as often as not, the townsmen have received muted treatment from Soviet scholarship.[34]

Whatever awkwardness has infused Soviet scholars' study of the townsmen, nevertheless, their work gives some sense of the effect that the period of transition had on the posad, both through its direct impact on the basic features of posad life and through a number of indirect influences on the cities and on state-administrative relations. In the long run, this socioeconomic transition proved decisive for the fate of the commune.

The enlivening of the rural economy struck a double blow directly at the economic interests of the townsmen. First, the presence of so many commercial-minded peasants in the cities, whether legally or illegally, made a mockery of the townsmen's claim to a monopoly of urban trade and manufacture. The peasants were there to share both the marketplace and the profits, and they were not about to be excluded. Second, the growth of rural enterprises reinforced rural self-sufficiency and thus helped to maintain the long-standing limitations on market opportunities available to the townsmen.[35] Indeed, the Soviet scholar V. N. Bernadskii boldly asserts that the emergence of rural manufacturing and commerce occurred "in a significant degree apart from the city, and perhaps even at the expense of the city."[36] In all likelihood he overstates his case, for the cities could not help but be drawn into any intensification of national economic life; the big fortunes amassed by some first-guild merchants attest to the fact. But even the first-guild merchants experienced rough times in the latter decades of the eighteenth century (though responsibility for their declining numbers and dwindling capital resources cannot be attributed solely to peasant competition: the inherent weaknesses of their own enterprise, along with rapidly mounting rates of taxation, must be given their due as well),[37] and it seems clear that the posad was not able to replenish the upper ranks of the guilds with men who had worked their way up from within the posad. In the second half of the century the guilds relied heavily on the trading peasantry for new blood.[38] That condition may be indicative of the health of the national economy, but it is also a sign that the posad economy was not flourishing during this period of transition. Most assuredly, initiative in national economic life lay outside the confines of the posad.

It was not just the economic interests of the posad that suffered from the new vigor in the rural economy; the traditional relationship that linked state and townsmen—a relationship that had defined the townsmen's economic prerogatives and established a basis for their defense—was put at risk. This serious danger to the posad order arose from the differing reactions of townsmen and state toward the changing economic scene. While the townsmen, predictably, looked backward, the state, somewhat less predictably, looked forward.

As was so often the case, it was competition from the outside, from the peasantry, that nurtured the townsmen's penchant to turn inward and to rally around their traditional claims to exclusivity in urban trade and manufacturing. The estate mentality of the townsmen, so clearly manifest in the instructions to the Great Commission, emerged at exactly that moment when the forward surge of peasant economic diversification had begun to make itself widely felt. True, the basic elements of that mentality had been present in posad society from the mid-seventeenth century on, but it was thanks to acutely felt economic and social threats that they were reasserted with such vigor and singleness of mind in the early years of Catherine's reign. There were, however, two unfortunate consequences of this reassertion of posad tradition. First, it was clearly out of phase with a changing socioeconomic reality, and therefore destined to fail. Second, it committed the posadskie liudi, by the force of logic, law, and tradition, to dependence on the state for protection rather than on their own resources as producers, merchants, and urban residents. This tack, too, was doomed to failure.

The problem, of course, is that the townsmen turned to the state at precisely that moment when the state had set its sail in quite another direction, one that turned away from the protection of special economic interests. The spirit of free trade was abroad in the land, and not surprisingly so, since its benefits would most surely fall upon the gentry and their economic protégés, the peasantry—and, it should quickly be noted, upon the state in the form of increased revenues. The reversal of government policy favoring monopolies, the continued extension of peasant trade privileges, and the opening-up of internal trade had all helped to undermine entrenched commercial interests—most often those of the townsmen. But the ultimate symbol of the new spirit lay neither in these actions nor in the few outspoken comments of Catherine II about free trade, but in the government decision of 1775 to open manufacturing to all parties. Henceforth, any subject of the crown could set up a manufacturing enterprise "without needing for this any permission from higher or lower authorities."[39] The posad had never really gotten full satisfaction from the government when it came to protection of vital economic interests, but it had at least received lip service to posad rights and privileges and some token assistance against threats to them. Now, however, the state was opting out, apparently abandoning the townsmen in a time of sharply felt economic distress.

DEMOGRAPHIC CHANGE

Thanks in part to substantial territorial acquisitions and in part to a steady, gradual natural increase, the population of the Russian empire grew from 15.6 million in 1719, the date of the first census revision, to 37.2 million in 1795. Allowing for roughly the same rate of growth for the twenty-four years not included in that reckoning, it seems likely that the population grew by slightly more than two and a half times from 1700 to 1800.[40] As for the cities, there may have been twice as many Russians living in them at the end of the century as at the beginning, though source problems make it difficult to be precise on this matter.[41] But even if the city population doubled, it remained well below ten percent of the nation's population throughout the period under study. Urbanization lay far in the future for Russia.

While changing conditions did permit the cities to make some sizable gains in population relative to the low number of urban dwellers at the beginning of the century, conditions were clearly incompatible with any sudden spurts of urban growth that would have led to a radical shift in the urban-rural balance. Restraints on mobility arose both from serfdom and from the generally restrictive character of social relations and made unlikely any large-scale shift of the rural population to the cities. Unhealthy conditions within the cities curtailed natural population growth. The need to extend the rudiments of city life to newly settled border areas worked against the concentration of population in the cities of central Russia and hence acted as a brake on the emergence of a more intensely developed urban milieu that would, of its own right, have fostered still more rapid urban population growth.[42] More cities, rather than rapidly expanding ones, was the order of the day. But for all the factors that worked against dramatic change in the urban population during the eighteenth century, the census data do have an important tale to tell. It is not so much a matter of growth per se, though growth there was, as of the changing composition of the urban population. A shift took place in the relative balance between the posadskie liudi and other urban residents that was of sufficient magnitude to alert the government to the changing character of the cities and ultimately to compel it to reevaluate its traditional understanding of the nature of the Russian city.

According to the tax rolls, although the number of posadskie liudi grew absolutely during the eighteenth century, their percentage of the total population of the empire remained constant. Depending on whose figures one takes—and there is considerable variation owing to incomplete study of the revision data—the posad population made up 2.3 to 3.2 percent of the total population between 1719 and 1786.[43] The stability of this relationship can be explained largely in terms of social and physical limitations on the growth of the urban population.

Quite apart from the restraining influence of serfdom on social mobility within the country, there were specific impedimenta to entry and exit from the posad, which helped to hold its membership at a relatively constant level. Leaving the posad, if only to relocate in another posad, had become extraordinarily difficult in the wake of the absolute prohibition on departure written into the *Ulozhenie* of 1649. That provision had been motivated in part by the government's desire to maintain a stable urban tax base, and its rigorous enforcement well into the eighteenth century attests to the continued adherence of the government to that principle. Yet there were times when this restrictive policy came into conflict with other state objectives and had to be set aside. In 1710, for example, Peter I ordered 15,000 craft masters to move to St. Petersburg, an action soon followed by a decree calling on large numbers of prosperous merchants to join him in his new commercial paradise.[44] Eventually, the requirements of the government itself and the needs of its commercial citizens brought about a relaxation of that most rigid article of the *Ulozhenie*; in 1744 a senatorial decree made resettlement of posad people legal provided that permission was obtained from the Main Magistracy.[45] This is one law that did not remain a dead letter, for in 1759 the entire posad population of Tomsk and environs was sent off to work in newly established factories at Nerchinsk.[46] But these cases were exceptions, brought on by particular exigencies of state administration. By and large the government sought to preserve a stable, well-distributed urban tax and service base.

It was not only the government which, for tax considerations, sought to keep the posad people confined to their legal residences. The communes themselves were most reluctant to let their members go, especially since those most eager to depart were usually the most successful businessmen and consequently the biggest taxpayers. Litigation between communes and those seeking exit from them dragged on interminably, and the decision did not by any means always favor the petitioner. Of course, not all those who were desirous of moving to another posad or who may have harbored thoughts of heading toward cities in the east or south bothered to go through legal channels; they simply left in the middle of the night or took extended trade journeys during the course of which they established residences in other parts of the country. To curb these practices, so potentially dangerous to the tax capabilities of a posad, the government threw up barriers even to temporary departures. A trip of more than thirty-two kilometers from the posad required a passport; persons applying for such passports had to pay in advance half of their yearly tax obligation.[47] As for outright exit from posad status— that privilege came, as noted earlier, to but a handful of the most ambitious and successful merchants and manufacturers.

If the posad did not readily let go of its members, neither did it open wide the door to outsiders, not even to those who were willing to assume the burdens of urban tiaglo. The process of entry into posad society was fraught with legalistic barriers. Peasants were the most likely candidates, but a long and costly road awaited the trading peasant seeking posad status. First, he had to secure permission from local and provisional government authorities, from his own rural commune, and from his landlord if he was a proprietary serf.[48] He then had to demonstrate not only that he engaged in trade and manufacturing, as had been the case in the seventeenth century, but also that he had sufficient capital to be enrolled in a guild. After that, he had to obtain the approval of the particular guild he wished to join. Finally, if the would-be merchant met all these tests, the government required him to pay double taxes, peasant and posad, until the next census.[49] These stringent requirements for entry into the posad not only served government fiscal interests, but also protected the commune against the incursion of marginal peasant traders whose ability to pay their full load of taxes was doubtful and who might become a burden for the posad wealthy at tax apportionment time. By limiting eligibility to truly successful peasant entrepreneurs that danger was obviated.

It might appear that the process was so arduous and the rewards so dubious that few would venture it. That was not the case, however. In the second half of the eighteenth century an ever-increasing number of peasants earned admission to the merchant guilds, although the absolute numbers were never great. Vartanov notes that the third census (1762) recorded 3,727 peasants in the process of becoming merchants. For Moscow province only, during the years 1742-1782, the number came to 1,506 men. But Vartanov goes on to argue that small as these numbers were relative to the total number of peasants engaged in commercial operations, the trading peasantry provided "the main source of filling up the ranks of the guild merchantry."[50] In the last two decades of the eighteenth century (when the posad commune was no longer the integral whole it was until 1775), for every ten guild merchants there was one trading peasant formally engaged in the process of becoming a merchant.[51] Thus, there was a small increase in the ranks of the urban commercial population from this source. The ranks of the posad were also swelled by the registration of whole villages engaged in mercantile and manufacturing operations, a matter that will be discussed later.

Another possible source of posad growth, the natural increase of the population, was limited by unhealthy conditions in the cities and by the poor medical services available to the townsmen. In times of plague, the losses were often staggering. Eighteen percent of the population of Kiev is believed to have perished in the plague of 1770-71. There were few doctors to help fight the disease, and the clergy steadfastly refused to approve the burning of the clothes of the dead, lest divine wrath direct some evil judgment on the city.[52] In Moscow the plague carried away between 50,000 and 100,000 people in the city itself and another 75,000 from the remainder of the province. The situation there degenerated until rioting broke out and rumors spread about the city that the doctors, secretly in alliance with the gentry, were spreading the disease rather than fighting it.[53] These are, admittedly, extreme cases; but one historian argues that in general the birth rate in the cities was not high enough to overcome the death rate.[54] Whether that assertion is correct or not, the unhealthful conditions in the city were clearly not conducive to a rapid growth of full-time urban residents.

The regulatory constraints on entry and exit from the posad precluded either a significant influx into or a large-scale exodus from the ranks of the posad population. That, combined with the limitations on a natural increase, kept the growth rate of the posad population roughly equal to that of the society as a whole.

The posadskie liudi, of course, were but one constituent element of the urban population. Any calculation of the total city population must include figures for city dwellers of other social background, but, unfortunately, reliable data on their presence are hard to come by. The figures usually given for the overall city population, 3 percent of the total population of the state for the early part of the eighteenth century and 4.1 percent for 1796, are based on Miliukov's tables.[55] They are quite misleading, however, for Miliukov regarded only the posadskie liudi as urban inhabitants, thus ignoring vast numbers of city dwellers of other social categories, and he underestimated the total population of the state. Recent estimates of the overall city population, confined largely to the second half of the eighteenth century—for which the data are more trustworthy—place the percentage of urban dwellers substantially higher. The Soviet historical demographer V. M. Kabuzan contends that city dwellers made up 8.3 percent of the total population late in the century, and Gilbert Rozman argues that the urban population ranged from 7.4 to 7.8 percent of the total population in 1744 to 8.4 to 8.8 percent in 1795.[56] The figures of Kabuzan and Rozman, the products of sophisticated techniques of analysis, clearly supersede population estimates derived from the narrowly based observations of Miliukov or Kizevetter. Unfortunately, the absence of trustworthy assessments of the city population for the early decades of the century makes it impossible to draw comparisons between the overall city population of the Petrine era and that of the second half of the eighteenth century.

The data are satisfactory, however, when it comes to an examination of the relationship of the posad population to the overall city population during the second half of the century, a period of significant social change. If one accepts Rozman's estimate that the overall city population ranged from 7.4 to 8.8 percent of the national population, then two important inferences can be drawn. First, the non-posad population of the cities was greater than the posad population from at least 1744 on. Whether the posad dwellers were always a minority is unclear, but that they were by the mid-eighteenth century seems firmly established. Indeed, Rozman states that the archival data he observed "Gave ample evidence that the *podat'* [taxable] strata formed a minority in the cities."[57] Second, the gap between the posad population and the remaining city dwellers was growing. In short, the cities were growing faster than their posady.

The explanations for this phenomenon vary, of course, from city to city. In St. Petersburg the number of people connected with one level or another of the bureaucracy mounted over the course of the century, along with those drawn from all walks of life who were attracted to centers of power. But for most cities, gains in population can be attributed to a massive influx of peasants seeking to ply trades or simply to hire themselves out as manual laborers. Some of these peasants became semipermanent residents who differed from posad people only in that they remained bound to their lords or communes and could, presumably, be recalled to agricultural pursuits. An even larger body of peasants appeared in the cities on a seasonal basis, usually during the winter months when outdoor activities came to a halt in the bitter cold. The same can also be said for the gentry, many of whom found winter in the city livelier, if not necessarily warmer. Contemporary observers estimated that the population of Moscow nearly doubled during the winter months.[58]

Some notion of the extent and character of this phenomenon can be derived from the experience of Moscow. The following figures reveal the growing presence of peasants who were sufficiently settled in the city to be registered by government authorities; there were, naturally, numerous peasants who managed to escape registration:[59]

Year	Continual taxable city people (posad people)	State peasants and serfs
1730	23,707	54,269
1788-1795	21,000	115,000

Still further evidence of the peasant influx is contained in the breakdown of the total city population by sex. In 1738, Moscow had 65,000 men and 73,000 women. By the period 1788-1795, these figures had reversed dramatically: 114,000 men and 61,000 women.[60] Only the large-scale migration of male workers without families could explain such a shift in the make-up of the city's population.

To be sure, Moscow was not all Russia, and there is no question that its economic predominance of the central area made it more attractive than most cities to peasants seeking income away from the village. Even so, there is evidence that, for all its incompleteness, suggests strongly that the migration of peasants to the city was a widespread phenomenon. There were, as noted earlier, the many instructions of city delegates to the Great Commission complaining about peasants who lived in the cities and competed with the local merchants. Then, there are data drawn from individual city records, such as the census figures for Penza during the years 1761-1762 which reveal a population of 502 merchants, 145 crafts-men, and 221 "trading peasants."[61] Finally, one might consider as a kind of indirect evidence the unlikelihood—given the poor sanitary conditions in the cities—that the overall increase in the city population during the century could be accounted for solely by the natural rate of increase of urban residents of all social classes.

Regrettably, more precise figures on this important trend are not avail-able. The problem is not so much one of scholarship, though better works based on archival records can be anticipated, as it is one of basic evidence. Some of the transients who flooded a city such as Moscow par-ticipated illegally in the city economy and made every effort to remain anonymous to the city authorities; others were present only for short pe-riods of time; still others settled in suburbs on the remote edges of the city where police power rarely extended. The government itself was basically ignorant of the size and make-up of the city population. Count Voron-tsov, head of the Commerce College, complained in 1775 that his office did not know "in round numbers how many merchants, guildsmen, craftsmen, and masters, and working people of all ages could be found in the cities of the state, trading and manufacturing within and outside the cities."[62] And at one point the Senate found it advisable to inform Potem-kin through a footnote to a report that city populations included "clerics, church dependents, postmen, one-courters, agricultural soldiers, former petty servitors, military personnel, Cherkassians, and Tatars."[63] The Senate might have added to this list of "uncounted" city dwellers the thousands of state peasants and serfs who were also present.

It was not just in established cities that commercially minded peasants congregated. They could also be found in increasing numbers in the vari-ous commercial and manufacturing suburbs that played such an impor-tant role in the expansion of rural enterprise. Because of their personal bondage to secular or clerical lords, however, these peasants remained legally classified as serfs regardless of their occupations, and their places of residence, though cities in terms of population concentration and eco-nomic function, were not cities in law. Ostashkov, mentioned earlier, was a prime example of such a settlement. Just how like posadskie liudi its peasant inhabitants were can be seen from the enrollment in 1753 of 589 Ostashkov traders into the merchant guilds. At that time, trade capi-tal valued at 300 rubles was necessary for entry into the ranks of the mer-chants, a figure that, it should be stressed, was attained by only a small percentage of officially registered posad "merchants."[64] This elevation of the top strata of Ostashkov's peasant-traders to merchant status was done in response to pleas by the parties involved, but it was only a temporary and inadequate expedient. The remaining peasants, rankled by the disabilities that their class status imposed upon economic enterprise, continually pressured the government to transform the entire suburb into a city and its peasants into posadskie liudi, with all the economic prerogatives attendant on that estate. The Ostashkov story was not an isolated phenomenon. Numerous other suburbs developed along the same lines, pressing toward identity as full-fledged cities of the realm.[65]

The impact of the flow of peasants into the cities is difficult to gauge. In many cases their residence there was temporary and their influence accordingly slight. In other cases, they contributed to burgeoning city populations, and their influence, whatever precisely it was, no doubt proved lasting. Whether the influx of peasants into a city actually changed the tenor of city life is unclear, though one might suspect a negative answer to the question. It would, after all, be as hard to argue that the peasants were qualitatively more rural than the townsmen, most of whom still kept gardens and a few head of stock, as it would be to suggest that the peasants were markedly less sophisticated than the average townsmen in commercial ventures. The confusion of posadskie liudi with muzhiki, if only for the purpose of social snobbery, does contain a kernel of truth. In the absence of testimony to the contrary, one must strongly suspect that the gradual migration of peasants to the cities produced no startling qualitative changes in urban life, such as those brought about in modern industrial cities by the influx of large groups of unskilled rural types.

But the peasants did come—to some cities at any rate—in substantial numbers, and it was the presence in the cities of individuals who, whatever their lifestyle, had no formal, legal urban role but who sought to claim one, that challenged the traditional role of the townsmen. Inexact as they are, population figures reveal a marked decline in the relative weight of the posad population within the cities themselves, to say nothing of the appearance of quasi cities inhabited wholly or mostly by peasants. That the townsmen's numbers were reduced, relatively speaking, does not of necessity imply a total eclipse of their social or economic position; in status and privilege they stood above peasants of all stripes; and the economic power of the first-guild merchants remained impressive right through the century. But it does mean that the proportion of townsmen to the total urban population was dropping and that in larger, more important cities, the posadskie liudi had become a decided minority of the population. The population of the city, as the Senate reminded Potemkin, included many people who were not formally registered, taxpaying members of the posad commune. And, as if this reality were not a sufficient challenge to the notion that city and posad were one and the same, there had sprung up the many commercial and manufacturing suburbs, whose inhabitants pleaded for recognition as merchants of the realm and urged that their suburbs be granted city status. Sooner or later, the government would have to come to grips with the demographic realities in the nation's cities; when that happened a new understanding of what constituted a city was bound to emerge.

DECLINING SERVICE RESPONSIBILITIES

Yet another set of developments under way in the early 1750s led to a modest decline in the state service responsibilities of the posad and foreshadowed more substantial alterations in the posad's service role in years to come. The obligations of service had, as noted earlier, fallen to different degrees on each posad, depending on available manpower, on what means of tax collecting the posad chose to pursue, and upon the ever-changing directives of the government. But most townsmen agreed that service burdens weighed intolerably heavily upon their shoulders. In the 1750s and 1760s two major reductions of service occurred, which, if they fell short of the posad dweller's ultimate dream of the total abolition of service, at least rendered it less burdensome and raised hopes of future reductions.

With the abolition in 1753-54 of internal customs duties there disappeared the need for hundreds of officials—appraisers, inspectors, toll and customs collectors—most of whom had been drawn from the posad population. This reform was particularly welcome, for customs collection assignments, which frequently entailed service far from home, had been one of the most detested obligations. Port and border customs remained in effect, of course, and merchants from border localities continued to assist in these operations, though there was a growing body of full-time, salaried customs officials who did the bulk of the work.[66]

More relief from service came in 1765 when the government ordered that the collection of revenue from the state liquor monopoly should be handled through franchises, that is, farmed out rather than undertaken by sworn men from the posad or by local magistracy or ratusha officials. From the 1730s on, all three methods had been used in continually varying proportions, and with quite different results. Figures from 1753 indicate that arrears in liquor revenues were less from those cities where it was handled by individuals with franchises than in cities where sworn men or the magistracy office did the collecting. Thus, in spite of a report by Count Fermor's commission investigating the wine and salt monopolies, which noted that revenue farming worked great hardship on the people, the government followed its fiscal nose and put all liquor collections on a franchise basis.[67]

This law had striking effects on service burdens in the cities. In the city of Kashin, for example, the total number of persons involved in service yearly was nearly halved after the new law took effect. In Tula, the number of persons employed as tax collectors of one kind or another dropped from seventy-six in 1766 to twenty-two in the following year, and twenty-seven the year after that.[68]

At the same time that reform of liquor revenue collection was under discussion, the government also turned its attention to the administration of the salt monopoly. Service by the posad population in the sale of salt constituted the second most burdensome obligation and was the cause of never-ending complaint. In 1761 the Senate recommended to the Main Magistracy that retired officers replace posad people in the sale of salt, with salaries to be funded by the local merchant population. The magistracy in turn responded by asking various local magistracies their opinion of the proposed change. The reply from Orel betrays a desire to be rid of the service obligation, and, at the same time, a deep-seated fear that if the service burden were let out of posad hands, things might become even worse. In effect, the Orel merchants approved of the proposed reform, insofar as the responsibilities of the local posad were limited to paying the officers' salaries. But if the posad were also to be made responsible for the full delivery of revenues, then the merchants preferred to keep the management of the monopoly in their own hands. The question boiled down to which arrangement hurt least. As it turns out, the government left the existing arrangements untouched.[69] In 1761 the government did, however, shift the responsibility for the sale of gunpowder from elected members of the posad to the artillery department, thus relieving the townsmen of one small but aggravating obligation.[70]

The reduction in service obligations brought about by the abolition of internal customs, the farming of liquor tax collections, and the transfer of the gunpowder-sale responsibility were not the result of a conscious policy on the part of the government to reduce this burdensome aspect of posad life. Each was, in its own way, an effort to seek better means of ensuring the greatest possible tax yield. If, in the case of commerce, the pursuit of that objective called for the elimination of pesky petty collections in the hope of spurring trade, then in matters of government monopolies, like salt or powder, it meant tightening up on the actual collection process. The goal of the reforms may not have been the modification of the service system, but that was, willy-nilly, one of its consequences. It seems clear from the events leading up to the alteration of the liquor tax collections and from the debates about the salt monopoly that the existing service arrangements were far from ideal, that the government was losing vast sums of money yearly. From the mid-1740s on, Kizevetter notes, there was an increasing preference within government for revenue farming, and it is not surprising to see it advanced as a remedy to the liquor tax collection problem.[71]

So it was that the first significant reductions in posad service came about. Yet it should also be noted that the government was not at that point prepared to abandon in principle the notion of service. Indeed, in the discussion of an alternative means of administering the salt monopoly, the government proposed merely to shift the burden on the posad from a personal to a financial one, and to impress another segment of the population into the actual collection of the taxes. It was still not within the powers of the state, both for financial considerations and for lack of manpower, to assimilate these processes into the growing bureaucratic structure of the state.[72] But the quest for alternatives to the old system was underway, and the first steps toward the elimination of service had been taken.

Economic developments, tentative new directions in government administrative policy, and demographic movements steadily ate away at the bases of posad society. Bit by bit they undermined the institutional forms that had maintained the traditional role of the posad in the state order of early modern Russia. The powerful economic and social currents emanating from the countryside broke down once and for all the economic privileges of the posad, not only through direct competition but also indirectly through the gradual withdrawal of state support for monopolistic practices within the economy. To have perfect symmetry, the collapse of the economic privileges of the posad should have been matched by a parallel reduction in their service obligations, for the very rationale of the service order had been a quid pro quo relationship—economic and social prerogatives in return for service. The truth is, however, that although the decline of service had begun, the initial moves in that direction were timid. Only certain services had been touched, while most remained. Yet the few steps taken by the government in this area reflect dissatisfaction with the results of the service system and suggest that still another area of posad life—one of equal importance with economic activity—had fallen out of step with the needs of a new era. Finally, the changing composition of the urban population brought out more sharply than ever the need for a new social basis for urban institutions. The townsmen were neither sufficiently numerous nor adequately representative of the whole city population—to say nothing of their limited capabilities—to take full responsibility for the maintenance and, ideally, the enhancement of city life. When all these changes broke upon them, the townsmen fell back, more or less futilely, upon traditional means of defending their traditional place in Russian society. The state, by contrast, quickly began to adjust to this new set of realities and was shortly to initiate measures to bring the institutions affecting urban life into line with them.

CHAPTER NINE

The Early Reforms
of Catherine II

NOT SINCE THE REIGN of Peter I had the townsmen and the cities received as much attention as they were to get from the government of Catherine II. Indeed, many elements of continuity can be found in the respective policies of these two monarchs toward the cities. Each sought to enhance Russia's cities by transforming the urban population into an economically strong and civic-minded social group. Each reached outside the country for ideas and models on which to fashion reform plans. And each relied heavily on the apparatus of the state in pursuit of his or her objectives. But there were important differences as well. Peter was far more visionary and impetuous, striving for his goals without always reckoning the cost, or even the possibility of their being achieved. Catherine, by contrast, appears to have operated, especially during the early years of her reign, with greater caution and whenever possible with a firmer grounding in the needs and capacities of the country. The exigencies of her position compelled her to be an astute political operator, a talent that required a clear sense of what could and could not be done. It was, in the last analysis, Catherine's ability to read the country and to react to changing conditions within it that gave her reign both a longevity and a brilliance few would have predicted on the morrow of the coup that overthrew Peter III.

As the preceding chapter has argued, there were a number of forces at work in the middle years of the eighteenth century which affected directly and indirectly both the townsmen and the cities. They brought under seige the estate character of posad society, transformed the cities, and eroded the service functions of the commune. In the process, the contradiction between the service-oriented institutional base of the commune and the kinds of institutions ideally needed by a major European power grew ever more acute. A crisis of the old city order was developing, one that virtually begged for resolution by the new government.

Catherine reacted to this situation quite vigorously. Early in her reign she asked the townsmen about their lot and received in response a vast store of data about their lives and aspirations. That information was to guide her in future years when she bestowed upon the townsmen a veritable flood of legislation touching nearly every aspect of their lives, from the physical character of their environment to their role in the administration of the state. The empress' interest in the business affairs of the merchants was but a single aspect of her concern for the overall economic development of the empire; her attention to the social status of the townsment but one phase of her efforts to bring system and order to the constituent elements of Russian society; and, finally, her alterations of urban administration but one part of her pursuit of a coherent governmental apparatus for a vast and growing empire. And all these aspirations were subsumed under yet another goal, the enhancement of the power and glory of the Russian state. The absolute monarchy was itself maturing in these years, refining and extending its abilities to govern, and its drive to control and direct social phenomena remained as strong as ever. It is in light of this broader context of national life that the fate of the townsmen and their unique institution, the commune, must be understood.

THE PROBLEMS DEFINED

In the first decade of Catherine's reign, the government explored in some depth the problems of the cities and their commercial and manufacturing inhabitants. From the proceedings of various committees, commissions, and standing government agencies, two recurrent preoccupations emerged: the socioeconomic problems of the Russian merchants and the shortcomings of the cities' contributions to the administration of the empire. Here were the two main areas in need of attention; in the exploration of them many of the elements of future reforms were first adumbrated.

The problems facing the merchantry demonstrated the degree to which social and economic considerations were inextricably intertwined. The instructions presented to the Great Commission made that point eloquently, as did a number of merchant presentations to the codification commission of Elizabeth. The demands of the merchants after all had centered primarily on the strengthening of their social prerogatives to be the urban mercantile and manufacturing estate of the realm. Only secondarily did they discuss purely economic matters. It was clear that efforts to improve the economic contribution of the townsmen to the national cause would, if they were to amount to anything at all, have to have an important social dimension. Either the estate privileges of old would have to be enforced—an unlikely eventuality given the strength of peasant enterprise and its social and political support—or they would have to be somehow modified or broken up. But the latter course had its hazards as well, for tinkering with the prerogatives of one estate could not help but raise bigger questions about social relations in the country.

The strain that socioeconomic changes forced upon the society can be observed not only in the testimony of the townsmen, but also in the more rarified discussions that took place in government councils. The Commission on Commerce of 1763-1767 had a fascinating debate over the proper means for upgrading mercantile affairs in Russia. The papers from this conference reveal a sharp conflict of opinion between the chairman, Ia. P. Shakhovskoi, and one of its members, G. N. Teplov, as to the advisability of retaining an economy based on a division of responsibility along estate lines.[1] To a large extent, the issue turned on the phenomenon of trading peasants. To Shakhovskoi, only those persons who had a clearly defined legal right to a profession ought to be allowed to practice it; to Teplov, such a formal restriction could only be harmful to the country, for the merchants (those formally registered on the posad tax rolls) were neither numerous nor rich enough to meet the society's mercantile needs. Thus, while Shakhovskoi argued that the improvement of commerce depended on the state's providing privileges and rewards for the successful merchants and legally restricting the access of others to the marketplace, Teplov counseled that commerce should be open to all comers, regardless of social background. Teplov's position was genuinely radical in two respects. First, its execution would have entailed major modifications in the social order of the country and the laws that backed up that order. Second, by arguing that the purely economic rewards of a relatively open market would be a sufficient stimulus to expansion, he challenged the traditional view of Russian officialdom, which held that such an expansion could come about only through state involvement in the economy and in social relations. The force of tradition weighed heavily in the deliberations of the government, making unlikely the acceptance of Teplov's views, with their potent ramifications for several basic state institutional relationships. But the way was not entirely clear, either, for an unqualified reassertion of the old estate approach to economic matters. Subsequent Catherinean legislation was to represent a compromise of sorts, but the very act of compromise itself hailed the end of an era.

Concern for the development of the mercantile economy and for the related goal of raising the merchants' capacities to pay taxes were nothing new. From time to time during the eighteenth century, the Russian government had returned to these matters, inspired, as often as not, by various Petrine policy initiatives. Where Catherine's government really broke ground with its predecessors was in its concern for the cities of the realm. This concern can be traced to two sources: the actual conditions of Russia's cities as Catherine encountered them in her first years in Russia and in office; and the failure of the cities to contribute as effectively as they ought to the administration of the state, a failure that had terrifying consequences at the time of Pugachev's rebellion.

Although it would be mistaken to judge city life solely by external features, nonetheless the condition of the streets, the style and construction of buildings, the presence or absence of parks—these and a host of other characteristics of the urban environment do testify to the values and customs of the inhabitants and to the efficacy of local governmental institutions in securing objectives commonly held within the community. In the case of Russia in the 1760s and 1770s, descriptions of cities varied little from those of a century past. And the tale is the same whether it comes from domestic or foreign sources. One historian of Iaroslavl' wrote of the poorly located, narrow, and muddy streets, of the cattle wandering about the town during the summer, grazing on the grass that had sprung up in the unpaved streets and squares. And, there were the almost daily fires that devastated large portions of the city.[2] The British visitor William Coxe gave a similar portrayal of the many towns he passed through on his extensive tour of Russia. His description of Dogorobush, a small town along the Smolensk-to-Moscow road, is typical. Dogorobush exhibited, "like Smolensk, though on a lesser scale, an inter-mixture of churches, houses, cottages, corn-fields, and meadows: some of the houses . . . were of brick covered with stucco and had the appearance of so many palaces when contrasted with the meanness of the surrounding hovels."[3] Moscow, too, was made up of the same components of elegance and extreme poverty, though the proportions of both were greater, owing to the many church and government buildings as well as to a burgeoning population. Only Petersburg seemed somehow qualitatively different from the other cities Coxe visited. For it he reserved, or deferred, judgment: "Not withstanding, however, all these improvements [made by Peter I and Catherine II], it bears every mark of an infant city, and is still . . . only an immense outline, which will require future empresses and almost future ages to complete."[4] Even when one discounts the cultural bias implicit in these judgments and makes an ecologically proper obeisance to the need for a dose of the bucolic in the urban environment, the fact remains that Russia's cities had failed to facilitate communications from one part of town to another, to provide decent housing, and to eliminate the continual fires, which, in addition to the death and injury they visited upon the population, wrought havoc on the continuity of economic activities. All this is to say nothing of the paucity of facilities for education, for public health, or for the cultural enrichment of the population.

As telling as the physical countenance of the cities may have been, it was the deplorable state of urban administration that most influenced subsequent government action. The various agencies charged with urban administration—the magistracies, the offices of governors and military governors, and, here and there, police offices—labored without adequate manpower or money. Moreover, they stumbled into each other's bailiwicks or sloughed off unwanted responsibilities onto one another's shoulders, thanks in part to their imprecisely defined and often conflicting jurisdictions. The legal recognition in 1764 of what had been the de facto control of the magistracy by the military governor, "the true guardian of the province entrusted to him," may have made the lines of responsibility more clear, but it did not visibly enhance the performance of local government.[5]

The practical consequences of these shortcomings were grievous. Reports reaching the desk of Catherine II shortly after her assumption of power told of the near-collapse of urban administration in a number of cities and towns. In some localities, there were disorders led by the magistracy officials who had their own bands of armed hoodlums. Many military governors acted with an equal disregard for law and order. In Novgorod, then at its nadir, the magistracy building had a straw roof, and economic activity in the town had all but come to a halt. According to some observers, only the presence of the army in Moscow prevented wholesale looting; as it was, there was mayhem enough on the streets. Catherine herself took note in an imperial decree of the large number of dead bodies that cluttered the streets of the capital.[6] In addition to outright asocial behavior, there were numerous instances of the evasion of responsibilities by officials. Elected officials of the magistracy, for example, made every effort to avoid performing their duties, which they regarded as burdensome impositions on their time and energies.[7] Though forty years had passed since the issuance of Peter's Main Magistracy Regulation, the goals of that farsighted sovereign seemed as remote as ever.

From the earliest years of Catherine's reign, the Russian government was moved by a strong sense of the importance of cities to the process of state administration. Already in 1763 a Commission on Cities convened to grapple with the problem of bringing into better alignment administrative districts, population density, and cities that might serve well as administrative centers. Whether the commission lacked a sense of urgency or whether it simply bogged down as did so many government commissions in the eighteenth century, one cannot say, but nine years of work produced only meager results.[8]

In the last analysis, it was not an abstract devotion to administrative reform that moved the government to action, it was the revolt of Emelian Pugachev. The disappearance of tens of thousands of square miles under the banners of the pretender and his corevolutionists revealed in letters too bold to be ignored the poverty of local administration. In a paradox of classic configuration, the nation's cities, which had been shaped predominantly by administrative considerations, turned out at the moment of truth to be incapable of contributing their share to the most fundamental task of governmental institutions—the protection of the established political system.

The Guberniia Statute of 1775 followed closely on the heels of the rebellion. Indeed, it would appear that the two were closely linked. According to Robert E. Jones, the Pugachev affair established in Catherine's mind a clear link between national security and local reform, and in doing so compelled her to recommend reforms that hitherto had not been acceptable. While the empress had been toying with administrative reform—entertaining proposals, making some modest changes of regulations, and the like—she had been unwilling to accept the crucial principle of elective offices in local administration, though the idea had been presented to her as early as 1762 in a memorandum from Prince Ia. P. Shakhovskoi. Moreover, an experiment along these lines undertaken by Governor Ia. E. Sivers (Johann Sievers) of Novgorod province had been ordered disbanded by the Senate. Yet, when Catherine sat down to work out the new scheme of provincial administration, she adopted this principle as a major constituent of the new administrative order.[9] That the empress should accept on the morrow of the rebellion a remedy she had rejected previously, and that she should accept it on the grounds of national security, only underscores the impact of the *Pugachevshchina* on her subsequent legislation. The cities were soon to be the beneficiaries of Catherine's reaction to that violent episode.

If local and national conditions provided the incentive to undertake urban reforms, a large and growing body of data on the cities, far greater than that at the disposal of earlier Russian governments, helped to shape the characteristics of the actual reform. Obviously one must avoid anachronism: Catherine and her advisors were not social scientists or social engineers in the twentieth-century manner and did not systematically use quantifiable data. Even so, information from a number of sources enhanced the government's understanding of what cities were like and contributed to the shaping of a new attitude toward them.

There were, first of all, census figures. Although they did not yield precise data about cities or even, on occasion, the right kind of data (for example, the census failed to record large peasant populations, transient or settled), and in spite of the fact that both government officials and agencies appear to have had a less than accurate knowledge of the urban population, the census data did provide evidence on the basic social groups of the state, such as the posadskie liudi, and gave some indication as to how these groups were distributed. This latter information proved useful in the drafting of the 1775 statute.

Second, one might mention yet again the instructions of the city delegates to the Great Commission. If, as many historians argue, the principal objective of the Great Commission was to inform the empress about her subjects and not to create a new code, then she was well served indeed by the plethora of data contained in them.[10] That this information, along with the complaints and recommendations of the townsmen, registered on the imperial consciousness can be seen from subsequent legislation, especially the Charter Granted to the Cities, which met at least partially many of the requests of the townsmen.[11]

Third, the government had access to better data about the physical properties of the cities. No doubt of far greater value than census data were the Registers (*Vedomosti*) sent to the Commerce College by local magistracies in 1764-65 and the descriptions of cities and districts composed after the reforms of 1775. These documents are particularly rich in data on city inhabitants, buildings, and economic enterprise.[12] Efforts at city planning also signified heightened government awareness of the physical conditions and needs of the cities. The Commission for Stone Building in St. Petersburg and Moscow, for example, an agency whose original charge had been to coordinate and plan the growth of these two cities, in time assumed a supervisory role over city planning throughout the state.[13]

Of all the actions taken during the early part of the reign of Catherine II, perhaps the one that exercised the most immediate impact on city affairs was the general survey, begun in 1766. Though it had been ordered to straighten out the confused land relationships in the countryside, it inevitably affected the cities as well. The surveyors needed to begin somewhere, and the regulations established the cities as the initial reference points. More precisely, the survey was to provide each city with meadowland surrounding the city at a distance of two kilometers in every direction. It was at the border of that meadow that the surveying of the countryside was to begin. Before the boundaries of the meadow could be established, however, the surveyors needed accurate information on the land occupied by the city itself. But that was information that did not exist, for the most part, since in the thinking of most governmental institutions, central and local, the city was the sum total of different orders of the population, not a territorial whole. To surmount this obstacle, the government empowered the Commission for Stone Building in St. Petersburg and Moscow to solicit, review, and approve of plans to be submitted by local government authorities. Requests for such plans always insisted that precise boundaries be included, and where they were not present, the commission did not hesitate to order walls (earthen elevations) built to make sure that clearly visible physical boundaries were present.

In the process of drawing up and revising city plans, the various agencies at work altered both the internal layout and the boundaries of many cities. In some cases, for example, overzealous planners laid out vast squares in the center of towns which, if brought into being, would have meant the razing of precious brick dwelling places. Much more common, however, were attempts by the planners to compact cities, often by moving the inhabitants of outlying suburbs (in one case a suburb of twenty-two homes was situated nine kilometers from the town to which it was ascribed) into the confines of the city proper. And there were several instances of relocation, usually carried out for the sake of finding a topographically more suitable site. Obviously, only relatively small cities, with no substantial churches or governmental buildings, could be so relocated. In addition to such changes in the geographic layout of towns, the survey also effected major changes in boundaries by the application of the norm of a two kilometer circumferential meadowland. For some cities, there was a net gain in territory, as land was taken from reserves of state properties to make up for local inadequacies. But for many cities, where the communal holdings were vast, the losses were proportionally great. Tambov lost 6,560 acres to the state.[14] According to Klokman, the surveyors placed in the hands of the gentry sizable pieces of urban land, once granted to the cities by the state; but he gives no comprehensive figures for this loss of one-time city land.[15]

As important as these alterations of the physical characteristics of the cities may have been, there can be no doubt that the most significant outcome of the general survey was the establishment of precise city limits. Here, at last, the physical side of the city was given definition in such a way as to embrace all of its parts and all of its population. As T. P. Efimenko points out, the survey was a necessary supplement to the city statute of 1785, for it would have been meaningless for the latter to speak of the rights inherent in city property were there no clear-cut understanding of what property the city had.

Precisely how all the information that came to the attention of Catherine's government—from personal observation to reports of various commissions and agencies—shaped subsequent policy toward the cities is a matter for specialized study, but there can be no doubt that its impact was considerable. The accumulated data and ideas spoke to the major themes that Catherine's urban reform legislation addressed and they frequently prefigured the principles on which those reforms were based. Concern for the improvement of commerce and the merchants' role in that process; the importance of cities to state administration; an awareness of the city as a spatial entity embracing a diverse and growing population; and the recognition of the inadequacy of the existing social basis of city government and the correlate need for new urban administrative institutions—all these matters received attention, in one way or another, in the great information-gathering process that marked the first decade of Catherine's reign.

THE FISCAL AND ECONOMIC REFORM MEASURES OF 1775

In 1775, after more than a decade of information gathering and deliberation, Catherine's government finally moved positively to meet some of the pressing issues affecting the nation's cities and their inhabitants. Although the provincial reform of that year, addressed chiefly to the administrative problems of the country, had a profound long-term impact on the cities, of much greater immediate importance to the posad registrants was a less well-known piece of legislation issued earlier in the same year. On March 17, 1775, an imperial manifesto, "Concerning the Most High Favors Granted to Various Estates on the Event of the Conclusion of Peace with the Ottoman Porte," called for a new structuring of the city population.[16] For the bulk of the eighteenth century, all posad taxpayers except those formally registered in craft guilds had been members of one of the three merchant guilds, and all, including the craftsmen, had been treated juridically as members of a single merchant estate. That was the case in spite of the obvious fact that a substantial percentage of them were in no way occupied with mercantile interests. The new law divided the former merchant community into two groups: those with capital less than 500 rubles, who were to be called *meshchane*; and those with capital above 500 rubles, who were to be known as merchants. Moreover, the law emancipated the merchants from poll-tax responsibility and asked from them instead "one percent yearly from the capital declared by them in good conscience."[17] Subsequent enabling legislation called for the formation of three guilds of merchants, again based on capital: first guild, more than 10,000 rubles; second guild, between 1,000 and 10,000 rubles, and third guild, 500 to 1,000 rubles.[18]

At least three specific objectives of government policy can be discerned

in this legislation. First, the law met one of the key demands of the leading guild merchants as expressed in their instructions to the Great Commission: namely, the elimination of the poll tax. This plea, it will be re-
called, appears to have been based on vanity, on a wounded sense of
social worth, for the merchants had contended that liability to the poll
tax placed them on a social level with bonded servants. Insofar as no loss
of revenue to the government occurred, it cost the state little to grant this
satisfaction to a select stratum of townsmen. Second, the law enabled the
government to "clean up," as Klokman puts it, the social categorization
of the townsmen—in particular, to remove from that group that the new
law called "merchants" all those who were insolvent or who had long
since abandoned mercantile activities, to say nothing of those who had
never engaged in trade at all.[19] This action, apart from its inherent logic,
seems to have been integrally related to the third objective—the creation
of a tax system that would hold out greater incentives for the true merchants of the realm and raise the amount of revenue flowing into the treasury. To deny that fiscal considerations were paramount in the issuance
of this law would be to swim upstream against a veritable flood tide of
administrative tradition. Indeed, the shifting of wealthy merchants onto
a tax system of one percent of declared capital did increase noticeably the
treasury's yearly take.[20]

In his assessment of the tax reform of 1775, S. M. Troitskii argues that
it represents "the development of the bourgeois principle of taxation of
the city population," a position also held by Klokman.[21] Presumably that
phrase signifies the ordering or categorizing of individuals solely on the
basis of wealth. There is a certain truth to this argument, for the old ties
of common profession and common subjection to taxes had been dis-
carded in favor of a division determined strictly by wealth. But it is
equally true that posad society had always been divided into ranks on the
basis of wealth, and the mutual responsibility principle was, in its own
way, a differential tax, falling most heavily on those most able to pay.
Furthermore, the practice of distinguishing among individuals on the
basis of their wealth long antedates the commercial and industrial revolu-
tions; one may wonder just how "bourgeois" such a notion is.

It may well be that the key to understanding the character of this tax
reform lies in the debates of the Commission on Commerce of 1767. In
the exchange over peasant trade and the possible opening up of the market place, Teplov had pointed to the need for accurate knowledge of the
capabilities of the merchant class—that is, just how numerous it was,
how many men were occupied with truly mercantile pursuits, and
whether they could reasonably be expected to get the job done on their
own.[22] If the 1775 tax reform did not provide all the qualitative informa-

tion that Teplov called for, it did at least achieve a rudimentary sorting out of the merchant population on the basis of their material assets. Whereas the third census had recorded a merchant population of 222,767 males, the registration that followed the new law listed only 24,470 merchants and 194,160 meshchane.[23] Through this act of separating those with significant capital—and in all probability reasonably successful business operations—from the dross of the former merchant estate, the government acknowledged, in effect, that economic diversity within the commune was so great as to make it unwise to continue treating all townsmen the same, at least as far as tax matters were concerned. But the government did not go on to draw the conclusion that this tenth part of the merchantry was not adequate for the mercantile needs of the country and that trade would therefore have to be made freely open to any who wished to be so occupied. Rather, the separation of merchant from meshshanin was but an indispensible prelude to a renewed round of government encouragement of the top stratum of merchants, just as Shakhovskoi had recommended to the Commission on Commerce. In freeing the merchants from the humiliation of the poll tax and the leveling effects of communal tax obligations, the government hoped to boost the efforts of the true merchants of the realm. Thus the 1775 tax reform must be seen as an effort to improve the state of Russian commerce, but an effort fully within the traditional framework of state-determined incentives and rewards for a specially designated, though now decidedly more elite, merchant estate.

Buried within this same decree of March 1775, however, was another provision affecting the economic affairs of the townsmen that moved in quite another direction. Article eleven declared that henceforth any subject of the crown could set up a manufacturing enterprise "without needing any permission from higher or lower authorities to do so." What was good for commerce—close government tutelage—was apparently not good for manufacture. Several sets of considerations figured in this dramatic departure from an estate-oriented economic order. First, there was pressure from gentry eager to diversify their incomes through manufacturing enterprises established by themselves or by their peasants. Second, it was obvious to the government that the merchants, for a variety of economic and social reasons, had not on the whole been inclined to invest heavily in manufacturing. Since the countryside had the initiative, the resources, and the labor, it would have been the height of folly to try to curb rural enterprise on the basis of ancient estate privileges. Finally, it should be noted that a great deal of talk was in the air in these years about freedom of economic activity. Even the empress was not immune from its influence.[24] It is doubtful that such notions weighed as heavily as practical considerations, but they certainly provided ready justification for this new departure in economic policy.

This crucial reform measure thus reflected, in its different parts, the essential conflict—between an economy based on closed social estates and one open to all members of society—that had confronted leading government figures at least from the time of the Commission on Commerce.[25] In mercantile matters, the reform followed what Daniel calls the restrictionist position: that is, it sought to limit commerce to a select segment of society and to maintain close ties between that group and the state. In manufacturing, however, the legislation broke new ground by allowing the rewards of the market place to determine economic behavior. The conflict was never to be wholly resolved during the reign of Catherine II but its very existence, along with legislation supporting a more open economy, marked a considerable evolution in state policy toward the nature of the economy and, indeed, toward the very character of the social order.

Needless to say, the provisions of the decree of March 17, 1775, struck at the very roots of the traditional order of the posad. The separation of merchants from meshchane and the assignment of qualitatively different tax liabilities to each group destroyed the principle on which the tax structure of the commune had always rested. Heretofore, all members of the commune had shared in the payment of taxes, roughly according to their ability to pay. Now, the most successful members were skimmed off —and with them went their capacity to make up for the deficiencies of the less well-to-do members. It followed, of necessity, that the tax burden of the meshchane was to be heavier than it had ever been, unless some new guidelines for levying taxes against these individuals were introduced. The increase in state revenue following the reform suggests, at the very least, that their burdens were not lessened. But the precise weight of tax burdens is a secondary concern. The real import of this tax reform can be found in the collapse of the principle of mutual responsibility (krugovaia poruka) that had for centuries bound the townsmen together in the fulfillment of their state tax obligations. With the collapse of mutual responsibility, the common liability of all posad registrants to tiaglo came to an end; a fatal blow had been struck at the juridical basis of the posad estate.

At the same time that the fiscal-administrative character of the commune was under attack, the promulgation of the doctrine of freedom of manufacturing weakened still further the already decaying estate prerogatives of the townsmen. Without government support, their claims to exclusive rights to urban trade and manufacture were destined to sound more hollow than ever. Most likely, the presence of these two measures in the same decree—itself a grab-bag of wildly unrelated articles—was a coincidence. Each responded to a specific set of circumstances, though of course one might argue that ultimately both reflected the changing socio-economic conditions of the country. Taken together they made the law of March 17, 1775, the most important government action bearing on the fate of the townsmen since 1649.

THE PROVINCIAL REFORM OF 1775

The landmark legislative measures outlined in the preceding section touched most directly the estate interests of the townsmen; they had little impact on the cities themselves, where there existed problems of quite a different order. The inability of the cities either to govern themselves adequately or to contribute what they ought to the general administration of the country constituted a major weakness in the organization of the state. It was a weakness that urgently demanded attention. A practical response was forthcoming in 1775 with the publication of the Provincial Statute. Strictly speaking, it would not be correct to call this an urban reform, for it did little to improve city life. Rather, it was a reform of state administration in which the cities occupied a central, indeed indispensable, place.

The basic goal of this reform was, in essence, to upgrade local administration and in the process to preclude a repetition of the Pugachev affair. To achieve that end, the reform built on two different, and in principle sometimes contradictory, concepts. On the one hand it reorganized and rationalized the bureaucratic structure of the empire. As Robert Jones argues, the reform concentrated at the new guberniia level responsibilities that had hitherto resided either in the capitals or in the counties, in the hope that at this intermediate level both overcentralization and local impotence could be avoided and that some progress might actually be achieved in the governance of the empire.[26] Furthermore, the reform instituted a number of new agencies directed specifically at the administration of legal, fiscal, and police affairs, thus giving an added impetus to the development of the state's bureaucratic apparatus. On the other hand, the reform also introduced, in however timid a measure, the elective principal into areas of administration where it had not previously existed. In order to draw the recently emancipated gentry into relatively unattractice provincial posts, the government designated as elective certain judicial and police-administrative positions. In particular, the elected status of the judge of the county court and of the *zemskii ispravnik* (the chief police officer in the rural areas), men directly supervised by no other officials—though ultimately responsible to guberniia-level officials

—gave a latitude of action that ran counter to a strictly hierarchical bureaucratic structure.[27] Somehow, it was hoped that the prestige of election and the relative independence from bureaucratic intervention might make service in the provinces if not as glamorous as service in the capitals, at least palatable.

These apparently contradictory administrative principles—bureaucratic rationalization and the ceding of certain administrative functions to relatively unsupervised elected local officials—were not the consequence of inadequacies of thought or of legislative draftsmanship. They represented a necessary compromise between the growing pretensions of absolute monarchy—with its handmaiden, the bureaucracy—and certain basic social realities in the Russian state.

The growth of absolute monarchy in eighteenth-century Russia seems to hold the key to the puzzling—and on the surface, non-Marxist—phenomenon of a state apparatus that, especially in its nineteenth-century manifestation, has often appeared divorced from the obvious interests of the ruling classes.[28] Inevitably, attention has come to rest on the bureaucracy, whose quasi-independent status made it the principal supporter of autocracy as well as the instrument through which state ends were served, even when they came in conflict with perceived interests of the dominant order of society.

There appears to be general agreement that the groundwork for Russian absolutism was laid during the reign of Peter I.[29] The elimination of the cumbersome prikaz system, the establishment of a new and more rational complement of administrative agencies, and the introduction of the Table of Ranks opened up the way for a new style of bureaucracy. The process, however, was both slow and complicated. The continued dominant role of the gentry in the major positions of state administration often frustrated the original intent of the Table of Ranks to move talented people to the top regardless of their origins. Moreover, problems of finance and education placed real limits to the growth and effectiveness of the bureaucracy. Even so, the bureaucracy was expanding numerically and in its capacity to administer. Troitskii argues that from the reign of Peter I through about 1770, three important developments helped to shape the new bureaucracy: a rationalization of the bureaucratic establishment; the supplanting of the notion of birth as the criterion for selection and advancement by the principles of length of tenure, talent, and education; and the appearance of money salaries for all officials.[30] A sense of the independence these developments gave to the bureaucracy can be observed in some of the reforms undertaken from the 1750s on, reforms that reflected a certain bourgeois influence, even though the bureaucrats who initiated them were themselves gentry. The economic reforms of P. I. Shuvalov would be a case in point. Shuvalov was the driving force behind the elimination of internal customs and tariffs, the setting of limits on interest rates for commercial loans, and the establishment of the St. Petersburg Bank for the Restoration of Commerce, and he was a supporter of protectionist duties with respect to foreign imports. The trends outlined by Troitskii accelerated in the early years of Catherine's reign, giving further impetus to the evolution of the bureaucracy into a separate "privileged stratum [*prosloika*] standing above the nation."[31]

More was at issue here than growing independence of outlook. The capacity of the bureaucracy to get things done also appears to have increased, if one can judge by the greater number of bureaucrats in service —though that is by no means a certain measure. In 1763 Catherine reformed the civil service, raising the total number of officials by 25 percent, to some 16,000 men.[32] Shortly after the execution of the provincial reform, the number of local officials alone was to exceed that figure.[33] What all this means, quite apart from the quality of performance of the bureaucrats, is that the central government was expanding its bureaucratic capacity, reaching out further and further through its hierarchically organized machinery toward the individual citizens who had, for the greater part of Russia's history, been only indirectly linked to the central government.

The growing independence of the bureaucracy, along with its enhanced capacity, served well the cause of the emerging absolutist state. As Robert Jones argues in his study of the nobility under Catherine II, there is every reason to believe that the empress would like to have extended bureaucratic absolutism still further, perhaps to the point of integrating the vast body of the peasantry into the state bureaucratic net.[34] But the Pugachev affair made it apparent that the state's administrative apparatus was not yet up to the ultimate test of government: the preservation of law and order in the face of seditious action. There could hardly be any thought of such an inadequate administration assuming direct control over millions of peasant souls. What was immediately necessary was the strengthening of the weakest link in the administrative chain, that of local administration. The stumbling block here, of course, was personnel. To whom was the government to entrust this vital responsibility? The question was rhetorical, for the state had little choice but to turn to the gentry. Thus, to attract the gentry into the provinces or to rouse from lethargy those already settled in the countryside, the state ceded— albeit reluctantly—a certain measure of political power to elected representatives of the gentry estate. The government hoped that in time a sense of corporate interest among the nation's landholders would come to the fore, bringing in its train responsible local government and a guarantee of internal security.[35] This accommodation between growing bureaucratic absolutism, on the one hand, and the realities of power and interest in the countryside, on the other, lies at the center of the provincial reform.

A similar tension can be observed in those aspects of the provincial reform that bear directly on the cities. The drive for rationalization was present, along with an extension of the bureaucratic apparatus further into the urban community. But many of the elements of old-style service remained in existence. They continued to function, of necessity, in those areas that lay beyond the limits of an ever-increasing state bureaucracy. In this contest between the new and the old, the state clearly seized the initiative: it adopted a new understanding of the character of the city and began to reshape the urban institutional complex. But service, while clearly on the defensive, had yet to be swept from the field.

To the end of establishing a more rational administrative system, the Provincial Statute called for the establishment of a network of heirarchically ordered and strategically located cities that would ensure the writ of the central government across the land. In the language of contemporary sociology, the cities would serve to organize "political-administrative space."[36] But it was not sufficient just to rearrange the cities on paper and to allocate to them new administrative responsibilities: someone had to be in charge in each city, someone whose task it was to make certain that the city and the institutions located within it met their administrative obligations. Accordingly, the law placed a single person in a position of authority over each city and town. For the capital cities, Moscow and St. Petersburg, this official was the *ober-politseimeister*; for the cities having garrisons, it was the commendant (*komendant*) of the garrison; for smaller cities, a new post, *gorodnichii*, was created. In popular usage the latter two officials came to be known as *namestniki*. These officials took responsibility for all police matters and for all administrative activities in their cities except for judicial ones, which fell under separate jurisdictions.[37]

The competences of the newly established officials paralleled those of the zemskii ispravnik, also a creation of the provincial reform.[38] This similarity of responsibility underlines the intent of the government to strengthen the forces of law and order throughout the country. Indeed, much was expected of the heads of city government: "the gorodnichii with words ought to encourage the inhabitants not only to every kind of permissible industry, craft, and manufacture, but even, in general, encourage all people living in the cities to good morals, love of fellowman, and orderly living."[39] The words, redolent of the Main Magistracy Regulation, suggest that old ambitions never died in eighteenth-century Russia: they just reappeared in new legislation. There was, however, one noteworthy difference between the zemskii ispravnik and the gorodnichii. Whereas the former official was to be elected by local gentry society, the latter was to be appointed by the crown, and not from among leaders of merchant society, but from the ranks of suitably experienced gentry administrators. This breach of symmetry was not without its reasons. The limited achievements of the magistracy in the area of local administration constituted a poor advertisement for the benefits of elective government in the hands of the townsmen. Moreover, the responsibilities of the city official were broader than those of his rural counterpart and thus called for a more experienced individual. But the most important consideration was simply that at this level of organization the government had no cause to give ground, for it had the capacity to fill these posts with its own appointees.[40]

With the appearance of these new city officials, for the first time the entire population of Russia's cities fell under the purview of a single administrative institution. The precedents for this move had been set earlier in Catherine's reign. The general survey had provided the government with a spatial definition of each city, thus making possible precise jurisdictional limits. Moreover, the precedent for a single urban authority had been set as well in the decree of December 14, 1766, which called for the election of deputies to the Great Commission by urban inhabitants of all classes (except peasants). First, however, the law called for the election of a city head (*gorodskoi golova*), or mayor, who would supervise the election of deputies. Whether or not the presence of the deputies and the city head implied, as Ditiatin suggests, that the city had become a juridical person remains unclear, especially given the vague legislative guidelines for the city head and the sparse evidence on the actual functioning of that office until 1785.[41] But the way had been paved for the new institutions of the provincial reform.

In creating the post of gorodnichii and subordinating to it the entire city population, the government implicitly modified its age-old practice of viewing the city as an agglomeration of isolable social groups, to be turned to for the performance of this or that task. In particular, the city could no longer be so closely identified with the posadskie liudi and the particular kinds of fiscal-administrative service they performed. The time had come to recognize the cities as entities in and of themselves and to provide them with institutions that honored that basic reality. A new view of the city had at last emerged.

If, however, the Provincial Statute treated the cities as a whole for police-administrative purposes, it did not regard all inhabitants of the cities as urban citizens. Here, more traditional principles of social organization won out. The law maintained the practice of separating the gentry, clergy, and raznochintsy—to say nothing of peasants, transient or settled—from the merchants, craftsmen, and hired workers; and it regarded as citizens only the latter three groups.[42] In effect, the trade and manufacturing class earned its right to citizenship through the magistracy, its own uniquely urban estate organ. The point comes through most clearly in judicial matters. Gentry and clergy who lived in the towns shared estate courts with their rural counterparts, and the same could be said for peasants residing in towns. But the commercial population had its own court, the magistracy, and even elected its officers. Thus urban citizenship amounted to little more than the selection of officials for an institution that served but a limited portion of the urban population.

This division of city inhabitants into citizens and noncitizens in some ways resembled Peter's Main Magistracy Regulation, which had equated "regular citizens" with the posadskie liudi and a handful of other individuals with special talents. But the tradition of viewing the tax-paying townsmen as the essential component of the city harks back still further, to the period when the Moscow tsars began to acquire their hold over the cities. It is a measure of the difficulty with which Russia threw off the shackles of custom that Catherine, for all her intent to update local administration, should have defined urban citizenship so narrowly while at the same time expanding the concept of the city in its administrative-police relations.

Along with its efforts to rationalize state administration, the provincial statute also extended the domain of the state's bureaucratic apparatus into areas of national life that it had previously been unable to reach in a direct manner. A whole new array of government institutions sprang up to handle a variety of state and local administrative matters, many of which had been at one time or another the responsibility of the magistracy, and almost all of which had in fact accumulated in the hands of governors and military governors. Financial matters, for example, were to be handled at the provincial level by the fiscal board (*kazennaia palata*), at the district level by the treasury (*kaznacheistvo*). These offices looked after the collection of taxes, supervised the financial activities of government organs, managed state incomes, farmed out liquor sales, and supervised private industry and trade.[43] The administration of schools, medical and charitable institutions, and reform schools fell to the newly created Bureau of Public Charities (*prikaz obshchestvennogo prizreniia*).[44] Each of these institutions was carefully integrated into the state bureaucratic network.

The import of this extension of the bureaucracy was clear. Instead of having to rely on the meager forces of the localities—particularly the unwilling townsmen through the service system—or upon the dubious energies of crown appointees such as the governors or military governors, the state moved directly into the business of local administration. In the process, old institutional structures became outmoded and either were modified or disappeared outright. The magistracy is a case in point.[45] The provincial statute took from the magistracy its many nonjudicial competences, the most important of which were financial, and transferred them to newly created agencies. The magistracy itself was reduced simply to a court of law for the townsmen. In small cities or rural posady this court was called the ratusha and in large ones the magistracy. Its members held office for three years and received no salary, a practice with some considerable historical precedent. And, the old organizational structure disintegrated completely. The local magistracies and ratushy were subordinated to the provincial-level magistracy, which itself was responsible to the Justice Chamber at the provincial level. Intermediate-level magistracies were abolished, and the Main Magistracy gradually wound down its operations and disappeared in 1782.[46] The magistracy had apparently ceased to function as a supervisor of service and as an organ of local administration.

Unquestionably, these new arrangements undermined the old service system, but they did not eliminate it entirely. Those who were formally considered urban citizens continued to collect taxes from their own subgroups, and many townsmen bore the traditional burdens of local administration, fire and watch duty, and quartering. Indeed, even the truncated magistracy operated on the basis of unpaid service. But things were not as they had been. The bureaucratic hierarchy had extended its dominion into urban affairs, and the townsmen's special role in the administration of the cities, though never vigorously exercised, had been substantially modified. The service relationship looked increasingly anachronistic.

THE EXECUTION OF THE PROVINCIAL REFORM OF 1775

The modifications of the service system that were implicit in the Provincial Statute, though hardly inconsequential, were not the most visible feature of the reform. After all, the deterioration of service was a slow process, already in motion well before 1775 and destined to continue for decades after that date. Far more dramatic was the impact of the reform on the cities as a whole, on their reorganization in the newly devised administrative system. As noted earlier, the reform assigned even greater responsibilities to the cities for the management of the realm than they had borne in the past. But it is one thing to legislate and another to execute legislation effectively. In the government's efforts to put the new administrative order in place after 1775, one can readily observe, side by side, both the urban weaknesses that complicated the reformers' tasks and the presence of developments that augured positively for the future.

Viewed in retrospect, the execution of the provincial reform looks to have been a complex and demanding exercise.[47] It called for the division of the country into provinces, with populations ranging from three hundred to four hundred thousand male inhabitants, and districts (*uezdy*), with populations in the range of twenty to thirty thousand male residents. For each unit, provincial and district, a central administrative city was required.[48] It was at this point that the difficulties began. Relative to its total area, Russia had few cities, and when their uneven distribution is taken into account, one can readily imagine that many areas would have no suitable administrative center. The problem was more acute for district seats than for provincial ones, since the demand for the latter was so much greater.

When governments are short of money, they are not above turning on the printing presses to make some. Similarly, when the Russian government found itself short of cities, it created the requisite number, with, there is reason to suspect, about the same degree of success as is encountered in printing money. In the decade following the issuance of the Provincial Statute, a total of 216 new cities appeared in Russia, a figure that constituted slightly more than forty percent of the total number of formally recognized cities in the state as of 1787.[49]

It would be misleading to suggest that the cities were created out of whole cloth. In fact, the process took the form of elevating to city status villages, settlements, posady, and suburbs that were appropriately located for administrative purposes. In the vast majority of cases, the honor of elevation to city status fell upon villages and suburbs inhabited by state or economic peasants, one-courters, and others who did not belong to private landholders. Where it was necessary to transform a privately-owned village into a new district seat, the government reimbursed the landowners generously for their loss; but by and large the government, in its desire not to offend the gentry, avoided the seizure of private land.[50]

There were more candidates available for elevation to city status than one might expect. The many suburbs and settlements whose thriving economies made them centers of competition for the townsmen could easily claim, at least in economic terms, to be worthy of city rank. Indeed, quite a number of them had higher levels of economic activity than many existing cities. And the precedent for transforming such communities into cities had already been set; the story of Ostashkov, recounted earlier, is a case in point. A similar example, this one a part of the provincial reform of 1775, concerned Rybnaia Sloboda. Strategically located on the Volga between its confluences with the rivers Mologa and Sheksna, it had long been known as a center of transit trade for the upper Volga basin. In addition to its busy wharves, a yearly fair and weekly markets contributed to its economic life. At the time of its transformation into a city, 638 people registered either as merchants or into the ranks of the tax-paying townsmen.[51] Though one can argue that it takes more than merchants and artisans to make a city, it can also be argued that such settlements had the potential to develop fuller forms of urban life than did many dying ancient fortress cities or small administrative cities with rurally oriented populations.

Just as it was impossible to find suitable existing cities to head up every new administrative unit, so too was it beyond the powers of the government to turn up on demand a satisfactory candidate for elevation to city status, as had been the case with Rybnaia Sloboda. Frequently the government fastened upon some tiny rural hamlet or village, whose only selling point was its geographical location, and transformed it into a city. Two towns in the Smolensk province, Ruposovo and Sychevka, serve as examples of this sad phenomenon. D. V. Volkhov, governor-general of Smolensk province, reported to the Senate that these two settlements were poor choices indeed to become cities, as they had very few merchants in them, "almost none of whom were literate."[52] Ruposovo had one church and five occupied households, counting the parish house. Moreover, he noted, the city was "in such a God-forsaken place, that no road led to it. A treasury official who has lived there three months has seen no one come or leave."[53] Klokman's exhaustive study of the changes in the city order following the publication of the provincial statute provides no statistical breakdown that would indicate what percentage of the 216 new towns fell roughly into the category of tiny, remote villages along the lines of Ruposovo and Sychevka. But the stress he places on the police-administrative character of the reform and the numerous references to hamlets-turned-cities leads one to believe that they were numerous. Moreover, he notes that in 1797 about one-fourth of the newly created cities were re-classified as *zashtatnye*, that is, demoted from their previous role as administrative centers.[54]

As Klokman indicates, there was more to the inability of many of these cities to function as planned than the failure of their economic configurations to conform to some ideal mode. In some cases, the inhabitants of the new cities proved reluctant, for understandable reasons of human inertia, to abandon their agricultural heritage and become merchants and townsmen just to suit the demands of bureaucratic symmetry.[55] Where such attitudes existed, an infinite number of decrees could not have created a city. In quite another vein, many new cities had difficulties achieving their intended role because of opposition from private or even state interests. The new merchants and townsmen of Petrozavodsk found themselves continually in conflict with the authorities of the metallurgical factories for whom they had been ascribed workers prior to their registration as tax-paying townsmen.[56]

In the absence of any rigorous quantitative study of the effects of the 1775 guberniia statute on the cities of Russia, one must, in the last analysis, be content with Klokman's cautious, mixed judgment. On the one hand, he points out that much good came of the reform. Many small, decaying or dead cities, quite often those that had never served as more than military strong points, were crossed off the list of cities.[57] That represents, no doubt, an achievement for the bureaucracy, insofar as its information should more nearly correspond to fact, but it is by no means clear that city development in Russia prospered as a result. Of more substance, however, was the elevation to the rank of city of numerous populated points that did have noticeably developed commercial and manufacturing activities, and which for that reason had the capability of exercising hegemony, both economic and political, over a limited hinterland.[58] Again, there is a caveat in order. Too close an identification of cities with a certain type and level of economic life leads ultimately to a narrow, distorted understanding of city. There can be , and are, administrative cities with little indigenous industry. Yet the ability of a settled point to serve as an effective administrative center depends upon its ability to exert control over the adjacent countryside. To the extent that the city has a large enough population, with the diversity that comes in the wake of numbers, or to the extent that it provides economic goods and services to those nearby, the city proportionately gains in its ability to function administratively. It is at this level of interpretation that Klokman's arguments, themselves stated in a more narrow, economically deterministic fashion, take on meaning. On the other hand, Klokman's tally sheet contains some negative entries. Many ill-qualified settlements, transformed by fiat into cities, failed miserably to become even rudimentary centers of state administration, thus negating the basic intent of the reform.[59] In sum, the state had more cities and it had liberated some quasi cities from dependence on feudal landholders; but it had not yet been able to extend the benefits of good and lawful administration to every nook and cranny of the empire.

It was, no doubt, the proper first step to allocate the cities about the newly created gubernii, and it would appear that the procedure was not without its benefits, both to bureaucratic rationality in a formal sense and to the socioeconomic life of the country. But the consequences of all this for the actual administration of the state remain less clear. On one count, and an important one at that, the reform would have to be adjudged a success: disorder of the kind that had so badly shaken the government was not to be visited upon the country again until the twentieth century, though here the credit may fall more properly to the rural aspects of the reform and to changes in the social conditions on the borders of the empire. Yet on another count, the reform seems to warrant substantially lower marks: there does not appear to have been any dramatic change in day-to-day local administration.[60] To be fair, it should be noted that the reform had been directed at creating new centers of power in guberniia-level institutions and not at wholly reshaping urban administration per se. In the process, it had created new offices in the cities —in particular, the gorodnichii—and expected much from their occupants. In fact, however, city administration remained incompletely reformed, a combination of bureaucratic agencies subject to direction from the center, on the one hand, and reliance on the remnants of the service system for the daily execution of a multitude of tasks, on the other. It was not a satisfactory arrangement, nor, given the changing character of the cities and of the state's attitude toward them, was it likely to be an enduring one.

CHAPTER TEN

The Later Reforms of Catherine II and the Fate of the Posad Commune

FROM THE PERSPECTIVE of the central government, the reforms of 1775 no doubt represented a significant step forward in urban policy. They addressed directly both the socioeconomic conditions of the townsmen and the administrative needs of the empire. The tax reform, in company with modest reductions in service, was designed to give aid and encouragement to the more prosperous members of the posad community, men on whom the government had chosen to rely for the expansion of the nation's commercial and manufacturing activities. The provincial reform, for its part, set new goals for the cities—albeit largely state-administrative ones—and sought to provide institutions appropriate to those goals through an extension of the state bureaucratic apparatus where possible and through locally elected officials where necessary.

As wide-ranging as these reforms were, one crucial area of urban life remained badly in need of attention: the administration of the internal life of the cities themselves. Not only did the cities lack the means for achieving the urban transformation that Peter I had dreamed of, they could scarcely handle even the basics of city management, matters of fundamental services that had gone undone or poorly done for centuries. And, as if the failure of existing arrangements was not damning enough, changing social relations and the enhanced state-administrative role of the cities rendered all the more urgent a restructuring of city administration.

The government was not unaware of the weakness of city administration: after all, it was a problem that had confronted Russian rulers for more than a century. But a problem identified is not automatically a problem solved, and in this case coming up with a satisfactory set of city administrative institutions proved a most difficult task indeed.

To begin with, the cities themselves were in flux, their populations growing and changing in composition, and their social relations evolving accordingly. These conditions made it hard to get an accurate sense of the reality on which any reform would have to be based, though it should be remembered that Catherine's government did a far better job than its predecessors had done in seeking out information to guide its work of reform.

Second, resolution of the problem of local administration was complicated by the limitations inherent in the central government's preferred method of reform: namely, extension of the central bureaucracy. That, of course, had been the underlying principle of many significant features of the provincial reform, and it continued to influence government policymakers in the period after 1775. The police reform of 1782 is a case in point. On April 8, 1782, there appeared the *Ustav blagochiniia*, literally, the Statute of Good Order, whose purpose was to supplement the provincial reform as it applied to the cities by reorganizing local police establishments. The law entrusted police operations in each locality to a board (*uprava blagochiniia*), which supervised a hierarchy of precinct and ward officers as well as the locally garrisoned military units that served as the coercive arm of police power. The board, in turn, was presided over by the oberpolitseimeister and the politseimeister in Petersburg and Moscow, respectively, by the gorodnichii in most cities, and by the oberkomendant and the gorodnichii in garrison towns.[1]

In keeping alive a state-wide network of police, all controlled hierarchically from the center, the *Ustav blagochiniia* paid homage to a concept that had its inception in the reign of Peter I.[2] Still another Petrine action found its way into the law: entrusting police officials with responsibilities other than those directly connected with the preservation of order and good morals. The law gave the police a handful of minor judicial tasks to perform, as well as the major burden of looking after the general condition (*blagoustroistvo*) of the city, a burden that ranged from the supervision of inns, restaurants, and taverns to the investigation of all deaths.[3]

Whether the reform actually brought improvement to local life cannot be assessed with any assurance at this time, owing to the paucity of studies of police operations. What does seem certain, however, is that the appearance of the *Ustav blagochiniia*, with its attempt to lump a number of diverse responsibilities into a single, hierarchically organized institution, reflects the government's continued adherence to the principle of bureaucratic solutions to problems of local administration.

But matters were not all that simple. As the provincial reform made abundantly clear, it was not within the state's capacity—for want of manpower and money—to extend the bureaucracy's net to cover all aspects of provincial life. Similarly, it was equally beyond the resources of the state to administer the cities wholly through elements of the bureaucratic structure. In both cases, some alternative solution had to be found.

And at that point one encounters the third, and by far the most thorny, problem that confronted the Russian government in its efforts to reform local administration, both in the countryside and the cities: namely, the problem of finding a secure social base on which to ground any reform.

In the case of the provincial reform, social relations in the countryside —in particular the predominance of the landed gentry—provided the ideal social basis for a new political institution, the zemskii ispravnik. If power (however carefully circumscribed and supervised) had to devolve into nonbureaucratic hands, what better individuals could one find than those elected by and from the most trusted estate of the realm, men with a vested interest in rural property?

In the case of the cities, however, finding a basis for new administrative institutions severely taxed the ingenuity of the country's leaders. The posadskie liudi, on whom so many responsibilities of city administration had fallen for so long, had shown themselves to be reluctant administrators for reasons which, if shortsighted in the long run, were completely understandable short-run responses to the burdens of service. Moreover, posad society itself was coming apart at this time, in no small measure thanks to the initiatives of a government that had mixed feelings about the competence of the trade-industrial population and an uncertain mind about how to encourage their development. All in all, the townsmen and the service system associated with them hardly qualified as a promising basis for a revamped city administration. But what other element of urban society stood ready and willing to take the lead? Surely not the gentry, with their newly enhanced leadership role in the countryside. And no other subset of the city population was either numerous enough or powerful enough to command even brief consideration as the raw material for new institutions of city management. There was, of course, an alternative to such an estate-oriented approach to the problem: namely, to devise a structure of urban government based simply on the principle of urban citizenship, open to all residents of the city irrespective of their formal estate or tax category (subject, perhaps, to some property qualifications, as was the custom of the age). But such an alternative, however modish in terms of Western European development, ran directly counter to the traditional basis of Russian society, and it did so at precisely the time when the government was itself engaged in the process of tidying up the social estates—particularly the landed gentry—by making clear their prerogatives and obligations and underwriting them with legal guarantees.

In short, any new political institution—and urban administration is just that—requires an identifiable and dependable social base if it is to enjoy any success. For the cities, the possibilities ranged from patching up the old service institutions and relying on the disintegrating posad commune to the introduction of city government independent of estate principles, based strictly on urban residence. It was a problem similar in many respects to that faced by the government in the area of economic development: that is, whether to maintain the old estate-oriented division of economic responsibilities (however breached it may have been in practice) or to open up economic activities to all and sundry. The decision in the case of city administration—like the decision on the economy —represented something of a compromise, an effort to achieve needed change without upsetting the social applecart. The famed Charter Granted to the Cities was not only a product of Catherine's self-educated fancies, but a genuine effort to find a viable basis for urban administration in a perplexing social milieu.

THE CHARTER GRANTED TO THE CITIES: THE SOCIAL BASIS

The crowning glory of Catherine's city legislation appeared on April 21, 1785, with the publication of the Charter of Rights and Privileges Granted to the Cities of the Russian Empire.[4] The charter was truly comprehensive in scope: it defined in precise terms the rights and duties of the major groups of the city population and it restructured the institutions of city government. However imperfectly, it laid the groundwork for the city order that was to endure—with a brief hiatus during the reign of Paul— until the Great Reforms of the mid-nineteenth century.

The charter itself was a curious document. Its ultimate goals, the creation of a new urban citizenry and of institutions that would make that citizenry effective masters of the cities, were ambitious in the extreme. Its coverage was no less ambitious, for it dealt with a wide range of social, economic, and political matters. Its sources were many and varied. Some, such as the city instructions to the Great Commission, reflected purely Russian needs and traditional ways to meet them. Other sources, including some of the instructions, relied heavily on various foreign statutes, primarily Swedish, Prussian, and Baltic. And the proceedings of government agencies constitute yet another source; a proposal drawn up in 1778 in the Senate, "A Plan concerning the privileges and obligations of the merchantry and meshchanstvo," foreshadowed several sections of the city statute.[5]

While there is much in this record that warrants praise, in particular the active search for new ideas and information, the document has, in fact, drawn fairly heavy fire from historians.[6] The basic shortcomings that have been identified might be summed up as follows: the legislators failed to integrate the disparate elements that contributed to the charter into a systematic body of legislation, suitably tailored to contemporary Russian conditions. To this charge must be added that of poor legislative draftsmanship, which left a number of issues in a shadowy legal limbo. Understandably, this major historical document is at once rewarding and maddening for scholars. For the legal historian it provides a wealth of inadequacies and contradictions that a systematic mind can uncover with obvious relish. For the social historian, the imprecise language, the artificiality of some of the social categories, and the unlikelihood that many of its prescriptions could ever take root in the inhospitable soil of Russia's cities make it difficult to handle judiciously. Finally, like so many pieces of Russian reform legislation, it failed to produce the dramatic changes in Russian urban life that were so long overdue.

But a close look at the charter in light of the weakening urban service system and of new directions in government policy suggests that it tackled some complicated issues in a manner that respected recent changes in urban life even as it looked forward toward a new city order. These features emerged clearly in those passages that dealt with basic social relations in the city. After addressing some outstanding matters concerning the social and economic position of the townsmen and the broader question of urban citizenship, the statute then moved on into uncharted waters, outlining a whole new foundation for social and political affairs in the cities. In the process, it took a necessary first step on the way to a comprehensive urban reform.

Any document focusing on Russian cities, if only from tradition, had to speak to the situation of the posad population. Such attention was all the more urgent in 1785, given the recent changes in the nature of the townsmen's communal life. The statute of 1775, which had been responsible for the formal stratification of the posadskie liudi into merchants and meshchane and for the destruction of the principle of mutual responsibility for taxes, had, after all, been largely a tax reform; and, as such, it had conveyed its important message for the townsmen in the terse, direct phrases of a fiscal document. It did not expand on the economic or social implications of its various articles. There was, as a consequence, need for a fuller statement of the government's reasons for breaking apart an age-old institution of urban life.

The 1785 Charter Granted to the Cities provided, more or less clearly, such a statement. First of all, it reaffirmed and elaborated upon the stratification of the posad people that had been inaugurated by the 1775 reform. The charter maintained the threefold division of the merchant guilds, but raised the amounts of declared capital requisite for entry into each guild. In particular, the shift from meshchanin to merchant required a declared capital of 1,000 rubles, as opposed to the 500 rubles called for in the 1775 law.[7] To be sure, inflation was a constant feature of Catherine's reign, and its presence could in part explain this modification of the requirements for guild membership. But it also seems likely that the government had in mind restricting entry into the guilds still further in order to draw a sharper distinction between those who were really merchants and those of diverse trades who had been casually referred to as merchants simply because of their registry in the posad tax roles.

This interpretation gains force from those sections of the charter that defined the rights and obligations of the various groups that had formerly made up the posad.[8] The first-guild merchants were expected to be involved with large-scale operations, foreign and domestic; the second guild with domestic trade, from region to region and at fairs; and the third guild with small trade in shops and in limited hinterlands about the cities. The language of the law was not exclusive; that is, it did not prohibit merchants of one guild from doing what merchants of another guild did. It merely stated that merchants of each particular guild were "not prohibited from but even encouraged to" undertake trade of a specified kind. In short, the guild merchantry was intended to be the social domain of those involved in significant mercantile activity, properly arranged, of course, in a hierarchy based on size of operations and correspondent wealth.

Other sections of the charter dealt extensively with the craft guilds and their activities (including a Crafts Statute with 117 points) and with the small producers and shopkeepers who made up the bulk of the meshchane (called in this document *posadskie*).[9] Again, the language was that of permission, rather than restriction, in the definition of economic rights. Indeed, there was in these articles of permission and encouragement a certain overlap from group to group—that is, the granting of a given set of permissible activities to more than one category of urban businessmen. This refusal to be absolutely rigid no doubt corresponded to existing conditions, but it may also have been intended to facilitate movement from one category to another.

Nevertheless, in spite of the relative openness of the guidelines for the commercial population, a clear hierarchy has been established among the trade and industrial population, one that was reinforced by a number of privileges bestowed upon the merchants. Most importantly, the guild merchants were freed from numerous state services, including the sale of salt, spirits, and the like; from jobs as inspectors, sworn men, porters, accountants, and guards; and from the provisioning of the court or state.[10] In law, at least, this article signaled the end of state service obligations for the upper echelon of the trade and industrial population. Other privileges either relieved the merchants of annoying burdens or granted them small but socially important honors. Permission for the merchants to fulfill their military obligations through the payment of a sum to be determined each year fell into the former category, as did the exemption of the first two guilds from the humiliation, not to say the pain, of corporal punishment.[11] Various gradations of equipage for each guild fell into the latter category. First-guild merchants could ride in a coach drawn by a pair, and second-guild merchants in a carriage drawn by a pair, but third-guild merchants could not travel in a carriage at all.[12] Obviously these privileges represent concessions, whole or partial, to requests put forward by the merchants in the city instructions to the Great Commission and thus can be regarded as efforts by the government to respond favorably to the complaints and needs of the townsmen.

There was far more, however, to the charter than an effort to assuage the feelings of Russia's tax-paying townsmen. The government's overriding goal in its dealings with the towns was to create a strong, prosperous mercantile class. The notion that such ends might be achieved by preferential treatment for the truly successful merchant had been around since at least the early years of Catherine's reign and the 1775 tax reform had laid an institutional basis for such treatment by separating merchants from nonmerchants. Now, in 1785, the government expanded the inducements to mercantile activity and, so that no one would underestimate the seriousness of the matter, enshrined the rights and privileges of the merchants in a document parallel to the one affirming the status of the foremost estate of the realm, The Charter to the Nobility.

The clear-cut differentiation of the constituent elements of the trade and industrial population and the special privileges granted its summit also confirmed the government decision, apparent already in 1775, to refuse to lend a hand in the maintenance of a closed, tightly knit urban commercial and manufacturing estate such as the posad population had once, with some justification, claimed to be. Should further evidence of this direction of government policy be required, it can be found in the provisions of the charter that granted peasants the right to sell goods of their own production in the cities.[13] With that permission, the government formally struck from the record a central feature of the townsmen's urban economic rights, though one that had shown itself to be largely a paper right, honored most often in the breach. The relationship of state and townsmen had traveled a long way from the government's official protection—as expressed in the settlement of the mid-seventeenth century—of exclusive posad economic interests to the relatively open attitude of Catherine's government toward the social character of nonagricultural economic activity.

Clarification of the position of the tax-paying townsmen was, as argued, a necessary prelude to any thoroughgoing urban reform. But it is also true that the townsmen constituted only one part of the urban population, and not a majority at that. Indeed, the old identification of city and posad, long anachronistic, had been effectively laid to rest by the reform of 1775. It was imperative, then, that a new and broader institutional and conceptual framework be constructed, one that would embrace all residents of the cities and thereby give them all an opportunity, theoretically at least, to participate in city life. As mentioned earlier, the general survey had paved the way for a territorial concept of the city and the election of city mayors had led to the concept of an urban electorate. It remained for the charter to spell out precisely what urban citizenship entailed.

Working on the premise that a city constitutes the sum of the population within its geographical confines, the charter regarded as citizens "all those who in the city are either old-time residents, or were born there or settled there, or have homes or other buildings or places or land, or who are registered in merchant or craft guilds, or who perform service for the city or who are registered in the tax roll and accordingly bear service burdens for the city."[14] In short, nearly everyone was covered by this definition except transient peasants. The concept of urban citizenship thus reached far beyond the confines of the posad, beyond even the broader interpretation of citizenship advanced by Peter I in his unsuccessful effort to diversify and enrich the urban setting. In so doing, it responded to the changing social composition of the cities as well as to the need for new institutional devices that could pave the way for broader participation in the life of the cities.

The concept of citizenship ceased to be an abstraction and gained real substance from Section D of the charter, which granted civil and property rights to all city inhabitants. The city dweller (referred to in this context as meshchanin—yet another example of the perplexing inexactitude in the drafting of the document)[15] was not to be deprived of his name, his life, or his property without proper and lawful judicial proceedings. Moreover, the law forbad slandering city dwellers by word or writing, and called for fines—amounts unspecified—to be paid by the offending parties.[16] Here one sees the empress fighting two separate, but ultimately related battles. The guarantees of due process for life and property followed from her pursuit of a *Rechstaat*, a well-ordered, legally based state where clear rules carefully observed are believed to hold great promise for stability and prosperity. The protection afforded the name of the merchant harks back to an older struggle, that is, to the need to enhance the social status of nongentry society, particularly urban merchants. Such protection, it will be recalled, had been proffered as far

back as the *Ulozhenie*, though only to a small subset of the urban population. One can, of course, read these actions of the empress as so many
manifestations of legislative symmetry, the balancing off of the rights
and privileges of the townsmen with those granted to the nobility in their
charter of the same year. No doubt there is some truth in such an interpretation. But the securing of the life, property, and name of the urban
dweller made sense on its own terms, for without such protection, the
townsmen, perennial victims of governmental arbitrariness and social
discrimination, could hardly be expected to contribute their full share to
the society. The towns and their inhabitants had become much too important in the eyes of the government to be left un-cared for.

Refinements of the social status of the trade and industrial population
and the annunciation of a broader and fuller definition of urban citizenship were necessary steps toward the creation of a new city order, but by
themselves they were not sufficient to establish a wholly adequate social
basis for such an order. Some means had to be found to bring together
into a cohesive society the disparate elements that made up the expanded
urban citizenry, elements that had long stood in hostile relationship to
one another. In particular, institutions had to be created that would at
one and the same time honor the traditional, if recently modified, institutions of the merchants, guild artisans, and meshchane, while at the same
time making it possible to accommodate the interests of the newly elevated citizens who were not part of the former posad milieu. It was in
search of such institutional arrangements that the charter departed from
policy lines already adumbrated to make its most creative contribution.

Specifically, the law called for the division of the citizens into six distinct categories: (1) real (*nastoiashchie*) citizens, that is, those who possessed property in the city; (2) merchants of all guilds; (3) artisans; (4)
foreigners from other states or from other cities engaged in industry in
the towns; (5) honorary (*imenitye*) citizens, an extremely mixed collection embracing artists, learned men, elected officials, bankers, wholesale
traders, and capitalists of any calling worth 50,000 rubles or more; (6)
posad people, that is, "those who feed themselves by industry, crafts, or
manual labor." The law guaranteed freedom of movement from category
to category. A pie seller, as soon as he amassed a fortune of 50,000
rubles, could join the company of the honorary citizens.[17]

It was the intention of the empress that these six groupings be more
than abstract divisions of the population for the purpose of recordkeep-
ing: each of them was to have a life of its own. The law empowered each
group to hold meetings at which common business would be discussed
and the election of various city officials could be held.[18]

Some of the groups possessed their own self-regulating institutions, such as the guilds of the merchants or the craft boards of the artisans. And there were, of course, a certain number of social privileges passed around: exemption from corporal punishment for merchants of the first two guilds and honorary citizens; permission for honorary citizens to have summer houses and gardens beyond the city limits; and rules of livery to mark off the upper strata of city society.[19]

It is not easy to ferret out the organizing principles of this peculiar division of the city population. Since no less than four groups—merchants, artisans, foreigners, and posad people (all of which had once been part of the posad commune)—could be engaged in trade in the broadest sense of the word, the division was not made according to occupation. Nor were the categories based on wealth. Nothing in the legislation suggested that a posad trader need be any poorer than a third-guild merchant or an artisan, although de facto that would likely be the case. Furthermore, the honorary-citizen grouping included artists and sculptors, men not generally known for their wealth, as well as bankers with a personal capital of 100,000 to 200,000 rubles. Nor was citizenship limited to those who held property in the towns, for persons in the last five categories did not need to own urban real estate in order to register in the city inhabitants' book. Finally, the groupings of real and of honorary citizens, by their all-inclusiveness, ran counter to the concept of estate divisions of society.[20]

Apparently Catherine had in mind the introduction of corporate organization into Russia's cities.[21] The principle operated at two levels. First, each of the six categories of city inhabitants was to have a corporate life of its own, based, presumably, on the shared interests of its members or on preexisting institutional arrangements such as merchant or craft guilds. It was expecting a great deal, however, to hope that each of these categories of citizens would coalesce into an efficient working unit, given the inconsistent principles on which the categories had been devised and given the fact that some of the categories had no basis whatsoever in social reality. On the second and more important level, the empress sought to apply the corporate principle to the city as a whole, for corporate powers are precisely what the statute entrusted to the citizens and their primary organization, the gathering of city society.

The appearance of this principle was wholly in keeping with other aspects of the sovereign's social and political policy—especially where the gentry were concerned. The corporate organization of gentry society, well under way in the 1770s, was confirmed by legislation of November 25, 1778 that formally endowed the local gatherings of the nobility with specific rights and privileges.[22] As Robert Jones argues, the growing corporate sense of the gentry during the decade 1775-1785, though at first frightening to the monarchy, proved beneficial to the state in the long run. It made possible the replacement of the old compulsory means of securing service from the gentry by a positive, and hence preferable, set of incentives, largely psychological in nature, which led them to participate in government at the local level out of motives of self interest or even of public interest. This emerging corporate structure of the landed gentry was capped off by the Charter Granted to the Nobility of 1785, a document that spelled out even more precisely the rights and duties of the premier estate of the realm.[23]

Bringing the corporate principle to bear on the reorganization of the cities proved a far more challenging undertaking. However divided gentry society may have been—and it took six subdivisions of the gentry to properly acknowledge distinctions of birth and origin of gentry status, even while trying to create a homogeneous set of principles to govern their actions—the fact remains that it had considerably more coherence going for it than did the amorphous lot of city dwellers. But it was precisely for the purpose of forging the urban citizenry into a new and effective estate that Catherine introduced the corporate idea. Indeed, evidence dating from the beginning of Catherine's reign argues that she wished to treat Russia's cities as a whole and to place all their residents in the same neat package. They would constitute her "middle kind of people" (*srednii rod*), in that they would fall into a distinct social group midway between the gentry and the peasantry. She laid out her view of this intermediate social group in her famous Instruction (*Nakaz*) designed to guide the deliberations of the deputies chosen to draft a new code of laws. "This class of men, of which one must speak, and from which the Empire is promised much benefit, when it will have received a constitution solid and tending to encourage good morals and love of work, is the middle estate [*l'Etat mitoyen*]."[24] The empress realized, however, that the middle estate of people did not at that time exist. In a letter dated April 6, 1766, to Marie-Therese Rodet Jeoffrin, Catherine observed that it was her duty to bring a middle estate into existence.[25]

To create this middle class was a task at once difficult and potentially dangerous. The difficulty lay precisely in the diversity of the urban population. How was one—even an enlightened empress—to draw together into a cohesive body gentry, peasants, raznochintsy, and the diverse remnants of posad society? Just because they all held residence in the city, there were no grounds for believing that they were willing to set aside the prejudices and enmities that had traditionally animated their mutual relations. In the unlikely event that a single estate could have been formed of such disparate materials, there lurked the potential for great danger to the government. To have turned all these people loose, linked only by common urban residence, would have meant abandoning many of the traditional forms of control that the government exercised over society through the means of clearly defined social groupings. There could be no predicting—and perhaps no controlling—what might be done by free and independent citizens of a town. Thus Catherine sought to accommodate tradition, the pressing forces of social change, her own views as to social organization, and the needs of the state by making all permanent residents of the cities into urban citizens, while keeping them fragmented in what she hoped would be manageable subgroups. Such an explanation makes the muddle of groups of city society seem less irrational than it does at first glance. Indeed, one might consider this section of the charter a most ingenious response to a problem of great difficulty for modernizing reformers everywhere: namely, how to create from the diverse elements of a hierarchical and traditional society a fluid, mobile, aggressive, and competent middle class. That Catherine was unsuccessful in her efforts, as Peter I had been before her, is perhaps less a measure of her failure as a reformer than of the difficulty of the task she confronted.

THE CHARTER GRANTED TO THE CITIES: ADMINISTRATIVE INSTITUTIONS

With the urban citizenry organized into what seemed—to the empress, at any rate—like rational and manageable subgroups, it remained only for the charter to provide political institutions whereby these varied groups could come together for the administration of local affairs. The charter sought to attain that end through the creation of three political institutions: the city society, the common council (*duma*), and the six-man council.

The largest of these bodies was the city society (*gradskoe obshchestvo*), which was composed of all city residents over the age of twenty-five years who had an income of at least fifty rubles a year.[26] Those who so qualified might be looked upon as the real citizens of their communities, for they alone possessed genuine political rights, over and above the rights of person and property that accrued to all who fell under the charter's broad definition of urban citizenship. These stiff property qualifications for the gathering of the city society essentially limited participation to merchants of the first two guilds and to a handful of honorary citizens. It could be argued that the old posad commune had been more representative, both in terms of property qualifications and of the spread of its members' occupations, than the gathering of the city society, supposedly a major organ of the new, all-inclusive urban citizenry.[27] It would probably be a mistake, however, to dwell on that apparent contradiction.

The precedent for singling out an elite for special treatment had already been set in the charter's handling of the socioeconomic affairs of the upper strata of the merchantry, and it seems clear that the political message of the charter was the same: help out the cities by giving the elite a stake in local political life. It was not, in the end, a policy very different from that which stood behind Catherine's reforms of local, or rural, administration. Nor was it entirely out of keeping with eighteenth-century notions of political franchise.

The charter, as it created and empowered the city society, provided the cities for the first time ever with a legal basis from which to launch an assault on their multitudinous problems. It called for regular meetings or gatherings (*sobranie*) every three years "in winter time"; it granted the society numerous signs and symbols of its identity, such as archives and seals; and it allowed for the establishment of a treasury in the name of city society.[28] In the judgment of Ditiatin, these features of the charter in effect granted the rights of a juridical person—that is, corporate rights— to the gathering of city society.[29] The city itself, therefore, through the instrument of the gathering, ceased to be the collection of isolated social groups it had once been, but became instead a legal entity with the capacity to act on behalf of the mutual interests of its members. The right of the cities to purchase land, for example, heretofore impossible under the law, was but one of the avenues opened up through the powers entrusted to city society.[30] Clearly a milestone had been reached in the legal history of the Russian city.

As significant as the introduction of the corporate principle may have been, the bulk of the charter's treatment of the gathering of city society focused on the precise set of political responsibilities the gathering was expected to dispatch at its triennial sessions. Members could bring to the attention of the governor all matters of community life that they felt warranted consideration, and they could make recommendations for action. They also checked on the condition of the registry books—the records of who belonged to what category of city dweller.[31] But these were, for the most part, bureaucratic exercises, without great influence on the affairs of the city. The real political power of the meeting of the city society lay in its right to elect officials for various posts in the city administration. The meeting elected the mayor, judges of the oral courts, elders in charge of the registry books, burgomistry, and ratmany to serve in the magistracy, and two city councilors to sit on the police board.[32] There is no finer example of the glaring inconsistencies that permeate this document than the election of these officials by the meeting of the city society. Only the mayor and the councilors who sat on the police board functioned in institutions that were city-wide in authority. The remaining officials worked in what were, basically, estate institutions. Yet they were elected not by the particular estate they served, but by a gathering that was theoretically an organ of the entire city population, an "all-estate" institution, as the language of the day would have it. Kizevetter found the conflict of these two organizing principles, the one based on a single estate, the other on all estates, particularly vexing.[33] Yet in the last analysis, those people who qualified for participation were more than likely to be wealthy merchants, who were the appropriate ones to select as magistracy officials. Here, the sloppiness of the legislation probably did not matter.

In addition to providing for periodic meetings of all the qualified citizens, the charter set up two representative institutions, the common council and the six-man council. The common council was the larger body, containing representatives chosen by each of the six categories of city inhabitants. Just how large it was depended on the size of the city and the composition of its population.[34] The electoral rules were complex, and the weightings accorded to the various social groups cannot be determined with certainty. Nevertheless, the law seems to have favored the wealthy, the educated, foreign merchants, and in the bigger cities, the guild craftsmen.[35] Whatever the breakdown may have been, the fact remains that the common council, with its representation from all six categories of city inhabitants, must have been more representative of the total urban population than was the gathering of the city society.

The charter granted to the common council a broad range of competences:

> 1) To supply to the inhabitants of the city the necessary means for their feeding or maintenance. 2) To protect the city from quarrels and suits from the surrounding cities and villages. 3) To preserve among the inhabitants of the city peace, quiet, and harmony. 4) To prohibit all that is contradictory to good order and good morals, leaving, however, matters relating to the part of the police to be fulfilled by positions and people established for this. 5) By the means of observing good faith and by all allowable means to encourage the import into the city and sale of all that can serve the welfare and advantage of the inhabitants. 6) To look after the solidity of public city buildings, to see to the construction of all that is needed, to the management of squares, trade concourses, wharves, warehouses, stores and things similar to this which can be necessary, advantageous, and useful for the city. 7) To be concerned about the growth of institutions under the bureau of public charities. 8) To settle doubts and problems about crafts and the merchant guilds on the basis of the regulations made about this.[36]

Then, after entrusting the council with these weighty tasks, the charter virtually precluded any action being taken by limiting the council to one sitting every three years.[37]

At that one session, however, the common council elected from among its ranks the members of the six-man council, one from each of the population categories.[38] This smaller board, premanently in session, became the effective executive arm of self-government in the cities. Again, the inadequacies of the legislation make it difficult to determine just how the six-man council was intended to operate. The law gave no guidelines for procedure and it said nothing about the relationship between the mayor and the council. But matters of that sort have a way of working themselves out in practice. Of much greater importance were the competences ascribed to the six-man council by the charter: the same ones assigned to the common council. In effect, then, it managed only the economy (*khoziaistvo*) of the city—building regulations, provisioning, street maintenance, regulation of commercial activities, and so forth.[39] The council had no responsibilities for tax collecting; that task resided with the fiscal board and the county treasury. Judicial matters were handled by the magistracies or by estate courts of the gentry. The police part of the statewide police hierarchy looked after the preservation of law and order. The only police power that the council possessed was that of preserving good order at markets and bazaars.

The law said a great deal more about the responsibilities of the six-man council, about its supervisory capacities, and about its relationships with other branches of city and central government. Characteristically, these articles were cloudy, occasionally contradictory, and sometimes incomplete. The relationship between the six-man council and the magistracy is a case in point.

The reform of 1775 had left the magistracy strictly a judicial body, though in fact it continued to perform many tasks connected with the activities of the commercial population of the towns. The Charter Granted to the Cities maintained in force the magistracy's estate court functions, but went on to add still others. They ranged from regulating weekly markets to supervising foreign merchants to keeping extensive real-estate records for the city.[40] Clearly, these were functions which, by any reasonable reading of the legislation, also fell under the competences granted to the common council and to the six-man council.

Thus the law had given over to an institution that was formally an estate court functions that it had already granted to institutions more representative of the entire community. The potential for conflict was substantial. One suspects that institutional inertia, namely, the fact that the magistracy had been dealing with such matters off and on since its inception, played a strong role in the drafting of this document.

The granting of the same responsibilities to two agencies of government distinctly different in composition and basic function was bad enough, but the charter rose to even greater heights of confusion when it spelled out the supervisory functions of higher-level magistracies. According to the law, guberniia-level magistracies had authority not only over magistracies in lesser cities—a wholly appropriate relationship—but over the common councils and six-man councils in such cities as well. Article 176 states that "whoever is unsatisfied with the common city council or with the six-man council, then let him take his complaints to the guberniia magistracy." Since the law had previously made clear that the guberniia magistracy was to be chosen only by merchants and meshchane, it would appear to be largely an estate institution (to the extent that these former posad registrants could still be said to compose an estate) and a judicial one at that. Yet it had been given jurisdiction over the entire city administrative apparatus.

Such logical inconsistencies and failures to sustain basic organizational principles have predictably drawn the fire of legal historians.[41] But, as suggested earlier, an assessment of this document ought not to turn solely upon its logical structure. The empress had set about the difficult task of remaking the cities, a task rendered all the more demanding by her cautious and wise refusal simply to tear up and throw away every vestige of the traditional order. If, for example, the magistracy had been around for the better part of the century exercising, for better or for worse, a kind of supervisory role over the affairs of the cities, then there was no reason to terminate that relationship just because it violated an abstract principle of organization which holds that some institutions ought to be estate-oriented while others ought to be all-estate in nature. It is a good deal harder, I confess, to justify the assignment of the same set of responsibilities to two different government agencies.

The real test of the charter as a document ought not to be based on a tally sheet of its contradictions and confusions, but on the appropriateness of the newly created institutions to changing social conditions, on the likelihood of their functioning effectively as political organs, and on the powers at their disposal. Judged on these counts, the charter merits praise while at the same time it raises cause for concern. On the positive side, the charter unambiguously recognized the cities as entities in themselves and thereby laid to rest, in formal institutional terms, the Muscovite city. It called for a new corporate basis for city society which, if it did not correspond directly to the social forces present in the city, represented an imaginative effort to transform those forces into a new urban estate. It also created a plausible set of administrative institutions that integrated these corporations for the sake of urban management. Through these innovations the foundations were laid both for a sense of urban citizenship and for concrete actions that could bring considerable benefit to the cities. But there were drawbacks to the document as well. A close examination suggests that the appearance of innovation and freshness conjured up by new offices and new titles can be misleading, especially where the new agencies of city administration were concerned. The cities were to have no independent institutions of self-rule; what they got was a set of administrative institutions with carefully delimited powers. The common council and the six-man duma, their lengthy list of competences notwithstanding, exercised authority primarily over the physical environment of the city. Other responsibilities of urban administration resided in other institutions of earlier provenance. Moreover, the newly created institutions could in no way be considered autonomous. Even the narrow areas under their control were subject to supervision and interference from the top officials in the provincial hierarchy, the namestniki and the governors. That relationship followed naturally from the dominant position reserved for the landed gentry in all governmental activities, at both the central and the local level. All this ought not be taken to mean that the reform was intrinsically meaningless: the symbolic value of having institutions to speak for and act on behalf of the city itself—and not the posad-city—should not be dismissed lightly, nor should the concrete powers of action, especially those connected with the acquisition and disposition of property in the name of the city, be overlooked. At the very least, the potential for the development of more effective urban administration inhered in the reform.

THE CHARTER GRANTED TO THE CITIES: THE EXECUTION OF THE LAW

No systematic study of the implementation of the Charter Granted to the Cities has yet been undertaken. Kizevetter and Ditiatin did address themselves to the subject as a part of broader works, but neither treated it exhaustively. Research is limited in part by the available sources and in part by the disruption brought about by Paul's decision to annul the charter as of September 4, 1800.[42] In the former case, the more readily available evidence tends, naturally, to pertain to Moscow and Petersburg and gives the customary capital-city bias. In the latter case, any complete evaluation of the reform becomes a matter of nineteenth-century history—Alexander I restored the previous legislation in toto in April of 1801—where the changes that were overtaking Russia make for a substantially different framework of interpretation.⁴³ Nevertheless, it is possible to answer tentatively a number of questions about the operation of the charter in the fifteen years that preceded its untimely demise.

Perhaps the most elementary question to ask is whether the reform was able to survive the overly ambitious and at times confused and contradictory legislation that brought it into being. The answer here is a simple affirmative. In the smaller cities, where the local population was neither sufficiently large nor diverse, it was impossible to maintain a full complement of the new urban institutions. Often the common council was supplanted by the gathering of city society, and the six-man council was staffed by three or four individuals who undertook as best they could to follow the charter's guidelines.⁴⁴ Another apparent shortcoming of the charter, at least from the perspective of legal historians, was that it seemed to allow individuals who qualified for more than one category of citizenship to have multiple political representation. This situation did arise on occasion. Iakov Khonkhen, a Riga miller, simultaneously served as an elder of his craft guild, belonged to the third merchant guild, and held office in the common council as a representative of the real (nastoiashchie) citizens.⁴⁵ But although such a practice violated the all-estate principle so dear to some historians, it does not seem to have offended any deepseated sense of equity among the townsmen. The granting of overlapping jurisdictions and duties to the common council and the six-man council, or to the two councils and the magistracy, was another potential source of difficulty, but actual practice tended to establish workable relationships. The common council in Moscow seems to have met more often than the law specified, mostly to add its confirmation to crucial decisions. By and large, however, the six-man council carried the brunt of the load, as the law intended, without serious conflicts with the common council or the magistracy.⁴⁶ It is useful to keep in mind in this regard that local government as exercised prior to 1785, especially by the magistracy, had not been characterized by vigorous efforts to extend jurisdictions or to add powers. If anything, the tradition had been to evade or to pass on responsibilities. There was not likely to be great competition for the council's tasks.

How well did the new institutions achieve the empress' objective of drawing all sorts of urban residents into the administration of the city? Here the evidence suggests that goal and achievement were far apart. Since the commercial and manufacturing population had always participated in city administration, the issue really turned on the involvement of other social groups—most notably, the gentry. Their willingness to participate in urban administration seemed to have been demonstrated during the first elections of mayors. At that time, many gentry stood for office and were duly elected.[47] But when it came time to select the members of the new city government, gentry became a scarce commodity. Those citizens of Riga who were elected to the common council from the ranks of real citizens (nastoiashchie) were petty bureaucrats, copiests, clerks, and the like. But there were no gentry involved.[48] The same thing held true for Moscow, at least between 1786 and 1789, where the highest officials elected to the common council as real citizens were collegiate assessors and one titular councillor.[49] The really powerful gentry who resided in the towns simply did not participate, and in a short while the petty servitors dropped out of the picture as well.

So it was that the new city institutions fell into the hands of the merchants, of the guild craftsmen, and of the less-prosperous posad people. Precisely who among these groups held the upper hand depended on the institution involved and, to some extent, on the size of the city. Apparently the gathering of city society tended to be dominated by wealthy citizens, particularly the guild merchants, who thus controlled the election of mayors, the magistracy, and other judicial functionaries, as well as of the police-board representatives.[50] The two councils, however, were more broadly based, including not only representatives of the guild merchants but craftsmen and petty traders as well, with a predominance of the latter.[51] The role of craftsmen and petty traders was most pronounced in the smaller cities, where wealthy guild merchants were few and far between; the guild merchants showed themselves far stronger in the councils of the economically more prosperous cities. Whatever the relative distribution of power may have been, one fact is clear: in the absence of gentry participation the majority of the officials in the newly created councils were individuals whose roots lay in the old posad society. In practice, therefore, the 1785 reform failed to achieve for its new administrative institutions a social base significantly different from that which had stood behind the posad-magistracy city order.

Such a failure surely boded ill for the new institutions of city government, but any firm assessment of their fate has to be based not on their social composition but on their performance of the tasks of city administration. On this count, there is little positive evidence to go on. The mundane regulatory acts that constituted the bulk of the council's work have left few traces in the historical record. What has survived is a body of evidence attesting to the difficulties encountered by the new institutions, which, in its turn suggests that they were able to do far less than the law had envisaged them doing.

It was, for example, some time before the Moscow six-man council had an office to work in, and even after one turned up, it lacked the necessary equipment. Collections of laws, data about the inhabitants of the city, even a city map were lacking.[52] Without such information the new city government could scarcely make a move. And, of course, there was the perennial problem of money. The cities made do with their old revenue sources: fines, small special levies, guild collections, and one percent from the liquor tax collections. A small fee for registration in the city residents' book constituted the only new income source granted by the charter. In the event that the city showed a deficit, it had to be made up by collections from the citizens or by borrowing from the merchant guilds.[53] The relative stability of income in St. Petersburg over a twelve-year period illustrates just how little the cities gained from the reform by way of resources to tackle their basic problems. In 1785, the income of the city was estimated at 20,000 to 30,000 rubles; by 1797, it had risen to 36,000 rubles.[54] Administrative salaries could easily have taken the bulk of that sum. When one allows for inflation, the gain becomes negligible.

As if the hurdles outlined above were not troublesome enough, the new city institutions confronted still another, and greater, barrier: interference from officials representing central-government institutions. The problems here took a variety of forms, running the gamut from indifference to outright infringement of rights. The Moscow common council, in a complaint to the provincial administration, contended that "various governmental agencies responded to communications of the council very sluggishly or not at all," mostly, the petitions explained, because these agencies were loath to recognize the council as an official governmental body.[55] At the other extreme, the governor of Moscow province and his board demanded that members of the city's six-man duma police the marketplaces and ferry landings to check on weights, measures, prices, and the like. Since the guild merchants were represented on the council, that demand clearly constituted a violation of the letter of the charter that exempted them from unpaid service; and more broadly interpreted, it seems a violation of the spirit of the reform as well.[56] Here, as in the case of the police, tradition demonstrated its stubbornness in the form of unpaid service being required by the state of its urban citizens.

Perhaps the most eloquent testimony to the shallow roots put out by the new institutions of city administration comes from an imperial decree of 1802, after the resurrection of the reform of 1785 had been undertaken. This decree noted that "no one of the inhabitants of Petersburg has any information about the measure or basis of responsibilities, either monetary or personal," and that "no one can with assurance define for himself the breadth of his obligations or the means of meeting them."[57] The citizens had no notion of their obligations because, among other things, the council had no idea what was going on. Indeed, the central document of the new city government, the city-inhabitants book, had been kept in full only three years, 1784-1788.[58] After that it fell into desuetude. Alexandrine policy toward the cities constituted but another variation on an old theme: special commissions to meet this or that pressing need of urban society, coupled with the presence in attenuated form of the "formal, legal" administrative institutions.[59]

This recounting of the implementation of the Charter Granted to the Cities may produce a sense of déjà vu. An institution of local government, staffed largely by people drawn from the urban mercantile population, inadequately funded, harassed by crown officials—was it not the magistracy in new clothes? In operation the similarity was considerable and real. But in principle, there were differences of moment. The pre-1785 magistracy had dealt at most with a single estate of the realm— though a decaying one. Moreover, it had served primarily as the supervisor of that estate's service obligations to the crown. Its urban administrative functions, though a part of the magistracy's duties from its inception, were clearly secondary. The post-1785 urban institutions differed on both counts. They were city institutions, even if some eligible citizens disdained to participate. And the objectives of these institutions were, for all intents and purposes, local. The state service component had largely disappeared. Thus the new institutions represented in principle something new and better, though it is another matter to demonstrate that they imparted positive new directions to the life of the nation's cities. In times of complexity and change, it was perhaps enough of an achievement merely to break even.

Both Kizevetter and Ditiatin lamented the fate of the Charter Granted to the Cities, especially the failure of the reform to diversify the social composition of local government or to reduce the final authority of crown officials over the entire urban milieu. Both men were devotees of the all-estate principle and seem to have felt that it held the key to the flowering of Russia's cities. But such a view, based in all likelihood on an anachronism, that is, their own liberal political views, was simplistic. Securing the participation of the gentry in urban government was hardly an adequate remedy for the problems at hand. It was not so much a matter of who ran local government as it was a matter of how well prepared they were to assert the rights of the towns against all comers. One cannot help but think that a more aggressive and innovative mercantile community might have got the job done better, especially if it were powerful enough to defend its interests against the central government. But such a mercantile community was not the legacy of Russia's history. In light of the inherent weakness of the townsmen, it is similarly unrealistic to expect that the reform would have weakened the hold of the central government on the cities. The state had been a powerful presence in the cities for centuries, and, if anything, it was gaining in its ability to manipulate the lives of the urban dwellers through a growing bureaucracy. In Russia, as elsewhere, the probability that an expanding bureaucratic establishment would voluntarily curtail its sphere of influence and cede some of its power to other political agencies in society was not very great.

THE FATE OF THE POSAD COMMUNE

In discussing the effects of the Catherinean reforms, this chapter and the preceding one have implied, without ever stating it as a fact, that the posad commune came to an end some time during the final third of the eighteenth century. Such an indirect approach is completely in keeping with the tradition established in the literature, which, with only an occasional exception, either ignores the subject or speaks obliquely on it.

General statements on the city, such as the one written by N. N. Firsov for the Granat' encyclopedia, do not address the issue at all, nor does the essay on *posadskie liudi* in the new *Soviet Historical Encyclopedia*.[60] The specialized literature, however, comes a good deal closer to the mark. Both Kizevetter and Klokman connect the fate of the posad commune with the introduction of the Charter Granted to the Cities of 1785. In Kizevetter's eyes, the commune constituted an organ of city self-administration (*samoupravlenie*), even if, as he was at great pains to demonstrate, the central government so often thwarted the exercise of the commune's prerogatives. Thus the new set of urban administrative institutions created by Catherine II effectively supplanted the posad commune in the latter's administrative capacity.[61] Klokman gives the same reform quite another reading. For him, economic developments in the latter half of the eighteenth century and their consequent social impact had led to the gradual weakening of the estate exclusivity (*zamknutost'*) of the posad commune. The reform of 1785 merely continued this process through "the broadening of the posad commune by the inclusion in it of representatives of other social categories in the city."[62] One direct, unambiguous comment on the ultimate resting place of the posad commune may be found in a recently published study on Russian population by Ia. E. Vodarskii. The tax reform of 1775, Vodarskii argues, "in fact destroyed the posad communes."[63] But he does not elaborate the point.

There is some truth to each of these arguments, but no one of them is of sufficient scope to yield up a wholly satisfactory explanation. In fact, it was a concatenation of events, trends, and legislative reforms that undermined the commune's chief characteristics and functions during Catherine's reign and brought about the demise of the commune as it had traditionally functioned. The decline of the posad's economic privileges

had severely eroded the townsmen's status as *the* commercial and manufacturing estate of the realm. The falling off of service responsibilities and
the transfer of local government operations to new administrative organs, purportedly of broader social composition, shifted many a burden
from the midst of the communal society. And the tax reform of 1775, in
eliminating the mutual responsibility for tax payments, severed the strongest bond that held together posad society. These phenomena occurred
over the course of decades and together they did in the commune. But
1775 was the crucial year. First, the opening-up of manufacturing to all
citizens was a formal slap in the face of the estate pretentions of the posad
and an act of symbolic importance. Second, and far more important, the
collapse of mutual responsibility separated forever the social groups that
had made up the commune. Henceforth, one must speak of this or that
group of townsmen, of merchants, of meshchane, or of craft guildsmen.
One cannot speak, as before, simply of posadskie liudi.

If the posad ended thus, it seems curious that scholars have been so
reluctant to address its fate directly. There is, perhaps, a simple explanation for that reticence, one that can shed further light on the fate of the
commune and, more generally, speak to the way in which change took
place in Russian society. It may well be that the commune's fortunes in
the late eighteenth century lay hidden behind a facade composed, on the
one hand, of the continued presence in Russian society of terminology
redolent of the old posad and, on the other hand, of the persistence of
certain institutional structures and operations, equally a part of the
posad heritage.

There is, to begin with, the very term *posad*. It appears again and
again in legislative memorials right into the nineteenth century. In most
cases it referred to small settlements of a quasi-urban character. A decree
of June 22, 1820, for example, declared that "the settlement Opechenskii
Riad in Novgorod province be renamed a posad and that its inhabitants
be granted all the rights and privileges that lawfully appertain to city
inhabitants."[64] Similar legislation can be found in the post-1785 period of
Catherine's reign.[65] Just as the term *posad* survived, so too did the appellation *posadskie*. In 1824 a lengthy piece of legislation issued to regulate
merchant and craft guilds and to define the role of other citizens in commercial matters contained a chapter entitled, "O meshchanakh i posad-
skikh." The chapter treated the two groups about equally, but the term
posadskie was rather consistently applied to rural types, to inhabitants of
the kind of posady just referred to.[66] Thus the old notion of the posad as
a territory inhabited by individuals engaged in crafts or trades persisted
into the nineteenth century, but with one significant change—whereas
previously a posad might have been either an integral part of a city or an

isolated entity in the countryside, it appears that in the nineteenth century the term was largely, but not exclusively, restricted to rural commercial settlements. Finally, terms describing social categories, such as *kuptsi* (merchants) or *tsekhi* (craft guilds), retained their validity long after the commune itself had come apart.

It was not just terminology that survived. Basic features of posad organization and functioning also lingered, particularly in tax matters. The traditional function of apportioning and collecting taxes continued in the nineteenth century, with, of course, the crucial difference that each group within the former posad population handled its own affairs. The merchant guilds through their elected elders handled taxes according to the provisions of the reform of 1775 and subsequent legislation.[67] Similarly, it is clear from that section of the *Svod zakonov* summarizing the tax laws that the meshchane as a group, through their elders, apportioned and collected state revenues assessed against them. Craft guilds had the same obligations.[68] Thus, these segments of the urban population, once part of the broader posad commune, themselves maintained the ancient tradition of serving as revenue agents of the state. Still another manifestation of the longevity of the service notion can be found in the magistracy's continued exercise of extrajudicial obligations, "appropriate to police and treasury administration."[69] And, of course, there were the above-mentioned service obligations imposed upon duma members—against their will and in violation of the letter of the law.

The changes that took place in Russian society in the eighteenth century modified significantly the salient features of posad life, but did not eliminate them root and branch. The estate principle suffered the loss of its economic dimension, but the notion of estates persevered. It was engrained in the social mentality of the townsmen as firmly as it was rooted in the police-administrative consciousness of the central bureaucracy. Social divisions, formalized in estates, could hardly disappear overnight. In a like manner, the self-administration and service functions of the posad people had their roots in the traditional service relationship that linked the Russian state with its citizens. Again, though change had laid bare the shortcomings of service for a society striving to keep up with its neighbors, the transformation of government and society together had not been of sufficient magnitude to render service entirely superfluous. Just as the forces of change broke apart the formal structure of the posad commune, so too the forces of custom and inertia kept alive, in varying states of health, many of its features. Traditional ways of getting things done are not dispensed with by the stroke of a legislator's pen. It should come as no surprise, then, that scholars have found the fate of the posad commune so elusive.

CHAPTER ELEVEN

Conclusion

In LOOKING BACK over the history of the posadskie liudi in the eighteenth century, one cannot help being struck by the contrast between a certain element of dynamism—represented by the enlivenment of the rural economy and the vigorous reform efforts of the Petrine and Catherinean governments—and a deep and persistent conservatism—manifested in the tradition-oriented behavior of the townsmen. It is this contrast, along with a comparison of Russia's townsmen with those of Western Europe, that has led the few historians who have written about the posady to display, almost without exception, a measure of disappointment with the modest role played by this social group in the history of early modern Russia. Their work is preoccupied with the weaknesses of the townsmen, with sins both of commission and omission: their shortcomings of commercial technique; their overly close and stultifying relationship with the state; their failure to develop positive, forward-looking ideas that would break the bonds of an estate mentality; and their general timidity, if not outright incompetence.[1] While none of these charges is without some foundation in fact, they have nonetheless been overdrawn, and it can be argued that they have often been advanced less from the compelling force of evidence than for their symbolic value. They represent for many historians the inadequacy of the Russian trade and industrial population in the face of the monumental tasks that history appears to have set for the bourgeoisie. Such judgments, of course, emerge from a perspective that holds, whether explicitly or implicitly, that Western European development provides a model for all societies.

It is undeniable that the nascent Russian middle class, the posadskie liudi, were far from being a driving force capable of sweeping away the feudal order and ushering in a new historical epoch. In many respects they showed themselves to be quite the opposite, that is, an archaic lot, abetting the survival of an old order in its time of crisis.[2] But one must be careful in drawing such judgments lest the townsmen be measured against a set of standards that are wholly extrinsic to their experience, standards that belong neither to the time nor place in which they moved. Justice to actors on the historical stage demands, first of all, that they be examined in terms of the real circumstances that governed their lives.

Russian townsmen operated in a complex world in the seventeenth and eighteenth centuries, and the factors that shaped posad life were numerous and varied. To begin with, the sheer size of the country meant that city development would have to be, in the words of the Soviet scholar Ia. M. Polianskii, "extensive, rather than intensive."[3] According to his argument, the expanding number of cities, a phenomenon that was itself a response to territorial acquisition and internal administrative needs, precluded the urbanization of any one part of the country and in the process ensured that large, socially complex, and economically powerful cities remained few and far between. Most of the cities that dotted the map of the realm thus waged an uphill struggle just to meet in a rudimentary manner the economic and administrative burdens incumbent on them; some failed outright. The resources, human and material, simply were not present.

Extensive development of cities need not entail an enfeebled product; but in the case of early modern Russia, a number of related considerations conspired to make it so. In part, the problem was one of numbers, of finding enough people to make the urban enterprise viable. On this count, the serf system clearly exercised a restraining influence on urban development. Though restrictions on mobility by no means cut off the flow of peasants to the cities, they did raise obstacles to that flow and, perhaps more importantly, made the shift of permanent residence from countryside to city extremely difficult. Although the cities did grow during the century, it seems hard to deny that serfdom restricted that growth and thus curtailed the human resources available to the cities.

In part, too, intensive urban development is a matter of wealth. Here, conditions within the cities, in particular the straitened economic circumstances of the posadskie liudi, worked against the development of a strong, aggressive urban order. Limitations of the domestic market, stiff foreign competition, unsophisticated business techniques, and the heavy burdens of tiaglo all restricted the accumulation of wealth in the hands of Russia's proto-bourgeoisie, a condition which, in turn, made it all the more difficult for them to meet their obligations as businessmen and citizens. To these hard realities of manpower and money ought to be added the matter of social status. The townsmen's subordinate role in the social hierarchy impeded their efforts to secure posad interests, especially where conflicts with the gentry and the gentry's rural dependents were involved. And as the eighteenth century wore on these socially inferior townsmen, devoted to an ever more anachronistic outlook on the social and economic order, had to confront an increasingly powerful and independent bureaucratic establishment. The point is clear: the individuals on whom an intensive development of the city order would have to depend lacked the strength to get the job done. The townsmen could barely meet the essential challenges of their daily existence, let alone lead the way toward broader notions of economic development or civic life.

The preceding argument has been developed largely without reference to the state (the obvious exception being, of course, taxation), and with good cause, for one cannot stress too much the limited capacities of the townsmen themselves. But it is also true that the activities of the state constituted the single most important influence on the lives of the townsmen. In one manner or another, the hand of the state could be seen in most essential relationships within the posad as well as in relationships between the posadskie liudi and other segments of Russian society. Building from land arrangements to the burdens of tiaglo and on to administrative matters, what the state structured for, received from, and expected of the townsmen added up to an enormous bill of particulars. It was precisely this bill of particulars that was responsible for the strong historiographic tradition holding the state accountable for the unsatisfactory condition of the towns and their inhabitants—that is, for the backwardness of urban Russia. Of course, the evidence was given a certain twist, commensurate with the intellectual climate of late nineteenth- and early twentieth-century Russia. The central government was made to appear both massive and willful, capable of penetrating the nooks and crannies of posad life, all to the purpose of serving the ends of that abstract entity, the state, as opposed to the ends of the people. And, of course, only a state jealous of its political prerogatives and suspicious of its citizens could have stifled so effectively all signs of urban autonomy.[4]

This tendency to blame the state for the failings of the townsmen, and, indeed, for the weakness of all elements of Russian society, continues to find expression in the literature, though the sharp, accusatory edges of the argument in its prerevolutionary manifestation have been blunted by the somewhat less value-charged rhetoric of social science. An excellent example of the old argument in new dress can be found in Hans Torke's exploration of the process whereby bureaucracy and society (both viewed in Weberian terms) emerged as independent forces on the Russian scene, parallel in essential character and function to bureaucracy and society in historic Western Europe. Though Torke's attention falls chiefly on the properties of these two institutional phenomena, the state stands always in the background, ready to assume its role as the ultimate arbiter of social relations. Autocracy, in his view, was "an over-developed form of absolutism," which, for political reasons—that is, its reluctance to yield up political power—refused independence not only to society or to the leading element of society, the gentry, but also denied that independence to its own chief agency of rule, the bureaucracy. This position is somewhat balanced by Torke's willingness to acknowledge that not all elements of society were ready for a more independent role and that the townsmen, for their part, effectively rebuffed the guarded efforts of the government to transfer some responsibility to them. But his overall emphasis is clear: political considerations led the state to restrict the budding estates of the realm.[5]

The state's profound influence on social relations is one of the persistent realities of early modern Russia. But care must be taken lest arguments developed from that basic reality become one-sided, ignoring what was in fact an interaction between state and society and in the process exaggerating or distorting the powers of the state. In the case at hand, while it would be folly to contend that the state was not the dominant partner in its relations with the townsmen, the fact remains that the links that bound state and posad arose not so much from the overwhelming strength of one party and the abject weakness of the other, as from the respective weaknesses of each. The inadequacies of the townsmen are obvious enough, and they can be accounted for in a significant degree by the inherent deficiencies of the Russian mercantile community. The weaknesses of the state, however, are less obvious. To understand them, matters of political power must be sorted out from those of administrative capacity, that is, the power to make decisions must be distinguished from the ability to effect them.

In political terms, the autocratic regime ruled the country with apparent ease. No social group, except perhaps the peasants rising in a *jacquerie*, could be considered a serious rival to the tsar's sovereignty. And yet, when it came down to the capacity to govern, both to manage the daily run of affairs and to carry through pressing reforms, the Russian state appeared considerably less forceful. In the countryside the state effectively surrendered control over vast numbers of its citizens, partly to secure and reward the service of the gentry, partly because the machinery of the state could not deal directly with so many souls. The urban service relationship emerged when neither the cities nor the central bureaucratic establishment proved up to the complex tasks of national administration. This stern necessity forced the state to look to the townsmen for vital assistance in a number of areas of state and local administration. To strengthen this relationship and, not incidentally, to promote the power and well-being of the nation, the state also found it desirable to protect and to foster urban economic enterprise, a policy that at the same time accommodated the basic interests of the posad community. All this is to say nothing of the failure of some of the more grandiose plans of Peter I and Catherine II to transform both the townsmen and the cities into models of middle-class behavior and organization.

If, then, the state's political power remained beyond challenge, the same cannot be said for its administrative abilities. Indeed, one might well adhere to J. L. H. Keep's assertion that in a sense the country was undergoverned, that the wherewithal for effective administration was conspicuously absent.[6] From such a perspective, what has appeared to many scholars a country suffering from an all-powerful, willful, and domineering state apparatus turns out in truth to be a rather badly administered one whose sovereign and bureaucracy grasped at every opportunity to rule or to compel others to rule in their behalf, lest the job simply not be done at all.

Urban service arose at a time when the state's bureaucratic machinery was just coming into its own and was far from being able to meet the challenges incumbent upon it *and* at a time when urban society itself had only the most limited administrative capabilities. The service arrangement did work, in the sense that it enabled the state to manage its affairs adequately, if not ideally, in a vital era of transition. But once the conditions that gave rise to and sustained service began to alter—in particular, once the central government grew in size and efficiency—the service system began to wind down, though the remnants of service that lingered after the reign of Catherine II suggest that a completely satisfactory replacement for it was hard to come by. The deterioration of service stands as a final piece of evidence of the inverse relationship between service and central-government power; and it reinforces the notion that service sprang from state weakness rather than from excessive state power.

Implicit in this history of the townsmen and the government lies yet another challenge to those who hold an inordinately strong state responsible for the rocky path of Russian development. One might well ask how the apparatus of a nation-state could grow so powerful while its cities and their nascent middle class remained so weak. Would not the state apparatus need the material wealth and human resources of the cities to reach such heights? Surely the rise of the modern nation-state in Western Europe is unthinkable without the contributions of its prosperous and powerful cities. The Russian nation-state, by contrast, had to make do with considerably less in the way of wealth and of individuals trained to manage complex administrative institutions; and the state order that emerged there, heavily dependent on the service of its citizens, represented a necessary accommodation with that reality. It goes without saying that the result of such an accommodation was a state less sophisticated and less effective than many of its European rivals.

All this is not to say that the townsmen did not find the state powerful and at times oppressive; from their perspective the state was an ominous force, demanding much and returning little. The origins of that condition, however, lay not in a simple, one-sided relationship, but in the paucity of resources available to both parties in the face of the exigencies of national development.

In the final analysis, then, the early history of the Russian middle class is firmly rooted in the difficulties of building a nation-state in a vast and relatively poor country. Such a perspective best accounts for the service relationship that took shape in the seventeenth century, just as it accounts for the strains and alterations put on that system in the eighteenth century when the interests of an expanding state and a traditional urban estate began to part ways. Moreover, it is from that perspective that the tug of war between continuity and change, so central a feature in the eighteenth century, stands out most clearly. The contrast of the old and the rooted, on the one hand, and the new and the sought after on the other, lay at the heart of the history of the posadskie liudi. One can see Kizevetter struggling to reconcile the ambitious goals of the sovereigns, goals with which he was largely in agreement, with the "dull and humdrum" realities of the posad life that his researches had uncovered. It is with an almost despairing resignation that he remarks in connection with the reforms of Peter I: "The new wine of the elevation of city culture was poured into the old skin of the tiaglo organization of the posad commune."[7] But that, of course, is precisely the point. The new wine could only be poured into the available skins, and the tiaglo relationship was both necessary and available. It was only in the latter decades of the eighteenth century that the government could begin to entertain the notion of altering the skins: but even that exercise, as it turned out, relied in practice as much on old materials as on new ones.

NOTES

BIBLIOGRAPHY

INDEX

Notes

A NOTE ON SOURCES

The following résumé is intended to provide the reader with a brief introduction to the principal sources on which this study has been based. The *Polnoe sobranie zakonov Rossiiskoi imperii* [Full Collection of Laws of the Russian Empire] is a basic source for the major reform legislation, and it also provides a running record of governmental policy decisions appropriate to the affairs of the townsmen and the cities. Developing trends within society, such as the growth of peasant trade or changes in tax policies, can be monitored—though not fully studied—through legal memorials in the *Polnoe sobranie zakonov*. For information on the attitudes of the townsmen, I have drawn heavily on the instructions (nakazy) of the city delegates to the Great Commission of Catherine II, materials found in the *Sbornik imperatorskogo russkogo istoricheskogo obshchestva* [Collection of the Imperial Russian Historical Society]. These two collections provide the bulk of the primary materials referred to in the study.

For information on the actual operations of posad society as well as more general developments in the Russian economy, society, and government, I have relied largely on secondary materials. Though the literature is not vast there are a number of works that stand out as landmarks in the historical writing on the posadskie liudi and Russia's cities. The seventeenth-century posad has been best described by P. P. Smirnov. In *Goroda Moskovskogo gosudarstva v pervoi polovine 17 veka* [Cities of the Moscow State in the First Half of the Seventeenth Century], one finds an extensive discussion of property and social relations in the Muscovite cities, along with a wealth of statistical detail about the make-up and movement of the urban population. Smirnov's other major work, *Posadskie liudi i ikh klassovaia bor'ba do serediny XVII veka* [The Posadskie Liudi and Their Class Struggle up to the Middle of the Seventeenth Century], is a less analytical and more narrative study than *Goroda*. It traces, mainly through extensive excerpts from primary sources, the relationship of the posad population to other social classes and to the state. Both of these works, with their extensive documentation and common-sense approach to the evidence, are indispensible to any study of the townsmen in the seventeenth century.

Three figures stand out in the literature on cities and on the posadskie liudi in the eighteenth century: I. I. Ditiatin, Iu. R. Klokman, and A. A. Kizevetter. Ditiatin's major work, *Ustroistvo i upravlenie gorodov Rossii* [The Structure and Administration of the Cities of Russia], represents a survey of the city order based on the legal memorials. It is a solid and reliable source of information about government policy toward the cities, though excessively legalistic. The works of Klokman represent the best products of Soviet scholarship on the topic. His major studies, *Ocherki sotsial'no-ekonomicheskoi istorii gorodov Severo-Zapada Rossii v seredine XVIII v.* [Outlines of the Social-Economic History of the Cities of the Northwest of Russia in the XVIII Century] and *Sotsial'no-ekonomicheskaia istoriia russkogo goroda: Vtoraia polovina XVIII veka* [The Social-Economic History of Russian Cities: The Second Half of the XVIII Century], focus on the cities as the loci of commercial and manufacturing activities and on the merchants, artisans, and workers who engaged in such labors. Thoroughly researched and lucidly written, Klokman's works yield a wealth of information both on the cities and on the industrial and commercial suburbs that dotted the central areas of the state. They also provide a useful introduction to the regional differentiation among Russia's cities.

As important as the above-cited works are, the most valuable contributions to the study of the posadskie liudi have come from the pen of A. A. Kizevetter. His massive study, *Posadskaia obshchina v Rossii XVIII st.* [The Posad Commune in Russia in the Eighteenth Century], builds carefully from archival records—principally those of the Main Magistracy—a comprehensive picture of the posad commune: who its members were; what services they performed; and how their communal organization operated. Although historians have subsequently cavilled at one aspect or another of this work, its basic characterization of posad society has yet to be challenged. All discussions of the commune in the eighteenth century proceed from this work. Kizevetter produced a number of other studies that supplement *Posadskaia obshchina* and broaden and deepen our knowledge of posad society, among them *Gorodovoe polozhenie Ekateriny II: 1785 goda* [The City Statute of Catherine II, 1785] and *Gil'diia Moskovskago kupechestva* [The Guilds of the Moscow Merchantry].

ABBREVIATIONS

Chteniia v O.I.D.R.	*Chteniia v Obshchestve istorii i drevnostei rossiiskikh pri Moskovskom universitete.*
L.G.P.I.	*Leningradskii gosudarstvennyi pedagogicheskii institut.*
PSZ	*Polnoe sobranie zakonov Rossiiskoi imperii.*
Sbornik I.R.I.O.	*Sbornik imperatorskogo russkogo istoricheskogo obshchestva.*
Svod Zakonov	*Svod zakonov rossiiskoi imperii.*
Zhurnal M.N.P.	*Zhurnal ministerstva narodnogo prosveshcheniia.*

INTRODUCTION

1. There exists no comprehensive review of the literature on Russian city history or on the posadskie liudi. The best available surveys of the literature have been compiled by Iu. R. Klokman. They are particularly useful for their evaluations of major authors, both prerevolutionary and Soviet, but there is a tendency

to overlook a number of less well known but useful works. Obviously, Klokman's essays are colored by his own emphasis on the socioeconomic characteristics of cities. Iu. R. Klokman, "Istoriografiia russkikh gorodov vtoroi poloviny XVII-XVIII v.," in *Goroda feodal'noi Rossii,* ed. N. M. Druzhinin et al. (Moscow, 1966), pp. 51-64; "Russkii gorod XVIII v. v sovremennoi burzhauznoi istoriografii," in *Kritika burzhuaznykh kontseptsii istorii Rossii perioda feodalizma,* ed. V. T. Pashuto, L. V. Cherepnin, and M. M. Shtrange (Moscow, 1962), pp. 324-351; *Sotsial'no-ekonomicheskaia istoriia russkogo goroda: Vtoraia polovina XVIII veka* (Moscow, 1967), pp. 6-26.

2. Russia's liberals, whose devotion to liberal political principles far outstripped their concern for private property rights, never related well to the mercantile and manufacturing community. Miliukov, in his historical writings, is perhaps an exception. Although he deplored the typical Muscovite merchants whose economic and political outlooks he found retrograde and slavish, he also hailed the appearance of a new third estate in Russia in the early twentieth century, one in which he could observe "those forces which created the cultural life of contemporary Europe: the force of capital and the force of knowledge." Just how comfortable he might have been in the real world of business we shall never know. P. N. Miliukov, *Ocherki po istorii russkoi kultury: Chast' pervaia: Naselenie, ekonomicheskii, gosudarstvennyi i soslovnyi stroi,* 6th ed. (St. Petersburg, 1909), p. 252.

3. Miliukov, *Ocherki,* p. 244.

4. P. A. Berlin, *Russkaia burzhuaziia v staroe i novoe vremia* (Moscow, 1922), p. 6.

5. A. A. Kizevetter, *Russkoe obshchestvo v vosemnadtsatom stoletii,* 2nd ed. (Rostov na Donu, 1905), p. 45.

6. This note of comparison with Western Europe resounds through a number of major studies. I. I. Ditiatin, author of *Ustroistvo i upravlenie gorodov Rossii,* I: *Goroda Rossii v XVIII stoletii* (St. Petersburg, 1875), begins his work with a lengthy analysis of the development of Western European cities. Miliukov's assessment of Russian cities and their inhabitants begins in a similar comparative manner (*Ocherki,* pp. 240-252). This same point of view runs through Berlin's study of the bourgeoisie. For each of them, urban autonomy was the main missing ingredient on the Russian urban scene.

7. Miliukov, *Ocherki,* pp. 241-243. Writing of the period beginning in the mid-fourteenth century and running through the end of the eighteenth, Ditiatin noted that "The majority of cities even in their external aspect were distinguished from villages and hamlets only by the number of cottages, and churches." On the conditions of cities at the accession of Catherine II, he noted that "The huge majority of cities according to their external aspect and prosperity are in no way distinguishable from villages." Ditiatin, *Ustroistvo,* I, 130, 373.

8. "In Moscow, every foreigner is taken to see the great cannon and the great bell—a cannon which is incapable of being fired and a bell which fell to the ground before it could be rung. Surprising city, in which most of the sights are so remarkable for their ineptitude—or is that bell without a tongue perhaps a hieroglyphic, a key to the true meaning of our huge country." P. Ia. Chaadaev, as

quoted in R. H. Hare, *Pioneers of Russian Social Thought* (London, 1951), p. 43.
In his famous "First Philosophical Letter," Chaadaev claimed that for Russia to
overcome its present condition of cultural isolation and shallowness, it was necessary for the country to relive—not superficially but in depth—the civilizing
experiences of mankind. In particular he respected the contribution of Christian-
ity to the making of Western European culture.

9. The Soviet position can be found in the above-cited historiographic articles of Klokman, as well as in the texts of his principal studies, *Sotsial'no-ekonomicheskaia istoriia* and *Ocherki sotsial'no ekonomicheskoi istorii gorodov
Severo-Zapada Rossii v seredine XVIII v.* (Moscow, 1960). See also B. B. Kafen-
guaz, "Gorod i gorodskaia reforma 1785 g.," in *Ocherki istorii SSSR: Period
feodalizma: Rossiia vo vtoroi polovine XVIII v.,* ed. A. I. Baranovich et al.
(Moscow, 1956), pp. 151-165.

10. Brief summary statements of the current Soviet perspective on urban
history can be found in the following reviews: Samuel H. Baron, "The Town in
'Feudal' Russia," *Slavic Review* 28, no. 1 (March 1969): 116-122; and J. M. Hittle,
rev. of *Ocherki sotsial'no-ekonomicheskoi istorii gorodov Severo-Zapada Rossii
v seredine XVII v.,* by Iu. R. Klokman, *Kritika* 1, no. 1 (Fall 1964): 14-21.

11. For an argument that economic weakness—and to a lesser extent "an
insufficiency of independent spiritual forces"—kept the Russian townsmen from
becoming a Western type bourgeoisie, see K. A. Pazhitnov, "Ocherk razvitiia
burzhuazii v Rossii," *Obrazovanie* 16, nos. 2a and 3 (1907): 3-5.

12. See, for example, Samuel H. Baron, "The Weber Thesis and the Failure
of Capitalist Development in 'Early Modern' Russia," *Jahrbucher für Geschichte
Osteuropas* 18 (1970): 320-336. Weber's notions have been applied more specifically to the economic activities of the Old Believers. For a discussion of this problem and bibliographic guidance, see Robert Crummey, *The Old Believers and the
World of Antichrist* (Madison, 1970), especially pp. 135-158.

13. Max Weber, *The City,* trans. and ed. Don Martindale and Gertrud Neuwirth (New York, 1962), p. 88. The complete statement reads: "To constitute a
full urban community a settlement must display a relative predominance of trade-
commercial relations with the settlement as a whole displaying the following features: 1. a fortification; 2. a market; 3. a court of its own and at least partially
autonomous law; 4. a related form of association; and 5. at least partial autonomy and autocephaly, thus also an administration by authorities in the election
of whom the burghers participated."

14. Gideon Sjoberg, *The Preindustrial City: Past and Present* (New York,
1960), pp. 108-144, 182-255.

15. For some general remarks on the low status of the townsmen and the
reasons for it see Pazhitnov, pp. 3-5.

16. Both Kliuchevskii and Ditiatin make the argument that the cities were
composed of diverse social groups. Ditiatin, for example, argues that the city
order that developed in the seventeenth century was "a collection of individuals
with no common ties, striving toward different ends—serving people of every
kind, ecclesiastics, agricultural and trade-industrial posad people, each drawing
his own tax burden [tiaglo]." *Ustroistvo,* I, 137. But such observations appear in

a context of regret over the unfortunate absence of Western principles of urban citizenship and autonomy. I have tried to shift the perspective and to state more positively what the characteristics of this city order were and how it came into being.

17. Institutional history is not without its detractors among contemporary historians, especially among those who pursue hidden motivations or who find institutions inherently too conservative and resistant to change. Yet the fact remains that groups of people, whole societies for that matter, do not go about the business of living in an entirely haphazard manner. See Geoffrey Barraclough, "What Is to Be Done about Medieval History?" *New York Review of Books* 14, no. 11 (June 4, 1970): 52-53. For a positive assessment of the contribution of the institutional approach to Russian history, see the review of Richard Pipes' *Russia under the Old Regime* by John Keep, "The Traditions of the Kremlin," *Times Literary Supplement*, June 20, 1975, pp. 697-698.

18. See, for example, the attack on Ditiatin's approach in Klokman, *Ocherki sotsial'no-ekonomicheskoi istorii*, p. 9. See also Gilbert Rozman, "Comparative Approaches to Urbanization: Russia, 1750-1800," in *The City in Russian History*, ed. Michael Hamm (Lexington, Kentucky, 1976), pp. 69-71.

19. There is, for example, in the works of Ditiatin, Kizevetter, and Miliukov, an implied regret that Russian cities did not enjoy true urban autonomy. Had such autonomy been present, the argument goes, then surely Russian historical development would have been different and, presumably, better. But the point is that circumstances were not conducive to urban autonomy; thus little is to be gained in the way of historical analysis by regretting its absence.

20. *PSZ*, XXIX, no. 22587 (August 10, 1807).

21. Leonard Reissman, "Urbanism and Urbanization," in *Penguin Survey of the Social Sciences 1965*, ed. Julius Gold (Baltimore, 1965), pp. 40-44.

22. Ia. E. Vodarskii, *Naselenie Rossii v kontse XVII-nachale XVIII veka* (Moscow, 1977), pp. 115-129.

1. TOWNS AND TOWNSMEN IN THE SEVENTEENTH CENTURY

1. A. I. Kopanev, "Naselenie russkogo gosudarstva v XVI veke," *Istoricheskie zapiski* 64 (1959): 239. P. P. Smirnov, *Goroda Moskovskogo gosudarstva v pervoi polovine 17 veke*, I, part 2 (Kiev, 1917), 128-129.

2. Sigismund von Herberstein, *Notes upon Russia*, trans. R. H. Major (1851; rpt. New York: Burt Franklin, 1963), I, 109.

3. V. P. Zagorovskii, *Belgorodskaia cherta* (Voronezh, 1969), pp. 252-253.

4. Smirnov, *Goroda*, I, part 2, 139-150.

5. Ibid., pp. 150-161. Zagorovskii, p. 245.

6. Smirnov, *Goroda*, I, part 2, 162-169.

7. S.M. Solov'ev, "Russkii gorod v XVII veke," *Sovremenik*, 37, division II (1853), 1-4. For a good, brief description of city (*gorod*) in its narrow sense of a fortified defense-administrative center, see the glossary in K. V. Bazilevich, *Gorodskie vosstaniia v Moskovskom gosudarstve XVII v.* (Moscow-Leningrad, 1936), p. 170.

8. Smirnov, *Goroda*, I, part 2, foldout opposite p. 346.

9. Smirnov, *Goroda*, I, part 1, 23-24.

10. Zagorovskii, pp. 244-245.

11. See Smirnov, *Goroda*, I, part 2, foldout opposite p. 346.

12. Ibid.

13. M. M. Bogoslovskii, "Gorodskaia reforma 1699 g.," in *Peter I: Materialy dlia biografii*, III (Leningrad, 1946), 245. Richard Hellie, *Enserfment and Military Change in Muscovy* (Chicago, 1971), pp. 124-126, 227-229.

14. For a succinct discussion of the origins of the term *posadskie liudi* see P. P. Smirnov, *Posadskie liudi i ikh klassovaia bor'ba do serediny XVII veka* (Moscow-Leningrad, 1947), I, 102-103.

15. *Ocherki istorii SSSR: Period feodalizma: XVII v.* (Moscow, 1955), p. 206. A. S. Lappo-Danilevskii, *Organizatsiia priamago oblozheniia v Moskovskom gosudarstve so vremen smuty do epokhi preobrazovanii* (St. Petersburg, 1890), pp. 124-125.

16. Lappo-Danilevskii, *Organizatsiia*, pp. 123-124.

17. A. N. Kopylov, "Gost' ," *Sovetskaia istoricheskaia entsiklopediia* (Moscow, 1963), IV, 609-610. For a much more extensive look at the gosti, see Samuel H. Baron, "Who Were the *Gosti?*" *California Slavic Studies* 7 (1973): 1-40.

18. P. I. Liashchenko, *Istoriia narodnogo khoziaistva SSSR, I: Dokapitalisticheskie formatsii* (Leningrad, 1947), 305.

19. S. M. Solov'ev, "Moskovskye kuptsy v XVII v.," *Sovremenik* 71 (1878): 431-432. The gosti advised against renewing English privileges, arguing that to do so would be harmful to the treasury and ruinous to the Russian merchants who could not compete.

20. Kopylov, "Gost'," pp. 609-610. M. M. Bogoslovskii, "Razbor sochineniia g. Kizevettera *Posadskaia obshchina v Rossii XVIII stoletiia*," *Chteniia v O. I. D. R.*, book 4, section 5 (1906), p. 28. Baron, "Who Were the *Gosti?*" pp. 18-19.

21. *Ocherki istorii SSSR: Period feodalizma: XVII v.*, p. 210.

22. Ibid., pp. 209-210. A. N. Kopylov, "Gostinaia sotnia," in *Sovetskaia istoricheskaia entsiklopediia*, IV (Moscow, 1963), 608-609.

23. Bogoslovskii, "Razbor," p. 29.

24. V. Snegirev, *Moskovskie slobody* (Moscow, 1947), pp. 3-6. "Sloboda," in *Sovetskaia istoricheskaia entsiklopediia*, XIII (Moscow, 1971), 42-43.

25. Ibid., p. 42. In Bogoslovskii's view, by the seventeenth century the Moscow suburbs were basically "tax organizations." Bogoslovskii, "Razbor," p. 34.

26. Ibid.

27. Ibid., pp. 28-33. Snegirev, pp. 16-44.

28. Smirnov, *Goroda*, I, part 1, 110, 112-113.

29. Smirnov, *Posadskie liudi*, I, 30.

30. Ibid., p. 82.

31. For brief discussions of the foreign suburbs see Snegirev, pp. 127-146; and E. A. Zviagintsev, "Slobody inostrantsev v Moskve XVII veka, "*Istoricheskii zhurnal*, no. 2-3 (1944), pp. 81-86. For a more substantial treatment see Samuel H. Baron, "The Origins of Seventeenth-Century Moscow's Nemeckaja Sloboda," *California Slavic Studies* 5 (1970): 1-18.

32. There were, of course, in any city of size some individuals who fitted into one of these categories—indigents and those living on the edge of the law.

33. Lappo-Danilevskii points out that in the first half of the seventeenth century it was frequently hard to distinguish posad people from peasants and that they were frequently taxed together. Lappo-Danilevskii, *Organizatsiia*, pp. 166-176.

34. Vodarskii, *Naselenie Rossii v kontse XVII-nachale XVIII veka*, pp. 131-134.

35. Smirnov, *Goroda*, I, part 1, 10.

36. B. N. Chicherin, "Dukhovnyia i dogovornyia gramoty velikikh i udel'-nykh kniazei," in *Opyty po istorii russkago prava* (Moscow, 1858), pp. 232-375. See also V. I. Sergeevich, *Russkiia iuridicheskiia drevnosti*, III: *Drevnosti russkago prava* (St. Petersburg, 1903), 24-25.

37. The *votchina* principle is discussed at length by Chicherin and by M. A. D'iakonov, *Ocherki obshchestvennogo i gosudarstvennogo stroia drevnei Rusi* (Moscow, 1908), pp. 200-294.

38. Smirnov, *Goroda*, I, part 1, 19-30.

39. The organized tax-paying community of a city or suburb. See Chapter 2.

40. The *svoezemtsi* were a class of rural small holders, neither privileged servitors nor peasants. In the sixteenth and seventeenth centuries, however, their position became precarious and they were for the most part absorbed by those two, more firmly rooted social groups.

41. Smirnov, *Goroda*, I, part 1, 43-55.

42. Ibid., pp. 61-74. In Smirnov's view, what was actually at stake in land transactions of all types was not ownership but right of possession.

43. Smirnov, *Goroda*, I, part 1, 31-36.

44. Sergeevich, pp. 232-234. Smirnov, *Goroda*, I, part 1, 57-58.

45. Ibid., pp. 110-113. Iu. R. Klokman, "Gorod v zakonodatel'stve russkogo absoliutizma vo vtoroi polovine XVII-XVIII vv.," in *Absoliutizm v Rossii* (*XVII-XVIII vv.*), ed. N. M. Druzhinin, N. I. Pavlenko, and L. V. Cherepnin (Moscow, 1964), p. 323.

46. The phrase is from Johann Philipp Kilburger, "Ot samogo znatnogo do samogo prostogo liubit kupechestvo," as quoted in I. M. Kulisher, *Istoriia russkoi torgovli do deviatnadtsatogo veka vkliuchetel'no* (St. Petersburg, 1923), p. 145. Giles Fletcher, *Of the Russe Commonwealth*, ed. Richard E. Pipes and John V. A. Fine, Jr. (Cambridge, Mass., 1966). Fletcher discusses the trade activities of the tsar (43v,44), of the monasteries (88v), and of the merchants and peasants (45v-49).

47. Kulisher, pp. 157-160. Baron, "The Weber Thesis," pp. 327-329.

48. Smirnov, *Posadskie liudi*, I, 195-196. Liashchenko, 1947 ed., I, 275-277.

49. Kulisher, p. 117.

50. Ibid., pp. 123-131.

51. Sergeevich contends that prior to the sixteenth century shop places in cities were held in private property. They became the property of the tsar in the sixteenth century primarily through confiscations. Sergeevich, pp. 235-241. Smirnov, to the contrary, contends that the tsar's claims to commercial areas

arose in Moscow and spread to new cities. Both are in agreement that in the early seventeenth century the tsar considered the property on which trade and manufacturing was carried out to be state land, similar to taxable (*chernoe*) property. Smirnov, *Goroda*, I, part 1, 62-72.

52. Kulisher, pp. 149, 153.

53. Ibid., p. 150.

54. Ibid., p. 143.

55. Danilova's figures for Iaroslavl' appear typical: one quarter of the shops dealt in comestibles, one quarter in hides, and one fifth in textiles and clothing. L. V. Danilova, "Torgovye riady Iaroslavlia v kontse XVII v.," in *Voprosy sotsial'no-ekonomicheskoi istorii i istochnikovedeniia perioda feodalizma v Rossii: Sbornik statei k 70-letiiu A.A. Novosel'skogo*, ed. N. V. Ustiugov (Moscow, 1961), p. 85.

56. Snegirev, pp. 74-80. S. V. Bakhrushin, "Remeslennye ucheniki v XVII v.," in *Nauchnye trudy*, II (Moscow, 1954), 101-117.

57. Smirnov, *Posadskie liudi*, I, 195-196. Smirnov, *Goroda*, I, part 1, 27-28.

58. Danilova, p. 86.

59. Liashchenko, 1939 ed., pp. 180-181.

60. Liashchenko, 1947 ed., I, 318.

61. Liashchenko, 1939 ed., p. 181. P. G. Liubomirov, "Rol' kazennogo, dvorianskogo, i kupecheskogo kapitala v stroitel'stve krupnoi promyshlennosti Rossii v XVII-XVIII vv.," *Istoricheskie zapiski* 16 (1945): 67.

62. Liubomirov, "Rol'," p. 73.

63. Ibid., pp. 65-72.

64. Karl Polanyi, "The Economy as Instituted Process," in *Trade and Market in the Early Empires*, ed. Karl Polanyi, Conrad Arensberg, and Harry Pearson (Glencoe, 1957), pp. 243-270.

65. Baron, "The Weber Thesis," pp. 327-331, 335.

66. Iurii Krizhanich, *Politika*, ed. M. N. Tikhomirov (Moscow, 1965), p. 413.

67. Liashchenko, 1939 ed., pp. 178-179.

68. Liashchenko relates that some silver items sold at nearly the cost of the metal. Low prices, as I am reminded by my colleagues in economics, are in part a function of extremely heavy competition, such as existed in seventeenth-century Russia. Liashchenko, 1947 ed., I, 269.

69. As quoted in Kulisher, p. 147.

70. I. T. Pososhkov, *Kniga o skudosti i bogatstve*, ed. B. B. Kafengauz (Moscow, 1937), p. 196.

71. For some provocative insights into Russian social and economic history from the Weberian perspective, see Baron's essay, "The Weber Thesis and the Failure of Capitalist Development in 'Early Modern' Russia."

72. "As soon as a provincial merchant became wealthy, the government immediately brought him to Moscow and drew him into its service. In such a fashion, a rich and independent merchantry could not be created in the provinces." Miliukov, *Ocherki*, p. 247. Ditiatin, *Ustroistvo*, I, 134-135.

2. THE TOWNSMEN AND THE STATE
IN THE EARLY SEVENTEENTH CENTURY

1. N. F. Demidova, "Biurokratizatsiia gosudarstvennogo apparata absoliutizma v XVII-XVIII vv.," in *Absoliutizm v Rossii,* ed. N. M. Druzhinin, N. I. Pavlenko, and L. V. Cherepnin (Moscow, 1964), pp. 214-215.

2. *Ocherki istorii SSSR: Period feodalizma: XVII v.,* p. 385. A. A. Kizevetter, *Mestnoe samoupravlenie v Rossii IX-XIX st.: Istoricheskii ocherk* (Moscow, 1910), p. 70.

3. While the majority of the top officials of the prikazy came from the serving aristocracy, candidates for the position of voevoda came from the middle ranks of the serving people. Demidova, "Biurokratizatsiia," p. 213.

4. Bogoslovskii, "Gorodskaia reforma 1699 g.," pp. 245-246, 325.

5. For an excellent description of the matters that fell under the military governor's purview, see Solov'ev, "Russkii gorod," pp. 11-13. A more structured list can be found in Kizevetter, *Mestnoe samoupravlenie,* p. 81.

6. Kizevetter, *Mestnoe samoupravlenie,* p. 56. Solov'ev points out that the police elders, in addition to caring for prisons and prisoners, were responsible for selling off the property of convicts and delivering the proceeds to the state. Solov'ev, "Russkii gorod," p. 15.

7. Kizevetter, *Mestnoe samoupravlenie,* pp. 56-57.

8. Ibid., pp. 81-84. See also Lappo-Danilevskii, *Organizatsiia,* pp. 120-121. For the unique make-up of the Moscow posad, see Bogoslovskii, "Razbor," pp. 28-33. *Tseloval'niki,* or sworn men, were elected members of the posad who performed state services, usually related to the collection of revenues. For a list of the kinds of duties performed by tseloval'niki, see Chapter 6, note 49.

9. Kizevetter, *Mestnoe samoupravlenie,* pp. 58-60.

10. Solov'ev, "Russkii gorod," p. 16.

11. Kizevetter, *Mestnoe samoupravlenie,* pp. 85-86.

12. Kizevetter discusses both the nature of the complaints and the government's efforts to remedy the problem. Among other actions, the government set up way stations on the road leading to and from Siberia to check the possessions of returning military governors for signs of sudden enrichment. Ibid., pp. 72-80. See also Solov'ev, "Russkii gorod," p. 14.

13. One must be careful not to fault the military governor too much. His office was not equipped to exercise broad regulatory functions over the daily lives of the city inhabitants. *Ocherki istorii SSSR: Period feodalizma: XVII v.,* p. 386.

14. Ibid., p. 211.

15. Ibid., p. 212.

16. Ibid., p. 210.

17. S. V. Bakhrushin, "Moskovskii miatezh 1648 g.," in *Sbornik statei v chest' Matvieia Kuz'micha Liubavskago* (Petrograd, 1917), p. 744.

18. D'iakonov, 1939 edition, p. 239.

19. Ibid. "The gosti, sovereign, and the gostinaia and sukonnaia hundreds are filled from all your state cities, by the best people from various suburbs, and we, your poor orphans, are ruined and we all become impoverished people; and,

sovereign, we have distinguished people, and these are selected into the gostinaia and sukonnaia sotni."

20. *Akty, sobrannye v bibliotekakh i arkhivakh Rossiiskoi imperii Arkheo-graficheskoiu Ekspeditsieiu Akademii nauk,* IV, document, no. 28, charter of July 31, 1648.

21. Kizevetter, *Mestnoe samoupravlenie,* pp. 72-73.

22. Solov'ev, "Russkii gorod," p. 14.

23. Ibid., p. 14.

24. Bakhrushin, "Moskovskii miatezh 1648 g.," p. 742.

25. "Novotorgovyi ustav," *PSZ,* I, no. 408 (April 22, 1667), article 35.

26. *Ocherki istorii SSSR: Period feodalizma: XVII v.,* pp. 422-423.

27. B. N. Chicherin, *Oblastnyia uchrezhdeniia Rossii v XVII-m veke* (Moscow, 1856), pp. 565-566.

28. Smirnov, *Posadskie liudi,* I, 157.

29. Ibid.

30. For a full discussion of the posad policy of Boris Godunov, see Smirnov, *Posadskie liudi,* I, 160-183.

31. Ibid., pp. 167, 177-178.

32. E. M. Tal'man, "Bor'ba posada Iaroslavlia s svetskimi i dukhovnymi feodalami v pervoi polovine XVII veka," *Istoricheskie zapiski* 20 (1946): 118.

33. Ibid., p. 119.

34. Smirnov, *Posadskie liudi,* I, 98.

35. Ibid., p. 119.

36. Ibid., p. 159.

37. Petitions of 1642 and 1646 complained that foreigners with and without charters were trading both wholesale and retail in the trade rows of Moscow. The plaint of unfair competition came through clearly: "They [foreign traders] are rich people, they do not draw us into their work; they trade alone and we are not able to act so, we are not bold." As quoted in Solov'ev, "Moskovskie kuptsi," p. 440.

38. See Chapter 1. Tal'man, pp. 100-101.

39. Smirnov, *Goroda,* I, part 2, 238. Chapter 5 in part 2 of his work contains a detailed treatment of the presence of nontaxable people in the cities.

40. For discussions of zakladnichestvo, see A. M. Pankratova, *Formiro-vanie proletariata v Rossii (XVII-XVIII vv.)* (Moscow, 1963), pp. 89-90; and Smirnov, *Posadskie liudi,* I, 325-328.

41. Tal'man, p. 100.

42. Smirnov, *Posadskie liudi,* I, 273.

43. Ibid., p. 167.

3. STATE POLICY IN THE SEVENTEENTH CENTURY AND THE EMERGENCE OF THE SERVICE CITY

1. P. P. Smirnov, *Posadskie liudi,* I, 354-387.

2. D'iakonov, p. 241.

3. Tal'man, p. 106.

4. M. F. Vladimirskii-Budanov, *Obzor istorii Russkago prava* (Kiev-St. Petersburg, 1900), p. 559.

5. Smirnov, *Posadskie liudi*, I, 400-402.

6. Vladimirskii-Budanov, p. 559.

7. Smirnov, *Posadskie liudi*, I, 403-406.

8. Ibid., pp. 406-409.

9. Ibid., pp. 425-427.

10. Ibid., p. 427.

11. Ibid., pp. 428-429.

12. Ibid., pp. 429-431.

13. Ibid., pp. 455-482.

14. Ibid., p. 475.

15. For a complete discussion of Morozov's policies, see Smirnov, *Posadskie liudi*, II, 5-131.

16. Ibid., pp. 79-88.

17. Ibid., p. 90.

18. Ibid., p. 91.

19. Bakhrushin, "Moskovskii miatezh 1648 g.," pp. 743-751.

20. *Sobornoe Ulozhenie 1649 g.*, ed. M. N. Tikhomirov and P. P. Epifanov (Moscow, 1961), chapter 19, articles 1, 5, 7.

21. Ibid., article 13.

22. Ibid., article 9.

23. Ibid., article 17.

24. Ibid., article 19.

25. Two exceptions were made for conditions already in existence: third sons of posad taxpayers enrolled in the musketeers could remain there, and posad people registered as cossacks before the Smolensk war could remain in service. *Sobornoe Ulozhenie 1649 g.*, chapter 19, articles 26, 27, 29.

26. A condition implicit in chapter 11, articles 1, 2, and 9 of the *Ulozhenie*, which eliminated the statute of limitations for the recovery of runaway serfs and their families.

27. N. N. Firsov, "Gorod v Rossii do kontsa XVIII veka," *Entsiklopediche-skii slovar'* (Granat'), 7th ed., XV (1912), 644. Kliuchevskii argues that the *Ulozh-enie* contributed to the process, under way during the seventeenth century, of the formation of an estate society, each group of which was beholden to the state. The state's principal goal in the *Ulozhenie* was "to seize control of the social grouping, having separated people according to hermetically sealed boxes, to forge national labor, having pressed it into the narrow frames of state demands, having enslaved private interests to it." *Sochineniia*, III, 145, 156-161.

28. Smirnov, *Posadskie liudi*, I, 96; II, 271. B. I. Syromiatnikov, *"Reguliar-noe" gosudarstvo Petra Pervogo i ego ideologiia: Chast' 1* (Moscow-Leningrad, 1943), pp. 129-137. There is yet another position—namely, that the intra-posad disputes that brought the rank and file posadskie liudi out against the privileged gosti and hundreds led to a reduction in the freedom of the urban population, but a reduction that "took place almost entirely at the behest of the townsmen them-selves." While there is something to say for this argument, it does play down the

interests of the state. See Richard Hellie, "Muscovite Law and Society: The *Ulozhenie* of 1649 as a Reflection of the Political and Social Development of Russia since the *Sudebnik* of 1589" (diss., University of Chicago, 1965), pp. 178, 257-259.

29. Throughout his work Smirnov stresses the coincidence of interests between the gentry and the townsmen. This view is disputed by Tikhomirov: "proof of the unity of posad people and the dvoriane is impossible to establish." For Tikhomirov, the events of 1648-1649 turn principally on the activities of the gentry. M. N. Tikhomirov, introduction to *Sobornoe Ulozhenie 1649 g.*, pp. 16-18. Bakhrushin, by way of contrast, stresses the importance of the Moscow posad people, not the dregs, but the rank and file. Bakhrushin, "Moskovskii miatezh 1648 g.," p. 740. Smirnov's vision, encompassing more aspects of the political scene in Moscow, remains the most persuasive.

30. Syromiatnikov, pp. 134, 137.

31. Smirnov, *Posadskie liudi*, II, 682.

32. D'iakonov, p. 244.

33. Solov'ev, "Moskovskii kuptsy," pp. 431-432.

34. K. V. Bazilevich, "Elementy merkantilizma v ekonomicheskoi politike pravitel'stva Alekseia Mikhailovicha," in *Uchenye zapiski Moskovskogo gosudarstvennogo universiteta: Vypusk 41* (Moscow, 1940), pp. 9-10.

35. *Ocherki istorii SSSR: Period feodalizma: XVII v.*, p. 137. The English were restricted to trading in Arkhangel only and had to pay the regular tariffs. N. N. Firsov, *Russkie torgovo-promyshlennye kompanii v pervoi polovine XVIII v.* (Kazan', 1896), pp. 9-11.

36. Bazilevich, "Elementy merkantilizma," p. 11.

37. The "Novotorgovyi ustav" can be found in *PSZ*, I, no. 408 (April 22, 1667). A discussion of the central features of the regulations in the context of Russian economic policy can be found in Bazilevich, "Elementy merkantilizma," pp. 28-30. See also E. V. Chistiakova, "Novotorgovyi ustav 1667 g.," in *Arkheograficheskii ezhegodnik za 1957 g.* (Moscow, 1958), pp. 102-126; and K. V. Bazilevich, "Novotorgovyi ustav 1667 g.: K voprosu o ego istochnikakh," *Izvestiia Akademiia Nauk SSSR, VII seriia, otdelenie obshchestvennykh nauk*, no. 7 (Moscow, 1932), pp. 589-622.

38. Bazilevich, "Novotorgovyi ustav 1667 g.," p. 619. For Marselis' role, see below.

39. The argument is Bazilevich's. Ibid., pp. 596-597.

40. "Novotorgovyi ustav," articles 48, 72, 73. For a brief review of the reuse of foreign metals see *Ocherki istorii SSSR: Period feodalizma: XVII v.*, pp. 430-432.

41. Bazilevich, "Elementy merkantilizma," pp. 12, 23-27.

42. Bazilevich, "Novotorgovyi ustav 1667 g.," pp. 599-619.

43. Bazilevich, "Novotorgovyi ustav 1667 g.," pp. 598-599; "Elementy merkantilizma," p. 28.

44. For a description of Pskov's troubles and the efforts of Ordyn-Nashchokin to remedy them, see Chicherin, *Oblastnyia uchrezhdeniia*, pp. 558-562; Bazilevich, "Novotorgovyi ustav 1667 g.," pp. 592-595.

45. Chicherin, *Oblastnyia uchrezhdeniia*, p. 562.

4. THE URBAN REFORMS OF PETER I

1. In 1716, for example, the government placed 1,776 belomestsy from various Moscow suburbs on the registers of the posad. E. I. Zaozerskaia, "Moskovskii posad pri Petre I," *Voprosy istorii*, no. 9 (1947), p. 27. The government had earlier made it possible for all city courts, taxable and nontaxable, to be sold to anyone in the city, thus giving posad dwellers a legal opportunity to secure nontaxable property. *PSZ*, IV, no. 1798 (June 15, 1700). Although complaints against peasant commercial activities continued through the century, complaints about belomestsy seem to have dropped off after the first few decades.

2. Bogoslovskii, "Gorodskaia reforma 1699 g.," p. 248.

3. Ibid., pp. 249-250. M. Z. Jedlicki, "German Settlement in Poland and the Rise of the Teutonic Order," in *The Cambridge History of Poland*, ed. W. F. Reddaway, J. H. Penson, O. Halecki and R. Dyboski (Cambridge, 1970), p. 133.

4. Bogoslovskii, "Gorodskaia reforma 1699 g.," pp. 254-258.

5. Ibid., pp. 254-255. The preambles to the legislation make this very point. See: *PSZ*, III, no. 1674 (January 30, 1699); and *PSZ*, III, no. 1675 (January 30, 1699).

6. Kizevetter, *Mestnoe samoupravlenie*, pp. 54-64.

7. Bogoslovskii, "Gorodskaia reforma 1699 g.," p. 300.

8. Ibid., p. 332.

9. Ibid., p. 331.

10. P. N. Miliukov, *Gosudarstvennoe khoziaistvo Rossii v pervoi chetverti XVIII stoletiia i reforma Petra Velikago*, 2nd ed. (St. Petersburg, 1905), pp. 91-92, 118.

11. Ditiatin, *Ustroistvo*, I, 181-182. Miliukov, *Gosudarstvennoe khoziaistvo*, p. 146.

12. Ditiatin, *Ustroistvo*, I, 193-194.

13. Ditiatin writes of a gradual decline and disappearance of the ratusha (*Ustroistvo*, I, 188), but the evidence suggests that the institution continued in operation in some towns right up to the appearance of the magistracy.

14. In 1711, for example, the Moscow ratusha attempted to arbitrate between two struggling factions of the Kaluga posad. Since the main issue at stake was tax apportionment, and since the Moscow ratusha's intervention aimed at securing maximum revenues from Kaluga, it is obvious that at least for this one troubled posad the Moscow ratusha continued to be involved directly in revenue collection for a few years after the provincial reform. A. V. Murav'ev, "Iz materialov po istorii klassovoi bor'by v Russkom gorode nachala XVIII veka," *Arkheograficheskii ezhegodnik za 1959 god* (Moscow, 1960), pp. 158-159.

15. Ibid., pp. 160, 161. A. V. Murav'ev, "Obrazovanie Moskovskogo magistrata," *Vestnik Moskovskogo universiteta*, III (Moscow, 1963).

16. Ditiatin, *Ustroistvo*, I, 194n.

17. "Reglament (ustav) gosudarstvennoi kommerts-kollegii," *PSZ*, V, no. 3318 (March 3, 1719).

18. Ibid., articles 15-20, 23.

19. Article 20 commands the Commerce College to look after police affairs in the towns and to make sure that the magistracies remove all possible hin-

drances to the business operations of the merchants.

20. As quoted in Ditiatin, *Ustroistvo*, I, 199.

21. Ibid., pp. 204-205.

22. "Reglament ili ustav glavnago magistrata," *PSZ*, VI, no. 3708 (January 17, 1721). The initial draft of the regulation was composed by Heinrich von Fick, a native of Hamburg who had entered Russian service in 1715. In 1718, after a period of study in Sweden, he had presented the tsar with a memorial calling for administrative reforms that would integrate central and local government institutions. His next major assignment appears to have been the first draft of the magistracy regulation. For a brief history of the text of the regulation see Ia. E. Vodarskii, "Proekt reglamenta glavnogo magistrata i ego redaktsii (1720g.)," *Problemy istochnikovedeniia*, X (Moscow, 1962), 195-207.

23. S. M. Solov'ev, *Istoriia Rossii s drevneishikh vremen*, XVIII, book 9 (Moscow, 1963), p. 486. "Instruktsiia magistratam," *PSZ*, VII, no. 4624 (December 30, 1724).

24. "Reglament . . . glavnago magistrata," chapters 5, 6.

25. Ibid., chapter 6.

26. Ibid.

27. Ibid., chapter 14.

28. Ibid., chapter 9.

29. Ibid., chapter 14.

30. Ibid., preamble.

31. "Tabel o rangakh . . . ," *PSZ*, VI, no. 3890 (January 24, 1722), ranks 8, 9, 10, 12.

32. Gentry, clergy, church dependents and foreigners were specifically excluded from the urban citizenry who were to be subject to the magistracy. "Reglament . . . glavnago magistrata," chapter 7.

33. Ibid.

34. "Instruktsiia magistratam," article 16.

35. "Reglament . . . glavnago magistrata," chapter 7.

36. Samuel H. Baron, "The Fate of the *Gosti* in the Reign of Peter the Great," *Cahiers du Monde Russe et Sovietique*, October-December, 1973, p. 509.

37. Ibid.

38. Ibid., pp. 510-511.

39. "Every art and craft should have their own special guilds [the document uses both *tsunfty* and *tsekhi* to refer to guilds] . . . or gatherings of craft people, and over them should be aldermen, according to the size of the city and the number of artisans it has, and also each craft and art has its own books, in which rules and regulations, rights and privileges of craft people should be kept." "Reglament . . . glavnago magistrata," chapter 7.

40. Ditiatin, *Ustroistvo*, I, 296-300.

41. F. Ia. Polianskii, *Gorodskoe remeslo i manufaktura v Rossii XVIII v.* (Moscow, 1960), p. 104.

42. In keeping with the early history of the magistracy reform, the craft guilds which it called for failed to appear. Supplementary legislation directed St. Petersburg officials to set up craft guilds and spelled out in detail their characteristics—including a seven-year apprenticeship followed by a test of skills. No mas-

ter then practicing, however, was to be made to join a guild involuntarily; thus a legal basis was provided for the nonexclusive character of Russian craft guilds. Ibid., pp. 104-105.

43. "Reglament . . . glavnago magistrata," chapter 21.

44. Ibid., chapter 20.

45. Ibid., chapter 10.

46. N. P. Eroshkin, *Ocherki istorii gosudarstvennykh uchrezhdenii dorevoliutsionnoi Rossii* (Moscow, 1960), p. 87.

47. "Reglament . . . glavnago magistrata," chapter 11.

48. Ibid., chapter 18.

49. Ibid., chapter 19.

50. Ibid., chapter 17.

51. *PSZ*, III, no. 1706 (October 27, 1699).

52. The company formed to trade with China was established in 1711. According to Lappo-Danilevskii it did not function beyond 1739 and was never successful. Basically, the merchants who made it up traded individually or through agents. A. S. Lappo-Danilevskii, *Russkiia promyshlennyia i torgovyia kompanii v pervoi polovine 18 stoletiia* (St. Petersburg, 1899), p. 99. The Spanish company apparently sailed only a single mission, even though the decree calling it into existence ordered the Commerce College to watch over it "as a mother over her children." N. N. Firsov, *Russkie torgovo-promyshlennye kompanii*, p. 23. *Ocherki istorii SSSR . . . Rossiia v pervoi chetverti XVIII v.*, ed. B. B. Kafengauz and N. I. Pavlenko (Moscow, 1954), p. 149.

53. For discussions of company organization and capitalization, see Liubomirov, pp. 65-99; and Lappo-Danilevskii, *Russkiia promyshlennyia i torgovyia kompanii*, pp. 3-61.

54. *Ocherki istorii Leningrada*, ed. M. P. Viatkin, I (Moscow-Leningrad, 1955), 58.

55. Kulisher, pp. 183-187. *Ocherki istorii Leningrada*, I, 86-87.

56. *Ocherki istorii Leningrada*, I, 132.

57. Ibid., pp. 158-162.

58. In 1721, Anton Divier, Police-master of the city, submitted to the Senate a city budget of 27,993 rubles, the greater part of which was to be allocated to new street lighting, while the remainder was to go for routine maintenance. The Senate granted him 5,000 rubles and promised to decide on the rest of the budget later. Ibid., p. 166.

59. Ibid., pp. 94-114.

60. Vodarskii, "Proekt," p. 207.

61. As if the right hand did not know what the left hand was doing, the government never worked out in legislative form the relationship of the two police forces, leaving unspecified the manner in which their functions, often overlapping, were to be allocated. Ditiatin, *Ustroistvo*, I, 234-235.

5. THE POSAD ECONOMY IN THE EIGHTEENTH CENTURY

1. In some cases, the very size of the provinces contributed to the weakness of the posady and the poverty of the merchants. In the 1760s, for example, the

Ufimskii uezd measured some 1,067 kilometers from border to border. Its two cities, Ufa and Tabynsk, were located at the relatively close distance of 96 kilometers. Given the communications of the day it was plainly impossible for the merchants of these two cities to serve the entire uezd; peasant traders naturally filled the gap. It is not surprising, then, that reports from the area to the government noted that few merchants could be found in these towns and that they were "not capitaled." Kulisher, p. 251.

2. A. A. Kizevetter, *Posadskaia obshchina*, pp. 158-160.

3. See Chapter 9.

4. N. L. Rubinshtein, "Vneshniaia torgovlia Rossii i russkoe kupechestvo vo vtoroi polovine XVIII v.," *Istoricheskie zapiski* 54 (1955): 350-360.

5. V. N. Iakovtsevskii, *Kupecheskii kapital v feodal'no-krepostnicheskoi Rossii* (Moscow, 1953), p. 59.

6. Kizevetter, *Posadskaia obshchina*, p. 141.

7. Rubinshtein, "Vneshniaia torgovlia," pp. 355-356.

8. *Ocherki istorii Leningrada*, I, 289; Rubinshtein, "Vneshniaia torgovlia," p. 346.

9. Kulisher, pp. 216-220.

10. Kulisher, p. 221; *Ocherki istorii Leningrada*, I, 290.

11. Iakovtsevskii, p. 75.

12. Ibid.

13. The apparent failure of Peter's efforts to set up foreign trade companies did not entirely quash the idea. In mid-century four more commercial companies were established (Astrakhan', Persian, Black Sea, and Caspian) but they did not enjoy a distinguished record and disappeared during the reign of Catherine II. A. S. Lappo-Danilevskii, *Russkiia promyshlenyia i torgovyia kompanii*, p. 99. His comprehensive study makes it clear that the more complex forms of company organization appeared most often in the realm of manufacturing. Merchant companies of complex organization appeared less frequently and tended to break up easily (ibid., p. 115).

14. For examples of single-owner firms taken from customs materials, see the studies by Rubinshtein and Iakovtsevskii. The borrowers with the largest outstanding loans at the Petersburg Bank for the Restoration of Commerce were all individual merchants. S. Ia. Borovoi, *Kredit i banki Rossii (seredina XVII v.-1861 g.)* (Moscow, 1958), p. 86.

15. Iakovtsevskii, p. 57.

16. *Ocherki istorii SSSR: Period feodalizma: Rossiia vo vtoroi polovine XVIII v.*, ed. A. I. Baranovich et al. (Moscow, 1956), p. 124.

17. B. B. Kafengauz, *Ocherki vnutrennego rynka Rossii pervoi poloviny XVIII veka* (Moscow, 1958), p. 168.

18. N. I. Pavlenko, "O nekotorykh stranakh pervonachal'nogo nakopleniia v Rossii," *Istoricheskie zapiski*, 54 (1955), 410.

19. For Shuvalov's personal stake in monopolistic enterprise see the article, "P. I. Shuvalov," *Russkii biograficheskii slovar'*, XV (St. Petersburg, 1911), 493-494.

20. Iakovtsevskii, p. 156.

21. Pavlenko, "O nekotorykh staranakh," p. 409. One crony of Potemkin is reputed to have supplied the army and navy with goods at triple the going price. F. Ia. Polianskii, *Pervonachal'noe nakoplenie kapitala v Rossii* (Moscow, 1958), p. 43.

22. Iakovtsevskii, p. 156.

23. Pavlenko, "O nekotorykh staranakh," pp. 406-407.

24. Traditionally, opposition to monopolies has been associated with Catherine II and her open advocacy of free trade. See, for example, A. S. Lappo-Danilevskii, *Ocherk vnutrennei politiki imperatritsy Ekateriny II* (St. Petersburg, 1893), p. 20. A more exhaustive study of the matter suggests that the movement away from monopolies was under way in the reign of Elizabeth, and that Shuvalov and his circle may have been the initiators of the change in policy (in a reversal of his earlier position). See N. L. Rubinshtein, "Ulozhennaia komissiia 1754-1766 gg. i ee proekt novogo ulozheniia 'O sostoianii poddannykh voobshche'," *Istoricheskie zapiski* 38 (1951): 245. As it turns out, even some of the merchants opposed monopolies.

25. Iakovtsevskii, pp. 154-156.

26. Ibid., pp. 75, 103. Themes of rural self-sufficiency run consistently through the literature. The capacity of the peasantry to produce items for domestic consumption receives persuasive treatment in V. N. Bernadskii, *Ocherki iz istorii klassovoi bor'by i obshchestvenno-politicheskoi mysli Rossii v tret'ei chetverti XVIII v.*, Uchenye zapiski LGPI im. A. I. Gertsena, no. 229 (Leningrad, 1962), pp. 69-70. The limited separation of town and country, a major theme of studies of the seventeenth century, figures in Polianskii's evaluation of the eighteenth century. F. Ia. Polianskii, *Gorodskoe remeslo i manufaktura v Rossii XVIII veka* (Moscow, 1958), p. 103.

27. The fundamental study of this phenomenon is that of B. B. Kafengauz, *Ocherki vnutrennego rynka*.

28. Lappo-Danilevskii, *Russkaia promyshlennyia i torgovyia kompanii*, p. 87.

29. Iakovtsevskii, p. 120.

30. For a discussion of this matter, see J. M. Hittle, "The City in Muscovite and Early Imperial Russia" (diss., Harvard University, 1969), pp. 213-216. The principal Soviet study of eighteenth-century foreign trade remains decidedly vague on the matter of balance of payments. See S. A. Pokrovskii, *Vneshniaia torgovlia i vneshniaia torgovaia politika Rossii* (Moscow, 1947), p. 120.

31. Foreign merchants also sold imported goods to Russian merchants on credit of six months to one year. Kulisher, pp. 241-244.

32. Iakovtsevskii, pp. 119-120.

33. Ibid., p. 124.

34. None of these measures proved particularly effective, however, as the foreign merchants either found ways around them or benefited from the government's lax enforcement of them. Ibid., pp. 120-122.

35. Kulisher, p. 225. In all fairness, however, it should be noted that Kulisher claims the Russians began to market their products more sensibly toward the end of the century, working from stocks on hand throughout the year, thus

freeing themselves from the almost total dependence on foreigners. Even so, the improvement was only relative, and the foreign commissionary agent remained a potent force on the export scene (ibid., p. 244).

36. See, for example, the works of Rubinshtein and Iakovtsevskii.

37. E. I. Zaozerskaia, "Torgi i promysly gostinoi sotni Srednego Povolzh'ia na rubezhe XVII-XVIII vv.," in *Petr Velikii: Sbornik statei* (Moscow-Leningrad, 1947), pp. 216-241.

38. N. I. Pavlenko, "Kupechestvo Pereiaslavlia-Riazanskogo v 30-kh godakh XVIII v.," in *Goroda feodal'noi Rossii*, ed. N. M. Druzhinin et al. (Moscow, 1966), pp. 437-445.

39. Kizevetter, *Posadskaia obshchina*, p. 142.

40. Iakovtsevskii, pp. 133-134.

41. Zaozerskaia, "Torgi i promysly," p. 233.

42. Borovoi, pp. 13-19, 45. The fact that the 6 percent ceiling on interest rates was repeated by legislation in 1764 suggests that it may well have been ignored.

43. Ibid., p. 32.

44. Ibid., pp. 83-93.

45. Ibid., p. 93. Polianskii, *Pervonachal'noe nakopleni*, pp. 92-98.

46. J-B. Scherer, *Histoire Raisonnée du Commerce de la Russie* (Paris, 1786), I, 123-140; Borovoi, p. 93; Kulisher, p. 144.

47. Iakovtsevskii, p. 39. In 1725 the copper ruble measured 18 by 19 centimeters and weighed three and one-half pounds. N. D. Mets, *Nash rubl'* (Moscow, 1960), p. 29.

48. Borovoi, pp. 83-91; Iakovtsevskii, pp. 39-40.

49. N. Chulkov, "Moskovskoe kupechestvo XVIII i XIX vv.," *Russkii Arkhiv* 12 (1907): 490.

50. Liubomirov, p. 99. M. I. Tugan-Baranovskii, *Russkaia fabrika v proshlom i nastoiashchem*, I (Moscow, 1926), 16-22.

51. Polianskii, *Gorodskoe remeslo*, p. 50.

52. See, for example, the lists of capital shares in Lappo-Danilevskii, *Russkiia promyshlennyia i torgovyia kompanii*, p. 28.

53. Ibid., p. 115. Lappo-Danilevskii attributes the break-up of companies in part to lowered risk and easier credit, but subsequent studies of credit and banking cast doubt on such an explanation. It seems more likely that the traditional preference for single-owner operations asserted itself after a relatively brief flirtation with more complex forms of organization encouraged by the government.

54. In 1724, when the partnership of Miklaev et al. dissolved, one partner received 360 shops (*stany*) and 760 workers. *Istoriia Moskvy* (Moscow, 1952), I, 27. The information on Tula comes from P. I. Liashchenko, *Istoriia narodnogo khoziaistva SSSR* (Leningrad, 1947), p. 394. For a general argument on the dispersed, domestic nature of eighteenth-century Russian manufacturing, see J. Koulischer [I. M. Kulisher], "La grande industrie aux XVII-e et XVIII-e siecles: France, Allemagne, Russie," in *Annales d'Histoire Economique et Sociele* (Paris, 1931), III, 39-46.

55. Iu. R. Klokman, "Gorod v zakonodatel'stve russkogo absoliutizma vo

vtoroi polovine XVII-XVIII vv.," in *Absoliutizm v Rossii (XVII-XVIII vv.)*, ed. N. M. Druzhinin, N. I. Pavlenko, and L. V. Cherepnin (Moscow, 1964), p. 328. At first serfs were assigned only to state enterprises, but following a report of V. N. Tatishchev in 1734, they were assigned to private concerns as well. *Khrestomatiia po istorii SSSR: XVIII v.* (Moscow, 1963), p. 95.

56. The relevant legislation: *PSZ*, VI, no. 3711 (January 18, 1721); *PSZ*, IX, no. 6858 (January 7, 1736); *PSZ*, XII, no. 9004 (July 27, 1744); *PSZ*, XIII, no. 9954 (March 12, 1752); *PSZ*, XV, no. 11490 (March 29, 1762).

57. Tugan-Baranovskii, p. 30. He places much of the responsibility for slow industrial development in Russia on the use of unproductive, unskilled compulsory labor.

58. Lappo-Danilevskii, pp. 30-43, 108.

59. Ibid., p. 108.

60. Kizevetter, *Posadskaia obshchina*, p. 141. Polianskii places the percentage of artisans at 18, based on figures for 1769. Polianskii, *Gorodskoe remeslo*, pp. 88-91.

61. *Ocherki istorii SSSR . . . Rossiia v pervoi chetverti XVIII v.*, pp. 78-79; *Istoriia Moskvy*, II, 12-13.

62. William Tooke, *View of the Russian Empire During the Reign of Catharine the Second and to the Close of the Eighteenth Century* (London, 1880), II, 54.

63. William Coxe, *Travels into Poland, Russia, Sweden and Denmark* (London, 1785), I, 309-310.

64. Polianskii, *Gorodskoe remeslo*, pp. 88-91.

65. Snegirev, p. 79. *Ocherki istorii SSSR . . . Rossiia v pervoi chetverti XVIII v.*, p. 75.

66. *Istoriia Moskvy* (Moscow, 1953), II, 237.

67. John Perry, *The State of Russia Under the Present Czar* (London, 1716), pp. 257-258; Coxe, I, 239.

68. Polianskii, *Gorodskoe remeslo*, p. 118.

69. Ibid., p. 73.

70. In the 1720s and 1730s only about 5 percent of the Moscow guild craftsmen were descendants of city artisans. Ibid., p. 122.

71. *Ocherki istorii SSSR . . . Rossiia v pervoi chetverti XVIII v.*, pp. 78, 82; *Ocherki istorii SSSR . . . Rossiia vo vtoroi polovine XVIII v.*, p. 96.

72. V. S. Ikonnikov, *Kiev v 1654-1855 gg.: Istoricheskii ocherk* (Kiev, 1904), pp. 62-63.

73. Polianskii, *Gorodskoe remeslo*, pp. 95, 101.

74. *Istoriia Moskvy*, II, 13.

75. Ibid., 12-13; *Ocherki istorii SSSR . . . Rossiia v pervoi chetverti XVIII v.*, pp. 78-79.

76. A. P. Polovnikov, *Torgovlia v staroi Rossii* (Moscow, 1958), p. 38.

77. Ibid. There is no solid study of the economic fortunes of the Russian merchants of the eighteenth century and trying to get a consensus on the subject from Soviet scholarship is a frustrating exercise. Iakovtsevskii stresses differentiation within the posad and focuses on the growing economic power of guild

merchants. But he is also aware that within the society at large the guild merchants were fast losing their monopoly position (if, I would argue, it ever existed). Volkov, while also noting the growth of a substantial commercial "bourgeoisie" within the nucleus of posad society, contends that the posadskie liudi from the 1720s to the 1780s constituted a "single estate of city dwellers, possessing an almost monopoly right to trade and industry." This judgment, playing down the role of peasant traders, seems to me to square much more closely with the stated aims of the posadskie liudi than with the realities of the marketplace, especially from mid-century on. At any rate, both men agree that the wealthy merchants flourished right through to the end of the century, even if there was outside competition. Volkov, "Formirovanie," pp. 194-197. V. N. Iakovtsevskii, "Torgovlia," in *Ocherki istorii SSSR . . . Rossiia vo vtoroi polovine XVIII v.*, pp. 131-147.

78. Iakovtsevskii, pp. 28, 42-47.

79. The role of peasant competition is treated at length in Chapter 8.

80. Polovnikov, pp. 41-44.

81. Kizevetter, *Posadskaia obshchina*, p. 141; Iakovtsevskii, p. 76.

82. Kh. D. Sorina, in her study of social relations in the cities of the Tver' area, speculates that many individuals on the tax rolls of Torzhok for whom no occupation was listed may well have lived by farming. Kh. D. Sorina, "K voprosu o protsesse sotsial'nogo rassloeniia goroda v sviazi s formirovaniem kapitalisticheskikh otnoshenii v Rossii v XVIII-nachale XIX v. (G. Tver')," *Uchenye zapiski Kalininskogo pedagogicheskogo instituta im. M. I. Kalinina*, no. 38 (Kalinin, 1964), p. 283.

83. Polianskii, *Gorodskoe remeslo*, p. 200.

84. Iakovtsevskii, p. 57.

85. On the basis of tax revenues, Polianskii provides an estimate of the total value of merchant capital in Russia in 1795—some 71,466,600 rubles. Though he provides no comparable estimate for earlier in the century, he implies that this figure represents a definite increase. Polianskii, *Pervonachal'noe nakoplenie*, p. 66. Iakovtsevskii, on the other hand, claims that both the number of merchants and the wealth under their control was declining between 1760 and 1824. The drop in tax revenues from merchants was particularly noticeable in the early years of the nineteenth century. As for the eighteenth century, he explains the figures in terms of increased taxes, which reduced overall capitalization, and capital concentration, which reduced the number of first-guild merchants. Iakovtsevskii, pp. 133-136.

6. THE POSAD COMMUNE IN THE EIGHTEENTH CENTURY

1. Kizevetter, *Posadskaia obshchina*, p. 624. Bogoslovskii takes issue on this point, arguing that eligibility for the posad tax roll could also be based simply on lengthy residence in a posad. Bogoslovskii, "Razbor," p. 9.

2. Kizevetter, *Posadskaia obshchina*, pp. 630-631.

3. Ibid., pp. 631-632.

4. See Chapter 9.

5. *PSZ*, XI, no 8504 (January 19, 1742), preamble.

6. Kizevetter, *Posadskaia obshchina*, pp. 128-130.

7. A. A. Kizevetter, *Gil'diia Moskovskago kupechestva* (Moscow, 1915), pp. 20-21.

8. Kizevetter, *Posadskaia obshchina*, p. 633. Moscow was the exception that proved the rule: it alone among Russia's cities possessing posad taxpayers did not have a common posad gathering. The failure to make this point constitutes a major shortcoming of Kizevetter's work. See Bogoslovskii, "Razbor," pp. 33-35.

9. Klokman, "Gorod," pp. 327-328.

10. Kizevetter, *Posadskaia obshchina*, p. 152.

11. Ditiatin, *Ustroistvo*, I, 295.

12. Kizevetter, *Posadskaia obshchina*, pp. 145-146.

13. *PSZ*, XXII, no. 16188 (April 21, 1785), article 123. The article contains 117 subpoints. Earlier, Catherine II had expressed guarded confidence in the guilds as a means of promoting handicraft production. "Mais ce qu'il y a de certain, c'est que les Communautés sont très utile pour le bon order dans les métiers, & qu'elles ne deviennent nuisible que lorsqu'elles limitent le nombre des ouvriers; puisque cela meme empeche l'augmentation des métiers." The excerpt comes from *Nakaz imperatritsy Ekateriny II, dannyi kommissii o sochinenii proekta novago ulozheniia*, ed. N. D. Chechulin (St. Petersburg, 1907), p. 113.

14. Only with the Charter Granted to the Cities of 1785 were these matters worked out in detail. Ditiatin, I, 296.

15. Polianskii, *Gorodskoe remeslo*, p. 108.

16. Ibid., p. 125.

17. Ibid., p. 142.

18. Ibid., p. 150.

19. Ibid., p. 146.

20. Ibid., p. 122.

21. Ibid., pp. 127-128.

22. Kizevetter, *Posadskaia obshchina*, pp. 638-640.

23. Ibid., p. 647.

24. Ibid., p. 641. He does not identify the city.

25. Ibid., p. 648.

26. A. A. Kizevetter, "Posadskaia obshchina v Rossii XVIII v.," in *Istoricheskie ocherki* (Moscow, 1912), p. 260.

27. Kizevetter, *Posadskaia obshchina*, pp. 653-657.

28. *PSZ*, VII, no. 4929 (June 15, 1726). Solov'ev, *Istoriia Rossii*, XVIII, book 9, pp. 589-590.

29. Eroshkin, pp. 134-144.

30. *PSZ*, VII, no. 5142 (August 18, 1727).

31. M. T. Florinsky, *Russia, A History and an Interpretation* (New York, 1955), I, 381. His phrase: "Soon adjudged to be too independent."

32. Murav'ev, "Obrazovanie," pp. 64-68.

33. According to Ditiatin, the Supreme Privy Council noted in 1727 that "the Russian merchants are almost ruined," and thus decided to put the military

governors in full charge of the cities. See I. I. Ditiatin, *Stoletie S.-Petersburg-skago gorodskago obshchestva 1785-1885* (St. Petersburg, 1885), pp. 9-10; and Ditiatin, *Ustroistvo*, I, 327-328.

34. *PSZ*, VIII, no. 5994 (March 18, 1732).

35. Anna also ordered that a magistracy be instituted in the newly founded city of Orenburg and even went so far as to provide it with the right to own property in its name. *PSZ*, IX, no. 6584 (June 7, 1734), articles 3, 4, 5, 7, 9, 12.

36. Ditiatin, *Ustroistvo*, I, 343-346.

37. Ultimately the Main Magistracy was placed under the watchful eye of the Senate. Ibid., pp. 343-347.

38. This quotation is from Ditiatin, *Stoletie*, p. 13. See also Klokman, *Sotsial'no-ekonomicheskaia istoriia*, p. 56.

39. Kizevetter, *Posadskaia obschchina*, pp. 663-664.

40. The term of office of the burgomistry varied during the course of the century. From 1721 until 1728 there was no limit on their term; from 1728 to 1731 new elections were held yearly; from 1731 to 1743 the term was three years; from 1743 on the term again became indefinite. Though the posady petitioned to have the three-year term reestablished, they were unsuccessful. Ibid., pp. 665-673.

41. Ibid., p. 696.

42. U. M. Poliakova, "V. V. Krestinin i obshchestvennaia bor'ba v Arkhangel'skom posade v 60-90-kh godakh XVIII v.," *Istoriia SSSR*, no. 2 (March-April, 1958), pp. 80-82.

43. Ibid., p. 774.

44. Ditiatin, *Ustroistvo*, I, 386-389.

45. Kizevetter, *Posadskaia obshchina*, p. 730.

46. Ibid., pp. 689-690.

47. *PSZ*, XIX, no. 14709 (December 14, 1773).

48. Kizevetter, *Posadskaia obshchina*, pp. 730 ff.

49. In his list of local services (*mirskiia sluzhby*) Kizevetter includes the following: work at the magistracy or ratusha as watchmen, errand boys, messengers, or office attendants; work at the Oral Court as judges and errand boys; work in police positions, chiefly supervision of subdivisions of the cities; work in the local town hall (*zemskaia izba*) as elders; work as supervisors of unlicensed trade; elders in trade rows, elders of merchant guilds, aldermen in craft guilds, notaries, brokers, and postal officials. Tax collection for direct and indirect taxes made up the bulk of the state services, along with service as accountants in the chancellery of the military governor. Ibid., p. 254.

50. For a comprehensive treatment of the service aspects of tiaglo see Kizevetter, *Posadskaia obshchina*, part II, chapters 1-6.

51. *Materialy dlia istorii Moskovskago kupechestva: Obshchestvennye prigovory*, I (Moscow, 1892), 15, nos. 8, 19, 22, 24.

52. *Sbornik I.R.I.O.*, vol. 123, pp. 446-447.

53. Bogoslovskii, "Razbor," p. 20.

54. Zaozerskaia, "Moskovskii posad," p. 26.

55. Kizevetter, *Posadskaia obshchina*, pp. 287-291.

56. V. N. Latkin, *Zakonodatel'nye komissii v Rossii v XVIII st.*, I (St. Petersburg, 1887), 461-463.

57. Ibid., p. 465.

58. For a full treatment of the tax component of tiaglo see Kizevetter, *Posadskaia obshchina*, part III, chapters 1-6.

59. Ibid., pp. 459-466.

60. Ibid., p. 467.

61. Ibid., p. 498.

62. Kizevetter, "Posadskaia obshchina," p. 252.

63. In fact the poll tax for posad registrants was eighty kopecks, but to it was added a quitrent tax (*obrochnyi sbor*) of forty kopecks. State peasants and peasants registered in posady paid this one ruble, twenty kopeck tax. From February 25, 1725 right through the century the bulk of the peasantry was taxed at seventy kopecks per soul. S. M. Troitskii, *Finansovaia politika russkogo absoliutizma v XVIII veke* (Moscow, 1966), pp. 114-123.

64. *Ocherki istorii SSSR . . . Rossiia v pervoi chetverti XVIII v.*, p. 222.

65. Kizevetter, "Posadskaia obshchina," p. 250.

66. Kizevetter, *Posadskaia obshchina*, pp. 448-449.

67. S. M. Troitskii, "Finansovaia politika russkogo absoliutizma vo vtoroi polovine XVII i XVIII vv.," in *Absoliutizm v Rossii (XVII-XVIII vv.)*, ed. N. M. Druzhinin, N. I. Pavlenko, and L. V. Cherepnin (Moscow, 1964), p. 317.

68. The *nakaz* from Mosal'sk, in *Sbornik I.R.I.O.*, vol. 107, pp. 33-34.

69. Kizevetter, "Posadskaia obshchina," p. 257.

70. Kizevetter, *Posadskaia obshchina*, pp. 51-53.

71. *PSZ*, XI, no. 8504 (January 19, 1742), article 11.

72. Eroshkin, pp. 143-171. Ditiatin, *Ustroistvo*, I, passim.

73. Legal relationships between crown officials and the local magistracies are not clear, but there is substantial agreement in the literature that the governors and military governors stood over the magistracies. Ditiatin, *Stoletie*, p. 13. Klokman, *Sotsial'no-ekonomicheskaia istoriia*, p. 56.

74. Ditiatin, *Ustroistvo*, I, 356-370.

75. In 1733 the government announced its resolve to establish police chiefs in about forty cities. The number of cities that actually had police officials appears to have been less than that figure and to have declined right up to the reign of Catherine II. Eroshkin, pp. 146-147. Ditiatin, *Ustroistvo*, I, 359.

76. *PSZ*, X, no. 7211 (March 28, 1737).

77. Apparently many police functions dealing with disorderly persons, fugitives, and criminals were handled by the military governors and governors, assisted by the garrisons at their command. Eroshkin, p. 146.

78. *Ocherki istorii Leningrada*, I, 171, 364, 374-5, 604. Some 1,200 watchmen were needed each night, an enormous burden for the public. Although no one, not even clergy, was exempt, in fact wealthy persons could buy their way out of service, thus increasing the obligations on the poor. Apparently by the end of the century this responsibility had disappeared, at least in St. Petersburg, where the police staff had some 500 guards on its payroll. How the watch responsibility was handled in smaller towns is unclear, though most likely it was handled by citizens in the same way as in the capitals.

79. Kizevetter, *Posadskaia obshchina*, pp. 542-543.

80. *PSZ*, XIII, no. 9754 (May 31, 1750).

81. The issue of posad revenues and expenditures is discussed in Kizevetter, *Posadskaia obshchina*, pp. 504-596. An interesting example of government subsidies applied to urban needs can be found in the record of William Coxe's visit to Russia. In Dogorobush, Viaz'ma, and Tver' he observed a number of substantial houses, brick covered with stucco, built at the empress' expense. Coxe, I, 218-219.

82. Kizevetter, *Posadskaia obshchina*, pp. 626-627.

83. *PSZ*, VIII, no. 5333 (September 12, 1728), article 26.

84. Kizevetter, "Posadskaia obshchina," p. 254.

85. The reluctance of the townsmen to maintain doctors at posad expense is a case in point. Some nakazy argued that the doctors treated only local gentry and therefore did not warrant support by townsmen. See V. N. Bochkarev, "Vrachebnoe delo i narodnoe prizrenie v Rossii XVIII veka," in *Sbornik statei v chest' Matvieia Kuz'micha Liubavskago* (Petrograd, 1917), pp. 445-451.

86. See Chapter 1.

7. THE POSAD ESTATE

1. A contemporary of Peter I, Ivan Tikhonovich Pososhkov (1652-1726), was the author of a memorandum of advice to the throne: *Kniga o skudosti i bogatstve* [Book about Poverty and Riches]. S. E. Desnitskii (c. 1740-1789), born into a Ukrainian merchant family, became a noted scholar of Russian law. He was particularly interested in social and economic matters. V. V. Krestinin (1729-1795), also of middle-class roots, wrote about trade and industry, especially in Arkhangel and the Russian north. For a Soviet perspective on select merchant-class authors, see *A History of Russian Economic Thought: Ninth through Eighteenth Centuries*, ed. John M. Letiche (Berkeley and Los Angeles, 1964).

2. The gentry case was put most forcefully by M. M. Shcherbatov in his "Razmyshleniia o ushcherbe torgovli . . . ," in *Chteniia v D.R.I.O.*, book 1 (January-March, 1860), pp. 135-140.

3. A representative collection of foreign observations can be found in Kulisher's history of trade. As an extreme example of adverse comparisons between the Russian and the Western European merchant, one might cite the following assertion of J-B. Scherer: "[In Russia] Il n'y a ne tiers-etat, ne bourgeois, ne marchands proprement dits; à l'exception du clergé, de la noblesse, et de l'etat militaire, tout est muschik, c'est-à-dire, serf." Scherer, *Histoire raisonnée due commerce de la Russie*, I, 104-105.

4. Both the content of the documents and the presence of merchant representatives of the cities at the commission argue strongly that they are basically representative of posad interests, and particularly the interests of the articulate, leading merchantry. For a somewhat different view see S. V. Voznesenskii, "Gorodskie deputatskye nakazy v Ekaterininskuiu komissiiu 1767 goda," *Zhurnal M.N.P.* (November 1909), pp. 89-119; (December 1909), pp. 241-284. The case for the value of these documents can be found in A. A. Kizevetter, "Proiskhozhdenie gorodskikh deputatskikh nakazov v Ekaterininskuiu komissiiu 1767 g.," in Kizevetter, *Istoricheskie ocherki*, pp. 209-241. See also V. N. Latkin, *Zakonodatel'nye komissii v Rossii v XVIII st.*

5. *Sbornik I.R.I.O.*, vol. 34, p. 5.

6. G. L. Vartanov, "Kupechestvo i torguiushchee krest'ianstvo tsentral'noi chasti Evropeiskoi Rossii vo vtoroi polovine XVIII veka," in *Uchenye zapiski L.G.P.I. im. A.I. Gertsena*, 229 (Leningrad, 1962), 163-176.

7. *Sbornik I.R.I.O.*, vol. 123, p. 468.

8. Ibid., vol. 107, p. 547.

9. Bernadskii, p. 75.

10. Klokman, "Gorod," p. 324.

11. Ibid.

12. *Sbornik I.R.I.O.*, vol. 107, p. 423.

13. Ibid., vol. 93, pp. 125-126.

14. Ibid., vol. 93, p. 132.

15. Bernadskii, pp. 78-79.

16. Ibid., p. 86.

17. Ibid., p. 76.

18. Latkin, I, 501-517.

19. Ibid., 501.

20. Polianskii, *Gorodskoe remeslo*, pp. 52-54.

21. Bernadskii, p. 81.

22. While I have attempted to derive these features of the posad outlook from the historical record left by the townsmen themselves, it is interesting to note how closely they mesh with a general assessment of the Russian character contained in Scherer's study; in particular the cautiousness and reluctance to innovate invite comparison. "Le Russe se plia pourtant au travail, mais par des degrés insensible, & plutôt à la fin par nécessité que par systeme. Malheureusement cette inertie, source de beaucoup de maux dans l'empire, est encore loin d'être déracinée. Renfermés dans l'intérieur de leurs maisons, dont ils sortent rarement, communiquant peu entr'eux, servilement attachés a leurs usages antiques & barbares, les Russes negligent les réformes les plus simples & les plus faciles qu'on leur indique, & montrent une indifférence incroyable pour certaines commoditiés de la vie que l'on voudroit leur procurer, & que la nature semble avoir enseignées aux peuples les plus sauvages. Toute nouveauté les effraye. Les raisons qu'ils en donnent révoltent quelque fois le bon sens, quelque fois aussi font gemir sur un état de misere profonde, dans lequel une administration très-vicieuse les enchaine." Scherer, I, pp. 88-89.

23. Rubinshtein, "Ulozhennaia komissiia 1754-1766 gg.," p. 249.

24. K. A. Pazhitnov, pp. 3-5.

25. "The Russian merchants, because they are subjected to the poll tax, find themselves in great contempt in the eyes of the bourgeoisie [meshchanstvo] of other European nations." *Sbornik I.R.I.O.*, vol. 107, pp. 33-34.

26. V. I. Sergeevich, untitled introduction to the collection of city nakazy: *Sbornik I.R.I.O.*, vol. 93, pp. vi-vii. Klokman, "Gorod," p. 327.

27. Sergeevich, ix. So distasteful was the quartering obligation that the merchants were willing partially to subsidize the construction of barracks. Latkin, I, 467.

28. Latkin, I, 485.

29. *PSZ*, V, no. 2789 (March 23, 1714), article 15.

30. The Karachev nakaz as quoted in Latkin, I, 489.

31. Coxe, *Travels*, I, 218-219.

32. Pazhitnov, pp. 2-3.

33. Sergeevich, v-vii. There is a brief discussion of the pattern of domestic serfholding by the townsmen of Tver' during the eighteenth century in Sorina, pp. 287-288.

34. Latkin, I, 489.

35. Ibid., 487.

36. N. I. Pavlenko, "Odvorianivanie russkoi burzhuazii v XVIII v.," *Istoriia SSSR*, no. 2 (1961), pp. 73-74. Other useful data on Moscow merchants who managed to attain gentry status can be found in N. Chulkov, pp. 489-501.

37. Pavlenko, "Odvorianivanie," p. 75.

38. Ibid., pp. 76-78.

39. Ibid., pp. 82-83.

40. Shcherbatov, pp. 135-140.

41. Pavlenko, "Odvorianivanie," pp. 86-87.

8. THE TRANSITIONAL ERA: 1750-1770

1. Tugan-Baranovskii, p. 31.

2. P. A. Khromov, *Ekonomicheskoe razvitie Rossii: Ocherki ekonomiki Rossii s drevneishikh vremen do Velikoi Okt. revol.* (Moscow, 1967), p. 115.

3. A. L. Shapiro, "K istorii krest'ianskikh promyslov i krest'ianskoi manu-faktury v Rossii XVIII v.," *Istoricheskie zapiski* 31 (1950): 152-153. The major study of textile production is I. V. Meshalin, *Tekstil'naia promyshlennost' krest'-ian Moskovskoi gubernii v XVIII i pervoi polovine XIX veka* (Moscow, 1950).

4. Henry Rosovsky, "The Serf Entrepreneur in Russia," *Explorations in Entrepreneurial History*, no. 6 (May 1954), pp. 352-357.

5. A detailed examination of Ostashkov can be found in Klokman, *Ocherki*, passim. For other treatments of the settlements and suburbs, see A. M. Razgon, "Promyshlennye i torgovye slobody i sela Vladimirskoi gubernii vo vtoroi polovine XVIII v.," *Istoricheskie zapiski* 32 (1950): 133-172; and Ia. E. Vodarskii, *Promyshlennye seleniia tsentral'noi Rossii v period genezisa i razvitiia kapitalizma* (Moscow, 1972).

6. Bernadskii, p. 67.

7. Rosovsky, p. 353.

8. Lappo-Danilevskii, *Russkiia promyshlennyia i torgovyia kompanii*, pp. 105-107.

9. *PSZ*, XII, no. 9438 (September 5, 1747); *PSZ*, XIV, no. 10285 (August 30, 1754); *PSZ*, XIV, no. 10914 (January 12, 1759). *Ocherki istorii Leningrada*, I, 71. For a more extensive discussion of the problem of social unrest and its relation to the legislation, see John T. Alexander, "Catherine II, Bubonic Plague, and the Problem of Industry in Moscow," *American Historical Review* 79, no. 3 (June 1974): 637-671.

10. Peter had instructed the Senate "to examine, and if there are not any obstacles, to allow each rank to trade equally with the same tariff, and in place of the tithe money, to tax in proportion to trade." As quoted in N. M. Druzhinin,

Gosudarstvennye krest'iane i reforma P. D. Kiseleva (Moscow-Leningrad, 1946), I, 78.

11. *PSZ*, VII, no. 4312 (September 27, 1723), articles 2, 4, 5.

12. M. Ia. Volkov, "Formirovanie gorodskoi burzhuazii v Rossii XVII-XVIII vv.," in *Goroda Feodal'noi Rossii*, ed. N. M. Druzhinin et al. (Moscow, 1966), pp. 199-200.

13. *PSZ*, XII, no. 9201 (August 19, 1745). The sentence in the text is a close paraphrase of the wording of the law.

14. The principal figure behind this reform, P. I. Shuvalov, had extensive commercial interests which could only be enhanced by a liberalization of internal trade. See M. Ia. Volkov, "Tamozhennaia reforma 1753-57 gg.," *Istoricheskie zapiski* 71 (1962): 135-143. For a brief discussion of steps taken by the gentry to diversify their income and of related conflicts with merchant interests at mid-century, see Arcadius Kahan, "The Costs of 'Westernization' in Russia: The Gentry and the Economy in the Eighteenth Century," *Slavic Review* 25, no. 1 (March 1966): 58-60.

15. *PSZ*, XIV, no. 10486 (December 1, 1755), chapter 2, article 1.

16. A particularly effective argument about the significance of peasant trade and manufacturing activities can be found in Vartanov's essay.

17. M. D. Chulkov, *Slovar' uchrezhdennykh v Rossii iarmarok izdannyi dlia obrashchaiushchikhsia v torgovle* (Moscow, 1788). For a more recent look at fairs, see N. L. Rubinshtein, "Russkaia iarmarka 18 veka," *Uchenye zapiski kafedry istorii narodov SSSR Moskovskogo oblastnogo pedagogicheskogo instituta*, part 1 (1939), pp. 5-28.

18. Klokman, *Ocherki*, p. 99.

19. Vartanov, pp. 180-181.

20. Khromov, pp. 145-149; Liashchenko, 1939 ed., pp. 244, 259.

21. Jerome Blum, *Lord and Peasant in Russia from the Ninth to the Nineteenth Centuries* (Princeton, 1961), pp. 448-453.

22. F. Ia. Polianskii, *Ekonomicheskoi stroi*, pp. 155-160; Vartanov, pp. 188-192.

23. This emphasis flowed naturally from their general criticism of imperial Russia, a criticism that was in all likelihood influenced by their liberal or radical personal political persuasions, and it flowed from their habit of comparing the shortcomings of Russia with the achievements of Western Europe. For examples of their comparative perspectives, see A. A. Kizevetter, "Novizna i starina v Rossii XVIII stoletiia: Rech' pered magisterskim disputom," in *Istoricheskie ocherki*, p. 272; and Miliukov, *Ocherki*, 1919 ed., pp. 240-242.

24. Kulisher, p. 144; Tugan-Baranovskii, pp. 20-50; Liashchenko, 1947 ed., p. 394. Arguments like these closely parallel the deprecatory remarks of Ditiatin, Kizevetter, and Miliukov on Russian urban development, and not surprisingly so, for the latter adduced similar kinds of evidence—descriptions of the physical state of the cities and rehearsals of the impoverished nature of civic life.

25. Kizevetter, "Posadskaia obshchina," p. 243.

26. One might list in this regard the works of Meshalin, Shapiro, Razgon, Vartanov, and Vodarskii.

27. If there is a common theme to this work, it might be represented by the

word "more": that is, more factories, more workers, more output, more trade, more traders, and more trading points. As often as not, the other term of the comparison is missing and without it wholly convincing proof of the dimensions of economic development cannot be said to be present.

28. See, for example, K. N. Serbina, *Ocherki iz sotsial'no-ekonomicheskoi istorii russkogo goroda: Tikhvinskii posad v XVI-XVIII vv.* (Moscow, 1951); Klokman, *Ocherki* and *Sotsial'no-ekonomicheskaia istoriia*; and Kafengauz, *Ocherki vnutrennego rynka.*

29. Stalinist periodization, which still exerts a powerful influence on Soviet scholarship, contends that the emancipation of the serfs in 1861 marks the definitive moment of transition from feudalism to capitalism. Of course, such a change could not occur overnight; it took some considerable time for the seeds of capitalism to come to maturity in the womb of Russian feudal society. Pursuant to that argument, Soviet historians have turned to the archives—fired, no doubt, by the spirit of socialist emulation—in an effort to demonstrate that the foundations of capitalism had been well laid in the eighteenth century—or possibly even earlier. After years of dispute there appears to be a growing consensus that the capitalistic uklad took shape in the second half of the eighteenth century, though the precise timing of its occurrence remains strongly contested. For a review of the arguments on the speed and extent of the economic transition, especially as it affected the eighteenth century, see *Perekhod ot feodalizmu k kapitalizmu v Rossii*, ed. V. I. Shunkov et al. (Moscow, 1969). Two lengthy reviews of that work are: Samuel H. Baron, "The Transition from Feudalism to Capitalism in Russia: A Major Soviet Historical Controversy," *American Historical Review* 77, no. 3 (June 1972): 715-729; and J. M. Hittle, review of *Perekhod . . .* , *Kritika* 7, no. 2 (Winter 1971): 97-110.

30. See Franklin F. Mendels, "Proto-industrialization: The First Phase of the Industrialization Process," *Journal of Economic History* 32, no. 1 (March 1972): 241-261; and Charles Tilly and Richard Tilly, "Agenda for European Economic History in the 1970's," *Journal of Economic History* 31, no. 1 (March 1971): 184-198.

31. Gilbert Rozman, *Urban Networks in Russia, 1750-1800, and Premodern Periodization* (Princeton, 1976).

32. The works of Klokman, Polianskii, and Iakovtsevskii stand out in this regard.

33. Polianskii, *Pervonachal'noe nakoplenie*, pp. 36-38.

34. *Perekhod* contains precious little information on cities or on the economic activities of the townsmen. This tendency also appears in general histories, which give only meager treatment to the townsmen.

35. Lappo-Danilevskii believes that small-scale rural operations were detrimental to merchant-run manufacturing enterprises. Lappo-Danilevskii, *Russkiia promyshlennyia i torgovyia kompanii*, p. 107.

36. Bernadskii, p. 69.

37. Iakovtsevskii, pp. 133-136.

38. Vartanov, p. 192.

39. *PSZ*, XX, no. 14275 (March 17, 1775), article 11.

40. V. M. Kabuzan, *Narodonaselenie Rossii v XVIII-pervoi polovine XIX v.* (Moscow, 1963), pp. 163, 171.

41. Polianskii suggests the city population may have quadrupled during the century, but these figures seem excessive, especially in light of recent, specialized demographic studies. Polianskii, *Gorodskoe remeslo*, p. 30.

42. Ibid., p. 36.

43. Kizevetter notes that the percentage of posadskie liudi in the total taxable population of the state remained stable. He gives the following percentages: first revision (1719), 3.2 percent; second revision (1744), 3.2 percent and third revision (1762), 3.1 percent. Kizevetter, *Posadskaia obshchina*, p. 113. The following table shows the posad population as a percentage of the total population of the state.

Year	Total population (male sex)	Posad population (male sex)	Posad percentage
1719	7,570,000	169,426	2.2
1762	11,200,000	228,365	2.0
1782	15,093,000	334,091	2.2

The total population figures come from V. M. Kabuzan, p. 164. They reflect the population of all of Russia covered by the censuses. The figures for the posadskie liudi come from the following sources: 1719—Kabuzan, pp. 118-119; 1762 (actually from a compilation of 1769 but close enough to the revision date)—Kizevetter, *Posadskaia obshchina*, p. 113; 1786 (based on archival research into the number of merchants, meshchane, and craft guildsmen)—Polianskii, *Gorodskoe remeslo*, p. 33.

44. V. Avseenko, *200 Let S.-Peterburga: Istoricheskii ocherk* (St. Petersburg, 1903), pp. 40-41.

45. Klokman, "Gorod," p. 329.

46. Ibid., p. 328.

47. Ibid., p. 329.

48. In Moscow province, two-thirds of the peasants registered to become merchants were economic peasants, that is, they came from land that had belonged to ecclesiastical institutions and church hierarchs before that land was taken over by the government in 1763-64. Vartanov, p. 190.

49. Although peasants seeking entry into the posad were formally restricted to applying for membership in the guild merchantry, in fact many of them sought simply to join the ranks of the nonguild posad people (after 1775, meshchane). The government strongly opposed this trend, but with limited success. In 1782 the practice was forbidden outright. Klokman, "Gorod," pp. 345-347.

50. Vartanov, pp. 186-192.

51. Ibid., pp. 194-196.

52. Ikonnikov, p. 44.

53. P. K. Alefirenko, "Chumnyi bunt v Moskve v 1771 g.," *Voprosy istorii,*

no. 4 (1947), p. 87. See also Alexander, "Catherine II, Bubonic Plague and the Problem of Industry in Moscow."

54. P. G. Ryndziunskii, "Goroda," in *Ocherki istorii SSSR: Period feodalizma: Rossiia vo votoroi chetverti XVIII v.* (Moscow, 1956), p. 193. He cites an unpublished study on population dynamics written by E. A. Zviagintsev.

55. Miliukov, *Ocherki*, p. 82.

56. Kabuzan's estimate comes from an unpublished manuscript cited by V. K. Iatsunskii in the latter's article "Nekotorye voprosy metodiki izucheniia istorii feodal'nogo goroda v Rossii," in *Goroda feodal'noi Rossii*, ed. N. M. Druzhinin et al. (Moscow, 1966), p. 87, n. 37. Rozman, "Comparative Approaches to Urbanization," p. 78.

57. Rozman, "Comparative Approaches to Urbanization," p. 77.

58. Polianskii, *Gorodskoe remeslo*, pp. 37-38.

59. M. Ia. Volkov, "Formirovanie gorodskoi burzhuazii v Rossii XVII-XVIII vv.," in *Goroda feodal'noi Rossii*, p. 196.

60. *Istoriia Moskvy*, II (Moscow, 1953), 306-308.

61. Polianskii, *Gorodskoe remeslo*, p. 49.

62. *PSZ*, XX, no. 14261 (March 2, 1775), article 1.

63. *Ocherki istorii SSSR: Period feodalizma: Rossiia vo vtoroi polovine XVIII v.*, ed. A. I. Baranovich (Moscow, 1956), p. 152.

64. In Kashin, for example, in 1744 only five of the town's sixty-four merchants had a capitalization exceeding 300 rubles. *Akademiia nauk SSSR: Trudy istoriko-arkheograficheskogo instituta. XV Materialy po istorii krest'ianskoi promyshlennosti XVIII i pervoi poloviny XIX v.*, I (Moscow-Leningrad, 1935), 249.

65. Klokman, *Ocherki*, pp. 124-140, 186-210, and *passim*.

66. Kizevetter, *Posadskaia obshchina*, pp. 254-270. *Ocherki istorii Leningrada*, I, 90. *Ocherki istorii SSSR . . . Rossiia vo vtoroi polovine XVIII v.*, p. 155.

67. Kizevetter, *Posadskaia obshchina*, p. 231. There were three basic ways of organizing service: through franchises (*na otkup*); through sworn men (*na vere*); and by the magistracy or by the whole posad society (*priniatie na magistraty i na posadskaia obshchestva*). The latter two differed chiefly as to responsibility: the sworn men were guaranteed by those who elected them; in the other situation either the magistracy office or the entire posad was responsible. From the 1730s on the government tried now one, now another of these methods for the liquor tax and customs collections. Ibid., pp. 211-248.

68. *Ocherki istorii SSSR . . . Rossiia vo vtoroi polovine XVIII v.*, p. 155.

69. Kizevetter, *Posadskaia obschchina*, p. 199.

70. Ibid., p. 202. For a study of the liquor and salt taxes as sources of government revenue, see S. M. Troitskii, *Finansovaia politika*, pp. 150-170.

71. Kizevetter, *Posadskaia obshchina*, pp. 234-236.

72. This argument is touched on in part by Kizevetter. "The small number of clerks in the chancelleries, the willfulness of the military college, with which it was difficult even for the Senate to cope, the extreme need among the people in view of the numerous and varied nature of service responsibilities—such were the conditions, unfavorable to the easing of the service burdens of the posad class." Ibid., p. 207.

9. THE EARLY REFORMS OF CATHERINE II

1. Wallace Daniel, "The Merchantry and the Problem of Social Order in the Russian State: Catherine II's Commission on Commerce," *Slavonic and East European Review* 15 (1977): 185-203.

2. *Iaroslavl': Ocherki po istorii goroda*, ed. P. Andreev et al. (Iaroslavl', 1954), p. 37. The Tomsk nakaz also contains a description of cattle wandering in the street. Bernadskii, p. 74.

3. Coxe, I, 222.

4. Ibid., p. 417.

5. As quoted in Ditiatin, *Ustroistvo*, I, 380.

6. Ibid., pp. 371-373.

7. Ibid., p. 384.

8. G. P. Makhnova, "Khod i rezul'taty administrativno-territorial'noi reformy 1775-1785 gg. v Rossii," *Voprosy geografii* 83 (1970): 134.

9. Robert E. Jones, "Catherine II and the Provincial Reform of 1775: A Question of Motivation," *Canadian Slavic Studies* 4 (1970): 497-508.

10. See, for example, V. Ulanov, "Nakaz i komissiia v sochinenii proekta novago ulozheniia," in *Tri veka: Rossiia ot smuty do nashego vremeni*, IV (Moscow, 1913), 237. Kizevetter, in a study of Catherine as legislator, argues that a major source of the second period of the empress' legislative activity (after 1775) was the fund of information that originated with the Great Commission. A. A. Kizevetter, "Imperatritsa Ekaterina II, kak zakonodatel'nitsa," in *Istoricheskie ocherki*, pp. 276-277.

11. The format of Latkin's study of the Great Commission is based on a comparison of the demands of the nakazy and the subsequent responses or failure of response by the government.

12. For an example see the published *Vedomost'* and *Opisanie* for Pereslavl'-Zalesskii in *Pereslavl'-Zalesskii: Materialy dlia istorii goroda XVII i XVIII stoletii*, ed. E. Belov (Moscow, 1884), pp. 25-30.

13. T. P. Efimenko, "K istorii gorodskogo zemleustroistva vremeni Ekateriny II," *Zhurnal M.N.P.* 54 (December 1914): 284. For a general study of the subject see Robert E. Jones, "Urban Planning and the Development of Provincial Towns in Russia, 1762-1796," in *The Eighteenth Century in Russia*, ed. J. G. Garrard (Oxford, 1973), pp. 321-344.

14. The preceding discussion of the general survey comes from Efimenko, pp. 291-301. The survey was called into being by a decree of September 19, 1765, and work began in earnest the following year. By 1843 some thirty-four provinces had been fully surveyed. *Sovetskaia istoricheskaia entsiklopediia*, IV (Moscow, 1963), 194.

15. Klokman, *Sotsial'no-ekonomicheskaia istoriia*, p. 59.

16. It is perhaps an imprecision to refer to this document of mixed content as a tax reform, but the majority of its articles do deal in one way or another with taxes. *PSZ*, XX, no. 14275 (March 17, 1775).

17. Ibid., article 47.

18. Klokman notes a law of May 25, 1775, which spelled out these precise

capital qualifications needed for registration in each of the merchant guilds. Klokman, *Sotsial'no-ekonomicheskaia istoriia*, p. 92. Eighteen months later a Senate decree indicated that there had been confusion in some localities concerning the implementation of the March 17, 1775 reform, as well as requests for clarification. This decree goes into some detail about the execution of the reform and provides a sample report to be made by localities to the Senate. *PSZ*, XX, no. 14516 (October 10, 1776).

19. Klokman, *Sotsial'no-ekonomicheskaia istoriia*, p. 90.

20. Ibid., p. 93.

21. Troitskii, "Finansovaia politika," p. 313.

22. Daniel, p. 197.

23. Klokman, *Sotsial'no-ekonomicheskaia istoriia*, p. 91.

24. "Commerce, for the most part, flourishes where there flowers independence and freedom [*vol'nost'u i svobodoiu*]," the empress wrote to N. Nepliuev. As quoted in A. S. Lappo-Danilevskii, *Ocherk vnutrennei politiki imperatritsy Ekateriny II*, p. 21.

25. In fact the movement away from monopolies and hence toward freer trade had begun before Catherine came to the throne, but it was during her reign that the broader implications of such a policy received full articulation.

26. Robert E. Jones, *The Emancipation of the Russian Nobility 1762-1785* (Princeton, 1973), pp. 222-223.

27. Ibid., p. 230.

28. A. Ia. Avrekh, "Russkii absoliutizm i ego rol' v utverzhdenii kapitalizma v Rossii," *Istoriia SSSR*, no. 2 (1968), pp. 82-104; A. L. Shapiro, "Ob absoliutizme v Rossii," *Istoriia SSSR*, no. 5 (1968), pp. 69-72; A. N. Chistozvonov, "Nekotorye aspekty problemy genizisa absoliutizma," *Voprosy Istorii*, no. 5 (1968), pp. 46-62; and M. Ia. Volkov, "O stanovlenii absoliutizma v Rossii," *Istoriia SSSR*, no. 1 (1970), pp. 90-104.

29. See, for example, S. M. Troitskii, *Russkii absoliutizm i dvorianstvo v XVIII v. Formirovanie biurokratii* (Moscow, 1974), p. 365. Other participants in the debate on absolutism are in argreement on this point. See Volkov, "O stanovlenii," p. 104.

30. Ibid., pp. 5-6, 294.

31. Ibid., pp. 365-366.

32. Jones, *Emancipation*, p. 179.

33. N. F. Demidova, "Biurokratizatsiia gosudarstvennogo apparata absoliutizma v XVII-XVIII vv.," *Absoliutizm v Rossii (XVII-XVIII vv.)*, ed. N. M. Druzhinin, N. I. Pavlenko, and L. V. Cherepnin (Moscow, 1964), p. 240.

34. Jones, *Emancipation*, pp. 298-299.

35. Ibid., pp. 260-272. Jones argues that in fact the government encouraged gentry to develop a corporate sense and to assume more responsibilities.

36. John Friedman, "Cities and Social Transformation," *Comparative Studies in Society and History*, IV (1961-1962), 92.

37. "Uchrezhdenie dlia upravleniia gubernii Vserossiiskoi imperii," *PSZ*, XX, no. 14392 (November 7, 1775), chapter 19, articles 253-254. To make certain that the decentralization implicit in the reform did not get out of hand, the name-

stniki were given powers that extended beyond local administration to state policy itself. M. P. Pavlova-Sil'vanskaia, "Sotsial'naia sushchnost' oblastnoi reformy Ekateriny II," *Absoliutizm v Rossii,* pp. 467-468.

38. Ibid., chapter 18.

39. Ibid., chapter 19, article 274.

40. Pavlova-Sil'vanskaia explains the exclusion of merchants from top urban administrative posts by reference to the economic weakness of merchant society. Their attention, she claims, centered on economic gains rather than on aspiring to political power. The nakazy, however, suggest that the merchants were not entirely lacking in political objectives. Pavlova-Sil'vanskaia, p. 481.

41. Ditiatin, *Ustroistvo,* I, 385-389. Ditiatin's eagerness to see the emergence of an all-estate city led him to value highly both the precedent cited here as well as the introduction of the new administrative heads of cities, embodied in the 1775 reform.

42. Ibid., p. 396.

43. "Uchrezhdenie," chapter 9, articles 117-123; chapter 11, articles 134-137.

44. Ibid., chapter 25, articles 378-394.

45. For details of the magistracy's legal fate under the new system, see Ibid., chapters 20, 21, and 22.

46. Eroshkin, pp. 168, 400-401.

47. A comprehensive treatment of the implementation of the provincial reform can be found in Klokman, *Sotsial'no-ekonomicheskaia istoriia,* pp. 100-109, 122-206.

48. "Uchrezhdenie," chapter 1, articles 1, 17.

49. Klokman, *Sotsial'no-ekonomicheskaia istoriia,* p. 202.

50. Ibid., pp. 125-126.

51. The suburb, upon becoming a city, was known as Rybinsk. Ibid., p. 159.

52. Ibid., p. 137.

53. Ibid.

54. Ibid., p. 319.

55. Ibid., pp. 103-104.

56. Ibid., pp. 104-107.

57. Ibid., p. 203.

58. Ibid., p. 204.

59. Ibid., pp. 205-206.

60. Ibid., p. 100.

10. THE LATER REFORMS OF CATHERINE II AND THE FATE OF THE POSAD COMMUNE

1. The board, in addition to its presiding officers, contained two appointed officers (*pristavy*), one each for criminal and civil affairs, and two councillors (*ratmany*), who were elected by the merchants. "Ustav blagochiniia ili politseiskii," *PSZ,* XXI, no. 15379 (April 8, 1782), articles 2, 3, 5-12. The hierarchical structure of the police apparatus and the responsibilities of officials at any given

level receive elaboration in later sections of the document. For an interpretation of the unclear articles of this document see Ditiatin, *Ustroistvo*, I, 463, note 1.

2. The structure of the police organization nationally was such that "a direct hierarchy existed from the Senate to the most distant ward supervisor." John P. LeDonne, "The Provincial and Local Police under Catherine the Great, 1775-1796," *Canadian Slavic Studies* 4, no. 3 (Fall 1970): 519.

3. "Ustav blagochiniia," articles 28-40, 70, 85-131. One might argue, as have many from the time the law appeared, that all those responsibilities were too much for a single agency to accomplish. See, for example, the brief, legally oriented survey of police institutions in Russia during the seventeenth and eighteenth centuries in I. E. Andreevskii, *Politseiskoe pravo* (St. Petersburg, 1874), pp. 96-97. Andreevskii contends that the townsmen found the *Ustav blagochiniia* unsatisfactory for a number of reasons, including the joining together of the judicial, criminal apprehension, and blagoustroistvo functions in a single agency. Andreevskii, who seems to think that a policy agency ought to consist of night guards, chimney inspectors, and the like, has his own reservations similar to those of the townsmen.

4. "Gramota na prava i vygody gorodam Rossiiskoi imperii," *PSZ*, XXII, no. 16188 (April 21, 1785).

5. For a thorough study of the textual history of the Charter to the Cities, see A. A. Kizevetter, *Gorodovoe polozhenie Ekateriny II 1785 g.: Opyt istoricheskogo komentariia* (Moscow, 1909). In a perceptive review of this book, Iu. V. Got'e suggests that Kizevetter gives undue weight to the German models for this legislation at the expense of changes in society which influenced the new legislation. *Zhurnal M.N.P.*, no. 9, section 2 (1909), pp. 206-219. Klokman stresses the influence of materials collected during the Great Commission and then given a preliminary working-out in the Senate's plan. Klokman, *Sotsial'no-ekonomicheskaia istoriia*, p. 112.

6. In his evaluation of the charter, Ditiatin refers frequently to the contradictory wording of the document as well as to the apparently conflicting principles on which it is based. Ditiatin, *Ustroistvo*, I, 417-459. See also Kizevetter, *Gil'diia*, p. 5 and "Gorodovoe polozhenie Ekateriny II," *Tri Veka*, pp. 260-266. The most comprehensive treatment of the charter, of course, is Kizevetter's *Gorodovoe polozhenie*.

7. "Gramota," article 114.

8. The precise characteristics of each guild are outlined in the "Gramota," articles 102-119.

9. Ibid., articles 123 (which contains the 117 points), 138-145.

10. Ibid., article 101.

11. Ibid., articles 99, 107, 113.

12. In a curious turn of phrase, third-guild merchants were forbidden "in summer and winter to harness more than one horse." Ibid., articles 106, 112, 119.

13. Ibid., article 24.

14. Ibid., article 77.

15. Section D of the "Gramota" is a fine example of the confusion caused by sloppy drafting. Its heading speaks of the "personal privileges of the city inhabi-

tants of the middle kind of people, or meshchane, in general." The problem arises from the use of meshchane. The legislation of 1775 gave that term a precise meaning, namely, those of the posad population not eligible for the merchant guilds. But in this section of the charter, the term appears to be used generically to embrace all city dwellers—merchants, craftsmen, hired laborers, everyone except perhaps the gentry, who were already covered in these matters by their own charter. My basis for giving the document such a reading consists primarily in the fact that these privileges were *not* specifically granted to guild merchants nor to "distinguished" (*imenitye*) citizens, though one would certainly expect them to be the first to receive such benefits. Thus the format of the legislation discusses first those general privileges of all city dwellers and then goes on to indicate precisely what extra privileges each group was to have. Latkin gives the document a similar reading, though he suggests that the gentry too were conceived of as belonging to the category of meshchane.

16. Ibid., articles 80-91. For an analysis of urban citizenship less sharp in legal matters than the work of Ditiatin and Kizevetter, but useful for its comparison of the condition of urban citizens (especially meshchane) with state peasants, see P. G. Ryndziunskii, *Gorodskoe grazhdanstvo doreformennoi Rossii* (Moscow, 1958), pp. 40-51.

17. Ibid., articles 63-68.

18. Ibid., articles 158-163.

19. Ibid., articles 106-107, 112-113, 119, 133-134.

20. Ditiatin argues that the divisions of the population contained in the charter are "almost exclusively of an estate character." Ditiatin, *Ustroistvo*, I, 420. If by estate character he has in mind the granting of special privileges to select groups of the population, then there is some merit to the argument. But the traditional estate (*soslovie*) relations in Russia had a much deeper and more consistent basis in economic relations and in service than can be found in the six groups of urban citizens as outlined in the charter.

21. The argument that corporate principles inspired both the charter to the nobility and the charter to the cities can be found in a discussion of Catherine's major domestic legislation by M. M. Bogoslovskii, "Uchrezhdenie dlia upravleniia gubernii i zhalovannyia gramoty Ekateriny II," in *Tri veka: Rossiia ot smuty do nashego vremeni*, ed. V. Kallash, IV (Moscow, 1913), 239-250.

22. Jones, *Emancipation*, pp. 267-268.

23. Ibid., pp. 244-272.

24. *Nakaz imperatritsy Ekateriny II*, p. 109.

25. *Sbornik I.R.I.O.*, vol. 1, p. 283.

26. "Gramota," articles 29, 50.

27. Kizevetter, *Gil'diia*, pp. 4-8; and his "Gorodovoe polozhenie Ekateriny II," in *Tri veka: Rossiia ot smuty do nashego vremeni*, IV (Moscow, 1913), 264.

28. "Gramota," articles 30, 39-44.

29. As Ditiatin notes, however, this juridical person is not composed of separate persons, but of separate groups, groups of an almost exclusively estate character. Ditiatin, *Ustroistvo*, I, 418-425.

30. Prior to this time, the only land in the towns set aside for the use of all

inhabitants was the common grazing land, guaranteed to the citizens by chapter 19, article 6 of the *Ulozhenie* of 1649. But, under that arrangement, the common remained the property of the tsar; the townsmen's privileges extended no further than its use, and that as individuals, not as a corporate body. All this changed with the charter. For a brief discussion of the evolving status of real property in the cities, see Ditiatin, *Ustroistvo*, I, 425-428.

31. Ibid., articles 36-37, 53-54.

32. Ibid., articles 31-34, 54.

33. This attitude permeates his essay on the statute. Kizevetter "Gorodovoe polozhenie," pp. 251-273. Just to demonstrate that there were inconsistencies even in the inconsistent principles, the magistracy officials at the provincial level continued to be elected by merchants and meshchane only—a truly estate-oriented arrangement left over from the 1775 provincial reform. "Gramota," article 32.

34. "Gramota," articles 158-163.

35. Ditiatin, *Ustroistvo*, I, 441.

36. "Gramota," article 167.

37. Ibid., article 158.

38. Ibid., articles 164-165.

39. The argument is Ditiatin's. *Ustroistvo*, I, 447. Kizevetter concurs that this was the case. *Gorodovoe polozhenie*, p. 373.

40. "Gramota," articles 9, 12, 25. For a discussion of the impact of the charter on the magistracy, see Kizevetter, *Gil'diia*, pp. 7-8.

41. Kizevetter, *Gil'diia*, p. 8.

42. The city duma in St. Petersburg died out sometime in 1797-1798. It was replaced by a Commission for Supplying the Residents with Provisions, Order, Residences, and Other Things, Pertaining to Police. In February of 1799 a similar commission was established in Moscow. Apparently the principle of representative institutions was completely abandoned. Ditiatin, *Ustroistvo*, II, 118-131.

43. *PSZ*, XXVI, no. 19811 (April 2, 1801).

44. Kizevetter, *Gorodovoe polozhenie*, pp. 330-333. In some cities where there were not enough qualified individuals to fill key posts, the government allowed the fifty-ruble tax qualification to be set aside and permitted meshchane who had some property to hold offices. *PSZ*, XXII, no. 16514 (March 11, 1787).

45. Kizevetter, *Gorodovoe polozhenie*, p. 340.

46. Ibid., p. 380.

47. I. I. Ditiatin, "K istorii 'Zhalovannykh gramot' dvorianstvu i gorodam, 1785 goda," *Russkaia mysl'*, no. 6 (1885), pp. 11-13.

48. Kizevetter, *Gorodovoe polozhenie*, p. 357.

49. Kizevetter, "Gorodovoe polozhenie," p. 267.

50. Kizevetter, *Gorodovoe polozhenie*, pp. 348-349.

51. Ibid., p. 349.

52. Ibid., pp. 389-390.

53. Ditiatin, *Stoletie*, p. 198; Kizevetter, *Gorodovoe polozhenie*, p. 392.

54. Ditiatin, *Stoletie*, p. 194.

55. Kizevetter, *Gorodovoe polozhenie*, p. 374.

56. Kizevetter, "Gorodovoe polozhenie," p. 268.

57. As quoted in Ditiatin, *Stoletie*, p. 199.

58. Ibid., p. 200.

59. W. Bruce Lincoln, "The Russian State and Its Cities: The Search for Effective Municipal Government, 1786-1842," *Jahrbucher für Geschichte Osteuropas* 17, no. 4 (1969): 531-554.

60. Firsov, "Gorod," pp. 632-656; M. Ia. Volkov, "Posadskie liudi" in *Sovetskaia istoricheskaia entsiklopediia*, XI (Moscow, 1968), 461-463. B. B. Kafengauz, although he discusses the posad commune in relation to key legislation of Catherine's reign, says nothing about the fate of the institution. B. B. Kafengauz, "Gorod i gorodskaia reforma 1785 g.," *Ocherki istorii SSSR . . . Rossiia vo vtoroi polovine XVIII v.*, pp. 157-162.

61. The fullest statement of this position is contained in Kizevetter, *Gil'diia*, pp. 1-22. In Kizevetter's formal defense of the work, he indicated that the old posad commune was "to a significant degree ruined before 1785," so that even if the legislation was a bit on the theoretical side, the ground had been prepared for it. "Disput A. A. Kizevettera," *Istoricheskii vestnik*, no. 2 (February 1904), p. 806.

62. Klokman, "Gorod," pp. 329-332.

63. Ia. E. Vodarskii, *Naselenie Rossii za 400 let (XVI-nachalo XX vv.)* (Moscow, 1973), p. 67. A less precise reference to the end of the commune can be found in Iakovtsevskii where he discusses the effects on the posad of the concentration of capital in the hands of the first-guild merchants. "Consequently, the 'motley' of the posad commune is a natural result of its historical development (the concentration of capital); the posad commune went from unity to differentiation and disintegration." Whether the commune was ever so united as Iakovtsevskii implies is of course doubtful. Iakovtsevskii, p. 138.

64. *PSZ*, XXXVII, no. 28325 (June 22, 1820).

65. *PSZ*, XXIII, no. 16765 (May 14, 1789). *PSZ*, XXIII, no. 17137 (July 4, 1793). In referring to the magistracy—or ratusha—in some small cities, the term posad was used synonymously with small town. *PSZ*, XXVII, no. 20099 (January 1, 1802).

66. *PSZ*, XXXIX, no. 30115 (November 14, 1824).

67. "Uchrezhdenie upravleniia obshchestvennykh del v gorode," *Svod zakonov*, II (1842), articles 3918-3921.

68. "Ustav o podatiakh," *Svod zakonov*, V (1842), articles 218-254.

69. Ibid., article 240. The ratusha (magistracy) shared with the city duma supervision over the apportionment and collection of taxes from the meshchane. "Uchrezhdenie upravleniia," article 4248. The magistracy and ratusha also controlled the issuance of passports to merchants and to the meshchane. *PSZ*, XXIII, no. 16971 (July 8, 1791).

11. CONCLUSION

1. See, for example: Kulisher, chapters 8-10; Kizevetter, "Novizna i starina," pp. 264-273; Berlin, pp. 3-40; Pazhitnov, pp. 2-25; Miliukov, *Ocherki*, pp. 246-252.

2. As if to underscore the failings of the posadskie liudi, Miliukov is at

pains to note the passing from the scene of the Moscow merchants. Miliukov, *Ocherki*, p. 252. See note 2 to the Introduction.

3. Polianskii, *Gorodskoe remeslo*, p. 36.

4. See, for a succinct statement of this position, Kizevetter, "Novizna i starina," pp. 268-273.

5. Hans J. Torke, "Continuity and Change in the Relations between Bureaucracy and Society in Russia, 1613-1861," *Canadian Slavic Studies* 5 (1971): 457-476; "More Light than Shade," *Canadian Slavic Studies* 6 (1972): 10-12.

6. John Keep, "Light and Shade in the History of the Russian Administration," *Canadian Slavic Studies* 6 (1972): 8.

7. Kizevetter, "Novizna i starina," p. 272.

Bibliography

Akademiia Nauk SSSR: Trudy istoriko-arkheograficheskogo instituta. XV. Materialy po istorii krest'ianskoi promyshlennosti XVIII i pervoi poloviny XIX v. Vol. 1. Moscow-Leningrad, 1935.

Akty, sobrannye v bibliotekakh i arkhivakh Rossiiskoi imperii Arkheograficheskoiu Ekspeditsieiu Akademii nauk. 4 vols. St. Petersburg, 1836-1838.

Alefirenko, P. K. "Chumnyi bunt v Moskve v 1771 g." *Voprosy istorii*, no. 4 (1947), pp. 82-88.

Alexander, John T. "Catherine II, Bubonic Plague, and the Problem of Industry in Moscow." *American Historical Review* 79, no. 3 (June 1974): 637-671.

Andreev, P., et al., eds. *Iaroslavl': Ocherki po istorii goroda.* Iaroslavl', 1954.

Andreevskii, I. E. *Politseiskoe pravo.* St. Petersburg, 1874.

Avrekh, A. Ia. "Russkii absoliutizm i ego rol' v utverzhdenii kapitalizma v Rossii." *Istoriia SSSR*, no. 2 (1968), pp. 82-104.

Avseenko, V. *200 Let S.-Peterburga: Istoricheskii ocherk.* St. Petersburg, 1903.

Bakhrushin, S. V. *Nauchnye trudy.* 4 vols. in 5 parts. Moscow, 1952-1959.

Baron, Samuel H. "The Fate of the *Gosti* in the Reign of Peter the Great." *Cahiers du Monde Russe et Sovietique*, October-December 1973, pp. 488-512.

—————. "The Origins of Seventeenth-Century Moscow's Nemeckaja Sloboda." *California Slavic Studies* 5 (1970): 1-18.

—————. "The Town in 'Feudal' Russia." *Slavic Review* 28, no. 1 (March 1969): 116-122.

—————. "The Transition from Feudalism to Capitalism in Russia: A Major Soviet Historical Controversy." *American Historical Review* 77, no. 3 (June 1972): 715-729.

—————. "The Weber Thesis and the Failure of Capitalist Development in 'Early Modern' Russia." *Jahrbucher für Geschichte Osteuropas* 18 (1970): 320-336.

—————. "Who Were the *Gosti?*" *California Slavic Studies* 7 (1973): 1-40.

Barraclough, Geoffrey. "What Is to Be Done about Medieval History?" *New York Review of Books* 14, no. 11 (June 4, 1970): 51-57.

Bazilevich, K. V. "Elementy merkantilizma v ekonomicheskoi politike pravitel'stva Alekseia Mikhailovicha." *Uchenye zapiski Moskovskogo gosudarstvennogo universiteta*, no. 41 (1940), pp. 3-34.

—————. *Gorodskie vosstaniia v Moskovskom gosudarstve XVII v.* Moscow-Leningrad, 1936.

————. "Novotorgovyi ustav 1667 g.: K voprosu o ego istochnikakh." *Izvestiia Akademiia Nauk SSSR: VII seriia: Otdelenie obshchestvennykh nauk*, no. 7 (1932), pp. 589-622.

Berlin, P. A. *Russkaia burzhuaziia v staroe i novoe vremia*. Moscow, 1922.

Bernadskii, V. N. *Ocherki iz istorii klassovoi bor'by i obshchestvenno-politicheskoi mysli Rossii v tret'ei chetverti XVIII v.* Uchenye zapiski LGPI im. A. I. Gertsena, vol. 229. Leningrad, 1962.

Blum, Jerome. *Lord and Peasant in Russia from the Ninth to the Nineteenth Centuries*. Princeton, 1961.

Bogoslovskii, M. M. *Petr I: Materialy dlia biografii*. 5 vols. Leningrad, 1940-1948.

————. "Razbor sochineniia g. Kizevettera *Posadskaia obshchina v Rossii XVIII stoletiia*." *Chteniia v Imperatorskom obshchestve istorii i drevnostei rossiiskikh*, book 4, section 5 (1906), pp. 1-36.

Borovoi, S. Ia. *Kredit i banki Rossii (seredina XVII v.-1861 g.)*. Moscow, 1958.

Chicherin, B. N. *Oblastnyia uchrezhdeniia Rossii v XVII-m veke*. Moscow, 1856.

————. *Opyty po istorii russkago prava*. Moscow, 1858.

Chistiakova, E. V. "Novotorgovyi ustav 1667 g." In *Arkheograficheskii ezhegodnik za 1957 g.*, pp. 102-126. Moscow, 1958.

Chistozvonov, A. N. "Nekotorye aspekty problemy genizisa absoliutizma." *Voprosy istorii*, no. 5 (1968), pp. 46-62.

Chulkov, M. D. *Slovar' uchrezhdennykh v Rossii iarmarok izdannyi dlia obrashchaiushchikhsia v torgovle*. Moscow, 1788.

Chulkov, N. "Moskovskoe kupechestvo XVIII i XIX vv." *Russkii Arkhiv* 12 (1907): 489-501.

Coxe, William. *Travels into Poland, Russia, Sweden and Denmark*. 2nd ed. 2 vols. London, 1785.

Daniel, Wallace. "The Merchantry and the Problem of Social Order in the Russian State: Catherine II's Commission on Commerce." *Slavonic and East European Review* 15 (1977): 185-203.

Danilova, L. V. "Torgovye riady Iaroslavlia v kontse XVII v." In *Voprosy sotsial'no-ekonomicheskoi istorii i istochnikovedeniia perioda feodalizma v Rossii: Sbornik statei k 70-letiiu A. A. Novosel'skogo*, ed. N. V. Ustiugov, pp. 85-90. Moscow, 1961.

D'iakonov, M. A. *Ocherki obshchestvennogo i gosudarstvennogo stroia drevnei Rusi*. Moscow, 1908.

"Disput A. A. Kizevettera." *Istoricheskii vestnik*, no. 2 (February 1904), pp. 803-807.

Ditiatin, I. I. "K istorii 'Zhalovannykh gramot' dvorianstvu i gorodam, 1785 goda." *Russkaia mysl'* (1885), no. 4, pp. 13-50; no. 5, pp. 1-38; no. 6, pp. 1-19; no. 7, pp. 1-19; no. 8, pp. 58-84.

————. *Stoletie S.-Peterburgskago gorodskago obshchestva 1785-1885*. St. Petersburg, 1885.

————. *Ustroistvo i upravlenie gorodov Rossii*, vol. I: *Goroda Rossii v XVIII stoletii*. St. Petersburg, 1875.

Druzhinin, N. M., N. I. Pavlenko, and L. V. Cherepnin, eds. *Absoliutizm v Rossii (XVII-XVIII vv.)*. Moscow, 1964.

Druzhinin, N. M., et al., eds. *Goroda feodal'noi Rossii.* Moscow, 1966.

Druzhinin, N. M. *Gosudarstvennye krest'iane i reforma P. D. Kiseleva.* 2 vols. Moscow-Leningrad, 1946-1958.

Efimenko, T. P. "K istorii gorodskogo zemleustroistva vremeni Ekateriny II." *Zhurnal ministerstva narodnogo prosveshcheniia,* n.s. 54 (December 1914), pp. 284-310.

Eroshkin, N. P. *Ocherki istorii gosudarstvennykh uchrezhdenii dorevoliutsionnoi Rossii.* Moscow, 1960.

Firsov, N. N. "Gorod v Rossii do kontsa XVIII veka." *Entsiklopedicheskii slovar'* (Granat'), 7th ed., vol. 15 (1912), pp. 632-656.

———. *Russkie torgovo-promyshlennye kompanii v pervoi polovine XVIII v.* Kazan', 1896.

Fletcher, Giles. *Of the Russe Commonwealth.* Ed. Richard E. Pipes and John V. A. Fine, Jr. Cambridge, Mass. 1966.

Florinsky, M. T. *Russia: A History and an Interpretation.* 2 vols. New York, 1955.

Friedman, John. "Cities and Social Transformation." *Comparative Studies in Society and History* 4 (1961-1962): 86-103.

Got'e, Iu. V. Review of *Posadskaia obshchina v Rossiia v XVIII st.* by A. A. Kizevetter. *Zhurnal ministerstva narodnogo prosveshcheniia,* no. 9, section 2 (1909), pp. 206-219.

Hare, Richard. *Pioneers of Russian Social Thought.* London, 1951.

Hellie, Richard. *Enserfment and Military Change in Muscovy.* Chicago, 1971.

———. "Muscovite Law and Society: The *Ulozhenie* of 1649 as a Reflection of the Political and Social Development of Russia since the *Sudebnik* of 1589." Diss., University of Chicago, 1965.

Herberstein, Sigismund von. *Notes upon Russia.* Trans. R. H. Major. 2 vols. 1851; rpt. New York, 1963.

A History of Russian Economic Thought: Ninth through Eighteenth Centuries. Ed. John M. Letiche. Berkeley and Los Angeles, 1964.

Hittle, J. M. "The City in Muscovite and Early Imperial Russia." Diss., Harvard University, 1969.

———. Review of *Ocherki sotsial'no-ekonomicheskoi istorii gorodov Severo-Zapada Rossii v seredine XVIII v.* by Iu. R. Klokman. *Kritika* 1, no. 1 (Fall 1964): 14-21.

———. Review of *Perekhod ot feodalizmu k kapitalizmu v Rossii. Kritika* 7, no. 2 (Winter 1971): 97-110.

Iakovtsevskii, V. N. *Kupecheskii kapital v feodal'no-krepostnicheskoi Rossii.* Moscow, 1953.

Ikonnikov, V. S. *Kiev v 1654-1855 gg.: Istoricheskii ocherk.* Kiev, 1904.

Istoriia Moskvy. 6 vols. Moscow, 1952-1959.

Jones, Robert E. "Catherine II and the Provincial Reform of 1775: A question of motivation." *Canadian Slavic Studies* 4, no. 3 (Fall 1970): 497-512.

———. *The Emancipation of the Russian Nobility 1762-1785.* Princeton, 1973.

———. "Urban Planning and the Development of Provincial Towns in Russia, 1762-1796." In *The Eighteenth Century in Russia,* ed. J. G. Garrard, pp. 321-344. Oxford, 1973.

Kabuzan, V. M. *Narodonaselenie Rossii v XVIII-pervoi polovine XIX v.* Moscow, 1963.

Kafengauz, B. B. *I. T. Pososhkov: Zhizn i deiatel'nost'.* Moscow, 1951.

―――. *Ocherki vnutrennego rynka Rossii pervoi poloviny XVIII veka.* Moscow, 1958.

Kahan, Arcadius. "The Costs of 'Westernization' in Russia: The Gentry and the Economy in the Eighteenth Century." *Slavic Review* 25, no. 1 (March 1966): 40-66.

Keep, John. "Light and Shade in the History of the Russian Administration." *Canadian Slavic Studies* 6 (1972): 1-9.

―――. "The Traditions of the Kremlin." *Times Literary Supplement,* June 20, 1975, pp. 697-698.

Khrestomatiia po istorii SSSR: XVIII v. Ed. L. G. Beskrovnyi and B. B. Kafengauz. Moscow, 1963.

Khromov, P. A. *Ekonomicheskoe razvitie Rossii: Ocherki ekonomiki Rossii s drevneishikh vremen do Velikoi Oktiabr'skoi revoliutsii.* Moscow, 1967.

Kizevetter, A. A. *Gil'diia Moskovskago kupechestva.* Moscow, 1915.

―――. *Gorodovoe polozhenie Ekateriny II 1785 g.: Opyt istoricheskogo komentariia.* Moscow, 1909.

―――. *Istoricheskie ocherki.* Moscow, 1912.

―――. *Mestnoe samoupravlenie v Rossii IX-XIX st.: Istoricheskii ocherk.* Moscow, 1910.

―――. *Posadskaia obshchina v Rossii XVIII st.* Moscow, 1903.

―――. *Russkoe obshchestvo v vosemnadtsatom stoletii.* 2nd ed. Rostov na Donu, 1905.

Kliuchevskii, V. O. *Sochineniia.* 8 vols. Moscow, 1956-1959.

Klokman, Iu. R. *Ocherki sotsial'no-ekonomicheskoi istorii gorodov Severo-Zapada Rossii v seredine XVIII v.* Moscow, 1960.

―――. "Russkii gorod XVIII v. v sovremennoi burzhauznoi istoriografii." In *Kritika burzhuaznykh kontseptsii istorii Rossii perioda feodalizma,* ed. V. T. Pashuto, L. V. Cherepnin, and M. M. Shtrange, pp. 324-351. Moscow, 1962.

―――. *Sotsial'no-ekonomicheskaia istoriia russkogo goroda: Vtoraia polovina XVIII veka.* Moscow, 1967.

Kopanev, A. I. "Naselenie russkogo gosudarstva v XVI veke." *Istoricheskie zapiski* 64 (1959): 233-254.

Koulischer, J. (I. M. Kulisher) "La grande industrie aux XVII-e et XVIII-e siècles: France, Allemagne, Russie." In *Annales d'Histoire Economique et Sociale,* vol. 3, pp. 39-46. Paris, 1931.

Krizhanich, Iurii. *Politika.* Ed. M. N. Tikhomirov. Moscow, 1965.

Kulisher, I. M. *Istoriia russkoi torgovli do deviatnadtsatogo veka vkliuchitel'no.* St. Petersburg, 1923.

Lappo-Danilevskii, A. S. *Ocherk vnutrennei politiki imperatritsy Ekateriny II.* St. Petersburg, 1893.

―――. *Organizatsiia priamago oblozheniia v Moskovskom gosudarstve so vremen smuty do epokhi preobrazovanii.* St. Petersburg, 1890.

————. *Russkiia promyshlennyia i torgovyia kompanii v pervoi polovine 18 sto-letiia*. St. Petersburg, 1899.

Latkin, V. N. *Zakonodatel'nye kommissii v Rossii v XVIII st*. Vol. 1. St. Petersburg, 1887.

LeDonne, John P. "The Provincial and Local Police under Catherine the Great, 1775-1796." *Canadian Slavic Studies* 4, no. 3 (Fall 1970): 513-528.

Liashchenko, P. I. *Istoriia narodnogo khoziaistvo SSSR*, vol. 1: *Dokapitalisti-cheskie formatsii*. Leningrad, 1947.

Lincoln, W. Bruce. "The Russian State and Its Cities: The Search for Effective Municipal Government, 1786-1842." *Jahrbucher für Geschichte Osteuropas* 17, no. 4 (1969): 531-554.

Liubomirov, P. G. "Rol' kazennogo, dvorianskogo, i kupecheskogo kapitala v stroitel'stve krupnoi promyshlennosti Rossii v XVII-XVIII vv." *Istoricheskie zapiski* 16 (1945): 65-99.

Makhnova, G. P. "Khod i rezul'taty administrativno-territorial'noi reformy 1775-1785 gg. v Rossii." *Voprosy geografii* 83 (1970): 133-147.

Materialy dlia istorii Moskovskago kupechestva: Obshchestvennye prigovory. Vol. 1. Moscow, 1892.

Mendels, Franklin F. "Proto-industrialization: The First Phase of the Industriali-zation Process." *Journal of Economic History* 32, no. 1 (March 1972): 241-261.

Meshalin, I. V. *Tekstil'naia promyshlennost' krest'ian Moskovskoi gubernii v XVIII i pervoi polovine XIX veka*. Moscow-Leningrad, 1950.

Mets, N. D. *Nash rubl'*. Moscow, 1960.

Miliukov, P. N. *Gosudarstvennoe khoziaistvo Rossii v pervoi chetverti XVIII stoletiia i reforma Petra Velikago*. 2nd ed. St. Petersburg, 1905.

————. *Ocherki po istorii russkoi kultury: Chast' pervaia: Naselenie, ekonomi-cheskii, gosudarstvennyi i soslovnyi stroi*, 6th ed. St. Petersburg, 1909.

Murav'ev, A. V. "Iz materialov po istorii klassovoi bor'by v Russkom gorode nachala XVIII veka." In *Arkheograficheskii ezhegodnik za 1959 god*, pp. 157-163. Moscow, 1960.

————. "Obrazovanie Moskovskogo magistrata." In *Vestnik Moskovskogo uni-versiteta*, vol. 3, pp. 64-68. Moscow, 1963.

Nakaz imperatritsy Ekateriny II, dannyi kommissii o sochinenii proekta novago ulozheniia. Ed. N. D. Chechulin. St. Petersburg, 1907.

Ocherki istorii Leningrada. 3 vols. Ed. M. P. Viatkin. Moscow-Leningrad, 1955-1957.

Ocherki istorii SSSR: Period feodalizma: XVII v. Ed. A. A. Novosel'skii and N. V. Ustiugov. Moscow, 1955.

Ocherki istorii SSSR: Period feodalizma: Rossiia v pervoi chetverti XVIII v. Ed. B. B. Kafengauz and N. I. Pavlenko. Moscow, 1954.

Ocherki istorii SSSR: Period feodalizma: Rossiia vo vtoroi chetverti XVIII v. Ed. A. I. Baranovich. Moscow, 1957.

Ocherki istorii SSSR: Period feodalizma: Rossiia vo vtoroi polovine XVIII v. Ed. A. I. Baranovich et al. Moscow, 1956.

Pankratova, A. M. *Formirovanie proletariata v Rossii (XVII-XVIII vv.)*. Moscow, 1963.

Pavlenko, N. I. "Odvorianivanie russkoi burzhuazii v XVIII v." *Istoriia SSSR,* no. 2 (1961), pp. 71-87.

———. "O nekotorykh strankah pervonachal'nogo nakopleniia v Rossii." *Istoricheskie zapiski* 54 (1955): 382-419.

Pazhitnov, K. A. "Ocherk razvitiia burzhuazii v Rossii." *Obrazovanie* 16, nos. 2a and 3 (1907): 1-23, 59-88.

Perekhod ot feodalizmu k kapitalizmu v Rossii. Ed. V. I. Shunkov et al. Moscow, 1969.

Pereslavl'-Zalesskii: Materialy dlia istorii goroda XVII i XVIII stoletii. Ed. E. Belov. Moscow, 1884.

Perry, John. *The State of Russia Under the Present Czar.* London, 1716.

Pokrovskii, S. A. *Vneshniaia torgovlia i vneshniaia torgovaia politika Rossii.* Moscow, 1947.

Polanyi, Karl. "The Economy as Instituted Process." In *Trade and Market in the Early Empires,* ed. Karl Polanyi, Conrad Arensberg, and Harry Pearson, pp. 243-269. Glencoe, 1957.

Poliakova, U. M. "V. V. Krestinin i obshchestvennaia bor'ba v Arkhangel'skom posade v 60-90-kh godakh XVIII v." *Istoriia SSSR,* no. 2 (March-April 1958), pp. 78-102.

Polianskii, F. Ia. *Ekonomicheskii stroi manufaktury v Rossii XVIII veka.* Moscow, 1956.

———. *Gorodskoe remeslo i manufaktura v Rossii XVIII v.* Moscow, 1960.

———. *Pervonachal'noe nakoplenie kapitala v Rossii.* Moscow, 1958.

Polnoe sobranie zakonov rossiiskoi imperii. 1st series. 1649-1825. 45 vols. St. Petersburg, 1830.

Polovnikov, A. P. *Torgovlia v staroi Rossii.* Moscow, 1958.

Pososhkov, I. T. *Kniga o skudosti i bogatstve.* Ed. B. B. Kafengauz. Moscow, 1937.

Razgon, A. M. "Promyshlennye i torgovye slobody i sela Vladimirskoi gubernii vo vtoroi polovine XVIII v." *Istoricheskie zapiski* 32 (1950): 133-172.

Reddaway, W.F., et al., eds. *The Cambridge History of Poland.* Cambridge, 1950.

Reissman, Leonard. "Urbanism and Urbanization." In *Penguin Survey of Social Sciences 1965,* ed. Julius Gould, pp. 36-55. Baltimore, 1965.

Rosovsky, Henry. "The Serf Entrepreneur in Russia." *Explorations in Entrepreneurial History,* no. 6 (May 1954), pp. 341-370.

Rozman, Gilbert. "Comparative Approaches to Urbanization: Russia, 1750-1800." In *The City in Russian History,* ed. Michael Hamm, pp. 69-85. Lexington, Kentucky, 1976.

———. *Urban Networks in Russia, 1750-1800, and Premodern Periodization.* Princeton, 1976.

Rubinshtein, N. L. "Russkaia iarmarka 18 veka." *Uchenye zapiski kafedry istorii narodov SSSR Moskovskogo oblastnogo pedagogicheskogo instituta,* part 1, pp. 5-28. Moscow, 1939.

———. "Ulozhennaia komissiia 1754-1766 gg. i ee proekt novogo ulozheniia 'O sostoianii poddannykh voobshche'." *Istoricheskie zapiski* 38 (1951): 208-251.

————. "Vneshniaia torgovlia Rossii i russkoe kupechestvo vo vtoroi polovine XVIII v." *Istoricheskie zapiski* 54 (1955): 343-361.

Ryndziunskii, P. G. *Gorodskoe grazhdanstvo doreformennoi Rossii.* Moscow, 1958.

Sbornik imperatorskogo russkogo istoricheskogo obshchestva. 148 vols. St. Petersburg, 1867-1916.

Scherer, J-B. *Histoire Raisonnée du Commerce de la Russie.* 2 vols. Paris, 1786.

Serbina, K. N. *Ocherki iz sotsial'no-ekonomicheskoi istorii russkogo goroda: Tikhvinskii posad v XVI-XVIII vv.* Moscow, 1951.

Sergeevich, V. I. *Russkiia iuridicheskiia drevnosti.* 3 vols. St. Petersburg, 1901-1903.

Shapiro, A. L. "K istorii krest'ianskikh promyslov i krest'ianskoi manufaktury v Rossii XVIII v." *Istoricheskie zapiski* 31 (1950): 136-150.

————. "Ob absoliutizme v Rossii." *Istoriia SSSR*, no. 5 (1968), pp. 69-82.

Shcherbatov, M. M. "Razmyshleniia o ushcherbe torgovli proiskhodiashchem vykhozhdeniem velikago chisla kuptsov v dvoriane i v ofitsery." *Chteniia v Imperatorskom obshchestve istorii i drevnostei rossiiskikh*, book 1 (January-March 1860), pp. 135-140.

Sjoberg, Gideon. *The Preindustrial City: Past and Present.* New York, 1960.

Smirnov, P. P. *Goroda Moskovskogo gosudarstva v pervoi polovine 17 veka.* Vol. 1, part 1: *Formy zemlevladeniia.* Kiev, 1917. Vol. 1, part 2: *Kolichestvo i dvizhenie naseleniia.* Kiev, 1919.

————. *Posadskie liudi i ikh klassovaia bor'ba do serediny XVII veka.* 2 vols. Moscow-Leningrad, 1947-1948.

Snegirev, V. *Moskovskie slobody.* Moscow, 1947.

Sobornoe Ulozhenie 1649 g. Ed. M. N. Tikhomirov and P. P. Epifanov. Moscow, 1961.

Solov'ev, S. M. *Istoriia Rossii s drevneishikh vremen.* 29 vols. in 15 books. Moscow, 1960-1966.

————. "Moskovskye kuptsy v XVII v." *Sovremenik* 71 (1878): 427-440.

————. "Russkii gorod v XVII veke." *Sovremenik* 37, division II (1853): 1-20.

Sorina, Kh. D. "K voprosu o protsesse sotsial'nogo rassloeniia goroda v sviazi s formirovaniem kapitalisticheskikh otnoshenii v Rossii v XVIII-nachale XIX v. (G. Tver')." In *Uchenye zapiski Kalininskogo pedagogicheskogo instituta im. M. I. Kalinina*, vol. 38, pp. 281-300. Kalinin, 1964.

Sovetskaia istoricheskaia entsiklopediia. Ed. E. M. Zhukov. Moscow, 1961-1976.

Svod zakonov Rossiiskoi imperii. 15 vols. St. Petersburg, 1842.

Syromiatnikov, B. I. *"Reguliarnoe" gosudarstvo Petra Pervogo i ego ideologiia: Chast' 1.* Moscow-Leningrad, 1943.

Tal'man, E. M. "Bor'ba posada Iaroslavlia s svetskimi i dukhovnymi feodalami v pervoi polovine XVII veka." *Istoricheskie zapiski* 20 (1946): 96-129.

Tilly, Charles and Richard. "Agenda for European Economic History in the 1970's." *Journal of Economic History* 31, no. 1 (March 1971): 184-198.

Tooke, William. *View of the Russian Empire During the Reign of Catharine the*

Second and to the Close of the Eighteenth Century. 2 vols. London, 1800.

Torke, Hans J. "Continuity and Change in the Relations between Bureaucracy and Society in Russia, 1613-1861." *Canadian Slavic Studies* 5 (1971): 457-476.

———. "More Light than Shade." *Canadian Slavic Studies* 6 (1972): 10-12.

Tri veka: Rossiia ot smuty do nashego vremeni. Ed. V. Kallash. 6 vols. Moscow, 1912-1913.

Troitskii, S. M. *Finansovaia politika russkogo absoliutizma v XVIII veke.* Moscow, 1966.

———. *Russkii absoliutizm i dvorianstvo v XVIII v. Formirovanie biurokratii.* Moscow, 1970.

Tugan-Baranovskii, M. I. *Russkaia fabrika v proshlom i nastoiashchem.* Vol. 1. Moscow, 1926.

Vartanov, G. L. "Kupechestvo i torguiushchee krest'ianstvo tsentral'noi chasti Evropeiskoi Rossii vo vtoroi polovine XVIII veka." In *Uchenye zapiski LGPI im. A. I. Gertsena,* vol. 229, pp. 162-196. Leningrad, 1962.

Vladimirskii-Budanov, M. F. *Obzor istorii Russkago prava.* Kiev-St. Petersburg, 1900.

Vodarskii, Ia. E. *Naselenie Rossii v kontse XVII-nachale XVIII veka.* Moscow, 1977.

———. *Naselenie Rossii za 400 let (XVI-nachalo XX vv.).* Moscow, 1973.

———. "Proekt reglamenta glavnogo magistrata i ego redaktsii (1720 g.)." In *Problemy istochnikovedeniia,* vol. 10, pp. 195-207. Moscow, 1962.

———. *Promyshlennye seleniia tsentral'noi Rossii v period genezisa i razvitiia kapitalizma.* Moscow, 1972.

Volkov, M. Ia. "O stanovlenii absoliutizma v Rossii." *Istoriia SSSR,* no. 1 (1970), pp. 90-104.

———. "Tamozhennaia reforma 1753-57gg." *Istoricheskie zapiski* 71 (1962): 134-157.

Voznesenskii, S. V. "Gorodskie deputatskye nakazy v Ekaterininskuiu komissiiu 1767 goda." *Zhurnal ministerstva narodnogo prosveshcheniia,* November 1909, pp. 89-119; December 1909, pp. 241-284.

Weber, Max. *The City.* Trans. and ed. Don Martindale and Gertrud Neuwirth. New York, 1962.

Zagorovskii, V. P. *Belgorodskaia cherta.* Voronezh, 1969.

Zaozerskaia, E. I. "Moskovskii posad pri Petre I." *Voprosy istorii,* no. 9 (1947), pp. 19-35.

———. "Torgi i promysly gostinoi sotni Srednego Povolzh'ia na rubezhe XVII-XVIII vv." In *Petr Velikii: Sbornik statei,* pp. 216-241. Moscow-Leningrad, 1947.

Zviagintsev, E. A. "Slobody inostrantsev v Moskve XVII veka." *Istoricheskii zhurnal,* no. 2-3 (1944), pp. 81-86.

Index